The Christ-Myth Theory
And Its Problems

ROBERT M. PRICE

The Christ-Myth Theory
And Its Problems

2011
American Atheist Press
Cranford, New Jersey

ISBN10: 1-57884-017-1
ISBN13: 978-1-57884-017-5

American Atheist Press
225 Cristiani Street
Cranford, NJ 07016
Voice: (908) 276-7300
FAX: (908) 276-7402

www.atheists.org

Library of Congress Cataloging-in-Publication Data

Price, Robert M., 1954-
  The Christ-myth theory and its problems / Robert M. Price.
    p. cm.
  ISBN 978-1-57884-017-5 (alk. paper)
  1. Jesus Christ--Mythological interpretations. I. Title.
  BT303.2.P74 2011
  232.9--dc23
                    2011028064

Dedication

To Hermann Detering
the greatest New Testament scholar of his generation

Acknowledgements

"The Quest of the Mythical Jesus" first appeared on the Robert M. Price MySpace page.

"Jesus at the Vanishing Point" was originally printed in The Historical Jesus: Five Views edited by James Beilby and Paul R. Eddy. Copyright (c) James K. Beilby and Paul Rhodes Eddy. Used by permission of Inter-Varsity Press PO Box 1400 Downers Grove, IL 60515. www.ivpress.com.

"New Testament Narrative as Old Testament Midrash" originally appeared in Jacob Neusner and Alan J. Avery Peck (eds.), Encyclopaedia of Midrash: Biblical Interpretation in Formative Judaism (E.J. Brill, 2005).

"Dubious Database: Second Thoughts on the Red and Pink Materials of the Jesus Seminar" first appeared in CSER Review (1/2) Winter/Spring 2006/07

"The Abhorrent Void" was originally published in Sources of the Jesus Tradition: Separating History from Myth, edited by R. Joseph Hoffmann (Amherst, NY: Prometheus Books, 2010), pp. 109-117; www. prometheusbooks.com.

"James the Just: Achilles Heel of the Christ Myth Theory?" was delivered as a paper at the Committee for the Scientific Examination of Religion Conference: "Scripture and Skepticism" Conference, Davis, CA. January 25-28, 2007.

"Does the Christ Myth Theory Require an Early Date for the Pauline Epistles?" first appeared in Thomas L. Thompson and Thomas Verenna, eds., Is This Not the Carpenter? The Question of the Historicity of the Figure of Jesus. Copenhagen International Seminar (Sheffield: Equinox Publishing, 2012)

"Revisiting the Pre-Christian Jesus" appears here for the first time.

"Worse Than Atheism" was delivered as a paper at the CFI Religion Under Examination conference, February 20, 2012.

Contents

Introduction:
The Quest of the Mythical Jesus

When, long ago, I first learned that some theorized that Jesus had never existed as an historical figure, I dismissed the notion as mere crankism, as most still do. Indeed, Rudolf Bultmann, supposedly the arch-skeptic, quipped that no sane person could doubt that Jesus existed (though he himself came surprisingly close to the same opinion, as did Paul Tillich). For a number of years I held a more or less Bultmannian estimate of the historical Jesus as a prophet heralding the arrival of the eschatological Kingdom of God, an end to which his parables, faith healings and exorcisms were directed. Jesus had, I thought, predicted the coming of the Son of Man, an angelic figure who should raise the dead and judge mankind. When his cleansing of the temple invited the unforgiving ire of the Sadducee establishment, in cahoots with the Romans, he sealed his own doom. He died by crucifixion, and a few days later his disciples began experiencing visions of him raised from the dead. They concluded that he himself was now to be considered the Son of Man, and they expected his messianic advent in the near future.

From this eminently reasonable position (its cogency reinforced by the postmortem unfolding of the messiahship of Lubavitcher Rebbe Menachem Mendel Schneerson) I eventually found myself gravitating to that crazy view, that Jesus hadn't existed, that he was mythic all the way down, like Hercules. I do not hold it as a dogma. I do not prefer that it be true. It is just that the evidence now seems to me to point that way. The burden of proof would seem to belong with those who believe there was an historical man named Jesus. I fully admit and remind the reader that all historical hypotheses are provisional and tentative. This one certainly is. And yet I do favor it. Why?

The Christ Myth Theory And Its Problems

I remember first encountering the notion that the Jesus saga was formally similar to the Mediterranean dying and rising god myths of saviors including Attis, Adonis, Tammuz/Dumuzi, Dionysus, Osiris, and Baal. I felt almost at once that the jig was up. I could not explain away those parallels, parallels that went right to the heart of the thing. I felt momentary respite when I read the false reassurances of Bruce M. Metzger (may this great man rest in peace), J.N.D. Anderson, Edwin Yamauchi (may I someday gain a tenth of his knowledge!), and others that these parallels were false or that they were later in origin, perhaps even borrowed by the pagans from Christianity. But it did not take long to discover the spurious nature of such apologetical special pleading. There *was* ample and early pre-Christian evidence for the dying and rising gods. The parallels were very close. And it was simply not true that no one ever held that, like Jesus, these saviors had been historical figures. And if the ancient apologists had not known that the pagan parallels were pre-Christian, why on earth would they have mounted a suicidal argument that Satan counterfeited the real dying and rising god *ahead of time*. That is like the fundamentalists of the nineteenth century arguing desperately that God created fossils of dinosaurs that had never existed.

And, yet, all of this scarcely proved that Jesus had not existed at all. Bultmann freely admitted that such myths clothed and shaped the form of resurrection belief among the early Christians, but he felt there had actually been certain Easter morning experiences, visions that might have given rise to a different explanation in a different age. I now think Bultmann's argument runs afoul of Ockham's Razor, since it posits redundant explanations. If you recognize the recurrence of the pagan savior myth in the Christian proclamation, then no need remains to suggest an initial "Big Bang" (Burton L. Mack) of an Easter Morning Experience of the First Disciples.

G.A. Wells, like his predecessors advocating the Christ Myth theory, discounted the gospel story of an historical Jesus, an itinerant teacher and miracle worker, on the grounds of its seeming absence from the Epistle literature, earlier than the gospels, implying that there was no Jesus tradition floating around in either oral or written form at the time Paul and Peter were writing letters. All they referred to was a supernatural Son of God who descended from heaven to vanquish the evil angels ruling the world, then returned heavenward to reign in divine glory till his second advent. Had Paul known of the teaching of Jesus, why did he not quote it when it would have settled this and that controversial question (*e.g.*, paying Roman taxes, celibacy for the Kingdom, congregational discipline)? Why does he seem to refer to occasional "commands of the Lord" in a manner so vague as to suggest charismatic revelations to himself? Why does he never mention Jesus having healed the sick or done miracles? How can he say the Roman Empire never punishes the righteous, only the wicked?

This is a weighty argument, but another makes it almost superfluous. Take the gospel Jesus story as a whole, whether earlier or later than the Jesus story of the Epistles; it is part and parcel of the Mythic Hero Archetype shared by cultures and religions worldwide and throughout history (Lord Raglan and then, later, Alan Dundes showed this in great detail.). Leave the gospel story on the table, then. You still do not have any truly historical data. There is no "secular" biographical information about Jesus. Even the seeming "facts" irrelevant to faith dissolve upon scrutiny. Did he live in Nazareth? Or was that a tendentious reinterpretation of the earlier notion he had been thought a member of the Nazorean sect? Did he work some years as a carpenter? Or does that story not rather reflect the crowd's pegging him as an expert in scripture, *à la* the Rabbinic proverb, "Not even a carpenter, or a carpenter's son could solve this one!'"? Was his father named Joseph, or is that an historicization of his earlier designation as the Galilean Messiah, Messiah ben Joseph? On and on it goes, and when we are done, there is nothing left of Jesus that does not appear to serve all too clearly the interests of faith, the faith even of rival, hence contradictory, factions among the early Christians.

The Christ Myth Theory And Its Problems

I admit that a historical hero might attract to himself the standard flattering legends and myths to the extent that the original lines of the figure could no longer be discerned. He may have lived nonetheless. Can we tell the difference between such cases and others where we can still discern at least some historical core? Apollonius of Tyana, itinerant Neo-Pythagorean contemporary of Jesus (with whom the ancients often compare him) is one such. He, too, seems entirely cut from the cloth of the fabulous. His story, too, conforms exactly to the Mythic Hero Archetype. To a lesser extent, so does Caesar Augustus, of whom miracles were told. The difference is that Jesus has left no footprint on profane history as these others managed to do. The famous texts of Josephus and Tacitus, even if genuine, amount merely to references to the preaching of contemporary Christians, not reporting about Jesus as a contemporary. We still have documentation from people who claimed to have met Apollonius, Peregrinus, and, of course, Augustus. It might be that Jesus was just as historical as these other remarkable individuals, and that it was mere chance that no contemporary documentation referring to him survives. But we cannot assume the truth of that for which we have no evidence.

A paragraph back, I referred to the central axiom of form criticism: that nothing would have been passed down in the tradition unless it was useful to prove some point, to provide some precedent. I am sorry to say that this axiom cancels out another, the Criterion of Dissimilarity: the closer a Jesus-saying seems to match the practice or teaching of the early Church, the greater likelihood that it stems from the latter and has been placed fictively into the speech or life of Jesus merely to secure its authority. Put the two principles together and observe how one consumes the other without remainder: all pericopae of the Jesus tradition owe their survival to the fact that they were useful. On the assumption that Christians saw some usefulness to them, we can posit a *Sitz-im-Leben Kirche* for each one. And that means it is redundant to posit a pre-Christian *Sitz-im-Leben Jesu* context. None of it need go back to Jesus.

Additionally, we can demonstrate that every hortatory saying is so closely paralleled in contemporary Rabbinic or Hellenistic lore that there is no particular reason to be sure this or that saying originated with Jesus. Such words commonly passed from one famous name to another, especially in Jewish circles, as Jacob Neusner has shown. Jesus *might* have said it, sure, but then he was just one more voice in the general choir. Is that what we want to know about him? And, as Bultmann observed, who remembers the great man quoting somebody else?

Another shocker: it hit me like a ton of bricks when I realized, after studying much previous research on the question, that virtually *every* story in the gospels and Acts can be shown to be very likely a Christian rewrite of material from the Septuagint, Homer, Euripides' *Bacchae*, and Josephus. One need not be David Hume to see that, if a story tells us a man multiplied food to feed a multitude, it is inherently much more likely that the story is a rewrite of an older miracle tale (starring Elisha) than that it is a report of a real event. A literary origin is always to be preferred to an historical one in such a case. And that is the choice we have to make in virtually every case of New Testament narrative. I refer the interested reader to my essay "New Testament Narrative as Old Testament Midrash," in Jacob Neusner and Alan J. Avery-Peck, eds., *Encyclopedia of Midrash,* in this collection. Of course I am dependent here upon many fine works by Randel Helms, Thomas L. Brodie, John Dominic Crossan, and others. None of them went as far as I am going. It is just that as I counted up the gospel stories I felt each scholar had convincingly traced back to a previous literary prototype, it dawned on me that there was virtually nothing left. None tried to argue for the fictive character of the whole tradition, and each offered some cases I found arbitrary and implausible. Still, their work, when combined, militated toward a wholly fictive Jesus story.

The Christ Myth Theory And Its Problems

It is not as if I believe there is no strong argument for an historical Jesus. There is one: one can very plausibly read certain texts in Acts, Mark, and Galatians as fossils preserving the memory of a succession struggle following the death of Jesus, who, therefore, must have existed. Who should follow Jesus as his vicar on earth? His disciples (analogous to the Companions of the Prophet Muhammad, who provided the first three caliphs)? Or should it be the Pillars, his own relatives (the Shi'ite Muslims called Muhammad's kinsmen the Pillars, too, and supported their dynastic claims)? One can trace the same struggles in the Baha'i Faith after the death of the Bab (Mirza Ali Muhammad): who should rule, his brother Subh-i-Azal, or his disciple Hussein Ali, Baha'Ullah? Who should follow the Prophet Joseph Smith? His disciples, or his son, Joseph, Jr.? When the Honorable Elijah Muhammad died, Black Muslims split and followed either his son and heir Wareeth Deen Muhammad or his former lieutenant Louis Farrakhan. In the New Testament, as Harnack and Stauffer argued, we seem to see the remains of a Caliphate of James. And that implies (though it does not prove) an historical Jesus.

And it implies an historical Jesus of a particular type. It implies a Jesus who was a latter-day Judah Maccabee, with a group of brothers who could take up the banner when their eldest brother, killed in battle, perforce let it fall. S.G.F. Brandon made a very compelling case for the original revolutionary character of Jesus, subsequently sanitized and made politically harmless by Mark the evangelist. Judging by the skirt-clutching outrage of subsequent scholars, Mark's apologetical efforts to depoliticize the Jesus story have their own successors. Brandon's work is a genuine piece of the classic Higher Criticism of the gospels, with the same depth of reason and argumentation. If there was an historical Jesus, my vote is for Brandon's version.

But I must point out that there is another way to read the evidence for the Zealot Jesus hypothesis. As Burton Mack has suggested, the political element in the Passion seems likely to represent an anachronistic confusion by Mark with the events leading to the fall of Jerusalem. When the Olivet Discourse warns its readers not to take any of a number of false messiahs and Zealot agitators for their own Jesus, does this not imply Christians were receiving the news of Theudas or Jesus ben Ananias or John of Gischala as news of Jesus' return? You don't tell people not to do what they're already not doing. If they were making such confusions, it would be inevitable that the events attached to them would find their way back into the telling of the Jesus story. It looks like this very thing happened. One notices how closely the interrogation and flogging of Jesus ben-Ananias, in trouble for predicting the destruction of the temple, parallels that of Jesus, ostensibly 40 years previously. We notice how Simon bar Gioras was welcomed into the temple with palm branches to cleanse the sacred precinct from the "thieves" who infested it, Zealots under John of Gischala. Uh-oh. Suppose these signs of historical-political verisimilitude are interlopers in the gospels from the following generation. The evidence for the Zealot Jesus evaporates.

I have not tried to amass every argument I could think of to destroy the historicity of Jesus. Rather, I have summarized the series of realizations about methodology and evidence that eventually led me to embrace the Christ Myth Theory. There may once have been an historical Jesus, but for us there is one no longer. If he existed, he is forever lost behind the stained glass curtain of holy myth. At least that's the current state of the evidence as I see it.

The present volume contains the major essays and papers I have written to set forth the case for the Christ Myth theory as well as my best attempts to deal with the major difficulties scholars have pointed out with it. There will be some overlap, but I think that is helpful, as certain of these points can use reiteration and can benefit from presentation from slightly different angles. I would like to thank the editors and publishers whose permissions to reprint this material have made this book possible.

Jesus at the Vanishing Point

At the outset of a controversial essay, let me try for a moment to make it easier for readers to resist the temptation to dismiss what I say based on tired stereotypes. I will argue that it is quite likely there never was any historical Jesus. Some will automatically assume I am doing apologetics on behalf of "village atheism," as some do. For what it may be worth, let me note that I began the study of the historical Jesus question as an enthusiastic would-be apologist. Eventually quite surprised to find myself disillusioned with "our" arguments, I shifted toward a more mainstream critical position more or less like Bultmann's. I was even more surprised, as the years went on, to find that I was having greater and greater difficulty poking holes in what I had regarded as extreme, even crackpot, theories. Finally and ironically, I wound up espousing them for reasons I will shortly be recounting. In all this time, while I gladly admit I wrote with some indignation against what Albert Schweitzer called "the twisted and fragile thinking of apologetics,"[1] I have never come to disdain Christianity.

Methodological Presuppositions

Which is the greatest commandment for historians? The first and greatest is the *Principle of Analogy*. It is for seeming failure to understand this important axiom that many hurl charges of "anti-supernaturalist bias" and "naturalistic presuppositions" in the study of the gospels. Historians do not have access to H.G. Wells's time machine. We cannot know what occurred in the past and thus do not dogmatize about it. We deal only in probabilities. How do we decide what probably did or probably did not happen in the past? When we are looking at an ancient account, we must judge it according to the analogy of our experience and that of our trustworthy contemporaries (people with observational skills, honest reporters, *etc.*, regardless of their philosophical or religious beliefs). There is no available alternative. Again, we weren't there and thus do not know that natural law always operated as it does now (the "Uniformitarianism" decried by "Scientific Creationists"), but there is no particular reason *not* to think so, and unless we do, we have no criterion at all. We will be at the mercy of old stories of people turning lead into gold, turning into werewolves, using magic to win battles. If in our experience it takes a whole army to defeat an army, we will judge improbable any ancient tale that has a single man defeating an army. What else can we do? So we will judge an account improbable if it finds no analogy to current experience. Regarding the gospels, for instance, this means that we will not reject out of hand stories in which Jesus heals the sick and casts out demons. We cannot do clinical follow-ups in these cases, but we do know such scenes may be found in our world today, and so they do not present a stumbling block to historical Jesus research. Even Bultmann admitted Jesus must have done what he and his contemporaries considered miracles.[2] (There may be other reasons for doubting it, of course, but not that it violates the Principle of Analogy.)

On the other hand, the historian must ask if an old account that does not fit the analogy of present-day experience does happen to match the analogy of legend or myth.

If it looks more like a legend than like any verifiable modern experience, what are we to conclude? If the story of Jesus walking on the water bears a strong resemblance to old stories in which Hermes, Pythagoras, the Buddha and others walk on water, mustn't we conclude we are probably dealing with a legend in the case of Jesus, too? We don't know. We weren't there. But we could say the same thing about the Hercules myths. Must we gravely admit it is entirely likely that the Son of Zeus killed the Hydra just because someone once said so?

The Principle of Analogy is simply a "surprise-free method,"[3] like that of the sociologist, the futurologist, the meteorologist.

These three specialists predict what probably will happen based upon current trends, and they can be wrong, since there are sometimes factors in play that are invisible to them. But what can they do? We do not reproach them because they are not oracles, infallibly predicting what will happen. Likewise, the historian does not claim clairvoyant knowledge of the past as Rudolf Steiner did. The historian, so to speak, "postdicts" based on traceable factors and analogy. *But it is all a matter of probabilities.* This is why gospel critics who reject the spectacular nature miracles of Jesus feel they must. They are judging those gospel reports "improbable." One may not be satisfied with this and decide to believe in them anyway, but that will be a matter of faith, *i.e.*, the will to believe, not of historical judgment, and the two must not be confused.

I will momentarily explain why I believe the Principle of Analogy compels us to go much further than this in our judgment of the historical Jesus question. But first, one more observation. The Principle of Analogy is important even in our choice of criteria for evaluating the sayings tradition. It underlies the Criterion of Dissimilarity (concerning which, more just below), but it also enters into the question of how we view the transmission of the sayings material. As is well known, Harald Riesenfeld and Birger Gerhardsson[4] urged critics to view the oral transmission of Jesus-sayings as analogous to the oral tradition of the Tannaim, the early Torah sages (if the term "rabbi" be deemed slightly anachronistic) who strove to be like "a plastered cistern that loses not a drop" (*Avot* 2:11), *i.e.*, not a word of one's master's teaching. That is a possible analogy, available in a closely related historical-cultural milieu, to be sure. But there is another, only slightly later, and that is the transmission of the hadith of Muhammad, which Muslims themselves were the first to realize had grown like a cancer to the point where only a century after Muhammad there were thousands of spurious sayings and precedents ascribed to him. Al-Bukhari, Muslim, and others began the process of weeding them out, but

The Christ Myth Theory And Its Problems

they retained a huge number, and today's Western, critical study of the hadith suggests virtually the whole corpus is inauthentic, that is, for the purpose of reconstructing Muhammad's teaching.[5] (For Al-Bukhari, Muslim bin Al-Hajjaj, and other early compilers of traditions, see Alfred Guillaume, *The Traditions of Islam: An Introduction to the Hadith Literature.* (Oxford University Press, 1924) pp. 26-35.) What all this means is that the early Muslim savants simply had no problem with fabricating hadith if they thought the content was valid.[6] It must have been no different for the creators of the *Pistis Sophia* and many Nag Hammadi gospels to coin of huge amounts of teaching and ascribe it to Jesus.[7] So were the gospel tradents more like the rabbis and their disciples, or more like the Muslim hadith-masters, or even the Nag Hammadi writers? Only a close scrutiny of the various sayings can tell us, if anything can. No *a priori* decision can short-circuit the critical process. One certainly cannot go into the study of the gospels armed with the assurance that the material *must* be authentic or inauthentic.

If the Principle of Analogy is the first historiographical commandment, the second, the *Criterion of Dissimilarity*, is like unto it. Norman Perrin formulated this axiom in its clearest form, though as he himself pointed out, it was nothing new. The idea is that no saying ascribed to Jesus may be counted as probably authentic if it has parallels in Jewish or early Christian sayings. Perrin was no fool. He understood well enough that if Jesus taught among Jewish colleagues, his opinions would frequently overlap theirs, and that if he founded a movement (even inadvertently!), the members of it would repeat his ideas.[8] But he was right: even in rabbinic sources it becomes clear that the same saying, not just the same sentiment, might be attributed to various rabbis (Jacob Neusner has made this even clearer),[9] and so the same was likely to be true with Jesus. Someone might naturally like a saying he heard without attribution and ascribe it to Jesus instead. This is all the more true in light of a discernible Judaizing tendency in early Christianity. And as for the early church, the contradictions between gospel sayings on eschatology, divorce, fasting, preaching to Gentiles and Samaritans, *etc.*, are most easily explained as the church ascribing their views to Jesus because they thought them valid inferences (or revelations from the Risen Lord).

No, I believe the opposition aroused by Perrin's proposal was because it made the game too difficult to play: too little data would be left, and so why not change the rules of the game? Indeed, I think Perrin's own application of the Criterion of Dissimilarity was selective and inconsistent. Worse yet, he failed to see that the Criterion of Dissimilarity must be all-devouring because of the central tenet of form-criticism, which is that in order to be transmitted, every gospel pericope must have had some pragmatic use. On that assumption, an entirely natural one as it appears to me, form critics sought with great ingenuity to reconstruct the *Sitz-im-Leben* of each and every gospel pericope, and with great success. (Again, remember that it is all a matter of probability; of course, it is speculative, but who has anything better to offer?) But Perrin did not seem to see that this meant that *every single* gospel bit and piece must have had a home in the early church, belonged to the early church (no big surprise! The gospels, after all, weren't written by Buddhists!), and thus *all* must be denied to Jesus by the Criterion of Dissimilarity. A saying may have been preserved because of its relevance, but it may as easily have been created, as many appear to have been, and so one must assume the latter. As F.C. Baur said, anything is possible, but what is probable? And if the Criterion of Dissimilarity is valid, then we must follow unafraid wherever it leads. I know many will protest at this point, saying I have reduced the criterion to its ultimate absurdity, demonstrated despite myself how wrong-headed it always was. But no: this is just to cut and run when the going gets tough. When one objects that the criterion is too strict because it doesn't leave us enough pieces of the puzzle, agnosticism is transforming into fideism. The objection presupposes the conclusion that there was a historical Jesus and that we ought to be able to find out about him.

The third commandment is to remember what an *Ideal Type* means. Conveniently forgetting it, many have ignored the importance of the Mystery Religions, the Θηειος ανηρ (divine man),[10] the dying and rising gods,[11] Mystery Religions,[12] and, most recently, Gnosticism,[13] for the historical Jesus question. An Ideal Type is a textbook definition made up of the regularly recurring features common to the phenomena in question. The Ideal Type most certainly does not ignore points of distinctiveness of the member phenomena, nor does it presuppose or require absolute likeness between all members of the envisioned category. Rather, the idea is that if discreet phenomena possess enough common features that a yardstick may be abstracted from them, then each member may be profitably measured and better understood against the yardstick. If the Ideal Type of "religion" includes the feature "belief in superhuman entities," then we do not conclude that Buddhism is not a religion after all. Rather, we turn around and use the yardstick of what is generally true of religions to better understand this particular exception.

Nor do we conclude that, since all members of the proposed category do not match up in every respect, that there is no such category after all. There is a natural range of variations on the theme, and it is only the broad theme that the Ideal Type sets forth. Neither do we expect that all typical features will be present in all specific cases. We do not deny there is such a thing as a form of miracle stories just because not every one of them contains, say, the feature of the skepticism of the onlookers, though most do.

Fourth, we must keep in mind that *Consensus is no criterion.* The truth may not rest in the middle. The truth may not rest with the majority. Every theory and individual argument must be evaluated on its own. If we appeal instead to "received opinion" or "the consensus of scholars," we are merely abdicating our own responsibility, as well as committing the fallacy of Appeal to the Majority. I dare say that, had we really been content to accede to received opinion, none of us would ever have entered the field of New Testament scholarship. I accept the dictum of Paul Feyerabend at this point. The only axiom that does not inhibit research is "Anything goes."[14] Let's just see *how far*. It matters neither whether a particular hypothesis comports easily with the majority paradigm nor with one's own other hypotheses. Since all must be but tentatively and provisionally held anyway, we must follow the evidence wherever it seems to be taking us in this or that particular case. We may wind up overturning and replacing the regnant paradigm, though in the meantime we will expect defenders of "normative science" to do their best defending the ramparts of their cherished paradigm — as they should, since a new one must show its worth by bearing the scrutiny of one's peers.[15]

In the same vein, the sixth commandment is to remember that *scholarly "conclusions" must be tentative and provisional, always open to revision.* Our goal is to try out this and that paradigm/hypothesis to see which makes the most natural sense of the evidence without "epicycling." We must seek the minimum of special pleading for fitting an item of recalcitrant evidence into the framework.

The Traditional Christ-Myth Theory

Virtually everyone who espoused the Christ-Myth theory has laid great emphasis on one question: *Why no mention of a miracle-working Jesus in secular sources?* Let me leapfrog the tiresome debate over whether the *Testimonium Flavianum* is authentic. For the record, my guess is that Eusebius fabricated it[16] and that the tenth-century Arabic version[17] represents an abridgement of the Eusebian original, not a more primitive, modest version. My opinion is that John Meier and others are rewriting a bad text to make it a good one, to rehabilitate it for use as a piece of evidence.[18] But who cares?

The Christ Myth Theory And Its Problems

It is all moot. The silence of the sources argument at most implies a Bultmannian version of a historical Jesus whose relatively modest activity as an exorcist and faith healer would not have attracted much attention, any more than the secular media cover Peter Popov today. It does not go all the way to imply there was no historical Jesus. (Indeed, it may even be circular in assuming there was either a real superman or a mythic superman, w/o a middle option of a mortal messiah.)

The second of the three pillars of the traditional Christ-Myth case is that *the epistles, earlier than the gospels, do not evidence a recent historical Jesus.* Setting aside the very late 1 Timothy, which presupposes the Gospel of John, the only gospel in which Jesus "made a good confession before Pontius Pilate"),[19] we should never guess from the epistles that Jesus died in any particular historical or political context, only that the fallen angels (Colossians 2:15), the archons of this age did him in, little realizing they were sealing their own doom (1 Corinthians 2:6–8). It is hard to imagine that the authors of Romans 13:3 and 1 Peter 2:13–14 (where we read that Roman governors punish only the wicked, not the righteous) believed that Jesus died at the order of Pontius Pilate. We should never even suspect he performed a single miracle, since none are mentioned. Did Paul think his Jesus had been a teacher? We just don't know, since his cherished "commands of the Lord" (1 Corinthians 7:10, *cf.* 25; 9:14), while they might represent quotations from something like the Q source, may as well be midrashically derived inferences from Old Testament commands of Adonai in the Torah, or even prophetic mandates from the Risen One.

Paul seems to know of a Last Supper of Jesus with his disciples, at which he instituted the Eucharist (1 Corinthians 11:23–26), but this is a weak reed. On the one hand, for reasons having nothing to do with Christ-Myth theory, some have pegged this piece of text as an interpolation.[20] On the other, suppose Paul did write it; Hyam Maccoby argued that in 1 Corinthians 11:23 we see Paul comparing himself with Moses, the one who receives material (in this case, cult law) directly from Adonai and passes it on to his fellow mortals. In other words, Paul does not mean he has received this tradition from other mortals who were present on the occasion, or even from their successors, but that, in human terms, the Last Supper pericope *originated with him*. He would have first apprehended it in a vision,[21] much as the nineteenth-century mystic Anna Katherina Emmerich[22] beheld in a series of visions the "dolorous passion of our Lord Jesus Christ," including "lost episodes" that made it into Mel Gibson's *The Passion of the Christ*. On Maccoby's entirely plausible reading, we would actually be seeing the beginnings of the historicization of the Christ figure here.

Finally, though the epistles name the Christian savior Jesus, it is quite possible, as Paul Couchoud suggested long ago,[23] that they attest to an even earlier stage of belief in which the savior received the honorific name "Jesus" only as of his postmortem exaltation. For Philippians 2:9–11, read without theological embarrassment, seems to intend that it was that name, exalted above all other names, that the savior received, not the title κυριος. Every voice acclaiming him Lord is instead paralleled with every knee bowing to him, both to occur at the mention of this new name, Jesus, now bestowed on him.

All the epistles seem to know is a Jesus Christ, Son of God, who came into the world to die as a sacrifice for human sin and was raised by God and enthroned in heaven. Some Mythicists (the early G.A. Wells[24] and Alvar Ellegård)[25] thought that the first Christians had in mind a Jesus who had lived as a historical figure, just not of the recent past, much as the average Greek believed Hercules and Achilles really lived somewhere back there in the past.[26] Others, like Earl Doherty,[27] believe the original Christology envisioned a Jesus who had never even appeared on earth (except in visions to his believers) and whose sacrificial death amid the angels had occurred in one of the lower havens, where these beings were located in ancient belief. Again, as the Son of Man, his death would be of a piece with the primordial death of the Primal Man Purusha in the Rig Veda (10:90), whose self-sacrifice in the heavens gave rise to the creation.[28]

But what about the one whom Paul calls "James the brother of the Lord" (Galatians 1:19)? Paul says he met him, so mustn't he have understood Jesus to be a figure of recent history? That is indeed a natural reading, but it is not the only one. Wells cautions that "brethren of the Lord" (1 Corinthians 9:5) may refer to a missionary brotherhood[29] such as the Johannine Epistles presuppose, and need not refer to literal siblings of the Lord any more than 1 Corinthians 3:9's "the Lord's co-laborers" means Paul and Apollos had offices down the hall from God as "the Lord's colleagues." After all, Paul does not say "James the brother of *Jesus*," and he might simply have meant to identify James as one of these itinerant evangelists. Wells's theory makes all the more sense in light of Walter Schmithals's argument[30] that in Galatians 1:19, Paul means by "apostles" (among whom he there counts James) simply itinerant preachers whose hub was Jerusalem; most of them were naturally out on the road at the time of Paul's visit, which is why he met only two who happened to be there: Cephas and James.

In any case, there is the Taiping Messiah Hong Xiuquan,[31] a nineteenth-century revolutionary leader: he proclaimed himself "the Little Brother of Jesus." Obviously he didn't mean he was a blood relative of the ancient Jesus of Nazareth. No doubt Hong Xiuquan believed in a historical Jesus, but what he had in mind was that he was the incarnation of a second heavenly Son-hypostasis of God. James' title may have implied something like that, especially since that is pretty much the same thing Gnostics meant when they called Thomas the Twin of Jesus, though they didn't think Jesus had been flesh-and-blood mortal.

Jesus: Sender or Recipient?

Wells and others have insisted that it is just inexplicable, on the usual understanding of a historical Jesus, why the epistles never quote him. To be sure, the epistles do contain many gems that sound like variants on sayings that are ascribed to Jesus in the gospels. But none of these are attributed to Jesus by the epistolarians. James D.G. Dunn asks us to believe that Paul and James did mean the reader to detect dominical logia at such points but thought it best to leave them as allusions for those who had ears to hear ("wink, wink, nudge, nudge").[32] With great respect to a great scholar, I must confess that this seems to me very strained. It is one of those arguments no one would take seriously except as a tool to extricate oneself from a tight spot. Surely if one wants to settle a question by appealing to the words of Jesus, one will make sure the reader understands that they are in fact words of Jesus — by saying so.

Along the same lines, Wells reasons that, if the writers of the New Testament epistles had access to anything like the sayings tradition of the Synoptics, they must surely have cited them when the same subjects came up in the situations they addressed. Is celibacy at issue (1 Corinthians 7:7, 25–35)? Why not quote Matthew 19:11–12? Tax-evasion (Romans 13:6)? Mark 12:17 would surely come in handy. Dietary laws (Romans 14:1–4; 1 Corinthians 8; Colossians 2:20–21) in contention? Mark 7:15 would made short work of that. Controversy over circumcision (Romans 3:1; Galatians 5:1–12)? Thomas 53 ought to settle that one fast. On the other hand, if there were originally no dominical sayings to settle the question, it is not hard to imagine that soon people would be coining them (as they still do today in illiterate congregations where debaters try to gain points by pulling a Jesus saying or a Bible verse out of their imaginations. No one can check to prove them wrong!)[33] — or attaching Jesus' name to a saying they already liked, to make it authoritative. It makes eminent sense to suggest, in the epistles, that we see early Christian sayings just before their attribution to Jesus.

Son of Scripture

We can observe the same tendency in the events predicated of Jesus. Scholars have always seen gospel echoes of the ancient scriptures in secondary coloring or redactional juxtaposition, but the more recent scrutiny of John Dominic Crossan,[34] Randel Helms,[35] Dale and Patricia Miller,[36] and Thomas L. Brodie[37] has made it appear likely that virtually the whole gospel narrative is the product of haggadic Midrash upon the Old Testament.

Earl Doherty has clarified the resultant understanding of the gospel writers' methodology. It has been customary to suppose that early Christians began with a set of remarkable facts, then sought after-the-fact for scriptural predictions for them. It has been supposed that Hosea 11:1 provided a pedigree for Jesus' childhood sojourn in Egypt, but that it was the story of the flight into Egypt that made early Christians go searching for the Hosea text. Now it seems, by contrast, that the flight into Egypt is midrashic all the way down. The words in Hosea 11:1 "my son," catching the early Christian eye, generated the whole story, since they assumed such a prophecy about the divine Son must have had its fulfillment. And the more apparent it becomes that most gospel narratives can be adequately accounted for by reference to scriptural prototypes, Doherty suggests,[38] the more natural it is to picture early Christians beginning with a more or less vague savior myth and seeking to lend it color and detail by anchoring it in a particular historical period and clothing it in scriptural garb.

We must now envision proto-Christian exegetes "discovering" for the first time what Jesus the Son of God had done and said "according to the scriptures" by decoding the ancient texts. Today's Christian reader learns what Jesus did by reading the gospels; his ancient counterpart learned what Jesus did by reading Joshua and

1 Kings. It was not a question of memory but of creative exegesis. Let me survey the Gospel of Mark to illustrate the extent of this midrashic borrowing.[39]

At Jesus' baptism (Mark 1:9–11) the heavenly voice conflates bits and pieces of Psalms 2:7; Isaiah 42:1; and Genesis 22:12 (LXX). In the Temptation narrative (Mark 1:12–13), the forty days of Jesus in the wilderness recall both Moses' period of forty years in the desert of Midian before returning to Egypt and the forty-day retreat of Elijah to the wilderness after the contest with Baal's prophets (1 Kings 19:5–7), where Elijah, like Jesus, is ministered unto by angels. The Q tradition shared by Matthew (4:1–11) and Luke (4:1–13) and possibly abridged by Mark, plays off the Exodus tradition in yet another way. Jesus resists the devil's blandishments by citing three texts from Deuteronomy, 8:3; 6:16; 6:13, all referring to trials in the wilderness.

The recruitment of the First Disciples (Mark 1:16–20) comes from Elijah's recruitment of Elisha in 1 Kings 19:19–21. Likewise, the calling of Levi in Mark 2:14. In the Capernaum exorcism story (Mark 1:21–28) the cry of the demoniac comes directly from the defensive alarm of the Zarephath widow in 1 Kings 17:18.

The incident of Peter's Mother-in-Law (1:29–31), too, is cut from the cloth of Elijah's mantle. In 1 Kings 17:8–16, Elijah meets the widow of Zarephath and her son, and he delivers them from imminent starvation. As a result she serves the man of God. In 2 Kings 4, Elisha raises from the dead the son of the Shunammite woman, who had served him. Mark has reshuffled these elements so that this time it is the old woman herself who is raised up from her illness, not her son, who is nonetheless important to the story (Peter), and she serves the man of God, Jesus.

The story of a paralyzed man's friends tearing off the roof and lowering him to Jesus (2:1–12) seems based on 2 Kings 1:2–17a, where King Ahaziah gains his affliction by falling from his roof through the lattice and languishes in bed. Mark has borrowed the substance of the withered hand healing (Mark 3:1–6) from the miracle of the Judean prophet of 1 Kings 13:1–7*ff.*

Mark has "sandwiched together" two previous pericopae, the choosing of the twelve and the embassy of relatives (Mark 3:13–35). We must imagine that previous to Mark someone had midrashically rewritten the Exodus 18 story of Moses heeding Jethro's advice to name subordinates, resulting in a scene in which choosing the twelve disciples was the idea of the Holy Family of Jesus. Originally we would have read of Jesus' welcoming his family. And as Jethro voices his concern for the harried Moses, suggesting he share the burden with a number of helpers (18:21–22), so we would have read that James or Mary advised the choice of assistants "that they might be with him, and that he might send them out to preach" (Mark 3:14). And Jesus would only then have named the Twelve. Mark, acting in the interest of a church-political agenda, has broken the story into two and reversed its halves so as to bring dishonor on the relatives of Jesus and to take from them the credit for choosing the Twelve (which is also why he emphasizes that Jesus "summoned those that he *himself* wanted," *i.e.*, it was all his own idea). Jesus, however, does not, like Moses, choose seventy (though Luke will restore this number, Luke 10:1), but only twelve, based on the choice of the twelve spies in Deuteronomy 1:23.

Matthew and Luke (hence the Q source) make an interesting addition to Jesus' response to the scribes. Luke 11:19–20, as usual, is probably closer to the Q original. Compressed into these verses is an unmistakable midrash upon the Exodus story of Moses' miracle contest with the magicians of Pharaoh. Initially able to match Moses feat for feat, they prove incapable of copying the miracle of the gnats and warn Pharaoh to give in, since "This is the finger of God" and no mere sorcery like theirs (Exodus 8:19).

The Stilling of the Storm (Mark 4:35–41) has been rewritten from Jonah's adventure, with additions from certain of the Psalms. The basis for the story can be recognized in Jonah 1:4–6;

1:15b–16a plus Psalm 107:23–29. The Gerasene Demoniac (5:1–20) mixes materials from Psalms 107:10, 4, 6, 14, and *Odyssey* 9:101–565. Jairus' Daughter and the Woman with the Issue of Blood (5:21–24, 35–43) are a complex retelling, again, of the tale of Elisha and the Shunammite woman (2 Kings 4). Jesus' rejection at home (Mark 6:1–6) goes back to the story of Saul as an improbable prophet in 1 Samuel 10:1–27.

Mark's version of the Mission Charge (6:7–13) may have been influenced by the practices of Cynic preachers, but they surely owe something to the Elisha stories. When Jesus forbids the missioners to "take along money nor two cloaks," he is warning them not to repeat Gehazi's fatal error; he had exacted from Naaman "a talent of silver and two cloaks" (2 Kings 5:22). The provision of a staff (Mark 6:8) may come from Gehazi's mission for Elisha to the Shunammite's son: "take my staff in your hand and go" (2 Kings 4:29a). Luke must have recognized this, since he returned to the same text to add to his own mission charge to the seventy (Luke 10:4b) the stipulation "and salute no one on the road," borrowed directly from Elisha's charge to Gehazi in 2 Kings 4:29b.

In the story of the death of the Baptizer (6:14–29), Herod Antipas' words to his step-daughter come from Esther 5:3. His painting himself into the corner, having to order John's execution, may come from Darius' bamboozlement in Daniel 6:6–15.

The basis for both miraculous feeding stories (Mark 6:30–44; 8:1–10) is the story of Elisha multiplying the twenty barley loaves for a hundred men in 2 Kings 4:42–44. The walking on the sea (Mark 6:45–52) looks to come from Psalms 107 (LXX: 106): 23–30; Job 9:8b. In debate with the scribes over purity rules (7:1–23), Jesus is made to cite the LXX of Isaiah 29:13, the Hebrew original of which would not really make the required point. Less obviously, there is also a significant reference to Elijah in v. 14, "and summoning the multitude again, he said to them, 'Listen to me, all of you, and understand.'" Here we are to discern a reflection of Elijah's gesture in 1 Kings 18: 30, "Then Elijah said to all the people, 'Come near to me.'"

In Mark 7:24–30 Jesus meets a foreign woman in the district of Tyre and Sidon, who requests his help for her child, and we find ourselves back with Elijah and widow of Sidonian Zarephath in 1 Kings 17:8–16. There the prophet encounters the foreigner and does a miracle for her and her son. In both cases the miracle is preceded by a tense interchange between the prophet and the woman in which the prophet raises the bar to gauge the woman's faith. The Syrophoenician parries Jesus' initial dismissal with a clever comeback; the widow of Zarephath is bidden to take her remaining meal and to cook it up for Elijah first, whereupon the meal is indefinitely multiplied. But why does Jesus call the poor woman and her daughter, by implication, dogs? Mark has taken it from 2 Kings 8:7–15. Mark 7:31–37 where Jesus is going from Tyre and Sidon to the Sea of Galilee, and cures a man who is deaf and unable to speak, is a midrash upon Isaiah 29:18 and 35:5–6. We probably ought to add Mark 8:22–26 and 10:46–52 as midrashic fulfillments of the same texts.

Jesus' ascent of the unnamed mountain and his Transfiguration (9:1–13) is Mark's version of Moses' ascent of Mount Sinai and his shining visage in Exodus 24 and 34:29. The Markan introduction, "And six days later" (9:2), must be understood as a pointer to the Exodus account, where the glory cloud covers the height for six days (v. 16). The glowing apparition of Jesus is most obviously derived from Exodus 34:29, but we must not miss the influence of Malachi 3:2, especially since Elijah, too, appears.

Mark connects again with the story of Elisha and the Shunammite (2 Kings 4) in his story of the deaf-mute epileptic (9:14–29). Elisha dispatched his disciple with his own potent staff to restore the Shunammite's dead son, but he could not (2 Kings 4:31). But Elisha succeeded where Gehazi failed (2 Kings 4:32–35).

The account of the disciples jockeying for position (Mark 9:33–37) reaches back to the Pentateuchal disputes between Moses and

Aaron and Miriam (Numbers 12) and/or Dathan and Abiram (Numbers 16). Mark returns to the same portion of Numbers for his story of the independent exorcist *etc.* (9:38–40). The man casting out demons outside of Jesus' retinue is based directly on Eldad and Medad (Numbers 11:24–30). John is a renamed Joshua who protested that "Eldad and Medad are prophesying in the camp," *i.e.*, "not following us" (Mark 9:38).

Mark modeled 10:13–16 where Jesus rebukes the disciples for chasing children away from him, on 2 Kings 4: again, the story of Elisha and the Shunammite. "And when she came to the mountain, to the man of God, she caught hold of his feet. And Gehazi came to thrust her away. But the man of God said, 'Let her alone, for she is in bitter distress, and the LORD has hidden it from me and has not told me' " (v. 27).

Jesus has just announced his impending death and resurrection, prompting James and John to venture, "Teacher, we want you to do for us whatever we may ask of you... Grant that we may sit in your glory, one at your right, one at your left" (Mark 10:35, 37). This comes from 2 Kings 2:9, "Ask what I shall do for you before I am taken from you." Hearing the request, Elijah reflects, "You have asked a hard thing" (v. 10), just as Jesus warns James and John, "You do not know what you are asking for."

The parallel stories of the preparation for the entry into Jerusalem and the passover supper (11:1–6; 14:12–16) alike derive from 1 Samuel chapter 9, where young Saul, while hunting to find lost asses encounters the prophet Samuel, by whom he is given a special meal and anointed ruler over Israel. Though Mark does not make it explicit, the scene of Jesus entering the holy city on donkeyback (11:7–11) is a fleshing out of Zechariah 9:9. The actions and words of the crowd come right from Psalms 118:26–27. The cursing the fig tree (11:12–14, 20) stems from Psalms 37:35–36. The cleansing of the Temple (11:15–18) must have in view Malachi's messenger of the covenant who will purify the sons of Levi (3:1–3, as hinted by Mark

The Christ Myth Theory And Its Problems

1:2 and 9:3), as well as the oracle of Zechariah 14:21b, "And there shall no longer be a trader in the house of the LORD of hosts on that day." The saying of Jesus is merely a conflation of Isaiah 56:7 and Jeremiah 7:11. The parable of the Wicked Tenants (12:1–12) with its vinyard, hedge, wine-press pit, and tower, has grown out of Isaiah 5:1–7 which concerns a vinyard that has a hedge around it, a pit for a wine vat, and a tower.

The whole apocalyptic discourse of Mark (Marks "Little Apocalypse") is a cento of scripture paraphrases and quotations: Mark 13:7 comes from Daniel 11:44; Mark 13:8 from Isaiah 19:2 and/or 2 Chronicles 15:6; Mark 13:12 from Micah 7:6; Mark 13:14 from Daniel 9:27 or 12:11 and Genesis 19:17; Mark 13:19 from Daniel 12:1; Mark 13:22 from Deuteronomy 13:2; Mark 13:24 from Isaiah 13:10; Mark 13:25 from Isaiah 34:4; Mark 13:26 from Daniel 7:13, and Mark 13:27 from Zechariah 2:10 and Deuteronomy 30:4

The seed of the Last Supper story (Mark 14:17–31) is Psalms 41:9. Matthew embellishes the enigmatic figure and fate of Judas. He gets the precise amount Judas was paid, 30 silver pieces, from Zechariah 11:11b. That Judas returned the money, throwing it into the Temple treasury, and that the priests decided to use it to buy the potter's field he drew from the Syriac version ("Cast it into the *treasury*"), then the Hebrew version ("Cast it to the *potter*"). How does Matthew know Judas hanged himself? That was the fate of David's traitorous counselor Ahithophel (2 Samuel 17:23), whom scribal tradition took to be the subject of Psalms 41:9, which the gospels applied to Judas.

Peter's avowal that he will not leave Jesus' side reminds us of Elisha's three avowals that he will not leave Elijah (2 Kings 2:2, 4, 6). Or Mark may have been thinking of Ittai's loyalty pledge to David (1 Samuel 15:21). The basis of the Garden of Gethsemane scene (14:32–52) is 2 Samuel chapters 15–16. Judas' betraying kiss (14:44–45) would seem to derive from 2 Samuel 20:7–10.

Mark borrowed from Daniel 6:4 LXX the scene of the crossfire of false accusations during the Sanhedrin trial (14:55–56). Mark 14:65, where Jesus suffers blows and mockery as a false prophet, comes from 1 Kings 22:24, "Then Zedekiah the son of Chenaanah came near and struck Micaiah on the cheek, and said, 'How did the spirit of the LORD go from me to speak to you?' And Micaiah said, '*Behold, you shall see* on that day when you go into an inner chamber to hide yourself.'" Jesus' silence at both trials before the Sanhedrin and Pilate (14:60–61; 15:4–5) comes from Isaiah 50:7; 53:7.

The substructure for the crucifixion in chapter 15 is, as all recognize, Psalm 22, from which derive all the major details, including the implicit piercing of hands and feet (Mark 15: 24//Psalms 22:16b), the dividing of his garments and casting lots for them (Mark 15:24//Psalms 22:18), the "wagging heads" of the mockers (Mark 15:29//Psalms 22:7), and of course the cry of dereliction, "My God, my God, why have you forsaken me?" (Mark 15:34// Psalms 22:1). Matthew adds another quote, "He trusts in God. Let God deliver him now if he desires him" (Matthew 27:43//Psalms 22:8), as well as a strong allusion ("for he said, 'I am the son of God' " 27:43b) to Wisdom of Solomon 2:12–20.

The darkness at noon comes from Amos 8:9, while the vinegar and gall come from Psalms 69:21. How odd that the first written account of the major event of the Christian story should be composed not of historical memories but of scripture passages out of context!

Joseph of Arimathea (Mark 15:42–47) is surely a combination of King Priam, who comes to Achilles' camp to beg the body of his son Hector, and the Patriarch Joseph who asked Pharaoh's permission to bury the body of Jacob in the cave-tomb Jacob had hewn for himself back beyond the Jordan (Genesis 50:4–5). The empty tomb narrative requires no source beyond Joshua chapter 10:18, 22, 26–27. The vigil of the mourning women reflects the women's mourning cult of the dying and rising god, long familiar in Israel (Ezekiel 8:14; Zechariah 12:11; Canticles 3:1–4).

We have not forgotten the Criterion of Dissimilarity; it is now evident that it must extend from sayings paralleled in Jewish sources to stories from the Jewish scriptures. If the gospel episode looks like a rewrite of an Old Testament story, it is multiplying explanations, *contra* Occam's Razor, to suggest that the episodes *also* actually happened to Jesus. And the Principle of Analogy applies here as well: which do the gospel stories resemble more closely: contemporary experience or ancient miracle tales? Which is more likely: that a man walked on water, glowed like the sun, and rose from the dead, or that someone has rewritten a bunch of well-known miracle stories?

Dying and Rising Gods

The Jesus story as attested in the epistles shows strong parallels to Middle Eastern religions based on the myths of dying and rising gods. (And this similarity is the third pillar of the traditional Christ-Myth pillar.) Originally celebrating the seasonal cycle and the yearly death and return of vegetation, these myths were reinterpreted later when peoples of the ancient nationalities relocated around the Roman Empire and in urban settings. The myths now came to symbolize the rebirth of the individual initiate as a personal rite of passage, namely new birth. Strong evidence from ancient stelae and tablets make clear that Baal and Osiris were believed to be dying and rising gods long before the Christian era. There is also pre-Christian evidence for the resurrection of Attis,[40] Adonis, and Dumuzi/Tammuz. All these survived into the Hellenistic and Roman periods, when they were available to influence Christianity. Apologists, understandably, have tried to minimize the parallels. In view of the archaeological evidence, it is only wishful thinking to claim that these other religions borrowed the common themes from Christianity. In any case the priority of the pagan versions ought to be obvious from the simple fact that church fathers and apologists from the ancient world admitted it by arguing that Satan had counterfeited the facts of the gospel and planted them in advance, much as modern Creationists have claimed Satan fabricated and planted the bones of non-existent dinosaurs, just to throw potential believers off the track.

J.Z. Smith[41] disdains the old Protestant propaganda accusing Catholicism of assimilating pagan myth and ritual, so he bends over backwards to try to make such borrowings impossible. This makes him take up the case of the conservative apologists. His particular approach is to aver that there never was a common myth of the dying and rising god. This he does by forgetting or obscuring the nature of the Ideal Type, as discussed above. Pointing out secondary, even trivial, differences between specific myths, he would have us deny they form a general type. But again, one might as well argue there is no such thing as a "religion" or a "miracle story" because the actual cases are not all exactly alike.

I must admit that when I first read of these mythic parallels in Gilbert Murray's *Five Stages of Greek Religion*,[42] it hit me like a ton of bricks. No assurances I received from any Christian scholar I read ever sounded like anything other than specious special pleading to me, and, believe me, I was disappointed. This was before I had ever read of the Principle of Analogy, but when I did learn about that axiom, I was able to give a name to what was so powerful in Murray's presentation. Yet I must admit that even this is not enough to make one discount the existence of a historical Jesus. It does not push us beyond Bultmann who reasoned that the resurrection faith, though based on Easter morning visions, was articulated in terms of these Mystery Religions myths. Bultmann regarded Christ-Myth theorists as insane.[43] And yet Bultmann was inconsistent: trying to have his cake for the queen of heaven and eat it, too. You mean, the first disciples *did* actually have visions of some type, persuading them that Jesus was risen, and then they adopted Mystery Religion parallels? Too many explanations. There is no more reason to posit a core experience than in the case of Attis. *And* yet, for all this, there still *might* have been a historical Jesus, even if there was no historical Easter morning experience. This is why the rest of the Jesus story is vital.

The Mythic Hero Archetype

I have already tried to give some idea of the extent to which the gospel story represents a tapestry of scripture quotes from the Old Testament. That is already enough to vitiate the use of gospel materials to reconstruct a life of Jesus. If you can explain it from systematic Old Testament borrowing, it is superfluous to look for anything else. But let me approach it from a slightly different angle, one equally powerful to my mind, namely that of the *Mythic Hero Archetype* compiled and delineated by Lord Raglan, Otto Rank, Alan Dundes[44] and others from the hero myths, both Indo-European and Semitic. Here are the twenty-two recurrent features, highlighting those appearing in the gospel story of Jesus. They make it pretty clear that it is not merely the death-and-resurrection complex in which the Jesus story parallels myth more than history.

1. *mother is a royal virgin*
2. *father is a king*
3. father related to mother
4. *unusual conception*
5. *hero reputed to be son of god*
6. *attempt to kill hero*
7. *hero spirited away*
8. *reared by foster parents in a far country*
9. *no details of childhood*
10. *goes to future kingdom*
11. is victor over king
12. marries a princess (often daughter of predecessor)
13. *becomes king*

14. *for a time he reigns uneventfully*
15. *he prescribes laws*
16. *later loses favor with gods or his subjects*
17. *driven from throne and city*
18. *meets with mysterious death*
19. *often at the top of a hill*
20. *his children, if any, do not succeed him* [*i.e., does not found a dynasty*]
21. *his body is not buried*
22. *nonetheless has one or more holy sepulchers*

Jesus' mother Mary is a virgin, though not of royal blood, though later apocrypha, as if to fill the lack, do make Mary Davidic. Joseph is "of the house of David," though he does not reign, but that is just the point: his heir, the true Davidic king, is *coming*. Mary and Joseph are not related. Jesus' conception is certainly unusual, being virginal and miraculous. Jesus is the Son of God, as more and more people begin to recognize. He is immediately persecuted by the reigning king, Herod the Great. In most hero tales, the persecutor is not only the reigning king but also the hero's father who may fear his son overthrowing him. This role has been split in the Jesus story, Joseph being a royal heir but not king, while another, Herod, sits on Joseph's rightful throne. Fleeing persecution, the hero takes refuge in a distant land, Egypt. Mary is not a foster parent, though Joseph is. There are no details about Jesus' childhood or upbringing. The one apparent exception, Jesus' visit to the temple when he is bar-mitzvah age (Luke 2:41–52), is itself a frequent hero mytheme, that of the child prodigy.

Jesus goes to Jerusalem to be acclaimed as king, though he eschews worldly power. Nonetheless, he comes into conflict with the rulers as if he had. He does not marry (though, again, as if to fill the gap, pious speculation has always suspected he married Mary Magdalene). Does Jesus have a peaceful reign, issuing laws? Not exactly. But while enjoying popular esteem as King of the Jews, for the moment unmolested, he does hold forth in the temple court, issuing teachings and moral commandments. Suddenly the once-ardent followers turn on him, demanding his blood. They drive Jesus out of the city to be crucified atop the hill of Golgotha. Though temporarily buried, his tomb turns up empty, and later various sites were nominated his burial place. He has no children, except in modern additions to the Jesus story in which he founded the Merovingian dynasty of medieval France.

Some of the heroes from whose stories scholars abstracted this list of features, this Ideal Type, were historical individuals, but inevitably their lives become encumbered by the barnacles of myth and legend. Dibelius called this tendency the Law of Biographical Analogy.[45] How do we know which ones have at least some historical basis? There will be collateral, "neutral" information about them, *e.g.*, details of upbringing, education, early plans, romances, likes and dislikes, physical appearance. In the case of Jesus there is absolutely none of this "secular" information. *Every* detail corresponds to the interest of mythology and epic.

Again, a basically historical figure will also be tied into the history of his times by well-documented events. Augustus Caesar and Cyrus of Persia would be good examples. Jesus Christ would not be. Consider the fact that at every point where the gospel story appears to obtrude upon contemporary history, there are serious difficulties in taking the narratives as historical. The Matthean Nativity story, in which Herod the Great persecutes baby Jesus, seems largely based on Josephus' nativity of Moses.[46] And besides, though Herod was a paranoid and a butcher, his many recorded atrocities do not include what one might consider a very conspicuous one: the butchery of all infants and toddlers in a particular town. And when the persecution of the infant hero is so common a theme in myth, it starts looking like a better alternative here, too.

At the other end of Jesus' career, we see him connected to the Sanhedrin, even to Caiaphas, whose tomb has been identified. But the difficulties attaching to a trial being held on Passover Eve, as well as the procedure and the grounds for a blasphemy verdict, have made many reject the historical accuracy of the story who have never entertained the Christ-Myth theory. There is also the suspicion that Jewish involvement was a creation fostered by the same tendency to whitewash the Romans that eventuated in the canonical sainthood of Pontius Pilate. And as for that worthy, it is by no means only Christ-Myth cranks and eccentrics who have rejected the story of Pilate trying to free Jesus as a piece of implausible fiction.[47] Who knows what happened? Maybe Herod the Great did try to kill the infant Messiah. Maybe the Sanhedrin did condemn Jesus as a blasphemer and a gutless Pilate finally gave in to their whims. But it does not seem very probable, and probability is the only coin in which the historian trades. He cannot build a story out of things that might possibly have happened. And this means that it is a chain of very weak links that binds Jesus to the circumstances of the first century.

Circularity and Historicity

Besides this, there are persistent alternative traditions as to when Jesus lived and died. Irenaeus thought Jesus was martyred under Claudius Caesar.[48] The Talmud makes Jesus the disciple of Rabbi Jeschua ben Perechiah and has him crucified in 83 BCE, when Alexander Jannaeus crucified so many Pharisees. The *Toledoth Jeschu* incorporated these long-lived traditions. Epiphanius reports them, too. [49] The Gospel of Peter assigns Jesus' condemnation to Herod Antipas, and (as Loisy suggested)[50] so did one of Luke's Passion sources. If Pilate had really turned the case over to Antipas, and the latter set Jesus free, why on earth does Jesus go back to Pilate? Only because Luke wants to use as much as he can of both an "L" story (*i.e.,* from a hypothetical "Lukan source," material private to "Luke") in which Antipas condemned Jesus, and Mark, in which it was Pilate who did the deed. How is it that such radically different estimates of Jesus' dates grew up side by side if there was a real event at the heart of it? We have already seen that no historical memory was available to Mark when he composed the first crucifixion account.

I am of the opinion that the varying dates are the residue of various attempts to anchor an originally mythic or legendary Jesus in more or less recent history. It would represent the ancient tendency toward euhemerism. In like manner, Herodotus had tried to calculate the dates of a hypothetically historical Hercules,[51] while Plutarch sought to pin Osiris down as an ancient king of Egypt.[52] Even the Christian Eusebius (in his *Chronological Tables* or *Summary of All Histories*) supposed that Medea and Jason really existed and dated them 780 years after the Patriarch Abraham. Ganymede and Perseus were historical figures, too, living some six centuries after Abraham. Why did the Christians bother trying to anchor Jesus in recent history? For the same reason that, according to Elaine Pagels's keen insight,[53] the Orthodox opposed the spiritual resurrection appearances of Jesus and preferred a version in which he showed up in the objective flesh to name apostles and give commands. As Arthur Drews had already posited,[54] *the urgency for historicizing Jesus was the need of a consolidating institution for an authoritative figurehead who had appointed successors and set policy* (exactly the advantage of Orthodoxy over subjectivistic Gnosticism according to Irenaeus, a true company man). It was exactly the logic whereby competing churches fabricated legends of their founding by this or that apostle: the apostle (or Jesus) could not be much older than the organization for which he is being appropriated as founder and authority.

All this implies it is utterly pointless even to ask whether there was sufficient time for legends to grow up around Jesus. Sufficient time — from *when*? It is anybody's guess when the tiny mutation of an honorific epithet of some Near Eastern dying-and-rising god took over Jesus as his name (as the Vedic Rudra became too holy or dangerous to say, and worshippers began to invoke him as "Siva," "Auspicious One").[55] Some god or savior was henceforth known as "Jesus," "Savior," and Christianity was off and running. The savior would eventually be supplied sayings borrowed from Christian sages, Jewish rabbis, and Cynics, and clothed in a biography drawn from the Old Testament. It is futile to object that monotheistic Jews would never have held truck with pagan godlings. We know they did in the Old Testament, though Ezekiel didn't like it much. And we know that first-century Judaism was not the same as Yavneh-era Judaism. There was no normative mainstream Judaism before Yavneh. And, as Margaret Barker has argued, there is every reason to believe that ancient Israelite beliefs, including polytheism, continued to survive despite official interdiction, from before the time of Josiah and Deuteronomy.[56] Barker suggests that the first Jesus-worshippers understood Jesus to be the Old Testament Yahweh, the Son of God Most High, or El Elyon, head of the Israelite pantheon from time immemorial. When he spoke of or to his Father, he meant El Elyon. And, according to Geo Widengren,[57] this ancient Yahweh was celebrated as a dying and rising god. When early Christians gave the Easter shout, "The Lord is risen!" they were only repeating the ancient acclamation, "Yahweh lives!" (Psalms 18:46), and they meant the same thing by it.

Bultmann, despite his disdain for the Christ Myth Theory, came perilously near to it when he argued that we know the *Dass* of Jesus but not the *Was*.[58] Maybe the *Was* was a myth, not a man. For if we are that short on historical content, it begins to look as if there never was any. Might there still have been a historical Jesus who, however, has been irretrievably lost behind the stained glass curtain of his own glorification? Indeed. But I should think the burden of proof lies with the one who would affirm such a Jesus.

The Christ Myth Theory And Its Problems

NOTES

1. Albert Schweitzer, *Out of my Life and Thought: An Autobiography*. Trans. C.T. Campion. (NY: Mentor / New American Library, 1953), pp. 185–186: "Because I am devoted to Christianity in deep affection, I am trying to serve it with loyalty and sincerity. In no wise do I undertake to enter the lists on its behalf with the crooked and fragile thinking of Christian apologetics, but I call on it to set itself right in the spirit of sincerity with its past and with thought in order that it may thereby become conscious of its true nature."

2. Rudolf Bultmann, *Jesus and the Word*. Trans, Louise Pettibone Smith and Erminie Huntress Lantero. (NY: Scribner's, 2nd ed, 1958), p. 173: "there can be no doubt that Jesus did the kind of deeds which were miracles to his mind and to the minds of his contemporaries… undoubtedly he healed the sick and cast out demons."

3. Herman Kahn and Anthony J. Wiener, *The Year 2000 — A Framework for Speculation on the Next Thirty-three Years* (NY: Macmillan, 1967), cited in Peter L. Berger, *A Rumor of Angels: Modern Society and the Rediscovery of the Sacred* (Garden City: Doubleday Anchor, 1970), pp.16–19. Benjamin B. Warfield adopted this "methodological atheism" as a matter of course in his scrutiny of Popish, Pentecostal, and pagan miracle stories in his *Counterfeit Miracles* (1918; rpt. London: Banner of Truth Trust, 1972).

4. Harald Riesenfeld, *The Gospel Tradition and its Beginnings: A Study in the Limits of 'Formgeschichte'* (London: Mowbray, 1957). Birger Gerhardsson, *Memory and Manuscript: Oral Transmission and Rabbinic Judaism in Early Christianity*. Trans. Eric J. Sharpe. (Uppsala: Almqvist & Wiksells, 1961). I believe that, in light of the more recent work of Jacob Neusner, the rabbinic model tends in exactly the opposite direction to that indicated by Reisenfeld and Gerhardsson. See Robert M. Price, "Messiah as Mishnah: The Problem of the Jesus-Attributed Saying." In Jacob Neusner, *Approaches to Ancient Judaism*. New Series Volume 13. University of South Florida Studies in the History of Judaism 164 (Atlanta: Scholars Press, 1998), pp. 1–19.

5. Henri Lammens, "The Koran and Tradition: How the Life of Muhammad Was Composed." Trans. Ibn Warraq. In Ibn Warraq, ed., *The Quest for the Historical Muhammad* (Amherst: Prometheus Books, 2000), pp. 169–187.

6. Ignaz Goldziher, *Etudes sur la Tradition Islamique*. Trans. L. Bercher (Paris: Adrien-Maisonneuve, 1952), pp. 58–59, 195, cited in Robert D. Smith, *Comparative Miracles* (NY: B. Herder Book Co., 1965), pp. 128–132. Ignaz Goldziher, *Introduction to Islamic Theology and Law*. Trans. Andras and Ruth Hamori. Modern Classics in Near Eastern Studies (Princeton: Princeton University Press, 1981), pp. 43–44. See also Alfred Guillaume, *The Traditions of Islam: An Introduction to the Study of the Hadith Literature* (NY: Oxford University Press, 1924), pp. 52–53, 78–79.

7. Christopher Tuckett, *Nag Hammadi and the Gospel Tradition: Synoptic Tradition in the Nag Hammadi Library*. Studies of the New Testament and its World (Edinburgh: T & T Clark, 1986). Majella Franzmann, *Jesus in the Nag Hammadi Writings* (Edinburgh: T & T Clark, 1996).

8. Norman Perrin, *Rediscovering the Teaching of Jesus* (NY: Harper & Row, 1976), p.39.

9. Jacob Neusner, *In Search of Talmudic Biography: The Problem of the Attributed Saying*. Brown Judaic Studies 70 (Chico: Scholars Press, 1984).

10. Jack Dean Kingsbury, *The Christology of Mark's Gospel* (Minneapolis: Fortress Press, 1989), pp. 33–37.

11. Jonathan Z. Smith, "Dying and Rising Gods," in *The Encyclopedia of Religion*, vol. 4, ed. Mircea Eliade (NY: Macmillan, 1987), pp. 521–527. See my refutation of Smith in Price, *Deconstructing Jesus*. (Amherst: Prometheus Books, 2000), pp. 88–91.

12. Helmut Koester, *Introduction to the New Testament: History, Culture and Religion of the Hellenistic Age* (Berlin: Walter de Gruyter,1987).

13. Michael Allen Williams, *Rethinking "Gnosticism": An Argument for Dismantling a Dubious Category* (Princeton: Princeton University Press, 1996). Karen L. King, *What Is Gnosticism?* (Cambridge: Belknap Press, 2003). If there's no such thing as Gnosticism, then there's no Buddhism or Presbyterianism, either.

14. Paul Feyerabend, *Against Method* (NY: Verso, Rev. ed., 1988), p. 14; see also chapter 3 on "counterinduction," pp. 24–32.

15. Thomas S. Kuhn, *The Structure of Scientific Revolutions* (Chicago: University of Chicago Press, 1962), p. 65.

16. Solomon Zeitlin, *Josephus on Jesus: With Particular Reference to the Slavonic Josephus and the Hebrew Josippon* (Philadelphia: Dropsie College for Hebrew and Cognate Learning, 1931), Chapter VII, "The Christ Passage in Josephus," pp. 61–70.

17. Shlomo Pines, *An Arabic Version of the Testimonium Flavianum and its Implications* (Jerusalem: Israel Academy of Sciences and Humanities, 1971.

18. Robert E. Van Voorst, *Jesus Outside the New Testament: An Introduction to the Ancient Evidence* (Grand Rapides: Eerdmans, 2000), pp. 88–104.

19. Robert M. Price, "Schleiermacher's Dormant Discovery." *Journal of Higher Criticism* (9/2) Fall 2002, pp. 203–216.

20. Jean Magne, 'Les paroles sur la coupe,' in Joel Delobel (ed.), *Logia: Les paroles de Jesus — The Sayings of Jesus: Memorial Joseph Coppens*. Bibliotheca ephemeridum theologicarum lovaniensum 59 (Leuven: Peeters/Leuven University Press, 1982), pp. 485–490; *From Christianity to Gnosis and From Gnosis to Christianity: An Itinerary through the Texts To and From the Tree of Paradise*. Trans. A.F.W. Armstrong; Brown Judaic Studies 286 (Atlanta: Scholars Press, 1993), p. 33. Cited in William O. Walker, Jr., *Interpolations in the Pauline Letters*. Journal for the Study of the New Testament Supplement Series 213 (London: Sheffield Academic Press, 2001), p. 19. *Cf.* Wells, *Jesus of the Early Christians*, p. 270: "In verses 22 and 33 Paul is urging the faithful to share the food in a decent and civilized way; while from verses 23 to 32 he is talking not of this ethical problem, but of the mystical properties of the Lord's body. Some have therefore regarded verses 23–32 as an interpolation." (Wells himself, however, is not convinced the passage is an interpolation.)

21. Hyam Maccoby, *Paul and Hellenism* (Philadelphia: Trinity Press International, 1991), pp. 92–93.

22. See the discussion of Emmerich and her novel in Albert Schweitzer, *The Quest of the Historical Jesus: A Critical Study of its Progress from Reimarus to Wrede*. Trans, W. Montgomery (NY: Macmillan, 1961), pp. 108–110.

23. Paul L. Couchoud, "The Historicity of Jesus: A Reply to Alfred Loisy," *Hibbert Journal* 37, no. 2 (1938), pp. 193–214. Couchoud, *The Creation of Christ: An Outline of the Beginnings of Christianity*. Trans. C. Bradlaugh Bonner (London: Watts & Co., 1939), p, 438.

24. G.A. Wells, *The Jesus of the Early Christians: A Study in Christian Origins.* London: Pemberton Books, 1971); Wells, *Who Was Jesus?* (London: Elek/Pemberton, 1975); Wells, *The Historical Evidence for Jesus* (Buffalo: Prometheus Books, 1988); Wells, *Who Was Jesus? A Critique of the New Testament Record* (LaSalle: Open Court, 1989).

25. Alvar Ellegård, *Jesus One Hundred Years Before Christ: A Study in Creative Mythology* (London: Century, 1999).

26. Paul Veyne, *Did the Greeks Believe in their Myths? An Essay on the Constitutive Imagination.* Trans. Paula Wissing (Chicago: University of Chicago Press, 1988), pp.17–18, 88.

27. Earl Doherty, *The Jesus Puzzle: Did Christianity Begin with a Mythical Christ?* Ottawa: Canadian Humanist Publications, 1999), pp. 120–122.

28. Wendy Doniger O'Flaherty, ed. and trans., *The Rig Veda: An Anthology* (Baltimore: Penguin Books, 1981), pp. 29–32.

29. Wells, *Jesus of the Early Christians*, pp. 141–142.

30. Walter Schmithals, *The Office of Apostle in the Early Church.* Trans. John E. Steely (Nashville: Abingdon Press, 1969), pp. 82–87.

31. Jonathan D. Spence, *God's Chinese Son: The Taiping Heavenly Kingdom of Hong Xiuquan* (NY: W.W. Norton & Company, 1996), pp. 46–49, 64–65.

32. James D.G. Dunn, "Jesus Tradition in Paul," in Bruce Chilton and Craig A. Evans (eds.), *Studying the Historical Jesus* (Leiden: E.J. Brill, 1994), pp. 177–178.

33. Nathan L. Gerrard, "The Holiness Movement in Southern Appalachia," in *The Charismatic Movement*, ed. Michael P. Hamilton (Grand Rapids: Eerdmans, 1975), p. 165.

The Christ Myth Theory And Its Problems

34. John Dominic Crossan, *The Cross That Spoke: The Origins of the Passion Narrative* (San Francisco: Harper & Row, Publishers, 1988).

35. Randel Helms, *Gospel Fictions*. (Buffalo: Prometheus Books, 1989).

36. Dale Miller and Patricia Miller. *The Gospel of Mark as Midrash on Earlier Jewish and New Testament Literature*. Studies in the Bible and Early Christianity 21 (Lewiston/Queenston/Lampeter: Edwin Mellen Press, 1990).

37. Thomas L. Brodie, "Luke the Literary Interpreter: Luke - Acts as a Systematic Rewriting and Updating of the Elijah-Elisha Narrative in 1 and 2 Kings." Ph.D. dissertation presented to Pontifical University of St. Thomas Aquinas, Rome. 1988.

38. Doherty, pp. 79–82, 225–230.

39. For the scriptural roots of all four gospels and Acts (and in greater detail), see Robert M. Price, "New Testament Narrative as Old Testament Midrash" in Jacob Neusner and Alan J. Avery Peck (eds.), *Encyclopedia of Midrash: Biblical Interpretation in Formative Judaism* (Leiden: E.J. Brill, 2005), Volume One, pp. 534–573. Besides Crossan, Helms, the Millers, and Brodie, I owe a great debt to the work of John Bowman, *The Gospel of Mark: The New Christian Jewish Passover Haggadah*. Studia Post-Biblica 8 (Leiden: E.J. Brill, 1965); J. Duncan M. Derrett, *The Making of Mark: The Scriptural Bases of the Earliest Gospel*. Volumes 1 and 2. Shipston-on-Stour (Warwickshire: P. Drinkwater, 1985); Frank Kermode, *The Genesis of Secrecy: On the Interpretation of Narrative*. The Charles Eliot Norton Lectures 1977–1978 (Cambridge: Harvard University Press, 1979); Wolfgang Roth, *Hebrew Gospel: Cracking the Code of Mark* (Oak Park: Meyer-Stone Books, 1988); and Rikki E. Watts, *Isaiah's New Exodus and Mark*. Wissenschaftliche Untersuchungen zum Neuen Testament 2. Reihe 88 (Tübingen: Mohr Siebeck, 1997).

40. Maarten J. Vermaseren, *Cybele and Attis: The Myth and the Cult*. Trans. A.M.H. Lemmers (London: Thames and Hudson, 1977), pp. 119–124. For other pre-Christian dying and rising deities, see Tryggve N.D. Mettinger, *The Riddle of Resurrection: "Dying and Rising Gods" in the Ancient Near East*. Coniectanea Biblica Old Testament Series 50. (Stockholm: Almqvist & Wiksell International, 2001).

41. Jonathan Z. Smith, *Drudgery Divine: On the Comparison of Early Christianities and the Religions of Late Antiquity.* Jordan Lectures in Comparative Religion, XIV, School of Oriental and African Studies, University of London (Chicago: University of Chicago Press, 1990).

42. Gilbert Murray, *Five Stages of Greek Religion* (Garden City: Doubleday Anchor Books, 3rd ed, 1951). "Preface to the Third Edition," pp. v–ix.

43. Bultmann, *Jesus and the Word*, p. 13: "Of course the doubt as to whether Jesus really existed is unfounded and not worth refutation. No sane person can doubt that Jesus stands as founder behind the historical movement whose first distinct stage is represented by the oldest Palestinian community." But one has to wonder whether Bultmann protests too much, knowing how close his critics charged he himself had come to such a view.

44. Alan Dundes, "The Hero Pattern in the Life of Jesus," in Robert A. Segal, ed., *In Quest of the Hero.* (Princeton: Princeton University Press, 1990).

45. Martin Dibelius, *From Tradition to Gospel* (NY: Scribner's, n.d.), pp. 104–108.

46. Josephus, *Antiquities of the Jews*, 2.9.2–3.

47. S.G. F. Brandon, *The Trial of Jesus of Nazareth* (NY: Stein and Day, 1968), Chapter Four: "The Scandal of the Roman Cross: Mark's Solution," pp. 81–106. Burton L. Mack, *A Myth of Innocence: Mark and Christian Origins* (Minneapolis: Fortress Press, 1991), pp. 293–296.

48. Irenaeus, *Demonstration* 74.

49. G.R.S. Mead, *Did Jesus Live 100 B.C.?* (New Hyde Park: University Books, 1968), Chapter VIII, "The Talmud 100 Years B.C. Story of Jesus," pp. 135–151; Chapter XVI, "The 100 Years B.C. Date in the Toldoth," pp. 302–323; Chapter XIX., "The 100 Years B.C. Date in Epiphanius," pp. 388–412.

50. Alfred F. Loisy, *The Origins of the New Testament*. Trans. L.P. Jacks. (London: Allen and Unwin, 1950), p. 167.

The Christ Myth Theory And Its Problems

51. Veyne, P. 32.

52. Plutarch, *Isis and Osiris* 13.

53. Elaine Pagels, *The Gnostic Gospels* (NY: Random House, 1979), Chapter I, "The Controversy over Christ's Resurrection: Historical Event or Symbol?" pp. 3–27.

54. Arthur Drews, *The Christ Myth*. Trans. C. DeLisle Burns. 3rd ed. (Amherst: Prometheus Books, 1998), pp. 271–272. *Cf.* Burton L. Mack, *The Lost Gospel: The Book of Q and Christian Origins* (San Francisco: HarperSanFrancisco, 1993): p. 207: "the myths of origin were written and imagined as having happened at a recent time and in a specific place." Also Veyne, p. 76: "Myth, this authorless 'it is said' that is confused with the truth, was reinterpreted as a historical or cultural memory which, starting with the eyewitnesses, would be handed down from generation to generation."

55. W.J. Wilkins, *Hindu Mythology, Vedic and Puranic* (Calcutta: Rupa and Company, 2nd ed., 1882, rpt. 1989), p. 266. In a hymn from the White Yajur Veda addressed to Rudra: "Thou art gracious [Siva] by name." Mahadev Chakravarti, *The Concept of Rudra Siva through the Ages* (Dehli: Motilal Banarsidass, 2nd rev. ed., 1994), p. 28: "The name Siva is euphemistic and is used as an attributive epithet not particularly of Rudra, but of several other Vedic deities. One of the earliest uses of Siva as a proper name of Rudra is found in the *Svetasvatara Upanisad*, in which the beginning of the cult of Rudra-Siva was traced."

56. Margaret Barker, *The Great Angel: A Study of Israel's Second God* (Louisville: Westminster/John Knox Press, 1992).

57. Geo Widengren, "Early Hebrew Myths and Their Interpretation." In S.H. Hooke, *Myth, Ritual, and Kingship: Essays on the Theory and Practice of Kingship in the Ancient Near East and in Israel* (NY: Oxford University Press, 1958), pp. 149–203.

58. Rudolf Bultmann, *Theology of the New Testament*. Trans. Kendrick Grobel. Scribner Studies in Contemporary Theology. (NY: Scribner's, 1955) II: p. 66.

New Testament Narrative as Old Testament Midrash

A. Introduction

The line is thin between extrapolating new meanings from ancient scriptures (borrowing the authority of the old) and actually composing new scripture (or quasi-scripture) by extrapolating from the old. By this process of midrashic expansion grew the Jewish *haggadah*, new narrative commenting on old (scriptural) narrative by rewriting it. *Haggadah* is a species of *hypertext*, and thus it cannot be fully understood without reference to the underlying text on which it forms a kind of commentary. The earliest Christians being Jews, it is no surprise that they practiced haggadic expansion of scripture, resulting in new narratives partaking of the authority of the old. The New Testament gospels and the Acts of the Apostles can be shown to be Christian haggadah upon Jewish scripture, and these narratives can be neither fully understood nor fully appreciated without tracing them to their underlying sources, the object of the present chapter.

Christian exegetes have long studied the gospels in light of Rabbinical techniques of biblical interpretation including allegory, midrash, and pesher. The discovery of the Dead Sea Scrolls lent great impetus to the recognition of the widespread use among New Testament writers of the pesher technique whereby prophetic proof texts for the divine preordination of recent events was sought, on the assumption that scripture could not become a dead letter simply because its original reference was in the past. What if the Holy Spirit had "smuggled" a second sense, prophetic of future events? Such references to events yet unborn would make no sense to readers who would never see them unfold, but could only be understood after the fact, out of context, virtually coded messages to the future. Sectarians like the Dead Sea Scrolls monks believed they had thus discovered predictions of their brotherhood and of their guru, the Teacher of Righteousness.

Slower (but still steady) in coming has been the realization of the wide extent to which the stories comprising the gospels and the Acts of the Apostles are themselves the result of haggadic midrash upon stories from the Old Testament (as we may call it here in view of the Christian perspective on the Jewish canon that concerns us). This was a way of expounding scriptural texts by retelling and embellishing them, sometimes with the slenderest residual connection with the original. The New Testament writers partook of a social and religious environment in which currents of Hellenism and Judaism flowed together and interpenetrated in numerous surprising ways, the result of which was not merely the use of several versions of the Old Testament texts, in various languages, but also the easy switching back and forth between Jewish and Greek sources like Euripides, Homer, and Mystery Religion traditions.

Earlier scholars (*e.g.*, John Wick Bowman), as many today (*e.g.*, J. Duncan M. Derrett), saw gospel echoes of the ancient scriptures in secondary coloring here or redactional juxtaposition of traditional Jesus stories there. But the more recent scrutiny of John Dominic Crossan, Randel Helms, Dale and Patricia Miller, and Thomas L. Brodie has made it inescapably clear that virtually the entirety of the gospel narratives and much of the Acts are wholly the product of haggadic midrash upon previous scripture.

Earl Doherty has clarified the resultant understanding of the gospel writers' methodology. It has been customary to suppose that early Christians began with a set of remarkable facts (whether few or many) and sought after the fact for scriptural predictions for them, the goal being to show that even though the founding events of their religion defied contemporary messianic expectation, they were nonetheless in better accord with prophecy, that recent events clarified ancient prophecy in retrospect. Thus modern scholars might admit that Hosea 11:1 ("Out of Egypt I have called my son") had to be taken out of context to provide a pedigree for the fact of Jesus' childhood sojourn in Egypt, but that it was the story of the flight into Egypt that made early Christians go searching for the Hosea text. Now it is apparent, just to take this example, that the flight into Egypt is midrashic all the way down. That is, the words in Hosea 11:1 "my son," catching the early Christian eye, generated the whole story, since they assumed such a prophecy about the divine Son must have had its fulfillment. And the more apparent it becomes that most gospel narratives can be adequately accounted for by reference to scriptural prototypes, Doherty suggests, the more natural it is to picture early Christians beginning with a more or less vague savior myth and seeking to lend it color and detail by anchoring it in a particular historical period and clothing it in scriptural garb.

We must now envision proto-Christian exegetes "discovering" for the first time what Jesus the Son of God had done and said "according to the scriptures" by decoding the ancient texts. Today's Christian reader learns what Jesus did by reading the gospels; his ancient counterpart learned what Jesus did by reading Joshua and 1 Kings. It was not a question of memory but of creative exegesis. Sometimes the signals that made particular scriptural texts attractive for this purpose are evident (like "my son" in Hosea 11:1, "Out of Egypt I have called my son."), sometimes not. But in the end the result is a new perspective according to which we must view the gospels and Acts as analogous with the Book of Mormon, an inspiring pastiche of stories derived creatively from previous scriptures by a means of literary extrapolation.

Our purpose here will be to review the bulk of the New Testament narratives, indicating in as brief a compass as possible how each has been derived from previous scripture. Mark will receive the most attention, as Matthew and Luke have used Mark as the basis of their narratives; there are fewer uniquely Matthean and Lukan items. John's Gospel and the Acts will receive more selective treatment, too, as John generally cannibalizes the Synoptic Gospels (or their underlying traditions, if one prefers) rather than deriving its material anew directly from scripture. Acts likewise draws more from other sources or creates freely. To anticipate, we will see how virtually any scriptural source was fair game, though the favorite tendencies are to draw from the Exodus saga and the Elijah and Elisha cycles. For his part, Mark relied about as heavily on the *Iliad* and the *Odyssey* (perhaps seeing the parallel between the adventurous wanderings of both Exodus and the *Odyssey* as well as a punning resemblance between their titles, or between Odysseus and the οδος of the itinerant Jesus; see Watts, pp. 124–128).

A far greater number of gospel Old Testament coincidences have been proposed than we will consider here. We will only consider those rendered compelling by the existence of striking parallels at crucial or numerous points, ignoring many, more subtle, suggestions that scholars have proposed as secondary implications of their basic theories. The danger is otherwise great that, in seeking to spot the ancient writers' own exegesis, we may ascribe to them our own creative midrash. What strikes our eye as an irresistible combination of fortuitous texts may not have occurred to them.

B. The Gospel of Mark

1. Introduction (1:1–3)

> 1. The beginning of the gospel of Jesus Christ, the Son of God. 2. As it is written in Isaiah the prophet, "Behold, I send my messenger before thy face, who shall prepare thy way; 3. the voice of one crying in the wilderness: Prepare the way of the Lord, make his paths straight —"

The syncretic flavor of Mark is at once evident from his reproduction of a piece of Augustan imperial propaganda and his setting it beside a tailored scripture quote. "The beginning of the gospel of Jesus Christ the Son of God" closely matches the formula found on a monument erected by the Provincial Assembly in Asia Minor (1st century BCE): "Whereas... Providence... has... brought our life to the peak of perfection in giving us Augustus Caesar... who, being sent to us and to our descendants as a savior..., and whereas... the birthday of the god has been for the whole world **the beginning of the gospel** (ευαγγελιον) **concerning him**, let all reckon a new era beginning from the date of his birth." (Helms, p. 24) As is well known, Mark proceeds to introduce as from Isaiah a conflation of passages, Malachi 3:1a, "Behold, I send my messenger/angel to prepare the way before me," and Exodus 23:20a, "Behold, I send a [LXX: my] messenger/angel before you, to guard you on the way," plus Isaiah 40:3, "A voice cries: 'In the wilderness prepare the way of the LORD; make straight in the desert a highway for our God." The messenger/angel has been made to refer to John the Baptizer, while the speaker seems to be Jesus. The wilderness is no longer, as originally, the place where the way is to be paved, but rather the location of the crying prophetic voice, that of John. The Dead Sea Scrolls sect had used the same Isaiah passage to prooftext their own desert witness.

2. Jesus' Baptism (1:9–11)

9. In those days Jesus came from Nazareth of Galilee and was baptized by John in the Jordan. 10. And when he came up out of the water, immediately he saw the heavens opened and the Spirit descending upon him like a dove; 11. and a voice came from heaven, "Thou art my beloved Son; with thee I am well pleased."

The scene in broad outline may derive from Zoroastrian traditions of the inauguration of Zoroaster's ministry. Son of a Vedic priest, Zoroaster immerses himself in the river for purification, and as he comes up from the water, the archangel Vohu Mana appears to him, proffering a cup and commissions him to bear the tidings of the one God Ahura Mazda, whereupon the evil one Ahriman tempts him to abandon this call. In any case, the scene has received vivid midrashic coloring. The heavenly voice (*bath qol*) speaks a conflation of three scriptural passages. "You are my beloved son, in whom I am well pleased" (Mark 1:11) combines bits and pieces of Psalms 2:7, the divine coronation decree, "You are my son. Today I have begotten you;" Isaiah 42:1, the blessing on the returning Exiles, "Behold my servant, whom I uphold, my chosen, in whom my soul delights;" and Genesis 22:12 (LXX), where the heavenly voice bids Abraham to sacrifice his "beloved son." And as William R. Stegner points out, Mark may have in mind a Targumic tradition whereby Isaac, bound on the altar, looks up into heaven and sees the heavens opened with angels and the Shekinah of God, a voice proclaiming, "Behold, two chosen ones, *etc.*" There is even the note that the willingness of Isaac to be slain may serve to atone for Israel's sins. Here is abundant symbolism making Jesus king, servant, and atoning sacrifice.

In view of parallels elsewhere between John and Jesus on the one hand and Elijah and Elisha on the other, some (Miller, p. 48) also see in the Jordan baptism and the endowment with the spirit a repetition of 2 Kings 2, where, near the Jordan, Elijah bequeaths "a double portion" of his own miracle-working spirit to Elisha, who henceforth functions as his successor and superior.

3. The Temptations (Mark 1:12–13)

12. The Spirit immediately drove him out into the wilderness.
13. And he was in the wilderness forty days, tempted by Satan; and he was with the wild beasts; and the angels ministered to him.

The forty days of Jesus in the wilderness recall both Moses' period of forty years in the desert of Midian before returning to Egypt (Bowman, p. 109) and the forty-day retreat of Elijah to the wilderness after the contest with Baal's prophets:

64

5. And he lay down and slept under a broom tree; and behold, an angel touched him, and said to him, "Arise and eat." 6. And he looked, and behold, there was at his head a cake baked on hot stones and a jar of water. And he ate and drank, and lay down again. 7. And the angel of the LORD came again a second time, and touched him, and said, "Arise and eat, else the journey will be too great for you." 8. And he arose, and ate and drank, and went in the strength of that food forty days and forty nights to Horeb the mount of God. (1 Kings 19:5–8).

There Elijah, like Jesus, is ministered unto by angels (Miller, p. 48). The Q tradition shared by Matthew (4:1–11) and Luke (4:1–13) and possibly abridged by Mark, plays off the Exodus tradition in yet another way. Jesus resists the devil's blandishments by citing three texts from Deuteronomy.

And he humbled you and let you hunger and fed you with manna, which you did not know, nor did your fathers know; that he might make you know that man does not live by bread alone, but that man lives by everything that proceeds out of the mouth of the LORD. (Deuteronomy 8:3)

You shall not put the LORD your God to the test, as you tested him at Massah. (Deuteronomy 6:16)

You shall fear the LORD your God, and him only shall you serve, and you shall cleave to him, and by his name you shall swear. (Deuteronomy 6:13 LXX)

All of these refer to trials of the people of Israel in the wilderness (the manna, Massa, and idolatry), which they failed, but which Jesus, embodying a new Israel, passes with flying colors.

4. Commencement of the Ministry (Mark 1:14–15)

14. Now after John was arrested, Jesus came into Galilee, preaching the gospel of God, 15. and saying, "The time is fulfilled, and the kingdom of God is at hand; repent, and believe in the gospel."

Only once he has completed the ordeal in the wilderness does Jesus begin his preaching of the near advent of the Kingdom of God. Bowman rightly observes the parallel to Moses leaving the wilderness, with Aaron, to announce to the children of Israel in the house of bondage that liberation would soon be theirs. (*ibid.*).

5. *Recruitment of the First Disciples (Mark 1:16–20)*

16. And passing along by the Sea of Galilee, he saw Simon and Andrew the brother of Simon casting a net in the sea; for they were fishermen. 17. And Jesus said to them, "Follow me and I will make you become fishers of men." 18. And immediately they left their nets and followed him. 19. And going on a little farther, he saw James the son of Zebedee and John his brother, who were in their boat mending the nets. 20. And immediately he called them; and they left their father Zebedee in the boat with the hired servants, and followed him.

As Bowman suggests (p. 157), Jesus summons James and John as well as Peter and Andrew, two pairs of brothers, as a gospel counterpart to Moses' recruiting his own unsuspecting brother Aaron at the analogous point in the Exodus story (4:27–28).

27. The LORD said to Aaron, "Go into the wilderness to meet Moses." So he went, and met him at the mountain of God and kissed him. 28. And Moses told Aaron all the words of the LORD with which he had sent him, and all the signs which he had charged him to do.

But the events, minimal as they are, come from Elijah's recruitment of Elisha in 1 Kings 19:19–21.

19. So he departed from there, and found Elisha the son of Shaphat, who was plowing, with twelve yoke of oxen before him, and he was with the twelfth. Elijah passed by him and cast his mantle upon him. 20. And he left the oxen, and ran after Elijah, and said, "Let me kiss my father and my mother, and then I will follow you." And he said

to him, "Go back again; for what have I done to you?" 21. And he returned from following him, and took the yoke of oxen, and slew them, and boiled their flesh with the yokes of the oxen, and gave it to the people, and they ate. Then he arose and went after Elijah, and ministered to him.

Likewise, the calling of Levi in Mark 2:14: "And as he passed on, he saw Levi the son of Alphaeus sitting at the tax office, and he said to him, 'Follow me.' And he rose and followed him." All are said to have abandoned their family livelihoods on the spot to follow the prophet.

6. Exorcism at Capernaum (Mark 1:21–28)

21. And they went into Capernaum; and immediately on the sabbath he entered the synagogue and taught. 22. And they were astonished at his teaching, for he taught them as one who had authority, and not as the scribes. 23. And immediately there was in their synagogue a man with an unclean spirit; 24. and he cried out, "What have you to do with us, Jesus of Nazareth? Have you come to destroy us? I know who you are, the Holy One of God." 25. But Jesus rebuked him, saying, "Be silent, and come out of him!" 26. And the unclean spirit, convulsing him and crying with a loud voice, came out of him. 27. And they were all amazed, so that they questioned among themselves, saying, "What is this? A new teaching! With authority he commands even the unclean spirits, and they obey him." 28. And at once his fame spread everywhere throughout all the surrounding region of Galilee.

Mark has set this first teaching and exorcism of Jesus at the town called Capernaum ("Village of Nahum") to hint at Nahum 1:15a (LXX), the only passage outside of Isaiah to use the term ευαγγελιζο– μενου in a strictly religious sense. "Behold upon the mountains the feet of him that brings glad tidings and publishes peace!" For Mark, that is of course Jesus. And so what better town for him to have begun bearing these gospel tidings than that of Nahum? (Miller, p. 58)

The Christ Myth Theory And Its Problems

The rude heckling of the local demoniac, "What have we to do with you, Jesus of Nazareth? Have you come to destroy us? I know who you are — the Holy One of God!" comes directly from the defensive alarm of the Zarephath widow in 1 Kings 17:18: "What have you against me, O man of God? You have come to me to bring my sin to remembrance, and to cause the death of my son!" (Miller, p. 76).

7. Peter's Mother-in-Law (Mark 1:29–31)

29. And immediately he left the synagogue, and entered the house of Simon and Andrew, with James and John. 30. Now Simon's mother-in-law lay sick with a fever, and immediately they told him of her. 31. And he came and took her by the hand and lifted her up, and the fever left her; and she served them.

This episode, too, is cut from the cloth of Elijah's mantle. In 1 Kings 17:8–16, Elijah meets the widow of Zarephath and her son, and he delivers them from imminent starvation.

8. Then the word of the LORD came to him, 9. "Arise, go to Zarephath, which belongs to Sidon, and dwell there. Behold, I have commanded a widow there to feed you." 10. So he arose and went to Zarephath; and when he came to the gate of the city, behold, a widow was there gathering sticks; and he called to her and said, "Bring me a little water in a vessel, that I may drink." 11. And as she was going to bring it, he called to her and said, "Bring me a morsel of bread in your hand." 12. And she said, "As the LORD your God lives, I have nothing baked, only a handful of meal in a jar, and a little oil in a cruse; and now, I am gathering a couple of sticks, that I may go in and prepare it for myself and my son, that we may eat it, and die." 13. And Elijah said to her, "Fear not; go and do as you have said; but first make me a little cake of it and bring it to me, and afterward make for yourself and your son. 14. For thus says the LORD the God of Israel, 'The jar of meal shall not be spent, and the

cruse of oil shall not fail, until the day that the LORD sends rain upon the earth.' " 15. And she went and did as Elijah said; and she, and he, and her household ate for many days. 16. The jar of meal was not spent, neither did the cruse of oil fail, according to the word of the LORD which he spoke by Elijah.

As a result she serves the man of God. In 2 Kings 4:27–37, Elisha raises from the dead the son of the Shunammite woman, who had served him.

32. When Elisha came into the house, he saw the child lying dead on his bed. 33. So he went in and shut the door upon the two of them, and prayed to the LORD. 34. Then he went up and lay upon the child, putting his mouth upon his mouth, his eyes upon his eyes, and his hands upon his hands; and as he stretched himself upon him, the flesh of the child became warm. 35. Then he got up again, and walked once to and fro in the house, and went up, and stretched himself upon him; the child sneezed seven times, and the child opened his eyes. 36. Then he summoned Gehazi and said, "Call this Shunammite." So he called her. And when she came to him, he said, "Take up your son." 37. She came and fell at his feet, bowing to the ground; then she took up her son and went out.

Mark has reshuffled these elements so that this time it is the old woman herself who is raised up from her illness, not her son, who is nonetheless important to the story (Peter), and she serves the man of God, Jesus. (Miller, 79).

8. The Healing of a Leper (Mark 1:40–45)

40. And a leper came to him beseeching him, and kneeling said to him, "If you will, you can make me clean." 41. Moved with pity, he stretched out his hand and touched him, and said to him, "I will; be clean." 42. And immediately the leprosy left him, and he was made clean. 43. And he sternly charged him, and sent him away at once, 44. and said to him, "See that you say nothing to any one; but go,

show yourself to the priest, and offer for your cleansing what Moses commanded, for a proof to the people." 45. But he went out and began to talk freely about it, and to spread the news, so that Jesus could no longer openly enter a town, but was out in the country; and people came to him from every quarter.

Bowman (p. 113) has suggested, with some plausibility, that the cleansing of this leper, placed thus early in Mark's story, is meant to recall the credential miracle vouchsafed by God to Moses, whereby he could turn his hand leprous white.

> 6. Again, the LORD said to him, "Put your hand into your bosom." And he put his hand into his bosom; and when he took it out, behold, his hand was leprous, as white as snow. 7. Then God said, "Put your hand back into your bosom." So he put his hand back into his bosom; and when he took it out, behold, it was restored like the rest of his flesh. (Exodus 4:6–7).

Jesus himself cannot manifest leprosy, even momentarily, perhaps, because he must remain the spotless lamb of God without blemish.

9. Healing the Paralytic (2 Kings 1:2–17a; Mark 2:1–12)

2 Kings 1:2. Now Ahaziah fell through the lattice in his upper chamber in Samaria, and lay sick; so he sent messengers, telling them, "Go, inquire of Baal-zebub, the god of Ekron, whether I shall recover from this sickness." 3. But the angel of the LORD said to Elijah the Tishbite, "Arise, go up to meet the messengers of the king of Samaria, and say to them, 'Is it because there is no God in Israel that you are going to inquire of Baal-zebub, the god of Ekron?' 4. Now therefore thus says the LORD, 'You shall not come down from the bed to which you have gone, but you shall surely die.' " So Elijah went. 5. The messengers returned to the king, and he said to them, "Why have you returned?" 6. And they said to him, "There came a man to meet us, and said to us, 'Go back to the king who

sent you, and say to him, Thus says the LORD, Is it because there is no God in Israel that you are sending to inquire of Baal-zebub, the god of Ekron? Therefore you shall not come down from the bed to which you have gone, but shall surely die.'" 7. He said to them, "What kind of man was he who came to meet you and told you these things?" 8. They answered him, "He wore a garment of haircloth, with a girdle of leather about his loins." And he said, "It is Elijah the Tishbite." 9. Then the king sent to him a captain of fifty men with his fifty. He went up to Elijah, who was sitting on the top of a hill, and said to him, "O man of God, the king says, 'Come down.'" 10. But Elijah answered the captain of fifty, "If I am a man of God, let fire come down from heaven and consume you and your fifty." Then fire came down from heaven, and consumed him and his fifty. 11. Again the king sent to him another captain of fifty men with his fifty. And he went up and said to him, "O man of God, this is the king's order, 'Come down quickly!'" 12. But Elijah answered them, "If I am a man of God, let fire come down from heaven and consume you and your fifty." Then the fire of God came down from heaven and consumed him and his fifty. 13. Again the king sent the captain of a third fifty with his fifty. And the third captain of fifty went up, and came and fell on his knees before Elijah, and entreated him, "O man of God, I pray you, let my life, and the life of these fifty servants of yours, be precious in your sight. 14. Lo, fire came down from heaven, and consumed the two former captains of fifty men with their fifties; but now let my life be precious in your sight." 15. Then the angel of the LORD said to Elijah, "Go down with him; do not be afraid of him." So he arose and went down with him to the king, 16. and said to him, "Thus says the LORD, 'Because you have sent messengers to inquire of Baal-zebub, the god of Ekron, — is it because there is no God in Israel to inquire of his word? — therefore you shall not come down from the bed to which you have gone, but you shall surely die.'" 17. So he died according to the word of the LORD which Elijah had spoken.

Mark 2:1. And when he returned to Capernaum after some days, it was reported that he was at home. 2. And many were gathered together, so that there was no longer room for them, not even about the door; and he was preaching the word to them. 3. And they came, bringing to him a paralytic carried by four men. 4. And when they could not get near him because of the crowd, they removed the roof above him; and when they had made an opening, they let down the pallet on which the paralytic lay. 5. And when Jesus saw their faith, he said to the paralytic, "My son, your sins are forgiven." 6. Now some of the scribes were sitting there, questioning in their hearts, 7. "Why does this man speak thus? It is blasphemy! Who can forgive sins but God alone?" 8. And immediately Jesus, perceiving in his spirit that they thus questioned within themselves, said to them, "Why do you question thus in your hearts? 9. Which is easier, to say to the paralytic, 'Your sins are forgiven,' or to say, 'Rise, take up your pallet and walk'? 10. But that you may know that the Son of man has authority on earth to forgive sins" — he said to the paralytic — 11. "I say to you, rise, take up your pallet and go home." And he rose, 12. and immediately took up the pallet and went out before them all; so that they were all amazed and glorified God, saying, "We never saw anything like this!"

As Roth (p. 56) shows, this story of a paralyzed man's friends tearing the thatch off a roof and lowering him to Jesus amid the crowd seems to be based on an Elijah story in 2 Kings 1:2–17a, King Ahaziah gains his affliction by falling from his roof through the lattice and languishes in bed. Mark's sufferer is already afflicted when he descends through the roof on his bed (pallet). He rises from his bed because whatever sin of his had earned him the divine judgment of paralysis was now pronounced forgiven on account of his friends' faith, though nothing is said of his own. King Ahaziah is pointedly not healed of his affliction because of his own pronounced lack of faith in the God of Israel: he had sent to the priests of the Philistine oracle god Baal-zebub to inquire as to his prospects. Elijah tells him he is doomed because of unbelief, a dismal situation reversed by Mark, who has Jesus grant forgiveness and salvation because of faith. Mark has preserved the Baal-zebub element for use in a later story: "And the scribes who came down from Jerusalem said, 'He is possessed by Beel-zebul, and by the prince of demons he casts out the demons'" (Mark 3:22).

10. The Withered Hand (1 Kings 13:1–6; Mark 3:1–6)

1 Kings 13:1. And behold, a man of God came out of Judah by the word of the LORD to Bethel. Jeroboam was standing by the altar to burn incense. 2. And the man cried against the altar by the word of the LORD, and said, "O altar, altar, thus says the LORD: 'Behold, a son shall be born to the house of David, Josiah by name; and he shall sacrifice upon you the priests of the high places who burn incense upon you, and men's bones shall be burned upon you.'" 3. And he gave a sign the same day, saying, "This is the sign that the LORD has spoken: 'Behold, the altar shall be torn down, and the ashes that are upon it shall be poured out'." 4. And when the king heard the saying of the man of God, which he cried against the altar at Bethel, Jeroboam stretched out his hand from the altar, saying, "Lay hold of him." And his hand, which he stretched out against him, dried up, so that he could not draw it back to himself. 5. The altar also was torn down, and the ashes poured out from the altar, according to the sign which the man of God had given by the word of the LORD. 6. And the king said to the man of God, "Entreat now the favor of the LORD your God, and pray for me, that my hand may be restored to me." And the man of God entreated the LORD; and the king's hand was restored to him, and became as it was before.

Mark 3:1. Again he entered the synagogue, and a man was there who had a withered hand. 2. And they watched him, to see whether he would heal him on the sabbath, so that they might accuse him. 3. And he said to the man who had the withered hand, "Come here." 4. And he said to them, "Is it lawful on the sabbath to do good or to do harm, to save life or to kill?" But they were silent. 5. And he looked around at them with anger, grieved at their hardness of heart, and said to the man, "Stretch out your hand." He stretched it out, and his hand was restored. 6. The Pharisees went out, and immediately held counsel with the Herodians against him, how to destroy him.

The Christ Myth Theory And Its Problems

Mark has borrowed the substance of this scene from the miracle of the Judean prophet of 1 Kings 13:1–6 (Helms, pp. 90–91). There the prophet confronts King Jeroboam in the Bethel temple and predicts Judean King Josiah's destruction of the rival altar. For this blasphemy Jeroboam orders his arrest, with surprising results: "the king stretched forth his hand (εξετεινεν... την χειρα αυτου) from the altar, saying, 'Take hold of him!' and his hand which he stretched forth against him withered (εξηρανθη), and he could not draw it back to himself" (v.4). In Mark, the man is a nobody, but the authorities are nonetheless present in the house of worship and waiting to pounce. The man's hand is already withered (εξηραμμενην) when Jesus calls him out. "'Stretch out your hand!' He stretched it out (την χειρα... εξετεινεν), and his hand was restored" (Mark 3:5). The anonymous prophet, too, heals the sufferer: "And King Jeroboam said to the man of God, 'Entreat the Lord your God, and let my hand be restored to me.' And the man of God entreated the Lord, and he restored the king's hand to him, and it became as before" (1 Kings 13:6 LXX). Whereas the withering and healing were the aftermath of the villains' attempt to arrest the prophet in 1 Kings, in Mark it is the healing of the withered hand which makes the villains plot to arrest him: "The Pharisees went out and immediately took council with the Herodians against him, how to destroy him" (3:6).

11. Choosing the Twelve; Embassy of Relatives Exodus 18:1–27; Mark 3:13–35)

Exodus 18:1. Jethro, the priest of Midian, Moses' father-in-law, heard of all that God had done for Moses and for Israel his people, how the LORD had brought Israel out of Egypt. 2. Now Jethro, Moses' father-in-law, had taken Zipporah, Moses' wife, after he had sent her away, 3. and her two sons, of whom the name of the one was Gershom (for he said, "I have been a sojourner in a foreign land"), 4. and the name of the other, Eliezer (for he said, "The God of my

father was my help, and delivered me from the sword of Pharaoh").
5. And Jethro, Moses' father-in-law, came with his sons and his wife
to Moses in the wilderness where he was encamped at the mountain of God. 6. And when one told Moses, "Lo, your father-in-law
Jethro is coming to you with your wife and her two sons with her,"
7. Moses went out to meet his father-in-law, and did obeisance and
kissed him; and they asked each other of their welfare, and went
into the tent. 8. Then Moses told his father-in-law all that the LORD
had done to Pharaoh and to the Egyptians for Israel's sake, all the
hardship that had come upon them in the way, and how the LORD
had delivered them. 9. And Jethro rejoiced for all the good which
the LORD had done to Israel, in that he had delivered them out of the
hand of the Egyptians. 10. And Jethro said, "Blessed be the LORD,
who has delivered you out of the hand of the Egyptians and out of
the hand of Pharaoh. 11. Now I know that the LORD is greater than
all gods, because he delivered the people from under the hand of
the Egyptians, when they dealt arrogantly with them." 12. And Jethro, Moses' father-in-law, offered a burnt offering and sacrifices to
God; and Aaron came with all the elders of Israel to eat bread with
Moses' father-in-law before God. 13. On the morrow Moses sat to
judge the people, and the people stood about Moses from morning
till evening. 14. When Moses' father-in-law saw all that he was doing for the people, he said, "What is this that you are doing for the
people? Why do you sit alone, and all the people stand about you
from morning till evening?" 15. And Moses said to his father-in-law,
"Because the people come to me to inquire of God; 16. when they
have a dispute, they come to me and I decide between a man and his
neighbor, and I make them know the statutes of God and his decisions." 17. Moses' father-in-law said to him, "What you are doing
is not good. 18. You and the people with you will wear yourselves
out, for the thing is too heavy for you; you are not able to perform
it alone. 19. Listen now to my voice; I will give you counsel, and
God be with you! You shall represent the people before God, and
bring their cases to God; 20. and you shall teach them the statutes
and the decisions, and make them know the way in which they must
walk and what they must do. 21. Moreover choose able men from

The Christ Myth Theory And Its Problems

all the people, such as fear God, men who are trustworthy and who hate a bribe; and place such men over the people as rulers of thousands, of hundreds, of fifties, and of tens. 22. And let them judge the people at all times; every great matter they shall bring to you, but any small matter they shall decide themselves; so it will be easier for you, and they will bear the burden with you. 23. If you do this, and God so commands you, then you will be able to endure, and all this people also will go to their place in peace." 24. So Moses gave heed to the voice of his father-in-law and did all that he had said. 25. Moses chose able men out of all Israel, and made them heads over the people, rulers of thousands, of hundreds, of fifties, and of tens. 26. And they judged the people at all times; hard cases they brought to Moses, but any small matter they decided themselves. 27. Then Moses let his father-in-law depart, and he went his way to his own country.

Mark 3:13. And he went up into the hills, and called to him those whom he desired; and they came to him. 14. And he appointed twelve, to be with him, and to be sent out to preach 15. and have authority to cast out demons: 16. Simon whom he surnamed Peter; 17. James the son of Zebedee and John the brother of James, whom he surnamed Boanerges, that is, sons of thunder; 18. Andrew, and Philip, and Bartholomew, and Matthew, and Thomas, and James the son of Alphaeus, and Thaddaeus, and Simon the Cananaean, 19. and Judas Iscariot, who betrayed him. Then he went home; 20. and the crowd came together again, so that they could not even eat. 21. And when his family heard it, they went out to seize him, for people were saying, "He is beside himself." 22. And the scribes who came down from Jerusalem said, "He is possessed by Beel-zebul, and by the prince of demons he casts out the demons." 23. And he called them to him, and said to them in parables, "How can Satan cast out Satan? 24. If a kingdom is divided against itself, that kingdom cannot stand. 25. And if a house is divided against itself, that house will not be able to stand. 26. And if Satan has risen up against himself and is divided, he cannot stand, but is coming to an end. 27. But no one can enter a strong man's house and plunder his goods, unless he first binds the strong man; then indeed he may plunder his house. 28. "Truly, I say to you, all sins will be forgiven the sons of men, and whatever blasphemies they utter; 29. but whoever blasphemes against the Holy Spirit never has forgiveness, but is guilty of an eternal sin" — 30. for they had said, "He has an unclean spirit." 31. And his mother and his brothers came; and standing outside they sent to him and called him. 32. And a crowd was sitting about him; and they said to him, "Your mother and your brothers are outside, asking for you." 33. And he replied, "Who are my mother and my brothers?" 34. And looking around on those who sat about him, he said, "Here are my mother and my brothers! 35. Whoever does the will of God is my brother, and sister, and mother."

We must imagine that previous to Mark someone had rewritten the story of Moses heeding Jethro's advice to name subordinates, resulting in a scene in which choosing the twelve disciples was the idea of the Holy Family of Jesus. Note the similarities between Mark 3 and Exodus 18. Just as Moses' father-in-law Jethro hears of Moses' successes and brings Moses' wife and sons to him (Exodus 18:1–5), so do the mothers and brothers of Jesus hear reports and journey to meet Jesus (Mark 3:21). Moses is constantly surrounded by suppliants (18:13–18), just like Jesus (3:20). Just as Moses' arriving family is announced ("Lo, your father-in-law Jethro is coming to you with your wife and her two sons with her" 18:6), so is Jesus' ("Behold, your mother and your brothers are outside looking for you," 3:31–32). "Moses went out to meet his father-in-law, and bowed down and kissed him; and they asked each other of their welfare, and went into the tent" (Exodus 18:7). Originally we would have read of Jesus' welcoming his family. And as Jethro voices his concern for the harried Moses, suggesting he share the burden with a number of helpers (18:21–22), so we would have read that James or Mary advised the choice of assistants "that they might be with him, and that he might send them out to preach" (Mark 3:14). And Jesus would only then have named the Twelve.

The Christ Myth Theory And Its Problems

Mark, acting in the interest of a church-political agenda, has broken the story into two and reversed its halves so as to bring dishonor on the relatives of Jesus (representing a contemporary faction claiming their authority) and to take from them the credit for naming the Twelve (which is also why he emphasizes that Jesus "summoned those that he *himself* wanted," *i.e.*, it was all his own idea. As the text now reads, Jesus chooses the disciples, and only subsequently do his interfering relatives arrive harboring doubts about his sanity, and he rebuffs them (Mark 3:33–35).

Jesus, however, does not, like Moses, choose seventy (though Luke will restore this number, Luke 10:1), but only twelve, based on the choice of the twelve spies in Deuteronomy 1:23, "The thing seemed good to me, and I took twelve men of you, one man for each tribe" (Miller, p. 117).

Sandwiched into the middle of this material is a controversy between Jesus and his scribal critics who allege that he performs his exorcisms only by virtue of being in league with Beel-zebul. Some manuscripts read "Beel-zebub," harking back to 2 Kings 1:2, 3. "Beel-zebul" denotes "Lord of the House," *i.e.*, of the world, a powerful patron of exorcists, while "Beel-zebub" means "Lord of the Flies," denoting an oracle, since the priests would hear a sound like buzzing, the voice of spirits telling the desired fortune. Jesus' reply to the charge seems to come from Isaiah 49:24 (Watts, pp. 148–149)

> Can the prey be taken from the mighty, or the captives of a tyrant be rescued? Surely thus says the LORD: Even the captives of the mighty shall be taken, and the prey of the tyrant be rescued, for I will contend with those who contend with you, and I will save your children.

and from 1 Samuel 2:25 ("If a man sins against a man, God will mediate for him; but if a man sins against the LORD, who can intercede for him?") (Miller, p. 136).

Matthew and Luke (hence the Q source) make an interesting addition to Jesus' response to the scribes. Luke's, as usual, is probably closer to the Q original: "If I by Beel-zebul cast out demons, by whom do your sons cast them out? Consequently, they shall be your judges. But if I cast out demons by the finger of God, then the kingdom of God has come upon you" (Luke 11:19–20). Compressed into these verses is an unmistakable midrash upon the Exodus story of Moses' miracle contest with the magicians of Pharaoh. Initially able to match Moses feat for feat, they prove incapable of copying the miracle of the gnats and warn Pharaoh to give in, since "This is the finger of God" and no mere sorcery like theirs (Exodus 8:19). The "sons" of the scribes correspond to the Egyptian magicians and can dispel the scribes' charge against Jesus if they would.

12. The Stilling of the Storm (Mark 4:35–41)

Jonah 1:4. But the Lord hurled a great wind upon the sea, and there was a mighty tempest on the sea, so that the ship threatened to break up. 5. Then the mariners were afraid, and each cried to his god... But Jonah had gone down into the inner part of the ship and had lain down, and was fast asleep. 6. So the captain came and said to him, 'What do you mean, you sleeper? Arise, call upon your god! Perhaps the god will give a thought to us, that we do not perish. [...] 15. So they took up Jonah and threw him into the sea, and the sea ceased from its raging. 16. Then the men feared the LORD exceedingly.

Psalms 107:23. Some went down to the sea in ships, doing business on the great waters; 24. they saw the deeds of the LORD, his wondrous works in the deep. 25. For he commanded, and raised the stormy wind, which lifted up the waves of the sea. 26. They mounted up to the heavens, they went down unto the depths; their courage melted away in their evil plight; 27. they reeled and staggered like drunken men, and were at their wits' end. 28. Then they cried to the LORD in their trouble, and he delivered them from their distress; 29. he made the storm be still, and the waves of the sea were hushed.

Mark 4:35. On that day, when evening had come, he said to them, "Let us go across to the other side." 36. And leaving the crowd, they took him with them in the boat, just as he was. And other boats were with him. 37. And a great storm of wind arose, and the waves beat into the boat, so that the boat was already filling. 38. But he was in the stern, asleep on the cushion; and they woke him and said to him, "Teacher, do you not care if we perish?" 39. And he awoke and rebuked the wind, and said to the sea, "Peace! Be still!" And the wind ceased, and there was a great calm. 40. He said to them, "Why are you afraid? Have you no faith?" 41. And they were filled with awe, and said to one another, "Who then is this, that even wind and sea obey him?"

Helms (pp. 76, 77) demonstrates how this story has been rewritten from Jonah's adventure, with additions from certain of the Psalms. The basis for the story can be recognized in Jonah 1:4–6 with elaboration via Psalms 107:23–29.

Mark was aware of a similar episode in the *Odyssey* 10:1–69, in which Odysseus set sail with his dozen ships from the Isle of Aeolus, the god of winds. Aeolus had given Odysseus a bag containing mighty winds in case he should be stalled in the doldrums. Odysseus falls asleep in the hold, and his men sneak a peek into the bag, letting the winds escape. The ships managed to survive the storm, but Odysseus rebuked his crew for their dangerous folly. MacDonald (pp. 68, 174–175) indicates the origin of Jesus' rebuke to the disciples here (Mark 1:40), as well as the puzzling detail in Mark 1:36 that Jesus and the disciples were accompanied by "other boats." It makes no sense in Mark and must be understood as a vestige of the *Odyssey*.

13. The Gerasene Demoniac (Psalms 107:4–14; Mark 5:1–20)

Psalms 107:4. Some wandered in desert wastes, finding no way to a city to dwell in; 5. hungry and thirsty, their soul fainted within them. 6. Then they cried to the LORD in their trouble, and he delivered them from their distress; 7. he led them by a straight way, till they reached a city to dwell in. 8. Let them thank the LORD for his steadfast love, for his wonderful works to the sons of men! 9. For he satisfies him who is thirsty, and the hungry he fills with good things. 10. Some sat in darkness and in gloom, prisoners in affliction and in irons, 11. for they had rebelled against the words of God, and spurned the counsel of the Most High. 12. Their hearts were bowed down with hard labor; they fell down, with none to help. 13. Then they cried to the LORD in their trouble, and he delivered them from their distress; 14. he brought them out of darkness and gloom, and broke their bonds asunder.

Mark 5:1. They came to the other side of the sea, to the country of the Gerasenes. 2. And when he had come out of the boat, there met him out of the tombs a man with an unclean spirit, 3. who lived among the tombs; and no one could bind him any more, even with a chain; 4. for he had often been bound with fetters and chains, but the chains he wrenched apart, and the fetters he broke in pieces; and no one had the strength to subdue him. 5. Night and day among the tombs and on the mountains he was always crying out, and bruising himself with stones. 6. And when he saw Jesus from afar, he ran and worshiped him; 7. and crying out with a loud voice, he said, "What have you to do with me, Jesus, Son of the Most High God? I adjure you by God, do not torment me." 8. For he had said to him, "Come out of the man, you unclean spirit!" 9. And Jesus asked him, "What is your name?" He replied, "My name is Legion; for we are many." 10. And he begged him eagerly not to send them out of the country. 11. Now a great herd of swine was feeding there on the hillside; 12. and they begged him, "Send us to the swine, let us enter them." 13. So he gave them leave. And the unclean spirits came out, and entered the swine; and the herd, numbering about two thousand, rushed down the steep bank into the sea, and were drowned in the sea. 14. The herdsmen fled, and told it in the city and in the country. And people came to see what it was that had happened. 15. And they came to Jesus, and saw the demoniac sitting there, clothed and in his right mind, the man who had had the legion; and they were afraid. 16. And those who had seen it told what had happened to the demoniac and to the swine. 17. And they began to beg Jesus to depart from their neighborhood. 18. And as he was getting into the boat, the man who had been possessed with demons begged him that he might be with him. 19. But he refused, and said to him, "Go home to your friends, and tell them how much the Lord has done for you, and how he has had mercy on you." 20. And he went away and began to proclaim in the Decapolis how much Jesus had done for him; and all men marveled.

Again, Mark has mixed together materials from scripture and from the *Odyssey*. Clearly, as MacDonald shows (pp. 65, 73, 173), the core of the story derives from *Odyssey* 9:101–565. Odysseus and his men come to shore in the land of the hulking Cyclopes, just as Jesus and his disciples arrive by boat in the land of the Gerasenes (or Gergesenes, supposedly the remnant of the ancient Girgashites, hence possibly associated with the mythical Anakim/Rephaim, Derrett, p. 102, who were *giants*). Goats graze in one landscape, pigs in the other. Leaving their boats, each group immediately encounters a savage man-monster who dwells in a cave. The demoniac is naked, and Polyphemus was usually depicted naked, too. The Cyclops asks Odysseus if he has come with intent to harm him, just as the Gerasene demoniac begs Jesus not to torment him. Polyphemus asks Odysseus his name, and the latter replies "Noman," while Jesus asks the demoniac his name, "Legion," a name reminiscent of the fact that Odysseus' men were soldiers. Jesus expels the *legion* of demons, sending them into the grazing swine, recalling Circe's earlier transformation of Odysseus' *troops* into swine. Odysseus contrives to blind the Cyclops, escaping his cave. The heroes depart, and the gloating Odysseus bids Polyphemus to tell others how he has blinded him, just as Jesus tells the cured demoniac to tell how he has exorcised him. As Odysseus' boat retreats, Polyphemus cries out for him to return, but he refuses. As Jesus is about to depart, the man he cured asks to accompany him, but he refuses. As MacDonald notes, sheer copying from the source is about the only way to explain why Jesus should be shown refusing a would-be disciple.

Psalm 107, whence details of the stilling of the storm were borrowed, has made minor contributions to this story as well. The detail of the demoniac having been chained up seem to come from Psalm 107's description of "prisoners in irons" (v. 10), who "wandered in desert wastes" (v. 4) and "cried to the LORD in their trouble" (v. 6), who "broke their chains asunder" (v. 14). It is also possible that Mark had in mind the Exodus sequence, and that he has placed the story here to correspond to the drowning of the Egyptian hosts in the Sea.

14. Jairus' Daughter and the Woman with the Issue of Blood (2 Kings 4:8–37; Mark 5:21–34, 35–43)

2 Kings 4:8. One day Elisha went on to Shunem, where a wealthy woman lived, who urged him to eat some food. So whenever he passed that way, he would turn in there to eat food. 9. And she said to her husband, "Behold now, I perceive that this is a holy man of God, who is continually passing our way. 10. Let us make a small roof chamber with walls, and put there for him a bed, a table, a chair, and a lamp, so that whenever he comes to us, he can go in there." 11. One day he came there, and he turned into the chamber and rested there. 12. And he said to Gehazi his servant, "Call this Shunammite." When he had called her, she stood before him. 13. And he said to him, "Say now to her, See, you have taken all this trouble for us; what is to be done for you? Would you have a word spoken on your behalf to the king or to the commander of the army?" She answered, "I dwell among my own people." 14. And he said, "What then is to be done for her?" Gehazi answered, "Well, she has no son, and her husband is old." 15. He said, "Call her." And when he had called her, she stood in the doorway. 16. And he said, "At this season, when the time comes round, you shall embrace a son." And she said, "No, my lord, O man of God; do not lie to your maidservant." 17. But the woman conceived, and she bore a son about that time the following spring, as Elisha had said to her. 18. When the child had grown, he went out one day to his father among the reapers. 19. And

he said to his father, "Oh, my head, my head!" The father said to his servant, "Carry him to his mother." 20. And when he had lifted him, and brought him to his mother, the child sat on her lap till noon, and then he died. 21. And she went up and laid him on the bed of the man of God, and shut the door upon him, and went out. 22. Then she called to her husband, and said, "Send me one of the servants and one of the asses, that I may quickly go to the man of God, and come back again." 23. And he said, "Why will you go to him today? It is neither new moon nor sabbath." She said, "It will be well." 24. Then she saddled the ass, and she said to her servant, "Urge the beast on; do not slacken the pace for me unless I tell you." 25. So she set out, and came to the man of God at Mount Carmel. When the man of God saw her coming, he said to Gehazi his servant, "Look, yonder is the Shunammite; 26. run at once to meet her, and say to her, Is it well with you? Is it well with your husband? Is it well with the child?" And she answered, "It is well." 27. And when she came to the mountain to the man of God, she caught hold of his feet. And Gehazi came to thrust her away. But the man of God said, "Let her alone, for she is in bitter distress; and the LORD has hidden it from me, and has not told me." 28. Then she said, "Did I ask my lord for a son? Did I not say, Do not deceive me?" 29. He said to Gehazi, "Gird up your loins, and take my staff in your hand, and go. If you meet any one, do not salute him; and if any one salutes you, do not reply; and lay my staff upon the face of the child." 30. Then the mother of the child said, "As the LORD lives, and as you yourself live, I will not leave you." So he arose and followed her. 31. Gehazi went on ahead and laid the staff upon the face of the child, but there was no sound or sign of life. Therefore he returned to meet him, and told him, "The child has not awaked." 32. When Elisha came into the house, he saw the child lying dead on his bed. 33. So he went in and shut the door upon the two of them, and prayed to the LORD. 34. Then he went up and lay upon the child, putting his mouth upon his mouth, his eyes upon his eyes, and his hands upon his hands; and as he stretched himself upon him, the flesh of the child became warm. 35. Then he got up again, and walked once to and fro in the house, and went up, and stretched himself upon him; the child sneezed seven times, and the child opened his eyes. 36. Then he summoned Gehazi and said, "Call this Shunammite." So he called her. And when she came to him, he said, "Take up your son." 37. She came and fell at his feet, bowing to the ground; then she took up her son and went out.

Mark 5:21. And when Jesus had crossed again in the boat to the other side, a great crowd gathered about him; and he was beside the sea. 22. Then came one of the rulers of the synagogue, Jairus by name; and seeing him, he fell at his feet, 23. and besought him, saying, "My little daughter is at the point of death. Come and lay your hands on her, so that she may be made well, and live." 24. And he went with him. And a great crowd followed him and thronged about him. 25. And there was a woman who had had a flow of blood for twelve years, 26. and who had suffered much under many physicians, and had spent all that she had, and was no better but rather grew worse. 27. She had heard the reports about Jesus, and came up behind him in the crowd and touched his garment. 28. For she said, "If I touch even his garments, I shall be made well." 29. And immediately the hemorrhage ceased; and she felt in her body that she was healed of her disease. 30. And Jesus, perceiving in himself that power had gone forth from him, immediately turned about in the crowd, and said, "Who touched my garments?" 31. And his disciples said to him, "You see the crowd pressing around you, and yet you say, 'Who touched me?'" 32. And he looked around to see who had done it. 33. But the woman, knowing what had been done to her, came in fear and trembling and fell down before him, and told him the whole truth. 34. And he said to her, "Daughter, your faith has made you well; go in peace, and be healed of your disease." 35. While he was still speaking, there came from the ruler's house some who said, "Your daughter is dead. Why trouble the Teacher any further?" 36. But ignoring what they said, Jesus said to the ruler of the synagogue, "Do not fear, only believe." 37. And he allowed no one to follow him except Peter and James and John the brother of James. 38. When they came to the house of the ruler of the synagogue, he saw a tumult, and people weeping and wailing loudly. 39. And when he had entered, he said to them, "Why do you make a tumult and weep? The child is not dead but sleeping." 40. And they laughed at him. But he put them all outside, and took the child's father and mother and those who were with him, and went in where the child was. 41. Taking her by the hand he said to her, "*Talitha cumi*"; which means, "Little girl, I say to you, arise." 42. And immediately the girl got up and walked (she was twelve years of age), and they were immediately overcome with amazement. 43. And he strictly charged them that no one should know this, and told them to give her something to eat.

Under the long-regnant paradigm of form-criticism this story was considered to be a complex of two prior tradition-units sandwiched together by Mark, and indeed it is easy to divide them into two distinct episodes. The story of Jairus and his daughter (vv. 21–23, 35–43, the phrase "while he was still speaking" referring originally to Jairus in v. 23) and that of the bleeding woman (vv. 24b–34), Mark having to add only 24a to tape the two together. But the more we recognize Mark's creative sophistication and view him as a real author, not just a scissors-and-paste editor as the form critics did, the more likely it seems that the two anecdotes began life as interdependent parts of a single story, a retelling of that of Elisha and the Shunammite woman (2 Kings 4). The Shunammite, a mother, has been replaced by a father, whose name Jairus means "he will awaken," winking to the readers as to the fictive character of the tale. Jairus, like his prototype, approaches the prophet abjectly pleading for help. The prophet, whether Jesus or Elisha, determines to go and raise the child despite the report that the child is already dead. Arriving, he seeks privacy (relative or absolute: Elisha excludes everyone, Jesus the crowd). He touches and speaks to the dead child, and the child rouses. The reaction is verbally almost verbatim. The Shunammite is "ecstatic with all this ecstasy" (εξεστησας... πασαν την εκστασιν ταυτην, 2 Kings 4:13 LXX), while Jairus and his wife are "ecstatic with great ecstasy" (εξεστησαν... εκστασει μεγαλη, Mark 5:42) (Helms, p. 66).

But what about the woman with the hemorrhage? She is the Shunammite, doubled! Jesus heals her of a reproductive problem just as Elisha had miraculously made it possible for the Shunammite to conceive. The woman had been plagued with the bleeding for twelve years, exactly the age of Jairus' daughter, the symbolic implication being that she was the daughter the bleeding woman had never been able to have, now, so to speak, restored to her. Why did Mark break up the story this way? For the most elementary of reasons: to provide narrative suspense, just as in the 2 Kings original, where we must follow the woman on the journey to Elisha and then endure the failed attempt of Gehazi to raise her son. As we will see, Mark liked the element of the disciple's failure, but instead of using it here, which would have made the story even more like its prototype, he has reserved it till later, in 9:18, 28.

The element of Jesus' healing energy being released upon contact, even without his say-so, may have been suggested by the story in 2 Kings 13:20–21, where a corpse, hastily stashed in Elisha's open mausoleum, strikes the bones of the prophet and is restored to life and vigor!

15. Rejection at Home (1 Samuel 10:1–27; Mark 6:1–6)

1 Samuel 10:1. Then Samuel took a vial of oil and poured it on his head, and kissed him and said, "Has not the LORD anointed you to be prince over his people Israel? And you shall reign over the people of the LORD and you will save them from the hand of their enemies round about. And this shall be the sign to you that the LORD has anointed you to be prince over his heritage. 2. When you depart from me today you will meet two men by Rachel's tomb in the territory of Benjamin at Zelzah, and they will say to you, 'The asses which you went to seek are found, and now your father has ceased to care about the asses and is anxious about you, saying, "What shall I do about my son?" ' 3. Then you shall go on from there further and come to the oak of Tabor; three men going up to God at Bethel will meet you there, one carrying three kids, another carrying three loaves of bread, and another carrying a skin of wine. 4. And they will greet you and give

you two loaves of bread, which you shall accept from their hand. 5. After that you shall come to Gibeath-elohim, where there is a garrison of the Philistines; and there, as you come to the city, you will meet a band of prophets coming down from the high place with harp, tambourine, flute, and lyre before them, prophesying. 6. Then the spirit of the LORD will come mightily upon you, and you shall prophesy with them and be turned into another man. 7. Now when these signs meet you, do whatever your hand finds to do, for God is with you. 8. And you shall go down before me to Gilgal; and behold, I am coming to you to offer burnt offerings and to sacrifice peace offerings. Seven days you shall wait, until I come to you and show you what you shall do." 9. When he turned his back to leave Samuel, God gave him another heart; and all these signs came to pass that day. 10. When they came to Gibeah, behold, a band of prophets met him; and the spirit of God came mightily upon him, and he prophesied among them. 11. And when all who knew him before saw how he prophesied with the prophets, the people said to one another, "What has come over the son of Kish? Is Saul also among the prophets?" 12. And a man of the place answered, "And who is their father?" Therefore it became a proverb, "Is Saul also among the prophets?" 13. When he had finished prophesying, he came to the high place. 14. Saul's uncle said to him and to his servant, "Where did you go?" And he said, "To seek the asses; and when we saw they were not to be found, we went to Samuel." 15. And Saul's uncle said, "Pray, tell me what Samuel said to you." 16. And Saul said to his uncle, "He told us plainly that the asses had been found." But about the matter of the kingdom, of which Samuel had spoken, he did not tell him anything. 17. Now Samuel called the people together to the LORD at Mizpah; 18. and he said to the people of Israel, "Thus says the LORD, the God of Israel, 'I brought up Israel out of Egypt, and I delivered you from the hand of the Egyptians and from the hand of all the kingdoms that were oppressing you.' 19. But you have this day rejected your God, who saves you from all your calamities and your distresses; and you have said, 'No! but set a king over us.' Now therefore present yourselves before the LORD by your tribes and by your thousands." 20. Then Samuel brought all the tribes of Israel near, and the tribe of Benjamin was taken by lot. 21. He brought the tribe of Benjamin near by its families, and the family of the Matrites was taken by lot; finally he brought the family of the Matrites near man by man, and Saul the son of Kish was taken by lot. But when they sought him, he could not be found. 22. So they inquired again of the LORD, "Did the man come hither?" and the LORD said, "Behold, he has hidden himself among the baggage." 23. Then they ran and fetched him from there; and when he stood among the people, he was taller than any of the people from his shoulders upward. 24. And Samuel said to all the people, "Do you see him whom the LORD has chosen? There is none like him among all the people." And all the people shouted, "Long live the king!" 25. Then Samuel told the people the rights and duties of the kingship; and he wrote them in a book and laid it up before the LORD. Then Samuel sent all the people away, each one to his home. 26. Saul also went to his home at Gibeah, and with him went men of valor whose hearts God had touched. 27. But some worthless fellows said, "How can this man save us?" And they despised him, and brought him no present. But he held his peace.

Mark 6:1. He went away from there and came to his own country; and his disciples followed him. 2. And on the sabbath he began to teach in the synagogue; and many who heard him were astonished, saying, "Where did this man get all this? What is the wisdom given to him? What mighty works are wrought by his hands! 3. Is not this the carpenter, the son of Mary and brother of James and Joses and Judas and Simon, and are not his sisters here with us?" And they took offense at him. 4. And Jesus said to them, "A prophet is not without honor, except in his own country, and among his own kin, and in his own house." 5. And he could do no mighty work there, except that he laid his hands upon a few sick people and healed them. 6. And he marveled because of their unbelief. And he went about among the villages teaching.

Miller and Miller (p. 167) point to 1 Samuel 10:1–27 as the likely source of Mark's episode of Jesus' frosty reception among his own townsfolk. Saul, newly appointed king of his people, is overcome by the prophetic afflatus and begins to speak in tongues ("prophesy,"

v. 10), whereupon "all who knew him previously" retort, "What has come over the son of Kish? Is Saul, too, among the prophets?" "Who is their father?" (v. 11). The upshot is that "it became a proverb, 'Is Saul, too, among the prophets?' " (v. 12). Just so, in Mark the people who had long known the local boy, now ostensibly a prophet, cannot believe it and raise the issue of Jesus' too-familiar family connections: a prophet must come from out of nowhere, not someone like us (*cf.* John 7:27–28, " 'When the Christ appears, no one will know where he comes from.' ...'You know me and you know where I come from, but I have not come of my own accord;' " James 5:17, "Elijah was a man with a nature like ourselves."). Jesus is merely the son of Mary and brother to James, Joses, Simon and Judas, just as Saul is nothing more than Kish's son. There is even the matching proverb in the case of Jesus: "A prophet is not without honor except in his home town and among his relatives and in his household."

16. Mission Instructions (Mark 6:7–13)

7. And he called to him the twelve, and began to send them out two by two, and gave them authority over the unclean spirits. 8. He charged them to take nothing for their journey except a staff; no bread, no bag, no money in their belts; 9. but to wear sandals and not put on two tunics. 10. And he said to them, "Where you enter a house, stay there until you leave the place. 11. And if any place will not receive you and they refuse to hear you, when you leave, shake off the dust that is on your feet for a testimony against them." 12. So they went out and preached that men should repent. 13. And they cast out many demons, and anointed with oil many that were sick and healed them.

These marching orders may have been influenced by the practices of Cynic preachers, but in their present form they surely owe something to the Elisha stories. When Jesus forbids the missioners to "take along money nor two cloaks," he is warning them not to repeat Gehazi's fatal error, aggrandizing himself at the expense of those the prophet serves; he had, unauthorized by Elisha, exacted from Naaman "a talent of silver and two cloaks" (2 Kings 5:22). (Roth, p. 50; Miller, p. 175). The provision of a staff (Mark 6:8) may come from Gehazi's mission for Elisha to the Shunammite's son: "take my staff in your hand and go" (2 Kings 4:29a). Luke must have recognized this, since he returned to the same text to add to his own mission charge to the seventy (Luke 10:4b) the stipulation "and salute no one on the road," borrowed directly from Elisha's charge to Gehazi in 2 Kings 4:29b, "If you meet anyone, do not salute him, and if anyone salutes you, do not reply."

17. The Death of the Baptizer (Mark 6:14–29)

14. King Herod heard of it; for Jesus' name had become known. Some said, "John the baptizer has been raised from the dead; that is why these powers are at work in him." 15. But others said, "It is Elijah." And others said, "It is a prophet, like one of the prophets of old." 16. But when Herod heard of it he said, "John, whom I beheaded, has been raised." 17. For Herod had sent and seized John, and bound him in prison for the sake of Herodias, his brother Philip's wife; because he had married her. 18. For John said to Herod, "It is not lawful for you to have your brother's wife." 19. And Herodias had a grudge against him, and wanted to kill him. But she could not, 20. for Herod feared John, knowing that he was a righteous and holy man, and kept him safe. When he heard him, he was much perplexed; and yet he heard him gladly. 21. But an opportunity came when Herod on his birthday gave a banquet for his courtiers and officers and the leading men of Galilee. 22. For when Herodias' daughter came in and danced, she pleased Herod and his guests; and the king said to the girl, "Ask me for whatever you wish, and I will grant it." 23. And he vowed to her, "Whatever you ask me, I will give you, even half of my kingdom." 24. And she went out, and said to her mother, "What shall I ask?" And she said, "The head of John the baptizer." 25. And she came in immediately with haste to the king, and asked, saying, "I want you to give me at once the head

of John the Baptist on a platter." 26. And the king was exceedingly sorry; but because of his oaths and his guests he did not want to break his word to her. 27. And immediately the king sent a soldier of the guard and gave orders to bring his head. He went and beheaded him in the prison, 28. and brought his head on a platter, and gave it to the girl; and the girl gave it to her mother. 29. When his disciples heard of it, they came and took his body, and laid it in a tomb.

In view of the preceding parallels, it is hardly a surprise that Mark would have people inferring that Jesus is the returned Elijah. Indeed, their opinion is righter than Mark lets on!

Usually scholars allow some core of historical reporting to underlie the story of the Baptizer's death (though any reading of Mark must be harmonized with some difficulty with Josephus), recognizing just a bit of biblical embellishment to the narrative. For instance, it is apparent to all that Herod Antipas' words to his step-daughter, "Whatever you ask of me I will give it to you, up to half my kingdom," comes from Esther 5:3. Herod's painting himself into the corner of having to order the execution of his favorite prophet may come from Darius' bamboozlement in the case of Daniel (Daniel 6:6–15) (Miller, p. 178). But it is possible that the whole tale comes from literary sources.

MacDonald (pp. 80–81, 176) shows how the story of John's martyrdom matches in all essentials the *Odyssey*'s story of the murder of Agamemnon (3:254–308: 4:512–547; 11:404–434), even to the point that both are told in the form of an analepsis or flashback. Herodias, like Queen Clytemnestra, left her husband, preferring his cousin: Antipas in the one case, Aegisthus in the other. This tryst was threatened, in Clytemnestra's case, by the return of her husband from the Trojan War, in Herodias', by the denunciations of John. In both cases, the wicked adulteress plots the death of the nuisance. Aegisthus hosted a banquet to celebrate Agamemnon's return, just as Herod hosted a feast. During the festivities Agamemnon is slain, sprawling amid the dinner plates, and the Baptizer is beheaded, his head displayed on a serving platter. Homer foreshadows danger awaiting the returning Odysseus with the story of Agamemnon's murder, while Mark anticipates Jesus' own martyrdom with that of John. The only outstanding difference, of course, is that in Mark's version, the role of Agamemnon has been split between Herodias' rightful husband (Philip according to Mark; another Herod according to Josephus) and John the Baptizer.

18. Multiplication of Loaves and Fish (2 Kings 4:42–44; Mark 6:30–44; 8:1–10)

2 Kings 4:42. A man came from Baal-shalishah, bringing the man of God bread of the first fruits, twenty loaves of barley, and fresh ears of grain in his sack. And Elisha said, "Give to the men, that they may eat." 43. But his servant said, "How am I to set this before a hundred men?" So he repeated, "Give them to the men, that they may eat, for thus says the LORD, 'They shall eat and have some left.'" 44. So he set it before them. And they ate, and had some left, according to the word of the LORD.

Mark 6:30. The apostles returned to Jesus, and told him all that they had done and taught. 31. And he said to them, "Come away by yourselves to a lonely place, and rest a while." For many were coming and going, and they had no leisure even to eat. 32. And they went away in the boat to a lonely place by themselves. 33. Now many saw them going, and knew them, and they ran there on foot from all the towns, and got there ahead of them. 34. As he went ashore he saw a great throng, and he had compassion on them, because they were like sheep without a shepherd; and he began to teach them many things. 35. And when it grew late, his disciples came to him and said, "This is a lonely place, and the hour is now late; 36. send them away, to go into the country and villages round about and buy themselves something to eat." 37. But he answered them, "You give them something to eat." And they said to him, "Shall we go and buy two hundred denarii worth of bread, and give it to them to eat?" 38. And he said to them, "How many loaves have you? Go and see." And when they had found out, they said, "Five, and two fish."

39. Then he commanded them all to sit down by companies upon the green grass. 40. So they sat down in groups, by hundreds and by fifties. 41. And taking the five loaves and the two fish he looked up to heaven, and blessed, and broke the loaves, and gave them to the disciples to set before the people; and he divided the two fish among them all. 42. And they all ate and were satisfied. 43. And they took up twelve baskets full of broken pieces and of the fish. 44. And those who ate the loaves were five thousand men.

Mark 8:1. In those days, when again a great crowd had gathered, and they had nothing to eat, he called his disciples to him, and said to them, 2. "I have compassion on the crowd, because they have been with me now three days, and have nothing to eat; 3. and if I send them away hungry to their homes, they will faint on the way; and some of them come a long way." 4. And his disciples answered him, "How can one feed these men with bread here in the desert?" 5. And he asked them, "How many loaves have you?" They said, "Seven." 6. And he commanded the crowd to sit down on the ground; and he took the seven loaves, and having given thanks he broke them and gave them to his disciples to set before the people; and they set them before the crowd. 7. And they had a few small fish; and having blessed them, he commanded that these also should be set before them. 8. And they ate, and were satisfied; and they took up the broken pieces left over, seven baskets full. 9. And there were about four thousand people. 10. And he sent them away; and immediately he got into the boat with his disciples, and went to the district of Dalmanutha.

As all acknowledge, the basis for both the miraculous feeding stories in Mark's gospel is the story of Elisha multiplying the twenty barley loaves for a hundred men in 2 Kings 4:42–44. There is in all three stories the initial assessment of how much food is available, the prophetic command to divide it among a hopelessly large number, the skeptical objection, puzzled obedience, and the astonishing climax in which not only all are fed, but they had leftovers as well! As Helms notes (p. 76) concerning the version of this story in the Gospel of John, John has gone back to the source to add a detail. He has made the servant (παιδαριον) of Elisha (LXX 4 Kings 4:41) into a boy (παιδαριον) whose five barley loaves Jesus uses to feed the crowd (John 6:9, "There is a lad here who has five barley loaves and two fish").

But there are more elaborate details in Mark's stories which do not come from 2 Kings. They come from the *Odyssey* 3:34–38, 63–68; 4:30, 36, 51, 53–58, 65–68 (MacDonald, pp. 89–90). The reason Mark has two feeding miracles is to emulate Homer, who has Odysseus' son Telemachus attend two feasts, and Mark has borrowed details from both. For the first feast, Telemachus and the disguised Athena sail to Pylos where King Nestor is presiding at a feast in honor of Poseidon. It is a sailors' feast, so only men are present. Four thousand, five hundred of them are seated in nine units of five hundred each. Everyone ate to satiety and there were leftovers. In Mark's first feast story, Jesus and his men also sail to the site of the meal. They encounter a group of five thousand men, ανδρες, males (no explanation is offered for this, a simple vestige of Homer). Jesus has them sit in discrete groups. After the Elisha-style miracle, everyone eats and is filled, and leftovers are gathered.

Homer's second feast witnesses Telemachus going overland to Sparta, just as in Mark's second episode, Jesus and the disciples walk to Galilee, where he meets the crowd of four thousand. This time, in both stories, there is no restriction to males. A servant of King Menelaus bids him send Telemachus and his companion away unfed, but the king will not, just as a disciple urges Jesus to send away the hapless crowd, and he will not. Everyone sits down to eat, in both cases, and in neither is there any mention of the elaborate arrangement of the diners as in the first feast scene. All are filled; leftovers are gathered. Mark has seemingly cast Jesus as Telemachus in both stories until the hero arrives at the banquet scene, whereupon he switches roles, having Jesus take the place of the hosts, Nestor and Menelaus.

19. Walking on the Sea (Psalms 107 [LXX: 106]: 23–30; Mark 6:45–52)

Psalms 107:23. They that go down to the sea in ships, doing business in many waters; 24. these men have seen the works of the Lord, and his wonders in the deep. 25. He speaks, and the stormy wind arises, and its waves are lifted up. 26. They go up to the heavens, and go down to the depths; their soul melts because of troubles. 27. They are troubled, they stagger as a drunkard, and all their wisdom is swallowed up. 28. Then they cry to the Lord in their affliction, and he brings them out of their distresses. 29. And he commands the storm, and it is calmed into a gentle breeze, and its ways are still. 30. And they are glad, because they are quiet; and he guides them to their desired haven.

Mark 6:45. Immediately he made his disciples get into the boat and go before him to the other side, to Beth-saida, while he dismissed the crowd. 46. And after he had taken leave of them, he went up on the mountain to pray. 47. And when evening came, the boat was out on the sea, and he was alone on the land. 48. And he saw that they were making headway painfully, for the wind was against them. And about the fourth watch of the night he came to them, walking on the sea. He meant to pass by them, 49. but when they saw him walking on the sea they thought it was a ghost, and cried out; 50. for they all saw him, and were terrified. But immediately he spoke to them and said, "Take heart, it is I; have no fear." 51. And he got into the boat with them and the wind ceased. And they were utterly astounded, 52. for they did not understand about the loaves, but their hearts were hardened.

To be sure, scriptural coloring is again in evidence, namely Psalm 107 (106) LXX. And see Job 9:8b, "who... trampled the waves of the sea"). But the body of the story Mark owes to Homer, this time the *Iliad* 24:332, 340–341, 345–346, 351–352 (MacDonald, pp. 148–153). Old King Priam is making the difficult journey to the Greek camp to beg the body of his son Hector. Father Zeus beholds the king's toiling progress and dispatches Hermes, guide to travelers, to aid him. "Under his feet he fastened the supple sandals, never-fading gold, that wing him over the waves and boundless earth with the rush of gusting winds... [Hermes] flew, the mighty giant-killer, touching down on Troy and the Helles-pont in no time and from there he went on foot." As Hermes approaches Priam and his servant, they fear he is a brigand who will slay them, but he reassures them, takes the reins of their mule cart and speeds them on their way, reaching Achilles' ship in no time flat. Finally he reveals his identity: "Old man, I am a god come down to you. I am immortal Hermes — my Father sent me here to be your escort, but now I will hasten back." Can anyone miss the parallel to Mark's story? The disciples are making poor head-way against the storm on their way to the far shore when they see the approaching Jesus, a sight inspiring fear, albeit for different reasons. They see him waking on the water, something Hermes also does to reach Priam, though without the latter seeing him do it. Once their divine visitor reassures them with a declaration ("I am..."), he joins them and they arrive at once at their destination.

Bowman (p.159) picks up the thread of the Exodus story with the mention of the disciples' obtuseness in Mark 6:52. They are said not to understand the feat they have just seen — because they had failed to learn anything from the miraculous feeding! The linking of the two would have to imply a reference back to a different but related pair of Moses' miracles, the dryshod pas-sage over the Sea and the provision of the manna. Despite seeing these, the children of Israel remained obdurate in their unbelief. Likewise the disciples. "Their hearts were hardened," just like Pharaoh's. The point is underscored, one might say too broadly, in 8:14–21 (Bowman, p. 180).

Mark 8:14. Now they had forgotten to bring bread; and they had only one loaf with them in the boat. 15. And he cautioned them, saying, "Take heed, beware of the leaven of the Pharisees and the leaven of Herod." 16. And they discussed it with one another, saying, "We have no bread." 17. And being aware of it, Jesus said to them, "Why do you discuss the fact that you have no bread? Do you not yet perceive or understand? Are your hearts hardened? 18. Having eyes do you not see, and having ears do you not hear? And do you not remember? 19. When I broke the five loaves for the five thousand, how many baskets full of broken pieces did you take up?" They said to him, "Twelve." 20. "And the seven for the four thousand, how many baskets full of broken pieces did you take up?" And they said to him, "Seven." 21. And he said to them, "Do you not yet understand?"

20. Jesus versus the Scribes (Mark 7:1–23)

Mark 7:1. Now when the Pharisees gathered together to him, with some of the scribes, who had come from Jerusalem, 2. they saw that some of his disciples ate with hands defiled, that is, unwashed. 3. (For the Pharisees, and all the Jews, do not eat unless they wash their hands, observing the tradition of the elders; 4. and when they come from the market place, they do not eat unless they purify themselves; and there are many other traditions which they observe, the washing of cups and pots and vessels of bronze.) 5. And the Pharisees and the scribes asked him, "Why do your disciples not live according to the tradition of the elders, but eat with hands defiled?" 6. And he said to them, "Well did Isaiah prophesy of you hypocrites, as it is written, 'This people honors me with their lips, but their heart is far from me; 7. in vain do they worship me, teaching as doctrines the precepts of men.' 8. You leave the commandment of God, and hold fast the tradition of men." 9. And he said to them, "You have a fine way of rejecting the commandment of God, in order to keep your tradition! 10. For Moses said, 'Honor your father and your mother'; and, 'He who speaks evil of father or mother, let him surely die'; 11. but you say, 'If a man tells his father or his mother, What you would have gained from me is Corban' (that is, given to God) — 12. then you no longer permit him to do anything for his father or mother, 13. thus making void the word of God through your tradition which you hand on. And many such things you do." 14. And he called the people to him again, and said to them, "Hear me, all of you, and understand: 15. there is nothing outside a man which by going into him can defile him; but the things which come out of a man are what defile him.16. If any man has ears to hear, let him hear. 17. And when he had entered the house, and left the people, his disciples asked him about the parable. 18. And he said to them, "Then are you also without understanding? Do you not see that whatever goes into a man from outside cannot defile him, 19. since it enters, not his heart but his stomach, and so passes on?" (Thus he declared all foods clean.) 20. And he said, "What comes out of a man is what defiles a man. 21. For from within, out of the heart of man, come evil thoughts, fornication, theft, murder, adultery, 22. coveting, wickedness, deceit, licentiousness, envy, slander, pride, foolishness. 23. All these evil things come from within, and they defile a man."

In debate with the scribes over purity rules, Jesus is made to cite the LXX of Isaiah 29:13, the Hebrew original of which ("And the Lord said: 'Because this people draw near with their mouth and honor me with their lips, while their hearts are far from me, and their fear of me is a commandment of men learned by rote…' ") would not really make the required point. Less obviously, there is also a significant reference to Elijah in v. 14, "and summoning the multitude again, he said to them, 'Listen to me, all of you, and understand.' " Here we are to discern a reflection of Elijah's gesture in 1 Kings 18: 30, "Then Elijah said to all the people, 'Come near to me;' and all the people came near to him." Elijah then restored the fallen altar of God and prepared for the miracle which would win the people back from idolatrous compromise with Baalism. We must infer that Mark regards the Judaism of the scribes as on a par with Baalism as a false religion which consistent Christians must shun. His point is much like that of Paul in Galatians, appealing to Christian readers to forswear Torah-observance.

21. The Syro-Phoenician Woman (1 Kings 17:8–16; Mark 7:24–30)

1 Kings 17:8. Then the word of the LORD came to him, 9. "Arise, go to Zarephath, which belongs to Sidon, and dwell there. Behold,

I have commanded a widow there to feed you." 10. So he arose and went to Zarephath; and when he came to the gate of the city, behold, a widow was there gathering sticks; and he called to her and said, "Bring me a little water in a vessel, that I may drink." 11. And as she was going to bring it, he called to her and said, "Bring me a morsel of bread in your hand." 12. And she said, "As the LORD your God lives, I have nothing baked, only a handful of meal in a jar, and a little oil in a cruse; and now, I am gathering a couple of sticks, that I may go in and prepare it for myself and my son, that we may eat it, and die." 13. And Elijah said to her, "Fear not; go and do as you have said; but first make me a little cake of it and bring it to me, and afterward make for yourself and your son. 14. For thus says the LORD the God of Israel, 'The jar of meal shall not be spent, and the cruse of oil shall not fail, until the day that the LORD sends rain upon the earth.'" 15. And she went and did as Elijah said; and she, and he, and her household ate for many days. 16. The jar of meal was not spent, neither did the cruse of oil fail, according to the word of the LORD which he spoke by Elijah.

Mark 7:24. And from there he arose and went away to the region of Tyre and Sidon. And he entered a house, and would not have any one know it; yet he could not be hid. 25. But immediately a woman, whose little daughter was possessed by an unclean spirit, heard of him, and came and fell down at his feet. 26. Now the woman was a Greek, a Syrophoenician by birth. And she begged him to cast the demon out of her daughter. 27. And he said to her, "Let the children first be fed, for it is not right to take the children's bread and throw it to the dogs." 28. But she answered him, "Yes, Lord; yet even the dogs under the table eat the children's crumbs." 29. And he said to her, "For this saying you may go your way; the demon has left your daughter." 30. And she went home, and found the child lying in bed, and the demon gone.

Jesus meets a foreign woman in the district of Tyre and Sidon, who requests his help for her child, and we find ourselves back with Elijah and widow of Sidonian Zarephath in 1 Kings 17:8–16. There the prophet encounters the foreigner and does a miracle for her and her son. In both cases the miracle is preceded by a tense interchange between the prophet and the woman in which the prophet raises the bar to gauge the woman's faith. The Syrophoenician parries Jesus' initial dismissal with a clever comeback; the widow of Zarephath is bidden to take her remaining meal and to cook it up for Elijah first, whereupon the meal is indefinitely multiplied (Roth, pp. 51–52; Miller, pp. 196–197).

Why does Jesus call the poor woman and her daughter, by implication, dogs? Mark has taken it from 2 Kings 8:7–15, where Elisha tells Hazael (a Syrian, like the woman in Mark), that he will succeed Ben-Hadad to the throne of Aram. He replies, "What is your servant, the dog, that he should accomplish this great thing?" In Mark, the question is whether the great deed shall be done *for* the "dog" (Roth, p. 44).

22. Healing of the Deaf and the Blind (Mark 7:31–37; 8:22–26)

Mark 7:31. Then he returned from the region of Tyre, and went through Sidon to the Sea of Galilee, through the region of the Decapolis. 32. And they brought to him a man who was deaf and had an impediment in his speech; and they besought him to lay his hand upon him. 33. And taking him aside from the multitude privately, he put his fingers into his ears, and he spat and touched his tongue; 34. and looking up to heaven, he sighed, and said to him, *"Ephphatha,"* that is, "Be opened." 35. And his ears were opened, his tongue was released, and he spoke plainly. 36. And he charged them to tell no one; but the more he charged them, the more zealously they proclaimed it. 37. And they were astonished beyond measure, saying, "He has done all things well; he even makes the deaf hear and the dumb speak." (Mark 7:31–38)

Bowman (p. 172) makes Mark 7:31–38 a midrash upon Isaiah 29:18 ("In that day the deaf shall hear the words of a book, and out of their gloom and darkness the eyes of the blind shall see") and Isaiah 35:5–6 ("Then the eyes of the blind shall be opened and the ears of the deaf *unstopped*; then shall the lame man leap like a hart, and the tongue of the mute sing for joy"). We probably ought to add the episodes of the blind man of Bethsaida

> Mark 8:22. And they came to Beth-saida. And some people brought to him a blind man, and begged him to touch him. 23. And he took the blind man by the hand, and led him out of the village; and when he had spit on his eyes and laid his hands upon him, he asked him, "Do you see anything?" 24. And he looked up and said, "I see men; but they look like trees, walking." 25. Then again he laid his hands upon his eyes; and he looked intently and was restored, and saw everything clearly. 26. And he sent him away to his home, saying, "Do not even enter the village."

and of Bar-Timaeus

> Mark 10:46. And they came to Jericho; and as he was leaving Jericho with his disciples and a great multitude, Bar-Timaeus, a blind beggar, the son of Timaeus, was sitting by the roadside. 47. And when he heard that it was Jesus of Nazareth, he began to cry out and say, "Jesus, Son of David, have mercy on me!" 48. And many rebuked him, telling him to be silent; but he cried out all the more, "Son of David, have mercy on me!" 49. And Jesus stopped and said, "Call him." And they called the blind man, saying to him, "Take heart; rise, he is calling you." 50. And throwing off his mantle he sprang up and came to Jesus. 51. And Jesus said to him, "What do you want me to do for you?" And the blind man said to him, "Master, let me receive my sight." 52. And Jesus said to him, "Go your way; your faith has made you well." And immediately he received his sight and followed him on the way.

who leaped up to follow Jesus, as midrashic fulfilments of the same texts. In the case of the blind man of Mark 8, we also have to reckon with influence from Genesis 19:11–13, where the angels of God blind the Sodomite welcoming committee and warn Lot and his family to flee the doomed city.

> Genesis 19:11. And they struck with blindness the men who were at the door of the house, both small and great, so that they wearied themselves groping for the door. 12. Then the men said to Lot, "Have you any one else here? Sons-in-law, sons, daughters, or any one you have in the city, bring them out of the place; 13. for we are about to destroy this place, because the outcry against its people has become great before the LORD, and the LORD has sent us to destroy it."

The gospel tradition writes off Bethsaida for its lack of responsiveness. In Matthew 11:21–22 its fate is likened to the doom of the Philistine cities of Tyre and Sidon: "Woe to you, Bethsaida! For if the mighty works done in you had been done in Tyre and Sidon, they would have repented long ago in sackcloth and ashes. But I tell you, it shall be more tolerable on the day of judgment for Tyre and Sidon than for you." The blind man of Bethsaida, then, is to escape the doomed city's eventual destruction.

Up to the acclamation of the crowd in v. 37, "He does all things well," implying he has passed some sort of milestone, Jesus has performed a total of sixteen miracles, meeting the quota set by Elisha, who himself doubled the number ascribed to his master Elijah. Jesus will go on to perform another eight (Roth, pp. 5–7).

23. The Transfiguration (Exodus 24:15–16: 34:29; Malachi 3:2; Mark 9:1–13)

> Exodus 24:15. Then Moses went up on the mountain, and the cloud covered the mountain. 16. The glory of the LORD settled on Mount Sinai, and the cloud covered it six days; and on the seventh day he called to Moses out of the midst of the cloud.

> Exodus 34:29. When Moses came down from Mount Sinai, with the two tables of the testimony in his hand as he came down from the mountain, Moses did not know that the skin of his face shone because he had been talking with God.

The Christ Myth Theory And Its Problems

Malachi 3:2. But who can endure the day of his coming, and who can stand when he appears? For he is like a refiner's fire and like fuller's soap.

Mark 9:1. And he said to them, "Truly, I say to you, there are some standing here who will not taste death before they see that the kingdom of God has come with power." 2. And after six days Jesus took with him Peter and James and John, and led them up a high mountain apart by themselves; and he was transfigured before them, 3. and his garments became glistening, intensely white, as no fuller on earth could bleach them. 4. And there appeared to them Elijah with Moses; and they were talking to Jesus. 5. And Peter said to Jesus, "Master, it is well that we are here; let us make three booths, one for you and one for Moses and one for Elijah." 6. For he did not know what to say, for they were exceedingly afraid. 7. And a cloud overshadowed them, and a voice came out of the cloud, "This is my beloved Son; listen to him." 8. And suddenly looking around they no longer saw any one with them but Jesus only. 9. And as they were coming down the mountain, he charged them to tell no one what they had seen, until the Son of man should have risen from the dead. 10. So they kept the matter to themselves, questioning what the rising from the dead meant. 11. And they asked him, "Why do the scribes say that first Elijah must come?" 12. And he said to them, "Elijah does come first to restore all things; and how is it written of the Son of man, that he should suffer many things and be treated with contempt? 13. But I tell you that Elijah has come, and they did to him whatever they pleased, as it is written of him."

Jesus' ascent of the unnamed mountain and his transfiguration there is, of course, Mark's version of Moses' ascent of Mount Sinai to receive the tablets of the Torah in Exodus 24:15–16. As Bowman notes (p. 190), the Markan introduction, "And six days later" (9:2), must be understood as a pointer to the Exodus account. God calls Moses up the mountainside to receive the tablets (Exodus 24:12), and he takes Joshua with him (v. 13). Once they make the climb, the glory cloud covers the height for six days (v. 16), and on the seventh the divine voice calls to Moses from the depth of the cloud. Mark has apparently foreshortened the process.

The glowing apparition of Jesus is most obviously derived from that of Moses in Exodus 34:29. But as Derrett (p. 159) points out, we must not miss the influence of Malachi 3:2, especially since Elijah, too, appears. This, then, is the prophesied return of Elijah, and Jesus' garments glow white "like no fuller on earth could have bleached them" (Mark 9:3).

Jesus appears like Moses, yet with Moses. He is the predicted prophet like Moses from Deuteronomy 18:15: "The LORD your God will raise up for you a prophet like me from among you, from your brothers. Him you shall heed." The heavenly voice reiterates this commandment in Mark 9:7, "This is my beloved son; listen to him" (Bowman, p. 193).

Peter's bumbling suggestion that three tabernacles be made, one each for Jesus, Moses and Elijah, apparently comes from earlier in Exodus 24, verse 4: "And Moses wrote all the words of the LORD. And he rose early in the morning, and built an altar at the foot of the mountain, and twelve pillars, according to the twelve tribes of Israel."

Derrett (p. 155) further traces the admonition of Jesus to conceal news of the vision till the Son of Man be raised from the dead (9:9) to similar warnings in Daniel 12:4a ("But you, Daniel, shut up the words, and seal the book, until the time of the end.") and Zephaniah 3:8a, LXX ("Therefore wait upon me, saith the Lord, *until the day when I rise up* as a witness.").

Scholars have puzzled over the intended reference when Mark has Jesus speak in v. 13 of prophetic writings detailing the sufferings of Elijah in his avatar as John the Baptizer. Does he refer to some writing that did not survive in the canon? The pseudepigraphical *Apocalypse of Elijah* gives no help. But we need not search so far afield. By now it is evident that the reference must be to the Elijah (and Elisha) tales of 1 and 2 Kings, which Mark took as a quarry of information about Jesus and John.

The Christ Myth Theory And Its Problems

24. The Deaf-Mute Epileptic (Exodus 32; Mark 9:14–29)

Exodus 32:1. When the people saw that Moses delayed to come down from the mountain, the people gathered themselves together to Aaron, and said to him, "Up, make us gods, who shall go before us; as for this Moses, the man who brought us up out of the land of Egypt, we do not know what has become of him." 2. And Aaron said to them, "Take off the rings of gold which are in the ears of your wives, your sons, and your daughters, and bring them to me." 3. So all the people took off the rings of gold which were in their ears, and brought them to Aaron. 4. And he received the gold at their hand, and fashioned it with a graving tool, and made a molten calf; and they said, "These are your gods, O Israel, who brought you up out of the land of Egypt!" 5. When Aaron saw this, he built an altar before it; and Aaron made proclamation and said, "Tomorrow shall be a feast to the LORD." 6. And they rose up early on the morrow, and offered burnt offerings and brought peace offerings; and the people sat down to eat and drink, and rose up to play. 7. And the LORD said to Moses, "Go down; for your people, whom you brought up out of the land of Egypt, have corrupted themselves, 8. they have turned aside quickly out of the way which I commanded them; they have made for themselves a molten calf, and have worshiped it and sacrificed to it, and said, 'These are your gods, O Israel, who brought you up out of the land of Egypt!'" 9. And the LORD said to Moses, "I have seen this people, and behold, it is a stiff-necked people; 10. now therefore let me alone, that my wrath may burn hot against them and I may consume them; but of you I will make a great nation." 11. But Moses besought the LORD his God, and said, "O LORD, why does thy wrath burn hot against thy people, whom thou hast brought forth out of the land of Egypt with great power and with a mighty hand? 12. Why should the Egyptians say, 'With evil intent did he bring them forth, to slay them in the mountains, and to consume them from the face of the earth'? Turn from thy fierce wrath, and repent of this evil against thy people. 13. Remember Abraham, Isaac, and Israel, thy servants, to whom thou didst swear by thine own self, and didst say to them, 'I will multiply your descendants as the stars of heaven, and all this land that I have promised I will give to your descendants, and they shall inherit it for ever.'" 14. And the LORD repented of the evil which he thought to do to his people. 15. And Moses turned, and went down from the mountain with the two tables of the testimony in his hands, tables that were written on both sides; on the one side and on the other were they written. 16. And the tables were the work of God, and the writing was the writing of God, graven upon the tables. 17. When Joshua heard the noise of the people as they shouted, he said to Moses, "There is a noise of war in the camp." 18. But he said, "It is not the sound of shouting for victory, or the sound of the cry of defeat, but the sound of singing that I hear." 19. And as soon as he came near the camp and saw the calf and the dancing, Moses' anger burned hot, and he threw the tables out of his hands and broke them at the foot of the mountain. 20. And he took the calf which they had made, and burnt it with fire, and ground it to powder, and scattered it upon the water, and made the people of Israel drink it. 21. And Moses said to Aaron, "What did this people do to you that you have brought a great sin upon them?" 22. And Aaron said, "Let not the anger of my lord burn hot; you know the people, that they are set on evil. 23. For they said to me, 'Make us gods, who shall go before us; as for this Moses, the man who brought us up out of the land of Egypt, we do not know what has become of him.' 24. And I said to them, 'Let any who have gold take it off'; so they gave it to me, and I threw it into the fire, and there came out this calf." 25. And when Moses saw that the people had broken loose (for Aaron had let them break loose, to their shame among their enemies), 26. then Moses stood in the gate of the camp, and said, "Who is on the LORD's side? Come to me." And all the sons of Levi gathered themselves together to him. 27. And he said to them, "Thus says the LORD God of Israel, 'Put every man his sword on his side, and go to and fro from gate to gate throughout the camp, and slay every man his brother, and every man his companion, and every man his neighbor.'" 28. And the sons of Levi did according to the word of Moses; and there fell of the people that day about three thousand men. 29. And Moses said, "Today you have ordained yourselves for the service of the LORD, each one at the cost of his son and of his brother, that he may bestow a blessing upon you this day." 30. On the morrow Moses said to the people, "You have sinned a great sin. And now I will go up to the LORD; perhaps I can make atonement for your sin." 31. So Moses returned to the LORD and said, "Alas, this people have sinned a great sin; they have made for themselves gods of gold. 32. But now, if thou wilt forgive their sin — and if not, blot me, I pray thee, out of thy book which thou hast written." 33. But the LORD said to Moses, "Whoever has sinned against me, him will I blot out of my book. 34. But now go, lead the people to the place of which I have spoken to you; behold, my angel shall go before you. Nevertheless, in the day when I visit, I will visit their sin upon them." 35. And the LORD sent a plague upon the people, because they made the calf which Aaron made.

Mark 9:14. And when they came to the disciples, they saw a great crowd about them, and scribes arguing with them. 15. And immediately all the crowd, when they saw him, were greatly amazed, and ran up to him and greeted him. 16. And he asked them, "What are you discussing with them?" 17. And one of the crowd answered him, "Teacher, I brought my son to you, for he has a dumb spirit; 18. and wherever it seizes him, it dashes him down; and he foams and grinds his teeth and becomes rigid; and I asked your disciples to cast it out, and they were not able." 19. And he answered them, "O faithless generation, how long am I to be with you? How long am I to bear with you? Bring him to me." 20. And they brought the boy to him; and when the spirit saw him, immediately it convulsed the boy, and he fell on the ground and rolled about, foaming at the mouth. 21. And Jesus asked his father, "How long has he had this?" And he said, "From childhood. 22. And it has often cast him into the fire and into the water, to destroy him; but if you can do anything, have pity on us and help us." 23. And Jesus said to him, "If you can! All things are possible to him who believes." 24. Immediately the father of the child cried out and said, "I believe; help my unbelief!" 25. And when Jesus saw that a crowd came running together, he rebuked the unclean spirit, saying to it, "You dumb and deaf spirit, I command you, come out of him, and never enter him again." 26. And after crying out and convulsing him terribly, it came out, and the boy was like a corpse; so that most of them said, "He is dead." 27. But Jesus took him by the hand and lifted him up, and he arose. 28. And when he had entered the house, his disciples asked him privately, "Why could we not cast it out?" 29. And he said to them, "This kind cannot be driven out by anything but prayer."

Coming as it does following Jesus' descent of the mountain of transfiguration, this episode seems to be intended as an analogue for the Golden Calf incident in Exodus 32 (Bowman, p. 199; Miller, p. 232). Moses is away with one of his lieutenants, Joshua, leaving Aaron in charge, and when he returns Aaron has completely lost control of the situation, treading the path of least resistance to idolatrous ruin. The conversion of Exodus' idol into Mark's demon is an easy one, given the later Jewish belief that "what pagans sacrifice they offer to demons and not to God" (1 Corinthians 10:20a). So Jesus and his inner circle return from the mountain to find the rest of the disciples making a bad show of things, unable to cast the demon out of a boy and facing the scorn of the crowd and his enemies.

And yet the conclusion is different, with only a mild rebuke to the unsuccessful disciples. While the punchline instructs early Christian exorcists to make sure they devote ample prayer to such cases in future, the clear lesson is that it takes nothing short of the man of God himself to do the deed, and here Mark connects again with the story of Elisha and the Shunammite (2 Kings 4, see above, under Mark 5:21–34, 35–43). There Elisha dispatched his disciple Gehazi with his own potent staff to restore the Shunammite's dead son, but he could not (2 Kings 4:31). The disciple did nothing wrong; it was just that the ultimate power was required, and Elisha succeeded where Gehazi failed (2 Kings 4:32–35), simply because he was Elisha and Gehazi was not. Even so, in Mark, Jesus is irreplaceable because he is the divine hero of the story.

The Christ Myth Theory And Its Problems

25. Jockeying for Position (Numbers 12:1–15; 16:1–35; Mark 9:33–37)

Numbers 12:1. Miriam and Aaron spoke against Moses because of the Cushite woman whom he had married, for he had married a Cushite woman; 2. and they said, "Has the LORD indeed spoken only through Moses? Has he not spoken through us also?" And the LORD heard it. 3. Now the man Moses was very meek, more than all men that were on the face of the earth. 4. And suddenly the LORD said to Moses and to Aaron and Miriam, "Come out, you three, to the tent of meeting." And the three of them came out. 5. And the LORD came down in a pillar of cloud, and stood at the door of the tent, and called Aaron and Miriam; and they both came forward. 6. And he said, "Hear my words: If there is a prophet among you, I the LORD make myself known to him in a vision, I speak with him in a dream. 7. Not so with my servant Moses; he is entrusted with all my house. 8. With him I speak mouth to mouth, clearly, and not in dark speech; and he beholds the form of the LORD. Why then were you not afraid to speak against my servant Moses?" 9. And the anger of the LORD was kindled against them, and he departed; 10. and when the cloud removed from over the tent, behold, Miriam was leprous, as white as snow. 11. And Aaron turned towards Miriam, and behold, she was leprous. And Aaron said to Moses, "Oh, my lord, do not punish us because we have done foolishly and have sinned. 12. Let her not be as one dead, of whom the flesh is half consumed when he comes out of his mother's womb." 13. And Moses cried to the LORD, "Heal her, O God, I beseech thee." 14. But the LORD said to Moses, "If her father had but spit in her face, should she not be shamed seven days? Let her be shut up outside the camp seven days, and after that she may be brought in again." 15. So Miriam was shut up outside the camp seven days; and the people did not set out on the march till Miriam was brought in again.

Numbers 16:1. Now Korah the son of Izhar, son of Kohath, son of Levi, and Dathan and Abi'ram the sons of Eli'ab, and On the son of Peleth, sons of Reuben, 2. took men; and they rose up before Moses, with a number of the people of Israel, two hundred and fifty leaders of the congregation, chosen from the assembly, well-known men; 3. and they assembled themselves together against Moses and against Aaron, and said to them, "You have gone too far! For all the congregation are holy, every one of them, and the LORD is among them; why then do you exalt yourselves above the assembly of the LORD?" 4. When Moses heard it, he fell on his face; 5. and he said to Korah and all his company, "In the morning the LORD will show who is his, and who is holy, and will cause him to come near to him; him whom he will choose he will cause to come near to him. 6. Do this: take censers, Korah and all his company; 7. put fire in them and put incense upon them before the LORD tomorrow, and the man whom the LORD chooses shall be the holy one. You have gone too far, sons of Levi!" 8. And Moses said to Korah, "Hear now, you sons of Levi: 9. is it too small a thing for you that the God of Israel has separated you from the congregation of Israel, to bring you near to himself, to do service in the tabernacle of the LORD, and to stand before the congregation to minister to them; 10. and that he has brought you near him, and all your brethren the sons of Levi with you? And would you seek the priesthood also? 11. Therefore it is against the LORD that you and all your company have gathered together; what is Aaron that you murmur against him?" […] 16. And Moses said to Korah, "Be present, you and all your company, before the LORD, you and they, and Aaron, tomorrow; 17. and let every one of you take his censer, and put incense upon it, and every one of you bring before the LORD his censer, two hundred and fifty censers; you also, and Aaron, each his censer." 18. So every man took his censer, and they put fire in them and laid incense upon them, and they stood at the entrance of the tent of meeting with Moses and Aaron. 19. Then Korah assembled all the congregation against them at the entrance of the tent of meeting. And the glory of the LORD appeared to all the congregation. 20. And the LORD said to Moses and to Aaron, 21. "Separate yourselves from among this congregation, that I may consume them in a moment." 22. And they fell on their faces, and said, "O God, the God of the spirits of all flesh, shall one man sin, and wilt thou be angry with all the congregation?" 23. And the LORD said to Moses, 24. "Say to the congregation, Get away from about the dwelling of Korah, Dathan, and Abiram." 25. Then Moses rose and went to Dathan and Abiram; and the elders of Israel followed him. 26. And he said to the congregation, "Depart, I pray you, from the tents of these wicked men, and touch nothing of theirs, lest you be swept away with all their sins." 27. So they got away from about the dwelling of Korah, Dathan, and Abiram; and Dathan and Abiram came out and stood at the door of their tents, together with their wives, their sons, and their little ones. 28. And Moses said, "Hereby you shall know that the LORD has sent me to do all these works, and that it has not been of my own accord. 29. If these men die the common death of all men, or if they are visited by the fate of all men, then the LORD has not sent me. 30. But if the LORD creates something new, and the ground opens its mouth, and swallows them up, with all that belongs to them, and they go down alive into Sheol, then you shall know that these men have despised the LORD." 31. And as he finished speaking all these words, the ground under them split asunder; 32. and the earth opened its mouth and swallowed them up, with their households and all the men that belonged to Korah and all their goods. 33. So they and all that belonged to them went down alive into Sheol; and the earth closed over them, and they perished from the midst of the assembly. 34. And all Israel that were round about them fled at their cry; for they said, "Lest the earth swallow us up!" 35. And fire came forth from the LORD, and consumed the two hundred and fifty men offering the incense.

Mark 9:33. And they came to Capernaum; and when he was in the house he asked them, "What were you discussing on the way?" 34. But they were silent; for on the way they had discussed with one another who was the greatest. 35. And he sat down and called the twelve; and he said to them, "If any one would be first, he must be last of all and servant of all." 36. And he took a child, and put him in the midst of them; and taking him in his arms, he said to them, 37. "Whoever receives one such child in my name receives me; and whoever receives me, receives not me but him who sent me."

This passage in Mark has long roots reaching back to the Pentateuchal disputes between Moses on the one hand and Aaron and

Miriam on the other (Numbers 12) or perhaps Dathan and Abiram (Numbers 16:1–33 *ff*) (Bowman, p. 205). These others covet Moses' special position before God and make trouble over it, but God himself intervenes to settle the issue in Moses' favor, just as Jesus does here. God preferred Moses as a leader precisely because he did not seek power: he "was very meek, more than all the men that were on the face of the earth" (Numbers 12:3) (Miller, p. 239), the same qualification Jesus stipulates for anyone who aims to be a leader among his flock (Mark 9:35).

26. The Independent Exorcist, etc. (Numbers 11:24–30; Mark 9:38–50)

Numbers 11:24. So Moses went out and told the people the words of the LORD; and he gathered seventy men of the elders of the people, and placed them round about the tent. 25. Then the LORD came down in the cloud and spoke to him, and took some of the spirit that was upon him and put it upon the seventy elders; and when the spirit rested upon them, they prophesied. But they did so no more. 26. Now two men remained in the camp, one named Eldad, and the other named Medad, and the spirit rested upon them; they were among those registered, but they had not gone out to the tent, and so they prophesied in the camp. 27. And a young man ran and told Moses, "Eldad and Medad are prophesying in the camp." 28. And Joshua the son of Nun, the minister of Moses, one of his chosen men, said, "My lord Moses, forbid them." 29. But Moses said to him, "Are you jealous for my sake? Would that all the LORD's people were prophets, that the LORD would put his spirit upon them!" 30. And Moses and the elders of Israel returned to the camp.

Mark 9:38. John said to him, "Teacher, we saw a man casting out demons in your name, and we forbade him, because he was not following us." 39. But Jesus said, "Do not forbid him; for no one who does a mighty work in my name will be able soon after to speak evil of me. 40. For he that is not against us is for us. 41. For truly, I say to you, whoever gives you a cup of water to drink because you bear the name of Christ, will by no means lose his reward. 42. "Whoever causes one of these little ones who believe in me to sin, it would be better for him if a great millstone were hung round his neck and he were thrown into the sea. 43. And if your hand causes you to sin, cut it off; it is better for you to enter life maimed than with two hands to go to hell, to the unquenchable fire 44. where their worm does not die, and the fire is not quenched. 45. And if your foot causes you to sin, cut it off; it is better for you to enter life lame than with two feet to be thrown into hell. 46. where their worm does not die, and the fire is not quenched. 47. And if your eye causes you to sin, pluck it out; it is better for you to enter the kingdom of God with one eye than with two eyes to be thrown into hell, 48. where their worm does not die, and the fire is not quenched. 49. For every one will be salted with fire. 50. Salt is good; but if the salt has lost its saltness, how will you season it? Have salt in yourselves, and be at peace with one another.

The man casting out demons outside of Jesus' retinue, intimidating poor John, is based directly on Eldad and Medad, members of the seventy elders who stayed in the camp when the rest followed Moses to the Tent of Meeting to receive prophetic inspiration. John is a renamed Joshua who protested that "Eldad and Medad are prophesying in the camp," *i.e.*, "not following us" (Mark 9:38). Jesus is depicted as being fully as broad-minded as Moses, happy to acknowledge the work of God where ever he hears of it (Bowman, p. 206; Miller, p. 242).

Among other attached preachments, v.41, "For whoever gives you a cup of water to drink because of your name of Christ, truly I say to you, he shall not lose his reward," especially as it is directly followed by a mention of children and their perils, recalls the story of the widow of Zarephath (1 Kings 17:10), of whom Elijah requested a drink. The reward? He saved her and her son from starvation (Miller, p. 241).

The warnings of hell fire to come (vv. 43–48) depend verbatim on Isaiah 66:24: "and they shall go forth and see the carcases of the men who have transgressed against me: for their worm shall not die, and their fire shall not be quenched..." (LXX)

27. Blessing Children (10:13–16)

> Mark 10:13. And they were bringing children to him, that he might touch them; and the disciples rebuked them. 14. But when Jesus saw it he was indignant, and said to them, "Let the children come to me, do not hinder them; for to such belongs the kingdom of God. 15. Truly, I say to you, whoever does not receive the kingdom of God like a child shall not enter it." 16. And he took them in his arms and blessed them, laying his hands upon them.

Jesus is indignant with the well-meaning but insensitive disciples who chase away parents approaching Jesus for his benediction on their infants. ("Don't push that baby in the Saviour's face!" *Monty Python's Life of Brian (of Nazareth)*, p. 124). Is it too much to suggest that Mark modeled the scene on a similar one in 2 Kings 4, again, the story of Elisha and the Shunammite? "And when she came to the mountain, to the man of God, she caught hold of his feet. And Gehazi came to thrust her away. But the man of God said, 'Let her alone, for she is in bitter distress, and the LORD has hidden it from me and has not told me'" (v. 27). The cause of her distress, of course, is the death of her son, and she seeks Elisha's divine blessing to restore him to life. Mark has generalized the scene and, so to speak, lowered the stakes, having matched the urgency and poignancy of the original in his Jairus story back in chapter 5.

28. The Request of James and John (2 Kings 2:1–10: Mark 10:32–45)

> 2 Kings 2:1. Now when the LORD was about to take Elijah up to heaven by a whirlwind, Elijah and Elisha were on their way from Gilgal. 2. And Elijah said to Elisha, "Tarry here, I pray you; for the

LORD has sent me as far as Bethel." But Elisha said, "As the LORD lives, and as you yourself live, I will not leave you." So they went down to Bethel. 3. And the sons of the prophets who were in Bethel came out to Elisha, and said to him, "Do you know that today the LORD will take away your master from over you?" And he said, "Yes, I know it; hold your peace." 4. Elijah said to him, "Elisha, tarry here, I pray you; for the LORD has sent me to Jericho." But he said, "As the LORD lives, and as you yourself live, I will not leave you." So they came to Jericho. 5. The sons of the prophets who were at Jericho drew near to Elisha, and said to him, "Do you know that today the LORD will take away your master from over you?" And he answered, "Yes, I know it; hold your peace." 6. Then Elijah said to him, "Tarry here, I pray you; for the LORD has sent me to the Jordan." But he said, "As the LORD lives, and as you yourself live, I will not leave you." So the two of them went on. 7. Fifty men of the sons of the prophets also went, and stood at some distance from them, as they both were standing by the Jordan. 8. Then Elijah took his mantle, and rolled it up, and struck the water, and the water was parted to the one side and to the other, till the two of them could go over on dry ground. 9. When they had crossed, Elijah said to Elisha, "Ask what I shall do for you, before I am taken from you." And Elisha said, "I pray you, let me inherit a double share of your spirit." 10. And he said, "You have asked a hard thing; yet, if you see me as I am being taken from you, it shall be so for you; but if you do not see me, it shall not be so."

Mark 10:32. And they were on the road, going up to Jerusalem, and Jesus was walking ahead of them; and they were amazed, and those who followed were afraid. And taking the twelve again, he began to tell them what was to happen to him, 33. saying, "Behold, we are going up to Jerusalem; and the Son of man will be delivered to the chief priests and the scribes, and they will condemn him to death, and deliver him to the Gentiles; 34. and they will mock him, and spit upon him, and scourge him, and kill him; and after three days he will rise." 35. And James and John, the sons of Zebedee, came forward to him, and said to him, "Teacher, we want you to do for us whatever we ask of you." 36. And he said to them, "What do you want me to do for you?" 37. And they said to him, "Grant us to sit, one at your right hand and one at your left, in your glory." 38. But Jesus said to them, "You do not know what you are asking. Are you able to drink the cup that I drink, or to be baptized with the baptism with which I am baptized?" 39. And they said to him, "We are able." And Jesus said to them, "The cup that I drink you will drink; and with the baptism with which I am baptized, you will be baptized; 40. but to sit at my right hand or at my left is not mine to grant, but it is for those for whom it has been prepared." 41. And when the ten heard it, they began to be indignant at James and John. 42. And Jesus called them to him and said to them, "You know that those who are supposed to rule over the Gentiles lord it over them, and their great men exercise authority over them. 43. But it shall not be so among you; but whoever would be great among you must be your servant, 44. and whoever would be first among you must be slave of all. 45. For the Son of man also came not to be served but to serve, and to give his life as a ransom for many."

This whole Markan episode comes right out of that of Elisha's request of Elijah just before his ascension. Only Mark's version reflects badly on James and John. The structure is exactly the same (Miller, p. 253). Just as Elijah has (a bit surreptitiously) announced his departure three times, Jesus has just announced for the third time his impending death and resurrection, prompting the brothers to venture, "Teacher, we want you to do for us whatever we may ask of you... Grant that we may sit in your glory, one at your right, one at your left" (Mark 10:35, 37). This comes from 2 Kings 2:9, "Ask what I shall do for you before I am taken from you." Hearing the request, Elijah reflects, "You have asked a hard thing" (v. 10), just as Jesus warns James and John, "You do not know what you are asking for." The Elijah-Elisha story cements the "apostolic succession" from one prophet to the other, whereas Mark's rewrite seems to pass over the two disciples to open the possibility of succession to anyone willing to follow Jesus (sacramentally?) along the way of martyrdom.

The Christ Myth Theory And Its Problems

29. Blind Bar-Timaeus (Isaiah 35:5a, 6a, 8a; Mark 10:46–52)

Isaiah 35:5. "Then shall the eyes of the blind be opened, and the ears of the deaf shall hear. 6. Then shall the lame man leap as an hart, and the toungue of the stammerers shall speak plainly; for water has burst forth in the desert, and a channel of water in a thirsty land. 7. And the dry land shall become pools, and a fountain of water shall be poured into the thirsty land; there shall be a joy of birds, ready habitations and marshes. 8. There shall be there a pure way, and it shall be called a holy way; and there shall not pass by there any unclean person, neither shall there be there an unclean way; but the dispersed shall walk on it, and they shall not go astray.

Mark 10:46. And they came to Jericho; and as he was leaving Jericho with his disciples and a great multitude, Bar-Timaeus, a blind beggar, the son of Timaeus, was sitting by the roadside. 47. And when he heard that it was Jesus of Nazareth, he began to cry out and say, "Jesus, Son of David, have mercy on me!" 48. And many rebuked him, telling him to be silent; but he cried out all the more, "Son of David, have mercy on me!" 49. And Jesus stopped and said, "Call him." And they called the blind man, saying to him, "Take heart; rise, he is calling you." 50. And throwing off his mantle he sprang up and came to Jesus. 51. And Jesus said to him, "What do you want me to do for you?" And the blind man said to him, "Master, let me receive my sight." 52. And Jesus said to him, "Go your way; your faith has made you well." And immediately he received his sight and followed him on the way.

As already noted, this story puts flesh on the skeleton of LXX Isaiah 35:5a, 6a, 8a: "Then shall the eyes of the blind be opened... then shall the lame man leap as an hart... And there shall be there a pure way, and it shall be called a holy way" (Miller, pp. 263–264). Thus Bar-Timaeus leaps up, is given his sight, and follows Jesus on the way. That he is not only blind but a beggar may come from the possible meaning of his name, as Derrett (p. 185) decodes it from Aramaic *Bar-teymah*, "son of poverty." In this, the fictive nature of the story is doubly clear.

MacDonald suggests (pp. 97–99) that Mark has created Bar-Timaeus as a Christian Tiresias, the blind seer of the *Odyssey*, since Bar-Timaeus distinguishes himself by spiritual insight; he recognizes Jesus as Son of David (Mark 10:48).

30. Preparation for the Entry to Jerusalem and the Passover Supper (1 Samuel 9:1–24; Mark 11:1–6; 14:12–16)

1 Samuel 9:1. There was a man of Benjamin whose name was Kish, the son of Abiel, son of Zeror, son of Becorath, son of Aphiah, a Benjaminite, a man of wealth; 2. and he had a son whose name was Saul, a handsome young man. There was not a man among the people of Israel more handsome than he; from his shoulders upward he was taller than any of the people. 3. Now the asses of Kish, Saul's father, were lost. So Kish said to Saul his son, "Take one of the servants with you, and arise, go and look for the asses." 4. And they passed through the hill country of Ephraim and passed through the land of Shalishah, but they did not find them. And they passed through the land of Shaalim, but they were not there. Then they passed through the land of Benjamin, but did not find them. 5. When they came to the land of Zuph, Saul said to his servant who was with him, "Come, let us go back, lest my father cease to care about the asses and become anxious about us." 6. But he said to him, "Behold, there is a man of God in this city, and he is a man that is held in honor; all that he says comes true. Let us go there; perhaps he can tell us about the journey on which we have set out." 7. Then Saul said to his servant, "But if we go, what can we bring the man? For the bread in our sacks is gone, and there is no present to bring to the man of God. What have we?" 8. The servant answered Saul again, "Here, I have with me the fourth part of a shekel of silver, and I will give it to the man of God, to tell us our way." 9. (Formerly in Israel, when a man went to inquire of God, he said, "Come, let us go to the seer"; for he who is now called a prophet was formerly called a seer.) 10. And Saul said to his servant, "Well said; come, let us go." So they went to the city where the man of God was. 11. As they went up the hill to the city, they met young maidens coming out to

draw water, and said to them, "Is the seer here?" 12. They answered, "He is; behold, he is just ahead of you. Make haste; he has come just now to the city, because the people have a sacrifice today on the high place. 13. As soon as you enter the city, you will find him, before he goes up to the high place to eat; for the people will not eat till he comes, since he must bless the sacrifice; afterward those eat who are invited. Now go up, for you will meet him immediately." 14. So they went up to the city. As they were entering the city, they saw Samuel coming out toward them on his way up to the high place. 15. Now the day before Saul came, the LORD had revealed to Samuel: 16. "Tomorrow about this time I will send to you a man from the land of Benjamin, and you shall anoint him to be prince over my people Israel. He shall save my people from the hand of the Philistines; for I have seen the affliction of my people, because their cry has come to me." 17. When Samuel saw Saul, the LORD told him, "Here is the man of whom I spoke to you! He it is who shall rule over my people." 18. Then Saul approached Samuel in the gate, and said, "Tell me where is the house of the seer?" 19. Samuel answered Saul, "I am the seer; go up before me to the high place, for today you shall eat with me, and in the morning I will let you go and will tell you all that is on your mind. 20. As for your asses that were lost three days ago, do not set your mind on them, for they have been found. And for whom is all that is desirable in Israel? Is it not for you and for all your father's house?" 21. Saul answered, "Am I not a Benjaminite, from the least of the tribes of Israel? And is not my family the humblest of all the families of the tribe of Benjamin? Why then have you spoken to me in this way?" 22. Then Samuel took Saul and his servant and brought them into the hall and gave them a place at the head of those who had been invited, who were about thirty persons. 23. And Samuel said to the cook, "Bring the portion I gave you, of which I said to you, 'Put it aside.'" 24. So the cook took up the leg and the upper portion and set them before Saul; and Samuel said, "See, what was kept is set before you. Eat; because it was kept for you until the hour appointed, that you might eat with the guests." So Saul ate with Samuel that day.

Mark 11:1. And when they drew near to Jerusalem, to Bethphage and Bethany, at the Mount of Olives, he sent two of his disciples, 2. and said to them, "Go into the village opposite you, and immediately as you enter it you will find a colt tied, on which no one has ever sat; untie it and bring it. 3. If any one says to you, 'Why are you doing this?' say, 'The Lord has need of it and will send it back here immediately.'" 4. And they went away, and found a colt tied at the door out in the open street; and they untied it. 5. And those who stood there said to them, "What are you doing, untying the colt?" 6. And they told them what Jesus had said; and they let them go.

Mark 14:12. And on the first day of Unleavened Bread, when they sacrificed the passover lamb, his disciples said to him, "Where will you have us go and prepare for you to eat the passover?" 13. And he sent two of his disciples, and said to them, "Go into the city, and a man carrying a jar of water will meet you; follow him, 14. and wherever he enters, say to the householder, 'The Teacher says, Where is my guest room, where I am to eat the passover with my disciples?' 15. And he will show you a large upper room furnished and ready; there prepare for us." 16. And the disciples set out and went to the city, and found it as he had told them; and they prepared the passover.

Both these stories, parallel to one another, alike derive from 1 Samuel chapter 9 (Miller, p. 325; Derrett, p. 187). Kish sends two men, his son Saul and a servant (1 Samuel 9:3), just as Jesus sends two disciples on each of these missions (Mark 11:1; 14:13). Saul and his companion were to find some runaway asses (9:3), while the disciples are to find a particular ass's colt (11:2). When Saul and the servant reach the city they are met by young women coming out to draw water (9:11); Jesus' disciples are told to look for a man carrying water (14:13). Like Saul and his companion, the two pairs enter the city. Saul and the other are told they will find the man they seek, the prophet Samuel, as soon as they enter the city (9:13), as Jesus tells his men they will find the colt tied as soon

121

as they enter the city (11:2). All transpires as predicted (9:6; 11:4; 14:16). Saul asks "Where is the house of the seer?" (9:18). Jesus tells the disciples to ask, "Where is my guest room?" (14:14). As in 9:20, Saul is told the missing asses have been located, so in 11:6 does Jesus say to assure the owner that his borrowed colt will be returned. In 9:19 Samuel oversees the preparation of a feast, and in 14:16 the disciples prepare the Passover.

The upper room of the Last Supper may also hark back to the second-story rooms provided for Elijah ("And he said to her, 'Give me your son.' And he took him from her bosom, and carried him up into the upper chamber, where he lodged, and laid him upon his own bed," 1 Kings 17:19) and Elisha ("Let us make a small roof chamber with walls, and put there for him a bed, a table, a chair, and a lamp, so that whenever he comes to us, he can go in there," 2 Kings 4:10) by bene-factors (Miller, p. 331). One of these Elijah first met by asking a drink of water from a woman God told him would provide for him (" 'Arise, go to Zarephath, which belongs to Sidon, and dwell there. Behold, I have commanded a widow there to feed you.' So he arose and went to Zarephath; and when he came to the gate of the city, behold, a widow was there gathering sticks; and he called to her and said, 'Bring me a little water in a vessel, that I may drink'," 1 Kings 17:9,10. He met her at the city gate, just as Jesus told the disciples to meet a man carrying water in a vessel as soon as they entered the city.)

31. The Entry into Jerusalem (Zechariah 9:9; Psalms 118:19–27; Mark 11:7–11)

Zechariah 9:9. Rejoice greatly, O daughter of Zion! Shout aloud, O daughter of Jerusalem! Lo, your king comes to you; triumphant and victorious is he, humble and riding on an ass, on a colt the foal of an ass.

Psalms 118:19. Open to me the gates of righteousness, that I may enter through them and give thanks to the LORD. 20. This is the gate of the LORD; the righteous shall enter through it. 21. I thank thee that thou hast answered me and hast become my salvation. 22. The stone which the builders rejected has become the head of the corner. 23. This is the LORD's doing; it is marvelous in our eyes. 24. This is the day which the LORD has made; let us rejoice and be glad in it. 25. Save us, we beseech thee, O LORD! O LORD, we beseech thee, give us success! 26. Blessed be he who enters in the name of the LORD! We bless you from the house of the LORD. 27. The LORD is God, and he has given us light. Bind the festal procession with branches, up to the horns of the altar!

Mark 11:7. And they brought the colt to Jesus, and threw their garments on it; and he sat upon it. 8. And many spread their garments on the road, and others spread leafy branches which they had cut from the fields. 9. And those who went before and those who followed cried out, "Hosanna! Blessed is he who comes in the name of the Lord! 10. Blessed is the kingdom of our father David that is coming! Hosanna in the highest!" 11. And he entered Jerusalem, and went into the temple; and when he had looked round at everything, as it was already late, he went out to Bethany with the twelve.

Though Mark does not make it explicit, it is evident that the scene of Jesus entering the holy city on donkeyback is a fleshing out of Zechariah 9:9. The actions and words of the crowd come right from Psalms 118:26–27, "Blessed is he who enters in the name of the LORD! ... Bind the festal procession with branches..." "Hosanna in the highest" comes from the Hebrew or Aramaic of "Save now!" in Psalms 118:25 and from Psalm 148 LXX: "Praise him in the highest!" (Helms, p. 104). Of course the Psalm means to offer its blessings on any pilgrim into the holy city.

32. Cursing the Fig Tree (Psalms 37:35–36; Mark 11:12–14, 20)

Psalms 37:35. I have seen a wicked man overbearing, and towering like a cedar of Lebanon. 36. Again I passed by, and, lo, he was no more; though I sought him, he could not be found.

Mark 11:12. On the following day, when they came from Bethany, he was hungry. 13. And seeing in the distance a fig tree in leaf, he went to see if he could find anything on it. When he came to it, he found nothing but leaves, for it was not the season for figs. 14. And he said to it, "May no one ever eat fruit from you again." And his disciples heard it. [...] 20. As they passed by in the morning, they saw the fig tree withered away to its roots.

As anyone can see, the tree is made to stand for unrepentant Jerusalem, and the episode is then seen (Miller, pp. 274–275) to stem from Psalms 37:35–36. Here is the source of Jesus *seeking* figs on the *tree* but *finding none*, and of the note that it was in *passing the spot again* they discovered the tree blasted.

33. Cleansing the Temple (Malachi 3:1–3; Zechariah 14:21b; Isaiah 56:7; Jeremiah 7:11; Mark 11:15–18)

Malachi 3:1. Behold, I send my messenger to prepare the way before me, and the Lord whom you seek will suddenly come to his temple; the messenger of the covenant in whom you delight, behold, he is coming, says the LORD of hosts. 2. But who can endure the day of his coming, and who can stand when he appears? For he is like a refiner's fire and like fullers' soap; 3. he will sit as a refiner and purifier of silver, and he will purify the sons of Levi and refine them like gold and silver, till they present right offerings to the LORD.

Zechariah 14:21b. And there shall no longer be a trader in the house of the LORD of hosts on that day.

Isaiah 56:7. My house shall be called a house of prayer for all the nations.

Jeremiah 7:11. Has this house, which is called by my name, become a den of robbers in your eyes?

Mark 11:15. 15. And they came to Jerusalem. And he entered the temple and began to drive out those who sold and those who bought in the temple, and he overturned the tables of the money-changers and the seats of those who sold pigeons; 16. and he would not allow any one to carry anything through the temple. 17. And he taught, and said to them, "Is it not written, 'My house shall be called a house of prayer for all the nations'? But you have made it a den of robbers." 18. And the chief priests and the scribes heard it and sought a way to destroy him; for they feared him, because all the multitude was astonished at his teaching.

Jesus' overthrow of the Temple service (not only does he scatter the livestock for offerings but somehow bans anyone carrying sacrificial vessels) is historically impossible as it reads here. The envisioned area is huge, and for Jesus to commandeer it like this would have required a military raid, something of which Mark's text seems oblivious. Though it is not unlikely that the story preserves some faded memory of the entry of Simon bar-Gioras into the Temple to clean out the robbers of John of Giscala on the eve of the Temple's destruction, the story may simply conflate various scripture passages, which it seems to do in any case. The "cleansing" must have in view that of Malachi's messenger of the covenant who will purify the sons of Levi (Malachi 3:1–3), as hinted by Mark 1:2, "As it is written in Isaiah the prophet, 'Behold, I send my messenger before thy face, who shall prepare thy way'," and 9:3, "and his garments became glistening, intensely white, as no fuller on earth could bleach them," as well as the oracle of Zechariah 14:21b, banning salesmen from the holy place. The saying of Jesus on that occasion is merely a conflation of Isaiah 56:7 and Jeremiah 7:11. The priests and scribes react to this disturbance by plotting to destroy Jesus, just as the priests, prophets, and people lay hold of Jeremiah and cry out, "You shall die!" when he likewise predicts the destruction of the city and the Temple (26:8) (Miller, p. 274).

34. *The Parable of the Wicked Tenants (Isaiah 5:1–7; Mark 12:1–12)*

Isaiah 5:1. Let me sing for my beloved a love song concerning his vineyard: My beloved had a vineyard on a very fertile hill. 2. He digged it and cleared it of stones, and planted it with choice vines; he built a watchtower in the midst of it, and hewed out a wine vat in it; and he looked for it to yield grapes, but it yielded wild grapes. 3. And now, O inhabitants of Jerusalem and men of Judah, judge, I pray you, between me and my vineyard. 4. What more was there to do for my vineyard, that I have not done in it? When I looked for it to yield grapes, why did it yield wild grapes? 5. And now I will tell you what I will do to my vineyard. I will remove its hedge, and it shall be devoured; I will break down its wall, and it shall be trampled down. 6. I will make it a waste; it shall not be pruned or hoed, and briers and thorns shall grow up; I will also command the clouds that they rain no rain upon it. 7. For the vineyard of the LORD of hosts is the house of Israel, and the men of Judah are his pleasant planting; and he looked for justice, but behold, bloodshed; for righteousness, but behold, a cry!

Mark 12:1. And he began to speak to them in parables. "A man planted a vineyard, and set a hedge around it, and dug a pit for the wine press, and built a tower, and let it out to tenants, and went into another country. 2. When the time came, he sent a servant to the tenants, to get from them some of the fruit of the vineyard. 3. And they took him and beat him, and sent him away empty-handed. 4. Again he sent to them another servant, and they wounded him in the head, and treated him shamefully. 5. And he sent another, and him they killed; and so with many others, some they beat and some they killed. 6. He had still one other, a beloved son; finally he sent him to them, saying, 'They will respect my son.' 7. But those tenants said to one another, 'This is the heir; come, let us kill him, and the inheritance will be ours.' 8. And they took him and killed him, and cast him out of the vineyard. 9. What will the owner of the vineyard do? He will come and destroy the tenants, and give the vineyard to others. 10. Have you not read this scripture: 'The very stone which the builders rejected has become the head of the corner; 11. this was the Lord's doing, and it is marvelous in our eyes'?" 12. And they tried to arrest him, but feared the multitude, for they perceived that he had told the parable against them; so they left him and went away.

All commentators call attention to the use of Isaiah 5:1–7 in this parable, and that surely is to account for one of its principal sources. MacDonald (p. 37) identifies the other in the *Odyssey*, where we discover the source (here and in other parables) of the absentee owner having left servants in charge of his estate while he is away on a long trip. The servants are not wicked, but the suitors are, the men who, assuming the long-absent Odysseus is dead, flock to his palace to woo his "widow" Penelope, eating her out of house and home for years. Their complete domination of the estates of Odysseus is threatened by the succession of Prince Telemachus, Odysseus' only son. They plot to kill him and so remove the last obstacle to their squatter's possession. He eludes their scheme. The caution of the Jewish leaders in the face of the veiled threat of the parable comes from the note in the *Odyssey* that the suitors had to tread lightly lest their brazenness finally push the people of Ithaca, Odysseus' subjects, too far and spark their wrath. Mark's result is a hybrid which applies Isaiah's judgment oracle not to the whole people but to their imagined usurping leaders and introduces the plot element of a rejected son.

Mark (12:10–11) returned to his recently-used Psalms 118 for the quotation from vv. 22–23 ("The stone which the builders rejected has become the head of the corner. This is the LORD's doing; it is marvelous in our eyes").

35. The Olivet Discourse (Mark 13:1–37)

Mark 13:1. And as he came out of the temple, one of his disciples said to him, "Look, Teacher, what wonderful stones and what wonderful buildings!" 2. And Jesus said to him, "Do you see these great buildings? There will not be left here one stone upon another, that will not be thrown down." 3. And as he sat on the Mount of Olives opposite the temple, Peter and James and John and Andrew asked him privately, 4. "Tell us, when will this be, and what will be the sign when these things are all to be accomplished?" 5. And Jesus began to say to them, "Take heed that no one leads you astray. 6. Many will come in my name, saying, 'I am he!' and they will lead many astray. 7. And when you hear of wars and rumors of wars, do not be alarmed; this must take place, but the end is not yet. 8. For nation will rise against nation, and kingdom against kingdom; there will be earthquakes in various places, there will be famines; this is but the beginning of the birth-pangs. 9. "But take heed to yourselves; for they will deliver you up to councils; and you will be beaten in synagogues; and you will stand before governors and kings for my sake, to bear testimony before them. 10. And the gospel must first be preached to all nations. 11. And when they bring you to trial and deliver you up, do not be anxious beforehand what you are to say; but say whatever is given you in that hour, for it is not you who speak, but the Holy Spirit. 12. And brother will deliver up brother to death, and the father his child, and children will rise against parents and have them put to death; 13. and you will be hated by all for my name's sake. But he who endures to the end will be saved. 14. "But when you see the desolating sacrilege set up where it ought not to be (let the reader understand), then let those who are in Judea flee to the mountains; 15. let him who is on the housetop not go down, nor enter his house, to take anything away; 16. and let him who is in the field not turn back to take his mantle. 17. And alas for those who are with child and for those who give suck in those days! 18. Pray that it may not happen in winter. 19. For in those days there will be such tribulation as has not been from the beginning of the creation which God created until now, and never will be. 20. And if the Lord had not shortened the days, no human being would be saved; but for the sake of the elect, whom he chose, he shortened the days. 21. And then if any one says to you, 'Look, here is the Christ!' or 'Look, there he is!' do not believe it. 22. False Christs and false prophets will arise and show signs and wonders, to lead astray, if possible, the elect. 23. But take heed; I have told you all things beforehand. 24. "But in those days, after that tribulation, the sun will be darkened, and the moon will not give its light, 25. and the stars will be falling from heaven, and the powers in the heavens will be shaken. 26. And then they will see the Son of man coming in clouds with great power and glory. 27. And then he will send out the angels, and gather his elect from the four winds, from the ends of the earth to the ends of heaven. 28. "From the fig tree learn its lesson: as soon as its branch becomes tender and puts forth its leaves, you know that summer is near. 29. So also, when you see these things taking place, you know that he is near, at the very gates. 30. Truly, I say to you, this generation will not pass away before all these things take place. 31. Heaven and earth will pass away, but my words will not pass away. 32. "But of that day or that hour no one knows, not even the angels in heaven, nor the Son, but only the Father. 33. Take heed, watch; for you do not know when the time will come. 34. It is like a man going on a journey, when he leaves home and puts his servants in charge, each with his work, and commands the doorkeeper to be on the watch. 35. Watch therefore — for you do not know when the master of the house will come, in the evening, or at midnight, or at cockcrow, or in the morning — 36. lest he come suddenly and find you asleep. And what I say to you I say to all: Watch."

The whole apocalyptic discourse of Mark is a cento of scripture paraphrases and quotations, and it will be sufficient simply to match each major verse to its source. Mark 13:7 ("And when you hear of wars and rumors of wars, do not be alarmed; this must take place, but the end is not yet.") comes from Daniel 11:44 ("But tidings from the east and the west shall alarm him, and he shall go forth with great fury to exterminate and utterly destroy many."). Mark 13:8 ("For nation will rise against nation, and kingdom against kingdom; there will be earthquakes in various places, there will be famines; this is but the beginning of the birth-pangs.") comes from Isaiah 19:2 ("And I will stir up Egyptians against Egyptians, and they will fight, every man against his brother and every man against his neighbor. City against city, kingdom against kingdom.") and/ or 2 Chronicles 15:6 ("They were broken in pieces, nation against nation and kingdom against kingdom."). Mark 13:12 ("And brother will deliver up brother to death, and the father his child, and children will rise against parents and have them put to death.") derives from Micah 7:6 ("for the son treats the father with contempt, the daughter rises up against her mother, the daughter-in-law against her mother-in-law; a man's enemies are the men of his own house."). Mark 13:14 ("But when you see the desolating sacrilege set up where it ought not to be (let the reader understand), then let those who are in Judea flee to the mountains.") is based on Daniel 9:27 ("And he shall make a strong covenant with many for one week; and for half of the week he shall cause sacrifice and offering to cease; and upon the wing of abominations shall come one who makes desolate, until the decreed end is poured out on the desolator.") and 12:11 ("And from the time that the continual burnt offering is taken away, and the abomination that makes desolate is set up, there shall be a thousand two hundred and ninety days.") as well as Genesis 19:17 ("And when they had brought them forth, they said, 'Flee for your life; do not look back or stop anywhere in the valley; flee to the hills, lest you be consumed.' "). Mark 13:19 ("For in those days there will be such tribulation as has not been from the beginning of the creation which God created until now, and never will be.") comes from Daniel 12:1 ("At that time shall arise Michael, the great prince who has charge of your people. And there shall be a time of trouble, such as never has been since there was a nation till that time; but at that time your people shall be delivered, every one whose name shall be found written in the book."). Mark 13:22 ("False Christs and false prophets will arise and show signs and wonders, to lead astray, if possible, the elect.") at least presupposes Deuteronomy 13:2–3 ("If a prophet arises among you, or a dreamer of dreams, and gives you a sign or a wonder, and the sign or wonder which he tells you comes to pass, and if he says, 'Let us go after other gods,' which you have not known, 'and let us serve them,' you shall not listen to the words of that prophet or to that dreamer of dreams; for the LORD your God is testing you, to know whether you love the LORD your God with all your heart and with all your soul."). Mark 13:24 ("But in those days, after that tribulation, the sun will be darkened, and the moon will not give its light") comes from Isaiah 13:10 ("For the stars of the heavens and their constellations will not give their light; the sun will be dark at its rising and the moon will not shed its light"), while Mark 13:25 ("and the stars will be falling from heaven, and the powers in the heavens will be shaken") derives from Isaiah 34:4 ("All the host of heaven shall rot away, and the skies roll up like a scroll. All their host shall fall, as leaves fall from the vine, like leaves falling from the fig tree."). Mark 13:26 ("And then they will see the Son of man coming in clouds with great power and glory") is obviously based upon Daniel 7:13 ("I saw in the night visions, and behold, with the clouds of heaven there came one like a son of man, and he came to the Ancient of Days and was presented before him."). Mark 13:27 ("And then he will send out the angels, and gather his elect from the four winds, from the ends of the earth to the ends of heaven.") comes from Zechariah 2:6–7 ("Ho! ho! Flee from the land of the north, says the LORD; for I have spread you abroad as the four winds of the heavens, says the LORD. Ho! Escape to Zion, you who dwell with the daughter of Babylon.") and/or Deuteronomy 30:3–4 ("then the LORD your God will restore your fortunes, and have compassion upon you, and he will gather you again from all the peoples where the LORD your God has scattered you. If your outcasts are in the uttermost parts of heaven, from there the LORD your God will gather you, and from there he will fetch you.") (Bowman, pp. 241–242, Miller, pp. 300–301).

36. The Anointing at Bethany (Mark 14:3–9)

Mark 14:3. And while he was at Bethany in the house of Simon the leper, as he sat at table, a woman came with an alabaster flask of ointment of pure nard, very costly, and she broke the flask and poured it over his head. 4. But there were some who said to themselves indignantly, "Why was the ointment thus wasted? 5. For this ointment might have been sold for more than three hundred denarii, and given to the poor." And they reproached her. 6. But Jesus said, "Let her alone; why do you trouble her? She has done a beautiful thing to me. 7. For you always have the poor with you, and whenever you will, you can do good to them; but you will not always have me. 8. She has done what she could; she has anointed my body beforehand for burying. 9. And truly, I say to you, wherever the gospel is preached in the whole world, what she has done will be told in memory of her."

Helms (pp. 98–100) is surely correct that the Johannine version of the Bethany anointing (John 12:1–8) most clearly reveals its origin in the resurrection mythology of the Egyptian Osiris (Mary and Martha=Isis and Nephthys; Lazarus=Eleazer=El-Osiris; Bethany=Beth-Annu, house of the Sun=Heliopolis).

John 12:1. Six days before the Passover, Jesus came to Bethany, where Lazarus was, whom Jesus had raised from the dead. 2. There they made him a supper; Martha served, and Lazarus was one of those at table with him. 3. Mary took a pound of costly ointment of pure nard and anointed the feet of Jesus and wiped his feet with her hair; and the house was filled with the fragrance of the ointment. 4. But Judas Iscariot, one of his disciples (he who was to betray him), said, 5. "Why was this ointment not sold for three hundred denarii and given to the poor?" 6. This he said, not that he cared for the poor but because he was a thief, and as he had the money box he used to take what was put into it. 7. Jesus said, "Let her alone, let her keep it for the day of my burial. 8. The poor you always have with you, but you do not always have me."

It is apparent that the story even as Mark knew it was already derived from Osiris. Just as Isis restored the slain Osiris to life by anointing him in some versions, the reference here to the un-named woman anointing Jesus for the day of his death and burial must originally have been set on that day, the day when she raised him from the dead. (The story of Joseph probably came ultimately from the same source, as numerous parallels make clear.)

37. The Last Supper (Mark 14:17–31)

Mark 14:17. And when it was evening he came with the twelve. 18. And as they were at table eating, Jesus said, "Truly, I say to you, one of you will betray me, one who is eating with me." 19. They began to be sorrowful, and to say to him one after another, "Is it I?" 20. He said to them, "It is one of the twelve, one who is dipping bread into the dish with me. 21. For the Son of man goes as it is written of him, but woe to that man by whom the Son of man is betrayed! It would have been better for that man if he had not been born." 22. And as they were eating, he took bread, and blessed, and broke it, and gave it to them, and said, "Take; this is my body." 23. And he took a cup, and when he had given thanks he gave it to them, and they all drank of it. 24. And he said to them, "This is my blood of the covenant, which is poured out for many. 25. Truly, I say to you, I shall not drink again of the fruit of the vine until that day when I drink it new in the kingdom of God." 26. And when they had sung a hymn, they went out to the Mount of Olives. 27. And Jesus said to them, "You will all fall away; for it is written, 'I will strike the shepherd, and the sheep will be scattered.' 28. But after I am raised up, I will go before you to Galilee." 29. Peter said to him, "Even though they all fall away, I will not." 30. And Jesus said to him, "Truly, I say to you, this very night, before the cock crows twice, you will deny me three times." 31. But he said vehemently, "If I must die with you, I will not deny you." And they all said the same.

All critics recognize the seed of the last supper story in Psalms 41:9, "Even my bosom friend, in whom I trusted, who ate my bread, has lifted his heel against me." Frank Kermode has traced (pp. 84–85) the logical process whereby the original, entirely and abstractly theological claim that Jesus had been "delivered up" (παρεδωκεν, Romans 8:32: "He who did not spare his own Son but gave him up for us all, will he not also give us all things with him?") has been narratized. From God having "handed over" his son for our sins grew the idea that a human agent had "betrayed" him (same Greek word). For this purpose, in line with anti-Jewish polemic, a betrayer named Judas was created. His epithet "Iscariot" seems to denote either *Ish-karya* (Aramaic for "the false one") or a pun on Issachar, "hireling" (Miller, p. 65), thus one paid to hand Jesus over to the authorities. Much of the Last Supper story is taken up with this matter because of the mention of the betrayer eating with his victim in Psalm 41.

It is interesting to see how Matthew embellishes the enigmatic figure and fate of Judas. First, he knows the precise amount Judas was paid, thirty silver pieces (Matthew 26:15, "And they paid him thirty pieces of silver."). He knows this from Zechariah 11:11b ("And they weighed out as my wages thirty shekels of silver.") How does he know that Judas returned the money, throwing it into the Temple treasury (Matthew 27:5, "throwing down the pieces of silver in the temple") and that the priests decided to use it to buy the potter's field (Matthew 27:7, "So they took counsel, and bought with them the potter's field")? The Syriac version of Zechariah reads: "Then the LORD said to me, 'Cast it into the treasury, this lordly price at which I was paid off by them. So I took the thirty shekels of silver and cast them into the treasury in the house of the LORD." The Hebrew of the same verse reads: "Cast it to the *potter, etc.*" How does Matthew know Judas hanged himself? That was the fate of David's traitorous counselor Ahithophel (2 Samuel 17:23b, "And he set his house in order, and hanged himself; and he died, and was buried in the tomb of his father."), whom scribal tradition took to be the subject of Psalms 41:9 ("Even my bosom friend in whom I trusted, who ate of my bread, has lifted his heel against me."), which the gospels applied to Judas (Helms, p. 106).

Almost secondary in the supper narrative is the bread and cup. Whatever the origin of the sacramental ritual underlying this etiological story, it has been interpreted here in scriptural terms as a covenant renewal. See the unmistakable connection with Exodus 24:8, "Behold the blood of the covenant which the LORD has made with you in accordance with these words."

In verse 26 Jesus and the disciples sing the traditional Passover hymn, which, as we will see, provided Mark the content of Jesus' introspection in the Garden of Gethsemane. Verse 27's quotation of Zechariah 13:7, "I will strike down the shepherd, and the sheep will be scattered," would seem to be the whole source for the subsequent scene where Jesus' disciples flee from the arresting party.

Peter avers that, no matter what the danger, he will not leave Jesus' side. In this he reminds us, not coincidentally, of Elisha's three avowals that he will not leave Elijah (2 Kings 2:2, 4, 6: "As the LORD lives, and as you yourself live, I will not leave you.") It seems not too much to suggest, with Roth (p. 17), that Mark has given Peter one such pledge and three betrayals of it. On the other hand (see below), Mark may have had in mind Ittai's loyalty pledge to David, "Wherever my lord the king shall be, whether for death or for life, there also will your servant be" (1 Samuel 15:21) (Miller, p. 332).

38. The Garden of Gethsemane (2 Samuel 15:30–37; 16:1–23; Mark 14:32–52)

2 Samuel 15:30. But David went up the ascent of the Mount of Olives, weeping as he went, barefoot and with his head covered; and all the people who were with him covered their heads, and they went up, weeping as they went. 31. And it was told David, "Ahithophel is among the conspirators with Absalom." And David said, "O LORD, I pray thee, turn the counsel of Ahithophel into foolishness." 32. When David came to the summit, where God was worshiped, behold, Hushai the Archite came to meet him with his coat rent and earth upon his head. 33. David said to him, "If you go on with me, you will be a burden to me. 34. But if you return to the city, and say

to Absalom, 'I will be your servant, O king; as I have been your father's servant in time past, so now I will be your servant,' then you will defeat for me the counsel of Ahithophel. 35. Are not Zadok and Abiathar the priests with you there? So whatever you hear from the king's house, tell it to Zadok and Abiathar the priests. 36. Behold, their two sons are with them there, Ahima-az, Zadok's son, and Jonathan, Abiathar's son; and by them you shall send to me everything you hear." 37. So Hushai, David's friend, came into the city, just as Absalom was entering Jerusalem.

2 Samuel 16:1. When David had passed a little beyond the summit, Ziba the servant of Mephibosheth met him, with a couple of asses saddled, bearing two hundred loaves of bread, a hundred bunches of raisins, a hundred of summer fruits, and a skin of wine. 2. And the king said to Ziba, "Why have you brought these?" Ziba answered, "The asses are for the king's household to ride on, the bread and summer fruit for the young men to eat, and the wine for those who faint in the wilderness to drink." 3. And the king said, "And where is your master's son?" Ziba said to the king, "Behold, he remains in Jerusalem; for he said, 'Today the house of Israel will give me back the kingdom of my father.'" 4. Then the king said to Ziba, "Behold, all that belonged to Mephibosheth is now yours." And Ziba said, "I do obeisance; let me ever find favor in your sight, my lord the king." 5. When King David came to Bahurim, there came out a man of the family of the house of Saul, whose name was Shimei, the son of Gera; and as he came he cursed continually. 6. And he threw stones at David, and at all the servants of King David; and all the people and all the mighty men were on his right hand and on his left. 7. And Shimei said as he cursed, "Begone, begone, you man of blood, you worthless fellow! 8. The LORD has avenged upon you all the blood of the house of Saul, in whose place you have reigned; and the LORD has given the kingdom into the hand of your son Absalom. See, your ruin is on you; for you are a man of blood." 9. Then Abishai the son of Zeruiah said to the king, "Why should this dead dog curse my lord the king? Let me go over and take off his head." 10. But the king said, "What have I to do with you, you sons of Zeruiah? If he is

cursing because the LORD has said to him, 'Curse David,' who then shall say, 'Why have you done so?' " 11. And David said to Abishai and to all his servants, "Behold, my own son seeks my life; how much more now may this Benjaminite! Let him alone, and let him curse; for the LORD has bidden him. 12. It may be that the LORD will look upon my affliction, and that the LORD will repay me with good for this cursing of me today." 13. So David and his men went on the road, while Shimei went along on the hillside opposite him and cursed as he went, and threw stones at him and flung dust. 14. And the king, and all the people who were with him, arrived weary at the Jordan; and there he refreshed himself. 15. Now Absalom and all the people, the men of Israel, came to Jerusalem, and Ahithophel with him. 16. And when Hushai the Archite, David's friend, came to Absalom, Hushai said to Absalom, "Long live the king! Long live the king!" 17. And Absalom said to Hushai, "Is this your loyalty to your friend? Why did you not go with your friend?" 18. And Hushai said to Absalom, "No; for whom the LORD and this people and all the men of Israel have chosen, his I will be, and with him I will remain. 19. And again, whom should I serve? Should it not be his son? As I have served your father, so I will serve you." 20. Then Absalom said to Ahithophel, "Give your counsel; what shall we do?" 21. Ahithophel said to Absalom, "Go in to your father's concubines, whom he has left to keep the house; and all Israel will hear that you have made yourself odious to your father, and the hands of all who are with you will be strengthened." 22. So they pitched a tent for Absalom upon the roof; and Absalom went in to his father's concubines in the sight of all Israel. 23. Now in those days the counsel which Ahithophel gave was as if one consulted the oracle of God; so was all the counsel of Ahithophel esteemed, both by David and by Absalom.

Mark 14:32. And they went to a place which was called Gethsemane; and he said to his disciples, "Sit here, while I pray." 33. And he took with him Peter and James and John, and began to be greatly distressed and troubled. 34. And he said to them, "My soul is very sorrowful, even to death; remain here, and watch." 35. And going a little farther, he fell on the ground and prayed that, if it were possible, the hour might pass from him. 36. And he said, "Abba, Father, all things are possible to thee; remove this cup from me; yet not what I will, but what thou wilt." 37. And he came and found them sleeping, and he said to Peter, "Simon, are you asleep? Could you not watch one hour? 38. Watch and pray that you may not enter into temptation; the spirit indeed is willing, but the flesh is weak." 39. And again he went away and prayed, saying the same words. 40. And again he came and found them sleeping, for their eyes were very heavy; and they did not know what to answer him. 41. And he came the third time, and said to them, "Are you still sleeping and taking your rest? It is enough; the hour has come; the Son of man is betrayed into the hands of sinners. 42. Rise, let us be going; see, my betrayer is at hand." 43. And immediately, while he was still speaking, Judas came, one of the twelve, and with him a crowd with swords and clubs, from the chief priests and the scribes and the elders. 44. Now the betrayer had given them a sign, saying, "The one I shall kiss is the man; seize him and lead him away under guard." 45. And when he came, he went up to him at once, and said, "Master!" And he kissed him. 46. And they laid hands on him and seized him. 47. But one of those who stood by drew his sword, and struck the slave of the high priest and cut off his ear. 48. And Jesus said to them, "Have you come out as against a robber, with swords and clubs to capture me? 49. Day after day I was with you in the temple teaching, and you did not seize me. But let the scriptures be fulfilled." 50. And they all forsook him, and fled. 51. And a young man followed him, with nothing but a linen cloth about his body; and they seized him, 52. but he left the linen cloth and ran away naked.

The basis of this whole scene can be found in 2 Samuel chapters 15–16 (Miller, p. 332). A weeping David, fleeing from his usurping son Absalom (a Judas figure), heads up the Mount of Olives and sends three of his allies (Sadoc, Achimaas and Jonathan, 15:27 LXX, "And the king said to Sadoc the priest, Behold, thou shalt return to the city in peace, and Achimaas thy son, and Jonathan the son of Abiathar"), back to Jerusalem. Jesus, too, heads up the mountain to the Garden of Gethsemane, where he will be overcome with sorrow. He leaves three disciples behind as he retreats into the recesses of the garden.

(Jesus, of course, is moving simultaneously with his betrayer, but, unlike David, he is aiming to converge with him, not to avoid him.)

David finds himself mocked and harassed by one Shimei, a partisan of Saul's dynasty. He curses the fallen king, and David's man Abishai offers to chop the mocker's head off, but David forestalls him, musing that apparently God has bidden Shimei to curse David, given the situation. So as they slink along in silence, Shimei continues to pelt the refugees with rocks. Here we find more elements underlying Mark's story. Abishai is the prototype of the unnamed disciple of Jesus (John fictively identifies him as Peter) who does attempt to behead Malchus in the arresting party. Shimei, another form of Shimeon or Simon, is the prototype for Simon who denies Jesus repeatedly, his stony missiles suggesting "Peter" as well. God having assigned Shimei to utter curses on David has become, in Mark's version, Jesus' prediction of Peter's denials, as well as Peter's calling down curses on himself (or on Jesus) in the high priest's courtyard (14:71).

But what of Jesus' prayer? That Mark is creating, not reporting, is evident from the fact that he has eliminated from the scene anyone who might have listened in on it. Mark derived the contents of the prayer from one of the traditional Passover hymns, which he has had Jesus sing at the close of the supper, Psalms 116:10–15, "My distress was bitter. In panic I cried, 'How faithless all men are!'... I will take in my hand the cup of salvation and invoke the LORD by name... A precious thing in the LORD's eyes is the death of those who die faithful to him" (Helms, p. 111).

Judas' betraying kiss (14:44–45) would seem to derive from 2 Samuel 20:7–10, where Joab, backed up by armed men, greets Amasa as a brother, kisses him, then stabs him (Miller, p. 337).

2 Samuel 20:7. And there went out after Abishai, Joab and the Cherethites and the Pelethites, and all the mighty men; they went out from Jerusalem to pursue Sheba the son of Bichri. 8. When they were at the great stone which is in Gibeon, Amasa came to meet

them. Now Joab was wearing a soldier's garment, and over it was a girdle with a sword in its sheath fastened upon his loins, and as he went forward it fell out. 9. And Joab said to Amasa, "Is it well with you, my brother?" And Joab took Amasa by the beard with his right hand to kiss him. 10. But Amasa did not observe the sword which was in Joab's hand; so Joab struck him with it in the body, and shed his bowels to the ground, without striking a second blow; and he died. Then Joab and Abishai his brother pursued Sheba the son of Bichri.

This identification, Helms notes (p. 117), is secured once we realize that Luke has modeled his version of Judas' miserable death upon that of Amasa. 2 Samuel 20:10 LXX tells us that Amasa's "bowels poured out ($\varepsilon\xi\varepsilon\chi\upsilon\theta\eta$) upon the ground," precisely as Luke tells us (Acts 1:18) that when Judas died, "he burst open, so that his entrails poured out ($\varepsilon\xi\varepsilon\chi\upsilon\theta\eta$)."

Amos 2:16, "And he who is stout of heart among the mighty shall flee away naked in that day," remains the most likely clue to the origin of the fleeing young man who loses his sole garment to escape naked (Mark 14:51) (Derrett, p. 252). "That day" sounded like a good reference to the momentous day of Jesus' passion.

Luke adds the element of an angel appearing beside the tormented Jesus to "strengthen" him (Luke 22:43), a detail borrowed from 1 Kings 19:7–8 LXX: "And the angel of the Lord returned again and touched him, and said to him, 'Arise, for the journey is far from thee.' And he arose, and ate and drank, and went in the *strength* of that meat forty days and forty nights to mount Horeb" (Helms, p. 109)

39. The Sanhedrin Trial (Daniel 6:4 LXX; Mark 14:53–72)

Daniel 6:4. "The governors and satraps sought ($\varepsilon\zeta\varepsilon\tauo\upsilon\nu$) to find ($\varepsilon\upsilon\rho\varepsilon\iota\nu$) occasion against Daniel, but they found against him no accusation."

Isaiah 53:7. "He was oppressed, and he was afflicted, yet he opened not his mouth; like a lamb that is led to the slaughter, and like a sheep that before its shearers is dumb, so he opened not his mouth."

1 Kings 22:24. "Then Zedekiah the son of Chenaanah came near and struck Micaiah on the cheek, and said, 'How did the spirit of the LORD go from me to speak to you?' And Micaiah said, 'Behold, you shall see on that day when you go into an inner chamber to hide yourself'."

Daniel 7:13. I saw in the night visions, and behold, with the clouds of heaven there came one like a son of man, and he came to the Ancient of Days and was presented before him. 14. And to him was given dominion and glory and kingdom, that all peoples, nations, and languages should serve him; his dominion is an everlasting dominion, which shall not pass away, and his kingdom one that shall not be destroyed.

Mark 14:53. And they led Jesus to the high priest; and all the chief priests and the elders and the scribes were assembled. 54. And Peter had followed him at a distance, right into the courtyard of the high priest; and he was sitting with the guards, and warming himself at the fire. 55. Now the chief priests and the whole council sought testimony against Jesus to put him to death; but they found none. 56. For many bore false witness against him, and their witness did not agree. 57. And some stood up and bore false witness against him, saying, 58. "We heard him say, 'I will destroy this temple that is made with hands, and in three days I will build another, not made with hands'." 59. Yet not even so did their testimony agree. 60. And the high priest stood up in the midst, and asked Jesus, "Have you no answer to make? What is it that these men testify against you?" 61. But he was silent and made no answer. Again the high priest asked him, "Are you the Christ, the Son of the Blessed?" 62. And Jesus said, "I am; and you will see the Son of man seated at the right hand of Power, and coming with the clouds of heaven." 63. And the high priest tore his garments, and said, "Why do we still need witnesses? 64. You have heard his blasphemy. What is your decision?"

The Christy Myth Theory And Its Problems

> And they all condemned him as deserving death. 65. And some began to spit on him, and to cover his face, and to strike him, saying to him, "Prophesy!" And the guards received him with blows. 66. And as Peter was below in the courtyard, one of the maids of the high priest came; 67. and seeing Peter warming himself, she looked at him, and said, "You also were with the Nazarene, Jesus." 68. But he denied it, saying, "I neither know nor understand what you mean." And he went out into the gateway. 69. And the maid saw him, and began again to say to the bystanders, "This man is one of them." 70. But again he denied it. And after a little while again the bystanders said to Peter, "Certainly you are one of them; for you are a Galilean." 71. But he began to invoke a curse on himself and to swear, "I do not know this man of whom you speak." 72. And immediately the cock crowed a second time. And Peter remembered how Jesus had said to him, "Before the cock crows twice, you will deny me three times." And he broke down and wept.

Mark borrowed from Daniel 6:4 LXX the scene of the crossfire of false accusations (Helms, p. 118). Of this Mark (14:55) has made the following: "The chief priests and the whole council sought (εζετουν) testimony against Jesus in order to kill him, but they found none (ουχ ηυρισκον)."

Mark 14:65, where Jesus suffers blows and mockery as a false prophet, comes from 1 Kings 22:24, "Then Zedekiah the son of Chenaanah came near and struck Micaiah on the cheek, and said, 'How did the spirit of the LORD go from me to speak to you?' And Micaiah said, 'Behold, you shall see on that day when you go into an inner chamber to hide yourself' " (Miller, p. 350). Mark has used Micaiah's retort, "Behold, you shall see..." as the model for Jesus' retort that his accusers/attackers will one day behold Jesus enthroned as the Son of Man from Daniel 7:13–14. It is interesting to speculate whether the doctrine of the second coming of Christ did not spring full-blown from Mark's reversal of order between the Son of Man's coming with the clouds and sitting on the throne in Daniel 7.

Jesus' silence at both trials before the Sanhedrin and Pilate (14:60–61; 15:4–5) comes from Isaiah 50:7 ("For the Lord GOD helps me; therefore I have not been confounded; therefore I have set my face like a flint, and I know that I shall not be put to shame") and 53:7 ("He was oppressed, and he was afflicted, yet he opened not his mouth; like a lamb that is led to the slaughter, and like a sheep that before its shearers is dumb, so he opened not his mouth.") (Crossan, p. 168).

40. The Scapegoat (Leviticus 16:7–10; Mark 15:1–15)

Leviticus 16:7. Then he shall take the two goats, and set them before the LORD at the door of the tent of meeting; 8. and Aaron shall cast lots upon the two goats, one lot for the LORD and the other lot for Azazel. 9. And Aaron shall present the goat on which the lot fell for the LORD, and offer it as a sin offering; 10. but the goat on which the lot fell for Azazel shall be presented alive before the LORD to make atonement over it, that it may be sent away into the wilderness to Azazel.

Mark 15:1. And as soon as it was morning the chief priests, with the elders and scribes, and the whole council held a consultation; and they bound Jesus and led him away and delivered him to Pilate. 2. And Pilate asked him, "Are you the King of the Jews?" And he answered him, "You have said so." 3. And the chief priests accused him of many things. 4. And Pilate again asked him, "Have you no answer to make? See how many charges they bring against you." 5. But Jesus made no further answer, so that Pilate wondered. 6. Now at the feast he used to release for them one prisoner for whom they asked. 7. And among the rebels in prison, who had committed murder in the insurrection, there was a man called Barabbas. 8. And the crowd came up and began to ask Pilate to do as he was wont to do for them. 9. And he answered them, "Do you want me to release for you the King of the Jews?" 10. For he perceived that it was out of envy that the chief priests had delivered him up. 11. But the chief priests stirred up the crowd to have him release for them Barabbas instead.

12. And Pilate again said to them, "Then what shall I do with the man whom you call the King of the Jews?" 13. And they cried out again, "Crucify him." 14. And Pilate said to them, "Why, what evil has he done?" But they shouted all the more, "Crucify him." 15. So Pilate, wishing to satisfy the crowd, released for them Barabbas; and having scourged Jesus, he delivered him to be crucified.

John Dominic Crossan has drawn attention to the singular importance for early Christian typology of the Leviticus 16 scapegoat ritual. He traces its development, as it picked up associations from Zechariah (see just below), on its way to the composition of the gospel narrative of the mocking, abuse, and crucifixion of Jesus. Although Crossan assumes the process began with a vague Christian memory/report of Jesus having been crucified, with no details, his own compelling charting of the midrashic trajectory strongly implies something subtly different, that the process began with something like Doherty's scenario of an even vaguer, ahistorical belief in the savior Jesus becoming progressively historicized by means of progressive biblical coloring, until the final stage of evolution was a crucifixion.

Crossan describes the scapegoat ritual as it was being practiced in early Christian times by reference to *Yoma* 6:2–6 , the *Epistle of Barnabas* chapter 7, Justin's *Dialogue with Trypho* 40, and Tertullian's *Against Marcion* 3:7. The goat was led out of the city walls. A crimson thread of wool was divided, half tied to a rock, half between the goat's horns. Along the way, the goat was abused by the crowd shouting, "Bear [sins] and begone! Bear and begone!" The crowd spat at it and goaded it along with pointed reeds till it arrived at the ledge where it was pushed over (Crossan, p. 119). Barnabas implies that in his day the woolen thread was tied onto a thorny bush, no longer a rock, a significant change (no less significant even if this was a misunderstanding, already marking a slippage of the "piercing" motif from the reed-poking to the wool-tying). Even *without reference to a passion narrative of any sort*, Barnabas and the Sibylline Oracles (8:294–301) apply the ritual in all its details to the death of the savior Jesus. Barnabas and others also attach to it the typology Zechariah 12:10 ("And I will pour out on the house of David and the inhabitants of Jerusalem a spirit of compassion and supplication, so that when they look on him whom they have *pierced*, they shall mourn for him as one mourns for an only child, and weep bitterly over him as one weeps over a firstborn") because of the catchword "piercing," derived from the reeds and thorns of the scapegoat ritual. From this it was a natural step to page through Zechariah to 3:1–5 and to associate the scapegoat-savior Jesus with the high priest Jesus (Joshua). There Jesus/Joshua is clothed in a crown (turban) and robe, which Barnabas, *et. al.*, "recognized" as an expansion of the two bits of crimson wool from the scapegoat ritual. Once this connection was made, it was easy for the wool motif to be segregated to the robe, the crown assimilating to the thorns to which the other thread had been tied, resulting in a crown of thorns (Crossan, p. 128). From these roots, as the passion narrative begins to form, the piercing motif takes several forms. When Jesus becomes a mock king (as in the Roman Saturnalia games or the mockery of Carrabas in Philo, *Flaccus* VI), the reeds that once poked the scapegoat have become the reed sceptre of the mock king (which his mockers seize and use to hit him) as well as the mock crown of thorns and the scraping bits of the scourging whip. Then, in a full-scale crucifixion narrative (involving, of course, the driving of the scapegoat Jesus outside the city walls), the piercing motif takes the form of the nails of crucifixion and finally the piercing lance of Longinus.

41. The Crucifixion (Psalms 22:1–18; Mark 15:21–41)

Psalms 22:1. My God, my God, why hast thou forsaken me? Why art thou so far from helping me, from the words of my groaning? 2.

The Christ Myth Theory And Its Problems

O my God, I cry by day, but thou dost not answer; and by night, but find no rest. 3. Yet thou art holy, enthroned on the praises of Israel. 4. In thee our fathers trusted; they trusted, and thou didst deliver them. 5. To thee they cried, and were saved; in thee they trusted, and were not disappointed. 6. But I am a worm, and no man; scorned by men, and despised by the people. 7. All who see me mock at me, they make mouths at me, they wag their heads; 8. "He committed his cause to the LORD; let him deliver him, let him rescue him, for he delights in him!" 9. Yet thou art he who took me from the womb; thou didst keep me safe upon my mother's breasts. 10. Upon thee was I cast from my birth, and since my mother bore me thou hast been my God. 11. Be not far from me, for trouble is near and there is none to help. 12. Many bulls encompass me, strong bulls of Bashan surround me; 13. they open wide their mouths at me, like a ravening and roaring lion. 14. I am poured out like water, and all my bones are out of joint; my heart is like wax, it is melted within my breast; 15. my strength is dried up like a potsherd, and my tongue cleaves to my jaws; thou dost lay me in the dust of death. 16. Yea, dogs are round about me; a company of evildoers encircle me; they have pierced my hands and feet — 17. I can count all my bones — they stare and gloat over me; 18. they divide my garments among them, and for my raiment they cast lots.

Mark 15:21. And they compelled a passer-by, Simon of Cyrene, who was coming in from the country, the father of Alexander and Rufus, to carry his cross. 22. And they brought him to the place called Golgotha (which means the place of a skull). 23. And they offered him wine mingled with myrrh; but he did not take it. 24. And they crucified him, and divided his garments among them, casting lots for them, to decide what each should take. 25. And it was the third hour, when they crucified him. 26. And the inscription of the charge against him read, "The King of the Jews." 27. And with him they crucified two robbers, one on his right and one on his left. 28. And the scripture was fulfilled which says, "He was reckoned with the transgressors." 29. And those who passed by derided him, wagging their heads, and saying, "Aha! You who would destroy the temple and build it in three days, 30. save yourself, and come down from the cross!" 31. So also the chief priests mocked him to one another with the scribes, saying, "He saved others; he cannot save himself. 32. Let the Christ, the King of Israel, come down now from the cross, that we may see and believe." Those who were crucified with him also reviled him. 33. And when the sixth hour had come, there was darkness over the whole land until the ninth hour. 34. And at the ninth hour Jesus cried with a loud voice, "*Eloi, Eloi, lama sabachthani?*" which means, "My God, my God, why hast thou forsaken me?" 35. And some of the bystanders hearing it said, "Behold, he is calling Elijah." 36. And one ran and, filling a sponge full of vinegar, put it on a reed and gave it to him to drink, saying, "Wait, let us see whether Elijah will come to take him down." 37. And Jesus uttered a loud cry, and breathed his last. 38. And the curtain of the temple was torn in two, from top to bottom. 39. And when the centurion, who stood facing him, saw that he thus breathed his last, he said, "Truly this man was the Son of God!" 40. There were also women looking on from afar, among whom were Mary Magdalene, and Mary the mother of James the younger and of Joses, and Salome, 41. who, when he was in Galilee, followed him, and ministered to him; and also many other women who came up with him to Jerusalem.

The substructure for the crucifixion in chapter 15 is, as all recognize, Psalm 22, from which derive all the major details, including the implicit piercing of hands and feet (Mark 15: 24a, "And they crucified him" // Psalms 22:16b, "a company of evildoers encircle me; they have pierced my hands and feet"), the dividing of his garments and casting lots for them (Mark 15:24b, "and divided his garments among them, casting lots for them, to decide what each should take." // Psalms 22:18, "they divide my garments among them, and for my raiment they cast lots"), the "wagging heads" of the mockers (Mark 15:29a, "And those who passed by derided him, wagging their heads" // Psalms 22:7, "All who see me mock at me, they make mouths at me, they wag their heads"), and of course the cry of dereliction, "My God, my God, why have you forsaken me?" (Mark 15:34 // Psalms 22:1, "My God, my

God, why hast thou forsaken me?"). Matthew adds another quote, "He trusts in God. Let God deliver him now if he desires him" (Matthew 27:43 // Psalms 22:8, "He committed his cause to the LORD; let him deliver him, let him rescue him, for he delights in him!"), as well as a strong allusion ("for he said, 'I am the son of God'" 27:43b) to Wisdom of Solomon 2:12–20, which underlies the whole story anyway (Miller, p. 362).

> 12. Let us lie in wait for the righteous man because he is inconvenient to us and opposes our actions; he reproaches us for sins against the law and accuses us of sins against our training. 13. He professes to have knowledge of God, and calls himself a child of the Lord. 14. He became to us a reproof of our thoughts; 15. the very sight of him is a burden to us because his manner of life is unlike that of others, and his ways are strange. 16. We are considered by him as something base, and he avoids our ways as unclean; he calls the last end of the righteous happy, and boasts that God is his father. 17. Let us see if his words are true, and let us test what will happen at the end of his life: 18. for if the righteous man is God's son he will help him and will deliver him from the hand of his adversaries. 19. Let us test him with insult and torture that we may find out how gentle he is and make trial of his forbearance. 20. Let us condemn him to a shameful death, for, according to what he says, he will be protected.

As for other details, Crossan (p. 198) points out that the darkness at noon comes from Amos 8:9 (" 'And on that day,' says the Lord GOD, 'I will make the sun go down at noon, and darken the earth in broad daylight'."), while the vinegar and gall come from Psalms 69:21 ("They gave me poison for food, and for my thirst they gave me vinegar to drink"). It is remarkable that Mark does anything but call attention to the scriptural basis for the crucifixion account. There is nothing said of scripture being fulfilled here. It is all simply presented as the events of Jesus' execution. It is we who must ferret out the real sources of the story. This is quite different, *e.g.*, in John, where explicit scripture citations are given, *e.g.*, for Jesus' legs not being broken to hasten his death (John 19:36, "For these things took place that the scripture might be fulfilled, 'Not a bone of him shall be broken'."), either Exodus 12:10 LXX ("and a bone of it ye shall not break"), Numbers 9:12 ("nor break a bone of it"), or Psalms 34:19–20 ("He keeps all his bones; not one of them is broken.") (Crossan, p. 168).

Whence did Mark derive the tearing asunder of the Temple veil, from top to bottom (Mark 15:38)? Perhaps from the death of Hector in the *Iliad* (MacDonald, pp. 144–145). Hector dies forsaken by Zeus. The women of Troy watched from afar off (as the Galilean women do in Mark 15:40), and the whole of Troy mourned as if their city had already been destroyed "from top to bottom," just as the ripping of the veil seems to be a portent of Jerusalem's eventual doom.

42. Joseph of Arimathea (Genesis 50:4–5; Mark 15:42–47)

Genesis 50:4. "And when the days of weeping for him were past, Joseph spoke to the household of Pharaoh, saying, "If now I have found favor in your eyes, speak, I pray you, in the ears of Pharaoh, saying, 5. 'My father made me swear, saying, "I am about to die: in my tomb which I hewed out for myself in the land of Canaan, there shall you bury me." Now therefore let me go up, I pray you, and bury my father; then I will return','"

Mark 15:42. And when evening had come, since it was the day of Preparation, that is, the day before the sabbath, 43. Joseph of Arimathea, a respected member of the council, who was also himself looking for the kingdom of God, took courage and went to Pilate, and asked for the body of Jesus. 44. And Pilate wondered if he were already dead; and summoning the centurion, he asked him whether he was already dead. 45. And when he learned from the centurion that he was dead, he granted the body to Joseph. 46. And he bought a linen shroud, and taking him down, wrapped him in the linen shroud, and laid him in a tomb which had been hewn out of the rock; and he rolled a stone against the door of the tomb. 47. Mary Magdalene and Mary the mother of Joses saw where he was laid.

Joseph is surely a combination of King Priam, who courageously comes to Achilles' camp to beg the body of his son Hector (MacDonald, p. 159) and the Patriarch Joseph who asked Pharaoh's permission to bury the body of Jacob in the cave-tomb Jacob had hewn for himself back beyond the Jordan Genesis 50:4–5) (Miller, p. 373).

43. The Empty Tomb (Mark 16:1–8)

Joshua 10:16. These five kings fled, and hid themselves in the cave at Makkedah. 17. And it was told Joshua, "The five kings have been found, hidden in the cave at Makkedah." 18. And Joshua said, "Roll great stones against the mouth of the cave, and set men by it to guard them; 19. but do not stay there yourselves, pursue your enemies, fall upon their rear, do not let them enter their cities; for the LORD your God has given them into your hand." 20. When Joshua and the men of Israel had finished slaying them with a very great slaughter, until they were wiped out, and when the remnant which remained of them had entered into the fortified cities, 21. all the people returned safe to Joshua in the camp at Makkedah; not a man moved his tongue against any of the people of Israel. 22. Then Joshua said, "Open the mouth of the cave, and bring those five kings out to me from the cave." 23. And they did so, and brought those five kings out to him from the cave, the king of Jerusalem, the king of Hebron, the king of Jarmuth, the king of Lachish, and the king of Eglon. 24. And when they brought those kings out to Joshua, Joshua summoned all the men of Israel, and said to the chiefs of the men of war who had gone with him, "Come near, put your feet upon the necks of these kings." Then they came near, and put their feet on their necks. 25. And Joshua said to them, "Do not be afraid or dismayed; be strong and of good courage; for thus the LORD will do to all your enemies against whom you fight."26. And afterward Joshua smote them and put them to death, and he hung them on five trees. And they hung upon the trees until evening; 27. but at the time of the going down of the sun, Joshua commanded, and they took them down from the trees, and threw them into the cave where they had hidden themselves, and they set great stones against the mouth of the cave, which remain to this very day.

Mark 16:1. And when the sabbath was past, Mary Magdalene, and Mary the mother of James, and Salome, bought spices, so that they might go and anoint him. 2. And very early on the first day of the week they went to the tomb when the sun had risen. 3. And they were saying to one another, "Who will roll away the stone for us from the door of the tomb?" 4. And looking up, they saw that the stone was rolled back; — it was very large. 5. And entering the tomb, they saw a young man sitting on the right side, dressed in a white robe; and they were amazed. 6. And he said to them, "Do not be amazed; you seek Jesus of Nazareth, who was crucified. He has risen, he is not here; see the place where they laid him. 7. But go, tell his disciples and Peter that he is going before you to Galilee; there you will see him, as he told you." 8. And they went out and fled from the tomb; for trembling and astonishment had come upon them; and they said nothing to any one, for they were afraid.

Crossan (p. 274) and Miller and Miller (pp. 219, 377) note that the empty tomb narrative requires no source beyond Joshua (=Jesus in Septuagint Greek, remember!) chapter 10. The five kings have fled from Joshua, taking refuge in the cave at Makkedah. When they are discovered, Joshua orders his men to "Roll great stones against the mouth of the cave and set men by it to guard them" (10:18). Once the mopping-up operation of the kings' troops is finished, Joshua directs: "Open the mouth of the cave, and bring those five kings out to me from the cave" (10:22). "And afterward Joshua smote them and put them to death, and he hung them on five trees. And they hung upon the trees until evening; but at the time of the going down of the sun, Joshua commanded, and they took them down from the trees, and threw them into the cave where they had hidden themselves, and they set great stones against the mouth of the cave, which remain to this very day" (10:26–27). Observe that here it is "Jesus" who plays the role of Pilate, and that Mark needed only to reverse the order of the main narrative moments of this story. Joshua 10: first, stone rolled away and kings emerge alive; second, kings die; third, kings are crucified until sundown. Mark: Jesus as King of the Jews is cruci-fied, where his body will hang till sundown; second, he dies; third, he emerges alive (Mark implies) from the tomb once the stone is rolled away.

The vigil of the mourning women likely reflects the women's mourning cult of the dying and rising god, long familiar in Israel (Ezekiel 8:14, "Behold, there sat women weeping for Tammuz;" Zechariah 12:11, "On that day the mourning in Jerusalem will be as great as the mourning for Hadad-Rimmon in the plain of Megiddo;" Canticles 3:1–4, "I sought him whom my soul loves; I sought him but found him not; I called him but he gave no answer," *etc.*).

C. The Gospel of Matthew

1. The Nativity of Jesus (Matthew 1:18; 2:1–23)

Matthew 1:18. Now the birth of Jesus Christ took place in this way. When his mother Mary had been betrothed to Joseph, before they came together she was found to be with child of the Holy Spirit; 19. and her husband Joseph, being a just man and unwilling to put her to shame, resolved to divorce her quietly. 20. But as he considered this, behold, an angel of the Lord appeared to him in a dream, saying, "Joseph, son of David, do not fear to take Mary your wife, for that which is conceived in her is of the Holy Spirit; 21. she will bear a son, and you shall call his name Jesus, for he will save his people from their sins." 22. All this took place to fulfil what the Lord had spoken by the prophet: 23. "Behold, a virgin shall conceive and bear a son, and his name shall be called Emmanuel" (which means, God with us). 24. When Joseph woke from sleep, he did as the angel of the Lord commanded him; he took his wife, 25. but knew her not until she had borne a son; and he called his name Jesus.

Matthew 2:1. Now when Jesus was born in Bethlehem of Judea in the days of Herod the king, behold, wise men from the East came to Jeru-salem, saying, 2. "Where is he who has been born king of the Jews?

For we have seen his star in the East, and have come to worship him."
3. When Herod the king heard this, he was troubled, and all Jerusalem
with him; 4. and assembling all the chief priests and scribes of the
people, he inquired of them where the Christ was to be born. 5. They
told him, "In Bethlehem of Judea; for so it is written by the prophet:
6. 'And you, O Bethlehem, in the land of Judah, are by no means least
among the rulers of Judah; for from you shall come a ruler who will
govern my people Israel'." 7. Then Herod summoned the wise men
secretly and ascertained from them what time the star appeared; 8. and
he sent them to Bethlehem, saying, "Go and search diligently for the
child, and when you have found him bring me word, that I too may
come and worship him." 9. When they had heard the king they went
their way; and lo, the star which they had seen in the East went before
them, till it came to rest over the place where the child was. 10. When
they saw the star, they rejoiced exceedingly with great joy; 11. and
going into the house they saw the child with Mary his mother, and
they fell down and worshiped him. Then, opening their treasures, they
offered him gifts, gold and frankincense and myrrh. 12. And being
warned in a dream not to return to Herod, they departed to their own
country by another way. 13. Now when they had departed, behold, an
angel of the Lord appeared to Joseph in a dream and said, "Rise, take
the child and his mother, and flee to Egypt, and remain there till I tell
you; for Herod is about to search for the child, to destroy him." 14.
And he rose and took the child and his mother by night, and departed
to Egypt, and remained there until the death of Herod. This was to
fulfil what the Lord had spoken by the prophet, "Out of Egypt have
I called my son." 16. Then Herod, when he saw that he had been
tricked by the wise men, was in a furious rage, and he sent and killed
all the male children in Bethlehem and in all that region who were
two years old or under, according to the time which he had ascertained from the wise men. 17. Then was fulfilled what was spoken
by the prophet Jeremiah: 18. "A voice was heard in Ramah, wailing
and loud lamentation, Rachel weeping for her children; she refused to
be consoled, because they were no more." 19. But when Herod died,
behold, an angel of the Lord appeared in a dream to Joseph in Egypt,
saying, 20. "Rise, take the child and his mother, and go to the land of

153

Israel, for those who sought the child's life are dead." 21. And he rose and took the child and his mother, and went to the land of Israel. 22. But when he heard that Archelaus reigned over Judea in place of his father Herod, he was afraid to go there, and being warned in a dream he withdrew to the district of Galilee. 23. And he went and dwelt in a city called Nazareth, that what was spoken by the prophets might be fulfilled, "He shall be called a Nazarene."

On the whole Matthew seems to have borrowed the birth story of Jesus from Josephus' retelling of the nativity of Moses. Whereas Exodus had Pharaoh command the systematic murder of Hebrew infants simply to prevent a strong Hebrew fifth column in case of future invasion, Josephus makes the planned pogrom a weapon aimed right at Moses, who in Josephus becomes a promised messiah in his own right. Amram and Jochabed, expecting baby Moses, are alarmed. What should they do? Abort the pregnancy? God speaks in a dream to reassure them.

"One of those sacred scribes, who are very sagacious in foretelling future events truly, told the king that about this time there would a child be borne to the Israelites, who, if he were reared, would bring the Egyptian dominion low, and would raise the Israelites; that he would excel all men in virtue, and obtain a glory that would be remembered through the ages. Which was so feared by the king that, according to this man's opinion, he commanded that they should cast every male child into the river, and destroy it... A man, whose name was Amram, ... was very uneasy at it, his wife being then with child, and he knew not what to do... Accordingly God had mercy on him, and was moved by his supplication. He stood by him in his sleep, and exhorted him not to despair of his future favours... 'For that child, out of dread for whose nativity the Egyptians have doomed the Israelites' children to destruction, shall be this child of thine... he shall deliver the Hebrew nation from the distress they are under from the Egyptians. His memory shall be famous whole the world lasts'." (*Jewish Antiquities*, II, IX, 2–3)

It is evident that Matthew has had merely to change a few names. Herod the Great takes the role of the baby-killing Pharaoh, and he is warned by his own scribes (along with the Magi) of the impending birth of a savior, whereupon he resolves to kill every child he has to in order to eliminate the child of promise. Joseph takes the place of Amram, though the precise cause of his unease is different. Mary takes the place of Jochabed. A dream from God steels Joseph, like Amram, in his resolve to go through with things.

The rest of Matthew's birth story is woven from a series of formulaic scripture quotations. He makes Isaiah 7:14 LXX ("Therefore the Lord himself shall give you a sign; behold, a virgin shall conceive in the womb, and shall bring forth a son, and thou shalt call his name Emmanuel.") refer to the miraculous virginal conception of Jesus. It is likely that he has in this case found a scripture passage to provide a pedigree for a widespread hagiographical mytheme, the divine paternity of the hero, which had already passed into the Christian tradition, unless of course this is the very door through which it passed.

It is revealing that Matthew's Magi learn from scribal exegesis of Micah 5:2 that the messiah must be born in Bethlehem: "But you, O Bethlehem Ephrathah, who are little to be among the clans of Judah, from you shall come forth for me one who is to be ruler in Israel, whose origin is from of old, from ancient days." This is the same way Matthew "knew" Jesus was born there — it had to be!

The flight of the Holy Family into Egypt comes equally from exegesis, this time of Hosea 11:1 ("Out of Egypt I have called my son"), which allows Matthew to draw a parallel between his character Joseph and the Genesis patriarch Joseph, who also went to Egypt. Matthew also seems here to want to foreshadow the death and resurrection of Jesus. Note that Isaiah 51:9–10 makes the exodus from Egypt into a historical replay of God's primordial victory over the sea dragon Rahab, equating Egypt with Rahab.

> Awake, awake, put on strength, O arm of the LORD; awake, as in days of old, the generations of long ago. Was it not thou that didst

cut Rahab in pieces, that didst pierce the dragon? Was it not thou that didst dry up the sea, the waters of the great deep; that didst make the depths of the sea a way for the redeemed to pass over?

Matthew also knew that Jonah was swallowed by a sea monster at God's behest, and he saw this as a prefiguration of Jesus' descent into the tomb (Matthew 12:40, "For as Jonah was three days and three nights in the belly of the whale, so will the Son of man be three days and three nights in the heart of the earth."). The flight into Egypt has the child Jesus already going down into Rahab, the belly of the sea beast.

The closest Matthew can come, via punning exegesis, to providing a proof text for Jesus having become known as "the Nazarene" would seem to be Judges 13:7, "The boy shall be a Nazirite to God from birth." He knew Jesus must be born in Bethlehem yet was called "Jesus of Nazareth," so he cobbled together a story whereby Jesus was born in Mary and Joseph's home in Bethlehem, only to relocate in Nazareth (after Egypt) to avoid the wrath of Archelaus (Matthew 2:22–23, "But when he heard that Archelaus reigned over Judea in place of his father Herod, he was afraid to go there, and being warned in a dream he withdrew to the district of Galilee. And he went and dwelt in a city called Nazareth, that what was spoken by the prophets might be fulfilled, 'He shall be called a Nazarene'."). Luke, on the other hand, working with the same two assumptions, contrived to have Mary and Joseph live in Nazareth but to be in Bethlehem for the census when the time came for Jesus to be born. In both cases, exegesis has produced narrative.

2. The Resurrection of Jesus (Matthew 27:62–28:20)

Matthew 27:62. Next day, that is, after the day of Preparation, the chief priests and the Pharisees gathered before Pilate 63. and said, "Sir, we remember how that impostor said, while he was still alive, 'After three days I will rise again.' 64. Therefore order the sepulchre to be made secure until the third day, lest his disciples go and steal him away, and tell the people, 'He has risen from the dead,' and the last fraud will be worse than the first." 65. Pilate said to them, "Take a guard of soldiers; go, make it as secure as you can." 66. So they went and made the sepulchre secure by sealing the stone and setting a guard.

Matthew 28:1. Now after the sabbath, toward the dawn of the first day of the week, Mary Magdalene and the other Mary went to see the sepulchre. 2. And behold, there was a great earthquake; for an angel of the Lord descended from heaven and came and rolled back the stone, and sat upon it. 3. His appearance was like lightning, and his raiment white as snow. 4. And for fear of him the guards trembled and became like dead men. 5. But the angel said to the women, "Do not be afraid; for I know that you seek Jesus who was crucified. 6. He is not here; for he has risen, as he said. Come, see the place where he lay. 7. Then go quickly and tell his disciples that he has risen from the dead, and behold, he is going before you to Galilee; there you will see him. Lo, I have told you." 8. So they departed quickly from the tomb with fear and great joy, and ran to tell his disciples. 9. And behold, Jesus met them and said, "Hail!" And they came up and took hold of his feet and worshiped him. 10. Then Jesus said to them, "Do not be afraid; go and tell my brethren to go to Galilee, and there they will see me." 11. While they were going, behold, some of the guard went into the city and told the chief priests all that had taken place. 12. And when they had assembled with the elders and taken counsel, they gave a sum of money to the soldiers 13. and said, "Tell people, 'His disciples came by night and stole him away while we were asleep.' 14. And if this comes to the governor's ears, we will satisfy him and keep you out of trouble." 15. So they took the money and did as they were directed; and this story has been spread among the Jews to this day. 16. Now the eleven disciples went to Galilee, to the mountain to which Jesus had directed them. 17. And when they saw him they worshiped him; but some doubted. 18. And Jesus came and said to them, "All authority in heaven and on earth has been given to me. 19. Go therefore and make disciples of all nations, baptizing them in the name of the Father and of the Son and of the Holy Spirit, 20. teaching them to observe all that I have commanded you; and lo, I am with you always, to the close of the age."

Matthew had before him Mark's empty tomb story and no other source except the Book of Daniel, from which he has embellished the Markan original at several points. (Matthew had already repaired to Daniel in his Pilate story, where the procurator declared, "I am innocent of the blood of this man," Matthew 27:24b, which he derived from Susanna 46 / Daniel 13:46 LXX: "I am innocent of the blood of this woman.") (Crossan, p. 97–98). First, Matthew has introduced guards at the tomb and has had the tomb sealed, a reflection of Nebuchadnezzer's sealing the stone rolled to the door of the lion's den with Daniel inside (6:17, "And a stone was brought and laid upon the mouth of the den, and the king sealed it with his own signet and with the signet of his lords, that nothing might be changed concerning Daniel."). Mark had a young man (perhaps an angel, but perhaps not) already in the open tomb when the women arrived. Matthew simply calls the character an angel and clothes him in a description reminiscent of the angel of Daniel chapter 10 (face like lightning as in Daniel 10:6, "His body was like beryl, his face like the appearance of lightning, his eyes like flaming torches, his arms and legs like the gleam of burnished bronze, and the sound of his words like the noise of a multitude.") and the Ancient of Days in Daniel chapter 7 (snowy white clothing as in Daniel 7:9, "thrones were placed and one that was ancient of days took his seat; his raiment was white as snow, and the hair of his head like pure wool"). He rolls the stone aside. The guards faint and become as dead men, particular dead men, as a matter of fact, namely the guards who tossed Shadrach, Meschach, and Abed-nego into the fiery furnace in (Daniel 3:22, "Because the king's order was strict and the furnace very hot, the flame of the fire slew those men who took up Shadrach, Meshach, and Abed-nego.").

To provide an appearance of the risen Jesus to the women at the tomb (something conspicuously absent from Mark), Matthew simply divides Mark's young man into the angel and now Jesus himself, who has nothing more to say than a lame reiteration of the angel's words. He appears again on a mountain in Galilee (Matthew 28:16) which he now says Jesus had earlier designated, though this is the first the reader learns of it. There he dispenses yet more Danielic pastiche: "All authority in heaven and on earth has been given to me." This is based on a conflation of two Greek versions of Daniel 7:14. In the LXX, "to him [the one like a son of man was] ... given the rule... the authority of him [the Ancient of Days]." In Theodotion, he receives "authority to hold all in the heaven and upon the earth." The charge to make all nations his disciples comes from Daniel 7:14, too: "that all people, nations, and languages should serve him" (Helms, p. 141).

D. The Gospel of Luke

1. The Nativities of Jesus and John (1 Samuel 1:1–28; 2:1–26; Luke 1:5–2:52)

1 Samuel 1:1. There was a certain man of Ramathaim-zophim of the hill country of Ephraim, whose name was Elkanah the son of Jeroham, son of Elihu, son of Tohu, son of Zuph, an Ephraimite. 2. He had two wives; the name of the one was Hannah, and the name of the other Peninnah. And Peninnah had children, but Hannah had no children. 3. Now this man used to go up year by year from his city to worship and to sacrifice to the LORD of hosts at Shiloh, where the two sons of Eli, Hophni and Phinehas, were priests of the LORD. 4. On the day when Elkanah sacrificed, he would give portions to Peninnah his wife and to all her sons and daughters; 5. and, although he loved Hannah, he would give Hannah only one portion, because the LORD had closed her womb. 6. And her rival used to provoke her sorely, to irritate her, because the LORD had closed her womb. 7. So it went on year by year; as often as she went up to the house of the LORD, she used to provoke her. Therefore Hannah wept and would not eat. 8. And Elkanah, her husband, said to her, "Hannah, why do you weep? And why do you not eat? And why is your heart

sad? Am I not more to you than ten sons?" 9. After they had eaten and drunk in Shiloh, Hannah rose. Now Eli the priest was sitting on the seat beside the doorpost of the temple of the LORD. 10. She was deeply distressed and prayed to the LORD, and wept bitterly. 11. And she vowed a vow and said, "O LORD of hosts, if thou wilt indeed look on the affliction of thy maidservant, and remember me, and not forget thy maidservant, but wilt give to thy maidservant a son, then I will give him to the LORD all the days of his life, and no razor shall touch his head." 12. As she continued praying before the LORD, Eli observed her mouth. 13. Hannah was speaking in her heart; only her lips moved, and her voice was not heard; therefore Eli took her to be a drunken woman. 14. And Eli said to her, "How long will you be drunken? Put away your wine from you." 15. But Hannah answered, "No, my lord, I am a woman sorely troubled; I have drunk neither wine nor strong drink, but I have been pouring out my soul before the LORD. 16. Do not regard your maidservant as a base woman, for all along I have been speaking out of my great anxiety and vexation." 17. Then Eli answered, "Go in peace, and the God of Israel grant your petition which you have made to him." 18. And she said, "Let your maidservant find favor in your eyes." Then the woman went her way and ate, and her countenance was no longer sad. 19. They rose early in the morning and worshiped before the LORD; then they went back to their house at Ramah. And Elkanah knew Hannah his wife, and the LORD remembered her; 20. and in due time Hannah conceived and bore a son, and she called his name Samuel, for she said, "I have asked him of the LORD." 21. And the man Elkanah and all his house went up to offer to the LORD the yearly sacrifice, and to pay his vow. 22. But Hannah did not go up, for she said to her husband, "As soon as the child is weaned, I will bring him, that he may appear in the presence of the LORD, and abide there for ever." 23. Elkanah her husband said to her, "Do what seems best to you, wait until you have weaned him; only, may the LORD establish his word." So the woman remained and nursed her son, until she weaned him. 24. And when she had weaned him, she took him up with her, along with a three-year-old bull, an ephah of flour, and a skin of wine; and she brought him to the house of the

LORD at Shiloh; and the child was young. 25. Then they slew the bull, and they brought the child to Eli. 26. And she said, "Oh, my lord! As you live, my lord, I am the woman who was standing here in your presence, praying to the LORD. 27. For this child I prayed; and the LORD has granted me my petition which I made to him. 28. Therefore I have lent him to the LORD; as long as he lives, he is lent to the LORD." And they worshiped the LORD there.

2:1. Hannah also prayed and said, "My heart exults in the LORD; my strength Is exalted in the LORD. My mouth derides my enemies, because I rejoice in thy salvation. 2. "There is none holy like the LORD, there is none besides thee; there is no rock like our God. 3. Talk no more so very proudly, let not arrogance come from your mouth; for the LORD is a God of knowledge, and by him actions are weighed. 4. The bows of the mighty are broken, but the feeble gird on strength. 5. Those who were full have hired themselves out for bread, but those who were hungry have ceased to hunger. The barren has borne seven, but she who has many children is forlorn. 6. The LORD kills and brings to life; he brings down to Sheol and raises up. 7. The LORD makes poor and makes rich; he brings low, he also exalts. 8. He raises up the poor from the dust; he lifts the needy from the ash heap, to make them sit with princes and inherit a seat of honor. For the pillars of the earth are the LORD'S, and on them he has set the world. 9. He will guard the feet of his faithful ones; but the wicked shall be cut off in darkness; for not by might shall a man prevail. 10. The adversaries of the LORD shall be broken to pieces; against them he will thunder in heaven. The LORD will judge the ends of the earth; he will give strength to his king, and exalt the power of his anointed."

11. Then Elkanah went home to Ramah. And the boy ministered to the LORD, in the presence of Eli the priest. 12. Now the sons of Eli were worthless men; they had no regard for the LORD. 13. The custom of the priests with the people was that when any man offered sacrifice, the priest's servant would come, while the meat was boiling, with a three-pronged fork in his hand, 14. and he would thrust it into the

pan, or kettle, or caldron, or pot; all that the fork brought up the priest would take for himself. So they did at Shiloh to all the Israelites who came there. 15. Moreover, before the fat was burned, the priest's servant would come and say to the man who was sacrificing, "Give meat for the priest to roast; for he will not accept boiled meat from you, but raw." 16. And if the man said to him, "Let them burn the fat first, and then take as much as you wish," he would say, "No, you must give it now; and if not, I will take it by force." 17. Thus the sin of the young men was very great in the sight of the LORD; for the men treated the offering of the LORD with contempt. 18. Samuel was ministering before the LORD, a boy girded with a linen ephod. 19. And his mother used to make for him a little robe and take it to him each year, when she went up with her husband to offer the yearly sacrifice. 20. Then Eli would bless Elkanah and his wife, and say, "The LORD give you children by this woman for the loan which she lent to the LORD"; so then they would return to their home.

21. And the LORD visited Hannah, and she conceived and bore three sons and two daughters. And the boy Samuel grew in the presence of the LORD. 22. Now Eli was very old, and he heard all that his sons were doing to all Israel, and how they lay with the women who served at the entrance to the tent of meeting. 23. And he said to them, "Why do you do such things? For I hear of your evil dealings from all the people. 24. No, my sons; it is no good report that I hear the people of the LORD spreading abroad. 25. If a man sins against a man, God will mediate for him; but if a man sins against the LORD, who can intercede for him?" But they would not listen to the voice of their father; for it was the will of the LORD to slay them. 26. Now the boy Samuel continued to grow both in stature and in favor with the LORD and with men.

Luke 1:5. In the days of Herod, king of Judea, there was a priest named Zechariah, of the division of Abijah; and he had a wife of the daughters of Aaron, and her name was Elizabeth. 6. And they were both righteous before God, walking in all the commandments and ordinances of the Lord blameless. 7. But they had no child, because

Elizabeth was barren, and both were advanced in years. 8. Now while he was serving as priest before God when his division was on duty, 9. according to the custom of the priesthood, it fell to him by lot to enter the temple of the Lord and burn incense. 10. And the whole multitude of the people were praying outside at the hour of incense. 11. And there appeared to him an angel of the Lord standing on the right side of the altar of incense. 12. And Zechariah was troubled when he saw him, and fear fell upon him. 13. But the angel said to him, "Do not be afraid, Zechariah, for your prayer is heard, and your wife Elizabeth will bear you a son, and you shall call his name John. 14. And you will have joy and gladness, and many will rejoice at his birth; 15. for he will be great before the Lord, and he shall drink no wine nor strong drink, and he will be filled with the Holy Spirit, even from his mother's womb. 16. And he will turn many of the sons of Israel to the Lord their God, 17. and he will go before him in the spirit and power of Elijah, to turn the hearts of the fathers to the children, and the disobedient to the wisdom of the just, to make ready for the Lord a people prepared." 18. And Zechariah said to the angel, "How shall I know this? For I am an old man, and my wife is advanced in years." 19. And the angel answered him, "I am Gabriel, who stand in the presence of God; and I was sent to speak to you, and to bring you this good news. 20. And behold, you will be silent and unable to speak until the day that these things come to pass, because you did not believe my words, which will be fulfilled in their time." 21. And the people were waiting for Zechariah, and they wondered at his delay in the temple. 22. And when he came out, he could not speak to them, and they perceived that he had seen a vision in the temple; and he made signs to them and remained dumb. 23. And when his time of service was ended, he went to his home. 24. After these days his wife Elizabeth conceived, and for five months she hid herself, saying, 25. "Thus the Lord has done to me in the days when he looked on me, to take away my reproach among men."

26. In the sixth month the angel Gabriel was sent from God to a city of Galilee named Nazareth, 27. to a virgin betrothed to a man whose

The Christ Myth Theory And Its Problems

name was Joseph, of the house of David; and the virgin's name was Mary. 28. And he came to her and said, "Hail, O favored one, the Lord is with you!" 29. But she was greatly troubled at the saying, and considered in her mind what sort of greeting this might be.

30. And the angel said to her, "Do not be afraid, Mary, for you have found favor with God. 31. And behold, you will conceive in your womb and bear a son, and you shall call his name Jesus. 32. He will be great, and will be called the Son of the Most High; and the Lord God will give to him the throne of his father David, 33. and he will reign over the house of Jacob for ever; and of his kingdom there will be no end." 34. And Mary said to the angel, "How shall this be, since I have no husband?" 35. And the angel said to her, "The Holy Spirit will come upon you, and the power of the Most High will overshadow you; therefore the child to be born will be called holy, the Son of God. 36. And behold, your kinswoman Elizabeth in her old age has also conceived a son; and this is the sixth month with her who was called barren. 37. For with God nothing will be impossible." 38. And Mary said, "Behold, I am the handmaid of the Lord; let it be to me according to your word." And the angel departed from her. 39. In those days Mary arose and went with haste into the hill country, to a city of Judah, 40. and she entered the house of Zechariah and greeted Elizabeth. 41. And when Elizabeth heard the greeting of Mary, the babe leaped in her womb; and Elizabeth was filled with the Holy Spirit 42. and she exclaimed with a loud cry, "Blessed are you among women, and blessed is the fruit of your womb! 43. And why is this granted me, that the mother of my Lord should come to me? 44. For behold, when the voice of your greeting came to my ears, the babe in my womb leaped for joy. 45. And blessed is she who believed that there would be a fulfillment of what was spoken to her from the Lord."

46. And Mary said, "My soul magnifies the Lord, 47. and my spirit rejoices in God my Savior, 48. for he has regarded the low estate of his handmaiden. For behold, henceforth all generations will call me blessed; 49. for he who is mighty has done great things for me, and

holy is his name. 50. And his mercy is on those who fear him from generation to generation. 51. He has shown strength with his arm, he has scattered the proud in the imagination of their hearts; 52. he has put down the mighty from their thrones, and exalted those of low degree; 53. he has filled the hungry with good things, and the rich he has sent empty away. 54. He has helped his servant Israel, in remembrance of his mercy, 55. as he spoke to our fathers, to Abraham and to his posterity for ever." 56. And Mary remained with her about three months, and returned to her home. 57. Now the time came for Elizabeth to be delivered, and she gave birth to a son. 58. And her neighbors and kinsfolk heard that the Lord had shown great mercy to her, and they rejoiced with her. 59. And on the eighth day they came to circumcise the child; and they would have named him Zechariah after his father, 60. but his mother said, "Not so; he shall be called John." 61. And they said to her, "None of your kindred is called by this name." 62. And they made signs to his father, inquiring what he would have him called. 63. And he asked for a writing tablet, and wrote, "His name is John." And they all marveled. 64. And immediately his mouth was opened and his tongue loosed, and he spoke, blessing God. 65. And fear came on all their neighbors. And all these things were talked about through all the hill country of Judea; 66. and all who heard them laid them up in their hearts, saying, "What then will this child be?" For the hand of the Lord was with him.

67. And his father Zechariah was filled with the Holy Spirit, and prophesied, saying, 68. "Blessed be the Lord God of Israel, for he has visited and redeemed his people, 69. and has raised up a horn of salvation for us in the house of his servant David, 70. as he spoke by the mouth of his holy prophets from of old, 71. that we should be saved from our enemies, and from the hand of all who hate us; 72. to perform the mercy promised to our fathers, and to remember his holy covenant, 73. the oath which he swore to our father Abraham, 74. to grant us that we, being delivered from the hand of our enemies, might serve him without fear, 75. in holiness and righteousness before him all the days of our life. 76. And you, child, will

be called the prophet of the Most High; for you will go before the Lord to prepare his ways, 77. to give knowledge of salvation to his people in the forgiveness of their sins, 78. through the tender mercy of our God, when the day shall dawn upon us from on high 79. to give light to those who sit in darkness and in the shadow of death, to guide our feet into the way of peace." 80. And the child grew and became strong in spirit, and he was in the wilderness till the day of his manifestation to Israel.

2:1. In those days a decree went out from Caesar Augustus that all the world should be enrolled. 2. This was the first enrollment, when Quirinius was governor of Syria. 3. And all went to be enrolled, each to his own city. 4. And Joseph also went up from Galilee, from the city of Nazareth, to Judea, to the city of David, which is called Bethlehem, because he was of the house and lineage of David, 5. to be enrolled with Mary, his betrothed, who was with child. 6. And while they were there, the time came for her to be delivered. 7. And she gave birth to her first-born son and wrapped him in swaddling cloths, and laid him in a manger, because there was no place for them in the inn. 8. And in that region there were shepherds out in the field, keeping watch over their flock by night. 9. And an angel of the Lord appeared to them, and the glory of the Lord shone around them, and they were filled with fear. 10. And the angel said to them, "Be not afraid; for behold, I bring you good news of a great joy which will come to all the people; 11. for to you is born this day in the city of David a Savior, who is Christ the Lord. 12. And this will be a sign for you: you will find a babe wrapped in swaddling cloths and lying in a manger." 13. And suddenly there was with the angel a multitude of the heavenly host praising God and saying, 14. "Glory to God in the highest, and on earth peace among men with whom he is pleased!" 15. When the angels went away from them into heaven, the shepherds said to one another, "Let us go over to Bethlehem and see this thing that has happened, which the Lord has made known to us." 16. And they went with haste, and found Mary and Joseph, and the babe lying in a manger. 17. And when they saw it they made known the saying which had been told them concerning this child;

18. and all who heard it wondered at what the shepherds told them. 19. But Mary kept all these things, pondering them in her heart. 20. And the shepherds returned, glorifying and praising God for all they had heard and seen, as it had been told them.

21. And at the end of eight days, when he was circumcised, he was called Jesus, the name given by the angel before he was conceived in the womb. 22. And when the time came for their purification according to the law of Moses, they brought him up to Jerusalem to present him to the Lord 23. (as it is written in the law of the Lord, "Every male that opens the womb shall be called holy to the Lord") and 24. to offer a sacrifice according to what is said in the law of the Lord, "a pair of turtledoves, or two young pigeons." 25. Now there was a man in Jerusalem, whose name was Simeon, and this man was righteous and devout, looking for the consolation of Israel, and the Holy Spirit was upon him. 26. And it had been revealed to him by the Holy Spirit that he should not see death before he had seen the Lord's Christ. 27. And inspired by the Spirit he came into the temple; and when the parents brought in the child Jesus, to do for him according to the custom of the law, 28. he took him up in his arms and blessed God and said, 29. "Lord, now lettest thou thy servant depart in peace, according to thy word; 30. for mine eyes have seen thy salvation 31. which thou hast prepared in the presence of all peoples, 32. a light for revelation to the Gentiles, and for glory to thy people Israel." 33. And his father and his mother marveled at what was said about him; 34. and Simeon blessed them and said to Mary his mother, "Behold, this child is set for the fall and rising of many in Israel, and for a sign that is spoken against 35. (and a sword will pierce through your own soul also), that thoughts out of many hearts may be revealed."

36. And there was a prophetess, Anna, the daughter of Phanuel, of the tribe of Asher; she was of a great age, having lived with her husband seven years from her virginity, 37. and as a widow till she was eighty-four. She did not depart from the temple, worshiping with fasting and prayer night and day. 38. And coming up at that very hour she gave thanks to God, and spoke of him to all who were

looking for the redemption of Jerusalem. 39. And when they had performed everything according to the law of the Lord, they returned into
Galilee, to their own city, Nazareth. 40. And the child grew and became strong, filled with wisdom; and the favor of God was upon him.

41. Now his parents went to Jerusalem every year at the feast of the
Passover. 42. And when he was twelve years old, they went up according to custom; 43. and when the feast was ended, as they were
returning, the boy Jesus stayed behind in Jerusalem. His parents
did not know it, 44. but supposing him to be in the company they
went a day's journey, and they sought him among their kinsfolk and
acquaintances; 45. and when they did not find him, they returned
to Jerusalem, seeking him. 46. After three days they found him in
the temple, sitting among the teachers, listening to them and asking them questions; 47. and all who heard him were amazed at his
understanding and his answers. 48. And when they saw him they
were astonished; and his mother said to him, "Son, why have you
treated us so? Behold, your father and I have been looking for you
anxiously." 49. And he said to them, "How is it that you sought me?
Did you not know that I must be in my Father's house?" 50.And
they did not understand the saying which he spoke to them. 51. And
he went down with them and came to Nazareth, and was obedient to
them; and his mother kept all these things in her heart. 52. And Jesus
increased in wisdom and in stature, and in favor with God and man.

The fundamental source of Luke's double nativity story is the nativity of Samuel. Eli becomes Simeon (and perhaps also Zachariah),
while barren Hannah becomes old Elizabeth (and Mary, too, if we
accept the majority of manuscripts' attribution of the Magnificat to
her instead of Elizabeth, 1:46–55). The Magnificat is clearly a paraphrase of Hannah's song in 1 Samuel 2:1–10. The repeated refrain
of Jesus' continuing growth in wisdom and favor with God and men
(2:40, 52, *cf.*, 1:80) comes directly from 1 Samuel 2:26, "Now the
boy Samuel continued to grow both in stature and in favor with the
LORD and with men."

The birth annunciation to Mary recalls those of Isaac (Genesis 17:19, "Sarah your wife shall bear you a son, and you shall call his name..."; 18:9–15) and Samson (Judges 13:2–5, "you shall conceive and bear a son... and he shall begin to deliver Israel..."). The story also borrows from the commissioning stories of Moses (Exodus 3:10–12) and Jeremiah (Jeremiah 1:4–8), where the servant of God objects to the divine summons and his objection is overruled (see Luke 1:18, 34).

A less familiar source for the Lukan nativity story is the nativity of Moses as told in Pseudo-Philo's *Biblical Antiquities*, where we read that, during Pharaoh's persecution of the Hebrew babies, Amram has determined to defy Pharaoh by having a son. God makes known his will by sending an angel to the virgin Miriam. "And the Spirit of God came upon Miriam one night, and she saw a dream and told it to her parents in the morning, saying, 'I have seen this night, and behold a man in a linen garment stood and said to me, "Go, and say to your parents, 'Behold, he who will be born from you will be cast forth into the water; likewise through him the water will be dried up. And I will work signs through him and save my people, and he will exercise leadership always' " ' " (9:10).

The angel Gabriel's predictions in Luke 1:32–33, 35 can be derived from an Aramaic version of Daniel found among the Dead Sea Scrolls: "[And when the Spirit] came to rest up[on] him, he fell before the throne. [Then Daniel rose and said,] 'O king, why are you angry; why do you [grind] your teeth? [The G]reat [God] has revealed to you [that which is to come.] ... [Peoples will make war,] and battles shall multiply among the nations, until [the king of the people of God arises... [All the peoples will serve him,] and he shall become gre[at] upon the earth... He will be called [son of the Gr]eat [God;] by his Name shall he be designated. He will be called the son of God. They will call him son of the Most High... His kingdom will be an eternal kingdom, and he will be righteous in all his ways" (4Q246, *The Son of God*).

When Mary visits her cousin Elizabeth, the latter's unborn child, John the Baptizer, leaps in the womb in greeting to acknowledge the greater glory of the unborn Jesus. Here, as G.R. Driver pointed out, Luke refers to Genesis 25:22 LXX, where Rebecca is in pain because her two rival sons strive within her as a sign of fraternal discord to come: "And the babes leaped within her." This precedent Luke seeks to reverse by having the older cousin, John, already deferring in the womb to his younger cousin. Here he has an eye on the rival John the Baptist sect whom he thus tries to conciliate and coopt.

2. The Centurion's Child and the Son of the Widow of Nain (1 Kings 17:1–24; Luke 7:1–17)

1 Kings 17:1. Now Elijah the Tishbite, of Tishbe in Gilead, said to Ahab, "As the LORD the God of Israel lives, before whom I stand, there shall be neither dew nor rain these years, except by my word." 2. And the word of the LORD came to him, 3. "Depart from here and turn eastward, and hide yourself by the brook Cherith, that is east of the Jordan. 4. You shall drink from the brook, and I have commanded the ravens to feed you there." 5. So he went and did according to the word of the LORD; he went and dwelt by the brook Cherith that is east of the Jordan. 6. And the ravens brought him bread and meat in the morning, and bread and meat in the evening; and he drank from the brook. 7. And after a while the brook dried up, because there was no rain in the land. 8. Then the word of the LORD came to him, 9. "Arise, go to Zarephath, which belongs to Sidon, and dwell there. Behold, I have commanded a widow there to feed you." 10. So he arose and went to Zarephath; and when he came to the gate of the city, behold, a widow was there gathering sticks; and he called to her and said, "Bring me a little water in a vessel, that I may drink." 11. And as she was going to bring it, he called to her and said, "Bring me a morsel of bread in your hand." 12. And she said, "As the LORD your God lives, I have nothing baked, only a handful of meal in a jar, and a little oil in a cruse; and now, I am gathering a couple of sticks, that I may go in and prepare it for myself and my son, that we may eat it, and die." 13. And Elijah said to her, "Fear not; go and do as you have said; but first make me a little cake of it and bring it to me, and afterward make for yourself

and your son. 14. For thus says the LORD the God of Israel, 'The jar of meal shall not be spent, and the cruse of oil shall not fail, until the day that the LORD sends rain upon the earth'." 15. And she went and did as Elijah said; and she, and he, and her household ate for many days. 16. The jar of meal was not spent, neither did the cruse of oil fail, according to the word of the LORD which he spoke by Elijah. 17. After this the son of the woman, the mistress of the house, became ill; and his illness was so severe that there was no breath left in him. 18. And she said to Elijah, "What have you against me, O man of God? You have come to me to bring my sin to remembrance, and to cause the death of my son!" 19. And he said to her, "Give me your son." And he took him from her bosom, and carried him up into the upper chamber, where he lodged, and laid him upon his own bed. 20. And he cried to the LORD, "O LORD my God, hast thou brought calamity even upon the widow with whom I sojourn, by slaying her son?" 21. Then he stretched himself upon the child three times, and cried to the LORD, "O LORD my God, let this child's soul come into him again." 22. And the LORD hearkened to the voice of Elijah; and the soul of the child came into him again, and he revived. 23. And Elijah took the child, and brought him down from the upper chamber into the house, and delivered him to his mother; and Elijah said, "See, your son lives." 24. And the woman said to Elijah, "Now I know that you are a man of God, and that the word of the LORD in your mouth is truth."

Luke 7:1. After he had ended all his sayings in the hearing of the people he entered Capernaum. 2. Now a centurion had a slave who was dear to him, who was sick and at the point of death. 3. When he heard of Jesus, he sent to him elders of the Jews, asking him to come and heal his slave. 4. And when they came to Jesus, they besought him earnestly, saying, "He is worthy to have you do this for him, 5. for he loves our nation, and he built us our synagogue." 6. And Jesus went with them. When he was not far from the house, the centurion sent friends to him, saying to him, "Lord, do not trouble yourself, for I am not worthy to have you come under my roof; 7. therefore I did not presume to come to you. But say the word, and let my servant be healed. 8. For I am a man set under authority, with soldiers under me: and I

171

say to one, 'Go,' and he goes; and to another, 'Come,' and he comes; and to my slave, 'Do this,' and he does it." 9. When Jesus heard this he marveled at him, and turned and said to the multitude that followed him, "I tell you, not even in Israel have I found such faith." 10. And when those who had been sent returned to the house, they found the slave well. 11. Soon afterward he went to a city called Nain, and his disciples and a great crowd went with him. 12. As he drew near to the gate of the city, behold, a man who had died was being carried out, the only son of his mother, and she was a widow; and a large crowd from the city was with her. 13. And when the Lord saw her, he had compassion on her and said to her, "Do not weep." 14. And he came and touched the bier, and the bearers stood still. And he said, "Young man, I say to you, arise." 15. And the dead man sat up, and began to speak. And he gave him to his mother. 16. Fear seized them all; and they glorified God, saying, "A great prophet has arisen among us!" and "God has visited his people!" 17. And this report concerning him spread through the whole of Judea and all the surrounding country.

Luke has used 1 Kings 17 as the basis for the two-miracle sequence here (Brodie, pp. 136–137). The original Elijah version stipulates (1 Kings 17:1) how the famine shall be relieved only by the prophetic word, just as the mere word of Jesus is enough to heal the centurion's servant/child at a distance (Luke 7:7b). Elijah journeys to the Transjordan where he will meet a Gentile in need, the widow of Zarephath (1 Kings 17:5, 10a), just as Jesus arrives in Capernaum to encounter a Roman centurion. Both Gentiles are in dire need, the widow about to succumb to starvation with her son (17:12), the centurion desperate to avert his son's/servant's imminent death (7:2–3). Once the facts are made known to the miracle worker, there is a series of commands (1 Kings 17:10c–13; Luke 7:8), and divine deliverance is secured, the multiplication of food in the one case (17:6), the return of health in the other (7:10).

It appears that Luke has drawn the story of the centurion's son from the wider gospel tradition, as it appears in both Matthew 8:513 (hence in Q) and John 4:46–54. It had already been derived from the Elijah story by early Christian scribes. But Luke has decided as well to add a new Jesus tale, unparalleled in other gospels, modeled upon the 1 Kings sequel to the story of Elijah and the widow. Whereas Elijah later raises from the dead the widow's son, Jesus next comes upon a funeral procession and raises the man about to be buried, again a widow's son, this time from Nain. Luke has decided to reserve one feature from the first Elijah episode to use in his second Jesus episode: the initial meeting with the widow at the city gate of Zarephath, which he makes the gate of Nain (even though historical Ain had no gate!).

But before this, Luke opens his second episode with the same opening from 1 Kings 17:17a: "And it happened afterward" // "after this..." The widow's son is dead (1 Kings 17:17b; Luke 7:12b). Elijah cried out in anguish (1 Kings 17:19–20), unlike Jesus, who, however, tells the widow not to cry (Luke 7:13). After a gesture (Elijah prays for the boy's spirit to return, v. 21; Jesus commands the boy to rise, 7:14), the dead rises, proving his reanimation by crying out (1 Kings 17:22; Luke 7:15). His service rendered, the wonder-worker "gave him to his mother" (1 Kings 17:24; Luke 7:15b, verbatim identical). Those present glorify the hero (1 Kings 17:24; Luke 7:16–17).

If Luke himself (as Brodie thinks, pp. 136–152) composed the first episode directly from the first Elijah episode, instead of taking it from Q, he will have also transferred the widow's lament that Elijah has come to punish her sins into the centurion's confession that he is unworthy to have Jesus come under his roof.

3. The Sinful Woman (2 Kings 4:1–7; 2 Kings 4:8–37; Luke 7:36–50)

2 Kings 4:1. Now the wife of one of the sons of the prophets cried to Elisha, "Your servant my husband is dead; and you know that your servant feared the LORD, but the creditor has come to take my two children to be his slaves." 2. And Elisha said to her, "What shall I do for you? Tell me; what have you in the house?" And she said, "Your

maidservant has nothing in the house, except a jar of oil." 3. Then he said, "Go outside, borrow vessels of all your neighbors, empty vessels and not too few. 4. Then go in, and shut the door upon yourself and your sons, and pour into all these vessels; and when one is full, set it aside." 5. So she went from him and shut the door upon herself and her sons; and as she poured they brought the vessels to her. 6. When the vessels were full, she said to her son, "Bring me another vessel." And he said to her, "There is not another." Then the oil stopped flowing. 7. She came and told the man of God, and he said, "Go, sell the oil and pay your debts, and you and your sons can live on the rest."

Luke 7:36. One of the Pharisees asked him to eat with him, and he went into the Pharisee's house, and took his place at table. 37. And behold, a woman of the city, who was a sinner, when she learned that he was at table in the Pharisee's house, brought an alabaster flask of ointment, 38. and standing behind him at his feet, weeping, she began to wet his feet with her tears, and wiped them with the hair of her head, and kissed his feet, and anointed them with the ointment. 39. Now when the Pharisee who had invited him saw it, he said to himself, "If this man were a prophet, he would have known who and what sort of woman this is who is touching him, for she is a sinner." 40. And Jesus answering said to him, "Simon, I have something to say to you." And he answered, "What is it, Teacher?" 41. "A certain creditor had two debtors; one owed five hundred denarii, and the other fifty. 42. When they could not pay, he forgave them both. Now which of them will love him more?" 43. Simon answered, "The one, I suppose, to whom he forgave more." And he said to him, "You have judged rightly." 44. Then turning toward the woman he said to Simon, "Do you see this woman? I entered your house, you gave me no water for my feet, but she has wet my feet with her tears and wiped them with her hair. 45. You gave me no kiss, but from the time I came in she has not ceased to kiss my feet. 46. You did not anoint my head with oil, but she has anointed my feet with ointment. 47. Therefore I tell you, her sins, which are many, are forgiven, for she loved much; but he who is forgiven little, loves little." 48. And he said to her, "Your sins are forgiven." 49. Then those who were at table with him began to say

among themselves, "Who is this, who even forgives sins?" 50. And he
said to the woman, "Your faith has saved you; go in peace."

According to Brodie (pp. 174–184), Luke has created his rather
cumbersome story of the sinful woman from a pair of Elisha's
miracles, the never-failing cruse of oil (2 Kings 4:1–7) and the
raising of the Shunammite's son (2 Kings 4:8–37; see discussion
above at Mark 5:21 *ff*, "Jairus' Daughter and the Woman with the
Issue of Blood"). The widow of Elisha's disciple is in financial
debt, with her creditors about to take her two children in payment
(2 Kings 4:1). In Luke's version, her arrears have become a debt of
sin (Luke 7:37, 40–42). Elisha causes her oil to multiply, becoming enough to pay her debt. Jesus' cancellation of the woman's
debt is less material but no less miraculous, as he pronounces her
forgiven (Luke 7:44–50). As for the oil, it has become the myrrh
with which the woman anoints Jesus' feet (Luke 7:38). In Luke's
version, Simon the Pharisee has invited the itinerant Jesus to dine
(Luke 7:36), a reflection of the Shunammite's invitation of Elisha
to stay and eat with her whenever passing by (2 Kings 4:8–11). As
a reward, Elisha grants her to conceive a son. Years later, he dies
of sunstroke, whereupon she journeys to Elisha for help, falling
at his feet (2 Kings 4:27), just as the suppliant woman anoints the
feet of Jesus (Luke 7:38). There is no need to posit Luke's creation
of the whole anointing story, the core of which he got from Mark
14:3–9, but he has substantially rewritten it in light of 2 Kings.

4. Appointment in Samaria (Luke 9:51–56)

Luke 9:51. When the days drew near for him to be received up, he
set his face to go to Jerusalem. And he sent messengers ahead of
him, 52. who went and entered a village of the Samaritans, to make
ready for him; 53. but the people would not receive him, because his
face was set toward Jerusalem. 54. And when his disciples James
and John saw it, they said, "Lord, do you want us to bid fire come

down from heaven and consume them?" 55. But he turned and rebuked them. 56. And they went on to another village.

The connection between Luke 9:51–56 and 2 Kings 1:1–2:1 (see the discussion of this passage at Mark 2:1–12, "Healing the Paralytic") is obvious to all in view of the explicit allusion in the one to the other (Luke 9:54). But Brodie shows (pp. 207–214) how the Lukan story is simply rewritten from its prototype. Luke has transferred the anticipation of the hero's being taken up into heaven from the end of the section of Elijah's clash with the Samaritan troops (2 Kings 2:1) to the beginning of the story of Jesus and the Samaritan village (Luke 9:51a). The king of Samaria has sent messengers to inquire of the oracle of Baal-zebub in Philistine Ekron, but Elijah meets them and turns them back (2 Kings 1:2–5). In Luke this has become the turning back of Jesus' messengers sent ahead to secure the night's accommodations in Samaria. The Samaritans are no longer those turned back but those who turn others back in their travels. The prophet is now the sender of the messengers, not their interceptor. Once the king of Samaria sends troops to apprehend Elijah, the latter calls down fire from the sky to consume them (2 Kings 1:9–10). The scene is repeated (vv. 1–12). The third time Elijah relents and comes along quietly (1 Kings 1:13–15). James and John want to repeat Elijah's miraculous destruction of the Samaritans (now villagers, not troops), but Jesus will have none of it. Instead he takes the role of the angel of the LORD who bade Elijah show mercy.

5. Calling a Ploughman (1 Kings 19:19–21; Luke 9:59–62)

1 Kings 19:19. So he departed from there, and found Elisha the son of Shaphat, who was plowing, with twelve yoke of oxen before him, and he was with the twelfth. Elijah passed by him and cast his mantle upon him. 20. And he left the oxen, and ran after Elijah, and said, "Let me kiss my father and my mother, and then I will follow you." And he said to him, "Go back again; for what have I done to you?"

176

21. And he returned from following him, and took the yoke of oxen, and slew them, and boiled their flesh with the yokes of the oxen, and gave it to the people, and they ate. Then he arose and went after Elijah, and ministered to him.

Luke 9:59. To another he said, "Follow me." But he said, "Lord, let me first go and bury my father." 60. But he said to him, "Leave the dead to bury their own dead; but as for you, go and proclaim the kingdom of God." 61. Another said, "I will follow you, Lord; but let me first say farewell to those at my home." 62. Jesus said to him, "No one who puts his hand to the plow and looks back is fit for the kingdom of God."

The stories of Jesus' calling Peter, Andrew, James, and John (Mark 1:16–20) and Levi (Mark 2:14) all seem to stem from Elijah summoning Elisha to become his disciple and successor (1 Kings 19:19–21). Elijah's throwing his mantle onto Elisha's shoulders would seem to anticipate his subsequent bequest of his authority to his successor, named first here, a literal "investiture." But Luke seems (Brodie, pp. 216–227) to have created another discipleship paradigm which implicitly critiques the prototype. In Luke 9:59–62, Jesus forbids what Elijah allows, that the new recruit should delay long enough to pay filial respects. Also, whereas plowing was for Elisha the worldly pursuit he must abandon for the prophetic ministry, for Luke plowing becomes the very metaphor for that ministry.

6. The Central Section (Luke 10:1–18:14)

Based on Mark's Transfiguration scene, which both take over directly (Matthew 17:1–8; Luke 9:28–36), Matthew and Luke depict Jesus as the Prophet like unto Moses, and each has him promulgating a new Torah. Matthew presents a whole new Pentateuch by organizing the teaching of Jesus into five great blocks: the Sermon on the Mount (chapters 5–7), the Mission Charge (chapter 10), the Parables chapter (13), the Manual of Discipline (chapters 18–19), and the denunciation on the Pharisees plus the Olivet Discourse (chapters 23–26; the cramming together of two themes in the fifth section only underlines his determination to squeeze the whole thing into five divisions, no matter how snug the fit!). By contrast, Luke thought it sufficient to have Jesus present a Deutero-Deuteronomy, a "second law" such as Moses offers in the Book of Deuteronomy. C.F. Evans ("The Central Section of St. Luke's Gospel," 1967) was the first to point this out. Just as Matthew did, Luke has both simply organized some traditional materials and also created some of his own based on suggestions in the scripture text he was emulating. It is particularly striking that Luke's material here in the central section follows the order of the corresponding topics from Deuteronomy,

a. Sending out Emissaries (Deuteronomy 1:1–46; Luke 10:1–3, 17–20)

Deuteronomy 1:1. These are the words that Moses spoke to all Israel beyond the Jordan in the wilderness, in the Arabah over against Suph, between Paran and Tophel, Laban, Hazeroth, and Dizahab. 2. It is eleven days' journey from Horeb by the way of Mount Seir to Kadesh-barnea. 3. And in the fortieth year, on the first day of the eleventh month, Moses spoke to the people of Israel according to all that the LORD had given him in commandment to them, 4. after he had defeated Sihon the king of the Amorites, who lived in Heshbon, and Og the king of Bashan, who lived in Ashtaroth and in Edrei. 5. Beyond the Jordan, in the land of Moab, Moses undertook to explain this law, saying, 6. "The LORD our God said to us in Horeb, 'You have stayed long enough at this mountain; 7. turn and take your journey, and go to the hill country of the Amorites, and to all their neighbors in the Arabah, in the hill country and in the lowland, and in the Negeb, and by the seacoast, the land of the Canaanites, and Lebanon, as far as the great river, the river Euphrates. 8. Behold, I have set the land before you; go in and take possession of the land which the LORD swore to your fathers, to Abraham, to Isaac, and to Jacob, to give to them and to their descendants after them'." 9. At that time I said to you, 'I am not able alone to bear you; 10. the LORD your God has multiplied you, and behold, you are this day as the stars of heaven for multitude. 11. May the LORD, the God of your fathers, make you a thousand times as many as you are, and bless you, as he has promised you! 12. How can I bear alone the weight and burden of you and your strife? 13. Choose wise, understanding, and experienced men, according to your tribes, and I will appoint them as your heads.' 14. And you answered me, 'The thing that you have spoken is good for us to do.' 15. So I took the heads of your tribes, wise and experienced men, and set them as heads over you, commanders of thousands, commanders of hundreds, commanders of fifties, commanders of tens, and officers, throughout your tribes. 16. And I charged your judges at that time, 'Hear the cases between your brethren, and judge righteously between a man and his brother or the alien that is with him. 17. You shall not be partial in judgment; you shall hear the small and the great alike; you shall not be afraid of the face of man, for the judgment is God's; and the case that is too hard for you, you shall bring to me, and I will hear it.' 18. And I commanded you at that time all the things that you should do. 19. "And we set out from Horeb, and went through all that great and terrible wilderness which you saw, on the way to the hill country of the Amorites, as the LORD our God commanded us; and we came to Kadesh-barnea. 20. And I said to you, 'You have come to the hill country of the Amorites, which the LORD our God gives us. 21. Behold, the LORD your God has set the land before you; go up, take possession, as the LORD, the God of your fathers, has told you; do not fear or be dismayed.' 22. Then all of you came near me, and said, 'Let us send men before us, that they may explore the land for us, and bring us word again of the way by which we must go up and the cities into which we shall come.' 23. The thing seemed good to me, and I took twelve men of you, one man for each tribe; 24. and they turned and went up into the hill country, and came to the Valley of Eshcol and spied it out. 25. And they took in their hands some of the fruit of the land and brought it down to us, and brought us word again, and said, 'It is a good land which the LORD our God gives us'." 26. Yet you would not go up, but rebelled against the command of the LORD your God; 27. and you murmured in your tents, and said, 'Because the LORD hated us he has brought us forth out of the land of Egypt, to give us into the hand of the Amorites, to destroy us. 28. Whither are we going up? Our brethren have made our hearts melt, saying, "The people are greater and taller than we; the cities are great and fortified up to heaven; and moreover we have seen the sons of the Anakim there".' 29. Then I said to you, 'Do not be in dread or afraid of them. 30. The LORD your God who goes before you will himself fight for you, just as he did for you in Egypt before your eyes, 31. and in the wilderness, where you have seen how the LORD your God bore you, as a man bears his son, in all the way that you went until you came to this place.' 32. Yet in spite of this word you did not believe the LORD your God, 33. who went before you in the way to seek you out a place to pitch your tents, in fire by night, to show you by what way you should go, and in the cloud by day." 34. And the LORD heard your words, and was angered, and he swore, 35. 'Not one of these men of this evil generation shall see the good land which I swore to give to your fathers, 36. except Caleb the son of Jephunneh; he shall see it, and to him and to his children I will give the land upon which he has trodden, because he has wholly followed the LORD!' 37. The LORD was angry with me also on your account, and said, 'You also shall not go in there; 38. Joshua the son of Nun, who stands before you, he shall enter; encourage him, for he shall cause Israel to inherit it. 39. Moreover your little ones, who you said would become a prey, and your children, who this day have no knowledge of good or evil, shall go in there, and to them I will give it, and they shall possess it. 40. But as for you, turn, and journey into the wilderness in the direction of the Red Sea'." 41. Then you answered me, 'We have sinned against the LORD; we will go up and fight, just as the LORD our God commanded us.' And every man of you girded on his weapons of war, and thought it easy to go up into the hill country. 42. And the LORD said to me, 'Say to them, Do not go up or fight, for I am not in the midst of you; lest you be defeated before your enemies.' 43. So I spoke to you, and you would not hearken; but you rebelled against the command of the LORD, and

were presumptuous and went up into the hill country. 44. Then the
Amorites who lived in that hill country came out against you and
chased you as bees do and beat you down in Seir as far as Hormah.
45. And you returned and wept before the LORD; but the LORD did
not hearken to your voice or give ear to you. 46. So you remained at
Kadesh many days, the days that you remained there.

Luke 10:1. After this the Lord appointed seventy others, and sent
them on ahead of him, two by two, into every town and place where
he himself was about to come. 2. And he said to them, "The harvest
is plentiful, but the laborers are few; pray therefore the Lord of the
harvest to send out laborers into his harvest. 3. Go your way; behold,
I send you out as lambs in the midst of wolves. […] 17. The seventy
returned with joy, saying, "Lord, even the demons are subject to us
in your name!" 18. And he said to them, "I saw Satan fall like lightning from heaven. 19. Behold, I have given you authority to tread
upon serpents and scorpions, and over all the power of the enemy;
and nothing shall hurt you. 20. Nevertheless do not rejoice in this,
that the spirits are subject to you; but rejoice that your names are
written in heaven."

Just as Moses had chosen twelve spies to reconnoiter the land
which stretched "*before your face*," sending them through the *cities* of the land of Canaan, so does Jesus send a second group, after
the twelve, a group of seventy, whose number symbolizes the nations of the earth who are to be conquered, so to speak, with the
gospel in the Acts of the Apostles. He sends them out "*before his
face*" to every *city* he plans to visit (in Canaan, too, obviously).

To match the image of the spies returning with samples of the
fruit of the land (Deuteronomy 1:25), Luke has placed here the Q
saying (Luke 10:2//Matthew 9:37–38), "The harvest is plentiful,
but the workers are few; therefore beg the Lord of the harvest to
send out more workers into his harvest."

And Jesus' emissaries return with a glowing report, just as
Moses' did.

The Christ Myth Theory And Its Problems

b. Judgment for Rejection (Deuteronomy 2–3:22; Luke 10:4–16)

Luke 10:4. Carry no purse, no bag, no sandals; and salute no one on the road. 5. Whatever house you enter, first say, 'Peace be to this house!' 6. And if a son of peace is there, your peace shall rest upon him; but if not, it shall return to you. 7. And remain in the same house, eating and drinking what they provide, for the laborer deserves his wages; do not go from house to house. 8. Whenever you enter a town and they receive you, eat what is set before you; 9. heal the sick in it and say to them, 'The kingdom of God has come near to you.' 10. But whenever you enter a town and they do not receive you, go into its streets and say, 11. 'Even the dust of your town that clings to our feet, we wipe off against you; nevertheless know this, that the kingdom of God has come near.' 12. I tell you, it shall be more tolerable on that day for Sodom than for that town. 13. "Woe to you, Chorazin! woe to you, Beth-saida! for if the mighty works done in you had been done in Tyre and Sidon, they would have repented long ago, sitting in sackcloth and ashes. 14. But it shall be more tolerable in the judgment for Tyre and Sidon than for you. 15. And you, Capernaum, will you be exalted to heaven? You shall be brought down to Hades. 16. He who hears you hears me, and he who rejects you rejects me, and he who rejects me rejects him who sent me."

Just as Moses sent messengers to Kings Og of Bashan and Sihon of Heshbon with terms of peace, so does Jesus send his seventy out with the offer of blessing: "Peace be to this house." The Israelite messengers are rebuffed, and God punishes them by sending Israel to decimate them. Jesus warns that in case of rejection (which does not in fact occur), the aloof cities will face divine judgment some time in the future. This mission charge material comes from Q (*cf.* Matthew 10). That it did not originate here with Luke borrowing it directly from Deuteronomy is evident from the fact that the hypothetical doom of the unresponsive towns is compared with those of Tyre and Sidon, not of Bashan and Heshbon. Perhaps Luke decided to use the Q material here because

182

it uses the image of the missionaries "shaking the dust" (*i.e.*, the contagion) of the village "from the soles of their feet" (Luke 10:10), matching the mention of "the sole of the foot" in Deuteronomy 2:5.

c. Praying to the Lord of Heaven and Earth (Deuteronomy 3:23–4:40; Luke 10:21–24)

Luke 10:21. In that same hour he rejoiced in the Holy Spirit and said, "I thank thee, Father, Lord of heaven and earth, that thou hast hidden these things from the wise and understanding and revealed them to babes; yea, Father, for such was thy gracious will. 22. All things have been delivered to me by my Father; and no one knows who the Son is except the Father, or who the Father is except the Son and any one to whom the Son chooses to reveal him." 23. Then turning to the disciples he said privately, "Blessed are the eyes which see what you see! 24. For I tell you that many prophets and kings desired to see what you see, and did not see it, and to hear what you hear, and did not hear it."

"At that time" Moses prayed to God, like unto whom there is none "in heaven or on earth" (Deuteronomy 2:23–24). In the Q saying Luke 10:21–24 // Matthew 11:25–27, perhaps itself suggested originally by the Deuteronomy text, Jesus "at that time" praised his divine Father, "Lord of heaven and earth" (Luke 10:21). Jesus thanks God for revealing his wonders to "children," not to the ostensibly "wise." In some measure this reflects the wording of Deuteronomy 4:6, where Moses reminds his people to cherish the commandments as their *wisdom* and 4:9, there he bids them tell what they have seen to their *children*. The Deuteronomic recital of all the wonders their eyes have seen (4:3, 9, 34, 36) may have inspired the Q blessing of the disciples for having seen the saving acts the ancient prophets and kings did not live to witness (Luke 10:23–24). Only note the antitypological reversal of Deuteronomy: for Q it is the ancients who failed to see what their remote heirs did see.

The Christ Myth Theory And Its Problems

The rest of the Q passage, Luke 10:22, may derive from Akhenaten's *Hymn to the Sun*: "O Aten, no man knoweth thee, save for thy son Akhenaten."

d. The Commandments and the Shema (Deuteronomy 5:1–33; 6:1–25; Luke 10:25–27)

Deuteronomy 5:1. And Moses summoned all Israel, and said to them, "Hear, O Israel, the statutes and the ordinances which I speak in your hearing this day, and you shall learn them and be careful to do them. 2. The LORD our God made a covenant with us in Horeb. 3. Not with our fathers did the LORD make this covenant, but with us, who are all of us here alive this day. 4. The LORD spoke with you face to face at the mountain, out of the midst of the fire, 5. while I stood between the LORD and you at that time, to declare to you the word of the LORD; for you were afraid because of the fire, and you did not go up into the mountain. He said: 6. 'I am the LORD your God, who brought you out of the land of Egypt, out of the house of bondage. 7. You shall have no other gods before me. 8. You shall not make for yourself a graven image, or any likeness of anything that is in heaven above, or that is on the earth beneath, or that is in the water under the earth; 9. you shall not bow down to them or serve them; for I the LORD your God am a jealous God, visiting the iniquity of the fathers upon the children to the third and fourth generation of those who hate me, 10. but showing steadfast love to thousands of those who love me and keep my commandments. 11. You shall not take the name of the LORD your God in vain: for the LORD will not hold him guiltless who takes his name in vain. 12. Observe the sabbath day, to keep it holy, as the LORD your God commanded you. 13. Six days you shall labor, and do all your work; 14. but the seventh day is a sabbath to the LORD your God; in it you shall not do any work, you, or your son, or your daughter, or your manservant, or your maidservant, or your ox, or your ass, or any of your cattle, or the sojourner who is within your gates, that your manservant and your maidservant may rest as well as you. 15. You shall remember that you were a servant in the land of Egypt, and the LORD your

God brought you out thence with a mighty hand and an outstretched arm; therefore the LORD your God commanded you to keep the sabbath day. 16. Honor your father and your mother, as the LORD your God commanded you; that your days may be prolonged, and that it may go well with you, in the land which the LORD your God gives you. 17. You shall not kill. 18. Neither shall you commit adultery. 19. Neither shall you steal. 20. Neither shall you bear false witness against your neighbor. 21. Neither shall you covet your neighbor's wife; and you shall not desire your neighbor's house, his field, or his manservant, or his maidservant, his ox, or his ass, or anything that is your neighbor's. 22. These words the LORD spoke to all your assembly at the mountain out of the midst of the fire, the cloud, and the thick darkness, with a loud voice; and he added no more. And he wrote them upon two tables of stone, and gave them to me. 23. And when you heard the voice out of the midst of the darkness, while the mountain was burning with fire, you came near to me, all the heads of your tribes, and your elders; 24. and you said, 'Behold, the LORD our God has shown us his glory and greatness, and we have heard his voice out of the midst of the fire; we have this day seen God speak with man and man still live. 25. Now therefore why should we die? For this great fire will consume us; if we hear the voice of the LORD our God any more, we shall die. 26. For who is there of all flesh, that has heard the voice of the living God speaking out of the midst of fire, as we have, and has still lived? 27. Go near, and hear all that the LORD our God will say; and speak to us all that the LORD our God will speak to you; and we will hear and do it.' 28. And the LORD heard your words, when you spoke to me; and the LORD said to me, 'I have heard the words of this people, which they have spoken to you; they have rightly said all that they have spoken. 29. Oh that they had such a mind as this always, to fear me and to keep all my commandments, that it might go well with them and with their children for ever! 30. Go and say to them, "Return to your tents." 31. But you, stand here by me, and I will tell you all the commandment and the statutes and the ordinances which you shall teach them, that they may do them in the land which I give them to possess. 32. You shall be careful to do therefore as the LORD your God

The Christ Myth Theory And Its Problems

has commanded you; you shall not turn aside to the right hand or to the left. 33. You shall walk in all the way which the LORD your God has commanded you, that you may live, and that it may go well with you, and that you may live long in the land which you shall possess.

Deuteronomy 6:1. "Now this is the commandment, the statutes and the ordinances which the LORD your God commanded me to teach you, that you may do them in the land to which you are going over, to possess it; 2. that you may fear the LORD your God, you and your son and your son's son, by keeping all his statutes and his commandments, which I command you, all the days of your life; and that your days may be prolonged. 3. Hear therefore, O Israel, and be careful to do them; that it may go well with you, and that you may multiply greatly, as the LORD, the God of your fathers, has promised you, in a land flowing with milk and honey. 4. Hear, O Israel: The LORD our God is one LORD; 5. and you shall love the LORD your God with all your heart, and with all your soul, and with all your might. 6. And these words which I command you this day shall be upon your heart; 7. and you shall teach them diligently to your children, and shall talk of them when you sit in your house, and when you walk by the way, and when you lie down, and when you rise. 8. And you shall bind them as a sign upon your hand, and they shall be as frontlets between your eyes. 9. And you shall write them on the door-posts of your house and on your gates. 10. And when the LORD your God brings you into the land which he swore to your fathers, to Abraham, to Isaac, and to Jacob, to give you, with great and goodly cities, which you did not build, 11. and houses full of all good things, which you did not fill, and cisterns hewn out, which you did not hew, and vineyards and olive trees, which you did not plant, and when you eat and are full, 12. then take heed lest you forget the LORD, who brought you out of the land of Egypt, out of the house of bondage. 13. You shall fear the LORD your God; you shall serve him, and swear by his name. 14. You shall not go after other gods, of the gods of the peoples who are round about you; 15. for the LORD your God in the midst of you is a jealous God; lest the anger of the LORD your God be kindled against you, and he destroy you from off the face of the earth. 16. You shall not put the LORD your God to the test, as you tested him at Massah. 17. You shall diligently keep the commandments of the LORD your God, and his testimonies, and his statutes, which he has commanded you. 18. And you shall do what is right and good in the sight of the LORD, that it may go well with you, and that you may go in and take possession of the good land which the LORD swore to give to your fathers 19. by thrusting out all your enemies from before you, as the LORD has promised. 20. When your son asks you in time to come, 'What is the meaning of the testimonies and the statutes and the ordinances which the LORD our God has commanded you?' 21. then you shall say to your son, 'We were Pharaoh's slaves in Egypt; and the LORD brought us out of Egypt with a mighty hand; 22. and the LORD showed signs and wonders, great and grievous, against Egypt and against Pharaoh and all his household, before our eyes; 23. and he brought us out from there, that he might bring us in and give us the land which he swore to give to our fathers. 24. And the LORD commanded us to do all these statutes, to fear the LORD our God, for our good always, that he might preserve us alive, as at this day. 25. And it will be righteousness for us, if we are careful to do all this commandment before the LORD our God, as he has commanded us.'

Luke 5:25. And behold, a lawyer stood up to put him to the test, saying, "Teacher, what shall I do to inherit eternal life?" 26. He said to him, "What is written in the law? How do you read?" 27. And he answered, "You shall love the Lord your God with all your heart, and with all your soul, and with all your strength, and with all your mind; and your neighbor as yourself."

These two chapters of Deuteronomy present both the Decalogue and the Shema (the great creedal declaration of Jewish monotheism). Luke presents but the tip of the iceberg when Jesus asks a scribe what he considers the gist of the Torah and the man replies with the Shema (adding Leviticus 19:18). Here Luke has rewritten Mark 12:28–34, which did list some of the Ten Commandments, albeit loosely. Luke's closing comment, "Do this and you will live," comes from Leviticus 18:5, "You shall therefore keep my statutes and my ordinances, by doing which a man shall live."

The Christ Myth Theory And Its Problems

It is not a case of Jesus being quoted as quoting the Leviticus text; rather it is evident Luke has refashioned the unacknowledged Levitical original into a fictive saying of Jesus.

e. (No) Mercy to the Foreigner (Deuteronomy 7:1–26; Luke 10:29–37)

Deuteronomy 7:1. When the LORD your God brings you into the land which you are entering to take possession of it, and clears away many nations before you, the Hittites, the Girgashites, the Amorites, the Canaanites, the Perizzites, the Hivites, and the Jebusites, seven nations greater and mightier than yourselves, 2. and when the LORD your God gives them over to you, and you defeat them; then you must utterly destroy them; you shall make no covenant with them, and show no mercy to them. 3. You shall not make marriages with them, giving your daughters to their sons or taking their daughters for your sons. 4. For they would turn away your sons from following me, to serve other gods; then the anger of the LORD would be kindled against you, and he would destroy you quickly. 5. But thus shall you deal with them: you shall break down their altars, and dash in pieces their pillars, and hew down their Asherim, and burn their graven images with fire. 6. "For you are a people holy to the LORD your God; the LORD your God has chosen you to be a people for his own possession, out of all the peoples that are on the face of the earth. 7. It was not because you were more in number than any other people that the LORD set his love upon you and chose you, for you were the fewest of all peoples; 8. but it is because the LORD loves you, and is keeping the oath which he swore to your fathers, that the LORD has brought you out with a mighty hand, and redeemed you from the house of bondage, from the hand of Pharaoh king of Egypt. 9. Know therefore that the LORD your God is God, the faithful God who keeps covenant and steadfast love with those who love him and keep his commandments, to a thousand generations, 10. and requites to their face those who hate him, by destroying them; he will not be slack with him who hates him, he will requite him to his face. 11. You shall therefore be careful to do the commandment, and the statutes, and the ordinances, which

I command you this day. 12. "And because you hearken to these ordinances, and keep and do them, the LORD your God will keep with you the covenant and the steadfast love which he swore to your fathers to keep; 13. he will love you, bless you, and multiply you; he will also bless the fruit of your body and the fruit of your ground, your grain and your wine and your oil, the increase of your cattle and the young of your flock, in the land which he swore to your fathers to give you. 14. You shall be blessed above all peoples; there shall not be male or female barren among you, or among your cattle. 15. And the LORD will take away from you all sickness; and none of the evil diseases of Egypt, which you knew, will he inflict upon you, but he will lay them upon all who hate you. 16. And you shall destroy all the peoples that the LORD your God will give over to you, your eye shall not pity them; neither shall you serve their gods, for that would be a snare to you. 17. "If you say in your heart, 'These nations are greater than I; how can I dispossess them?' 18. you shall not be afraid of them, but you shall remember what the LORD your God did to Pharaoh and to all Egypt, 19. the great trials which your eyes saw, the signs, the wonders, the mighty hand, and the outstretched arm, by which the LORD your God brought you out; so will the LORD your God do to all the peoples of whom you are afraid. 20. Moreover the LORD your God will send hornets among them, until those who are left and hide themselves from you are destroyed. 21. You shall not be in dread of them; for the LORD your God is in the midst of you, a great and terrible God. 22. The LORD your God will clear away these nations before you little by little; you may not make an end of them at once, lest the wild beasts grow too numerous for you. 23. But the LORD your God will give them over to you, and throw them into great confusion, until they are destroyed. 24. And he will give their kings into your hand, and you shall make their name perish from under heaven; not a man shall be able to stand against you, until you have destroyed them. 25. The graven images of their gods you shall burn with fire; you shall not covet the silver or the gold that is on them, or take it for yourselves, lest you be ensnared by it; for it is an abomination to the LORD your God. 26. And you shall not bring an abominable thing into your house, and become accursed like it; you shall utterly detest and abhor it; for it is an accursed thing.

The Christ Myth Theory And Its Problems

> Luke 10:29. But he, desiring to justify himself, said to Jesus, "And who is my neighbor?" 30. Jesus replied, "A man was going down from Jerusalem to Jericho, and he fell among robbers, who stripped him and beat him, and departed, leaving him half dead. 31. Now by chance a priest was going down that road; and when he saw him he passed by on the other side. 32. So likewise a Levite, when he came to the place and saw him, passed by on the other side. 33. But a Samaritan, as he journeyed, came to where he was; and when he saw him, he had compassion, 34. and went to him and bound up his wounds, pouring on oil and wine; then he set him on his own beast and brought him to an inn, and took care of him. 35. And the next day he took out two denarii and gave them to the innkeeper, saying, 'Take care of him; and whatever more you spend, I will repay you when I come back.' 36. Which of these three, do you think, proved neighbor to the man who fell among the robbers?" 37. He said, "The one who showed mercy on him." And Jesus said to him, "Go and do likewise."

To Deuteronomy's stern charge to eradicate the heathen of Canaan without mercy (7:2), itself a piece of long-after-the-fact jingoism, not an historical incitement to genocide, Luke poses this uniquely Lukan parable, that of the Good Samaritan, in which the despised foreigner/heretic is filled with mercy (Luke 10:33) for a Jew victimized by thugs. Like all the uniquely Lukan parables, this one is the evangelist's own creation. By contrast, Matthew knew of no such sympathy of Jesus for Samaritans (Matthew 10:5). This parable, like the uniquely Lukan narrative of the Samaritan leper (17:1–19), reflects Luke's interest in the Samaritan mission (Acts 8:5–17 *ff.*), shared with John (John 4:1–42). The parable of the Good Samaritan, like most of Luke's, is a genuine story, no mere extended simile, and it compares two type-characters, in this case the indifferent priest and Levite versus the compassionate Samaritan, just as Luke elsewhere contrasts the Prodigal and his straight-arrow brother, Lazarus and the Rich Man, the Pharisee and the Publican, the Widow and the Unjust Judge, Mary and Martha, the Importunate Friend and

his Unresponsive Friend. The contrast with Moses' mercilessness
is of a piece with Luke's Elijah/Jesus contrast in Luke 9:54, where
Jesus shows mercy to Samaritans, unlike his counterpart Elijah who
barbecued them (2 Kings 1:10, 12).

f. Not by Bread Alone (Deuteronomy 8:1–3; Luke 10:38–42)

Deuteronomy 8:1. "All the commandment which I command you
this day you shall be careful to do, that you may live and multiply,
and go in and possess the land which the LORD swore to give to your
fathers. 2. And you shall remember all the way which the LORD your
God has led you these forty years in the wilderness, that he might
humble you, testing you to know what was in your heart, whether
you would keep his commandments, or not. 3. And he humbled
you and let you hunger and fed you with manna, which you did not
know, nor did your fathers know; that he might make you know that
man does not live by bread alone, but that man lives by everything
that proceeds out of the mouth of the LORD.

Luke 10:38. Now as they went on their way, he entered a village;
and a woman named Martha received him into her house. 39. And
she had a sister called Mary, who sat at the Lord's feet and listened
to his teaching. 40. But Martha was distracted with much serving;
and she went to him and said, "Lord, do you not care that my sister
has left me to serve alone? Tell her then to help me." 41. But the
Lord answered her, "Martha, Martha, you are anxious and troubled
about many things; 42. one thing is needful. Mary has chosen the
good portion, which shall not be taken away from her."

Luke has created the story of Mary and Martha as a commentary on
Deuteronomy 8:3, "Man does not live by bread alone, but... man
lives by every word that proceeds from the mouth of the LORD."
Luke has opposed the contemplative Mary who hungers for Jesus'
("the Lord's") "words" with the harried Martha ("Lady of the
House," hence an ideal, fictive character), whose preoccupation

191

with domestic chores, especially cooking and serving, threatens to crowd out spiritual sustenance (*cf.* Deuteronomy 8:11–14). It is not unlikely that the passage is intended to comment in some way on the issue of celibate women and their various roles in the church of Luke's day (*cf.* 1 Timothy 5:3–16).

g. *Fatherly Provision (Deuteronomy 8:4–20; Luke 11:1–13)*

Luke 11:1. He was praying in a certain place, and when he ceased, one of his disciples said to him, "Lord, teach us to pray, as John taught his disciples." 2. And he said to them, "When you pray, say: "Father, hallowed be thy name. Thy kingdom come. 3. Give us each day our daily bread; 4. and forgive us our sins, for we ourselves forgive every one who is indebted to us; and lead us not into temptation." 5. And he said to them, "Which of you who has a friend will go to him at midnight and say to him, 'Friend, lend me three loaves; 6. for a friend of mine has arrived on a journey, and I have nothing to set before him'; 7. and he will answer from within, 'Do not bother me; the door is now shut, and my children are with me in bed; I cannot get up and give you anything'? 8. I tell you, though he will not get up and give him anything because he is his friend, yet because of his importunity he will rise and give him whatever he needs. 9. And I tell you, Ask, and it will be given you; seek, and you will find; knock, and it will be opened to you. 10. For every one who asks receives, and he who seeks finds, and to him who knocks it will be opened. 11. What father among you, if his son asks for a fish, will instead of a fish give him a serpent; 12. or if he asks for an egg, will give him a scorpion? 13. If you then, who are evil, know how to give good gifts to your children, how much more will the heavenly Father give the Holy Spirit to those who ask him!"

Deuteronomy compares the discipline meted out to Israel by God with the training a father gives his son, then reminds the reader of the fatherly provision of God for his children in the wilderness and promises security, prosperity, and sufficient food in their new land. Luke matches this with his version of the Q Lord's Prayer, sharing the same general themes of fatherly provision and asking God to spare his children "the test," recalling the "tests" sent upon the people by God in the wilderness. Luke adds the Q material about God giving good gifts to his children (Luke 11:9–13//Matthew 7:7–11), certainly the point of the Deuteronomy text, together with his own parable of the Importunate Friend, which (like its twin, the parable of the Unjust Judge, 18:1–8, also uniquely Lukan) urges the seeker not to give up praying "How long, O Lord?"

h. Vanquishing Strong Enemies (Deuteronomy 9:1–10:11; Luke 11:14–26)

Luke 11:14. Now he was casting out a demon that was dumb; when the demon had gone out, the dumb man spoke, and the people marveled. 15. But some of them said, "He casts out demons by Beelzebul, the prince of demons"; 16. while others, to test him, sought from him a sign from heaven. 17. But he, knowing their thoughts, said to them, "Every kingdom divided against itself is laid waste, and a divided household falls. 18. And if Satan also is divided against himself, how will his kingdom stand? For you say that I cast out demons by Beel-zebul. 19. And if I cast out demons by Beel-zebul, by whom do your sons cast them out? Therefore they shall be your judges. 20. But if it is by the finger of God that I cast out demons, then the kingdom of God has come upon you. 21. When a strong man, fully armed, guards his own palace, his goods are in peace; 22. but when one stronger than he assails him and overcomes him, he takes away his armor in which he trusted, and divides his spoil. 23. He who is not with me is against me, and he who does not gather with me scatters. 24. When the unclean spirit has gone out of a man, he passes through waterless places seeking rest; and finding none he says, 'I will return to my house from which I came.' 25. And when he comes he finds it swept and put in order. 26. Then he goes and brings seven other spirits more evil than himself, and they enter and dwell there; and the last state of that man becomes worse than the first."

The Christ Myth Theory And Its Problems

On the eve of Israel's entrance into the land, Moses reviews their fathers' sorry history of rebellion yet promises victory over stronger nations including the half-mythical Anakim, descended from a race of titans. Later haggadah made these Sons of Anak descendants of the miscegenation between the Sons of God understood as fallen angels and the daughters of men (Genesis 6:1–6). Thus it is no surprise for Luke to discern a parallel between this text and the Q/Mark account of the Beel-zebul controversy, where Jesus exorcises demons (fallen angels?), despoiling Satan, the strong man, of his captives. According to the analogy, the poor hapless demoniacs are like the promised land of Canaan, while the demons possessing the wretches are like the Anakim holding the land until God casts them out because of their wickedness, even though like Satan their chief they are far stronger than any mere mortal.

As noted in the discussion of the Beel-zebul controversy in Mark (section B.11 above), the Q comparison of Jesus with the "sons" of the Pharisees and his own use of "the finger of God" to cast out demons must derive from a midrash upon the Exodus contest between Moses and the priest-magicians of Pharaoh. But Luke anchors it precisely at this point because of the Deuteronomic reference to "the finger of God" writing the commandments upon the stone tables. The "strong man" element of both Markan and Q versions of the Beel-zebul episode also originated elsewhere, in Isaiah 49:24, but it seemed to fit the Deuteronomic reference to stronger nations here. That is, though the Beel-zebul controversy does stem from scriptural sources, it was pre-Lukan material which he then placed at a particular point in his sequence because of its perceived analogy to the piece of Deuteronomy he needed to parallel.

i. Impartiality and Clear Vision (Deuteronomy 10:12–11:32; Luke 11:27–36)

Deuteronomy 10:12. "And now, Israel, what does the LORD your God require of you, but to fear the LORD your God, to walk in all his ways, to love him, to serve the LORD your God with all your heart and with all your soul, 13. and to keep the commandments and statutes of the LORD, which I command you this day for your good? 14. Behold, to the LORD your God belong heaven and the heaven of heavens, the earth with all that is in it; 15. yet the LORD set his heart in love upon your fathers and chose their descendants after them, you above all peoples, as at this day. 16. Circumcise therefore the foreskin of your heart, and be no longer stubborn. 17. For the LORD your God is God of gods and Lord of lords, the great, the mighty, and the terrible God, who is not partial and takes no bribe. 18. He executes justice for the fatherless and the widow, and loves the sojourner, giving him food and clothing. 19. Love the sojourner therefore; for you were sojourners in the land of Egypt. 20. You shall fear the LORD your God; you shall serve him and cleave to him, and by his name you shall swear. 21. He is your praise; he is your God, who has done for you these great and terrible things which your eyes have seen. 22. Your fathers went down to Egypt seventy persons; and now the LORD your God has made you as the stars of heaven for multitude.

Deuteronomy 11:1. "You shall therefore love the LORD your God, and keep his charge, his statutes, his ordinances, and his commandments always. 2. And consider this day (since I am not speaking to your children who have not known or seen it), consider the discipline of the LORD your God, his greatness, his mighty hand and his outstretched arm, 3. his signs and his deeds which he did in Egypt to Pharaoh the king of Egypt and to all his land; 4. and what he did to the army of Egypt, to their horses and to their chariots; how he made the water of the Red Sea overflow them as they pursued after you, and how the LORD has destroyed them to this day; 5. and what he did to you in the wilderness, until you came to this place; 6. and what he did to Dathan and Abiram the sons of Eliab, son of Reuben; how the earth opened its mouth and swallowed them up, with their households, their tents, and every living thing that followed them, in the midst of all Israel; 7. for your eyes have seen all the great work of the LORD which he did. 8. You shall therefore keep all the commandment which I command you this day, that you may be strong, and go in and take possession of the land which you are going over to possess, 9. and that you may live long in the land which the LORD swore to your fathers to give to them and to their descendants, a land flowing with milk and honey. 10. For the land which you are entering to take possession of it is not like the land of Egypt, from which you have come, where you sowed your seed and watered it with your feet, like a garden of vegetables; 11. but the land which you are going over to possess is a land of hills and valleys, which drinks water by the rain from heaven, 12. a land which the LORD your God cares for; the eyes of the LORD your God are always upon it, from the beginning of the year to the end of the year. 13. "And if you will obey my commandments which I command you this day, to love the LORD your God, and to serve him with all your heart and with all your soul, 14. he will give the rain for your land in its season, the early rain and the later rain, that you may gather in your grain and your wine and your oil. 15. And he will give grass in your fields for your cattle, and you shall eat and be full. 16. Take heed lest your heart be deceived, and you turn aside and serve other gods and worship them, 17. and the anger of the LORD be kindled against you, and he shut up the heavens, so that there be no rain, and the land yield no fruit, and you perish quickly off the good land which the LORD gives you. 18. "You shall therefore lay up these words of mine in your heart and in your soul; and you shall bind them as a sign upon your hand, and they shall be as frontlets between your eyes. 19. And you shall teach them to your children, talking of them when you are sitting in your house, and when you are walking by the way, and when you lie down, and when you rise. 20. And you shall write them upon the doorposts of your house and upon your gates, 21. that your days and the days of your children may be multiplied in the land which the LORD swore to your fathers to give them, as long as the heavens are above the earth. 22. For if you will be careful to do all this commandment which I command you to do, loving the LORD your God, walking in all his ways, and cleaving to him, 23. then the LORD will drive out all these nations before you, and you will dispossess nations greater and mightier than yourselves. 24. Every place on which the sole of your foot treads shall be yours; your territory shall be from the wilderness and Lebanon and from the River, the river Euphrates, to the western sea. 25. No man shall be able to stand against you; the LORD your God will lay the fear of you and the dread of you upon all the land that you shall tread, as he promised you. 26. "Behold, I set before you this day a blessing and a curse: 27. the blessing, if you obey the commandments of the LORD your God, which I command you this day, 28. and the curse, if you do not obey the commandments of the LORD your God, but turn aside from the way which I command you this day, to go after other gods which you have not known. 29. And when the LORD your God brings you into the land which you are entering to take possession of it, you shall set the blessing on Mount Gerizim and the curse on Mount Ebal. 30. Are they not beyond the Jordan, west of the road, toward the going down of the sun, in the land of the Canaanites who live in the Arabah, over against Gilgal, beside the oak of Moreh? 31. For you are to pass over the Jordan to go in to take possession of the land which the LORD your God gives you; and when you possess it and live in it, 32. you shall be careful to do all the statutes and the ordinances which I set before you this day.

Luke 11:27. As he said this, a woman in the crowd raised her voice and said to him, "Blessed is the womb that bore you, and the breasts that you sucked!" 28. But he said, "Blessed rather are those who hear the word of God and keep it!" 29. When the crowds were increasing, he began to say, "This generation is an evil generation; it seeks a sign, but no sign shall be given to it except the sign of Jonah. 30. For as Jonah became a sign to the men of Nineveh, so will the Son of man be to this generation. 31. The queen of the South will arise at the judgment with the men of this generation and condemn them; for she came from the ends of the earth to hear the wisdom of Solomon, and behold, something greater than Solomon is here. 32. The men of Nineveh will arise at the judgment with this generation and condemn it; for they repented at the preaching of Jonah, and behold, something greater than Jonah is here. 33. No one after lighting a lamp puts it in a cellar or under a bushel, but on a stand, that those who enter may see the light. 34. Your eye is the lamp of your body; when your eye is sound, your whole body is full of light; but when it is not sound, your body is full of darkness. 35. Therefore be careful lest the light in you be darkness. 36. If then your whole body is full of light, having no part dark, it will be wholly bright, as when a lamp with its rays gives you light."

Again, Luke has done his best to match up previously existing gospel traditions with themes from the next bit of Deuteronomy. To the exaltation of God as impartial to all, no respecter of persons, Luke matches (and, not unlikely, creates on the basis of Mark 3:31–35) an anecdote showing that not even the mother of Jesus is higher in God's sight than the average faithful disciple.

Corresponding to the warning for Israel not to repeat the sins of the Canaanites and so repeat their doom, Luke matches the Q material on how even ancient non-Israelites better appreciated the divine witness of their day than did Jesus' contemporaries (Luke 11:29–32 // Matthew 12:39–42).

Finally, Luke places the Q material about the eye being the lamp of the body (Luke 11:34–36 // Matthew 6:22–23) in tandem with Deuteronomy 11:18's charge to cherish the commandments in one's heart and to place them as frontlets on one's forehead. Presumably, the unstated middle term of transition from the one image to the other was Psalms 19:8 ("the precepts of the LORD are right, rejoicing the heart; the commandment of the LORD is pure, enlightening the eyes") or perhaps Psalms 119:105 ("Your word is a lamp for my feet and a light for my path.").

j. Clean and Unclean (Deuteronomy 12:1–16; Luke 11:37–12:12)

Deuteronomy 12:1. "These are the statutes and ordinances which you shall be careful to do in the land which the LORD, the God of your fathers, has given you to possess, all the days that you live upon the earth. 2. You shall surely destroy all the places where the nations whom you shall dispossess served their gods, upon the high mountains and upon the hills and under every green tree; 3. you shall tear down their altars, and dash in pieces their pillars, and burn their Asherim with fire; you shall hew down the graven images of their gods, and destroy their name out of that place. 4. You shall not do so to the LORD your God. 5. But you shall seek the place which the LORD your God will choose out of all your tribes to put his name and make his habitation there; thither you shall go, 6. and thither you shall bring your burnt offerings and your sacrifices, your tithes and the offering that you present, your votive offerings, your freewill offerings, and the firstlings of your herd and of your flock; 7. and there you shall eat before the LORD your God, and you shall rejoice, you and your households, in all that you undertake, in which the LORD your God has blessed you. 8. You shall not do according to all that we are doing here this day, every man doing whatever is right in his own eyes; 9. for you have not as yet come to the rest and to the inheritance which the LORD your God gives you. 10. But when you go over the Jordan, and live in the land which the LORD your God gives you to inherit, and when he gives you rest from all your enemies round about, so that you live in safety, 11. then to the place which the LORD your God will choose, to make his name dwell there, thither you shall bring all that I command you: your burnt offerings and your sacrifices, your tithes and the offering that you present, and all your votive offerings which you vow to the LORD. 12. And you shall rejoice before the LORD your God, you and your sons and your daughters, your menservants and your maidservants, and the Levite that is within your towns, since he has no portion or inheritance with you. 13. Take heed that you do not offer your burnt offerings at every place that you see; 14. but at the place which the LORD will choose in one of your tribes, there you shall offer your burnt offerings, and there you shall do all that I am commanding you. 15. "However, you may slaughter and eat flesh within any of your towns, as much as you desire, according to the blessing of the LORD your God which he has given you; the unclean and the clean may eat of it, as of the gazelle and as of the hart. 16. Only you shall not eat the blood; you shall pour it out upon the earth like water.

Luke 11:37. While he was speaking, a Pharisee asked him to dine with him; so he went in and sat at table. 38. The Pharisee was astonished to see that he did not first wash before dinner. 39. And the Lord said to him, "Now you Pharisees cleanse the outside of the cup and of the dish, but inside you are full of extortion and wickedness. 40. You fools! Did not he who made the outside make the inside also? 41. But give for alms those things which are within; and behold, everything is clean for you. 42. But woe to you Pharisees! for you tithe mint and rue and every herb, and neglect justice and the love of God; these you ought to have done, without neglecting the others. 43. Woe to you Pharisees! for you love the best seat in the synagogues and salutations in the market places. 44. Woe to you! for you are like graves which are not seen, and men walk over them without knowing it." 45. One of the lawyers answered him, "Teacher, in saying this you reproach us also." 46. And he said, "Woe to you lawyers also! for you load men with burdens hard to bear, and you yourselves do not touch the burdens with one of your fingers. 47. Woe to you! for you build the tombs of the prophets whom your fathers killed. 48. So you are witnesses and consent to the deeds of your fathers; for they killed them, and you build their tombs. 49. Therefore also the Wisdom of God said, 'I will send them prophets and apostles, some of whom they will kill and persecute,' 50. that the blood of all the prophets, shed from the foundation of the world, may be required of this generation, 51. from the blood of Abel to the blood of Zechariah, who perished between the altar and the sanctuary. Yes, I tell you, it shall be required of this generation. 52. Woe to you lawyers! for you have taken away the key of knowledge; you did not enter yourselves, and you hindered those who were entering." 53. As he went away from there, the scribes and the Pharisees began to press him hard, and to provoke him to speak of many things, 54. lying in wait for him, to catch at something he might say.

12:1. In the meantime, when so many thousands of the multitude had gathered together that they trod upon one another, he began to say to his disciples first, "Beware of the leaven of the Pharisees, which is hypocrisy. 2. Nothing is covered up that will not be revealed, or hidden that will not be known. 3. Therefore whatever you have said in the dark shall be heard in the light, and what you have whispered in private rooms shall be proclaimed upon the housetops. 4. I tell you, my friends, do not fear those who kill the body, and after that have no more that they can do. 5. But I will warn you whom to fear: fear him who, after he has killed, has power to cast into hell; yes, I tell you, fear him! 6. Are not five sparrows sold for two pennies? And not one of them is forgotten before God. 7. Why, even the hairs of your head are all numbered. Fear not; you are of more value than many sparrows. 8. And I tell you, every one who acknowledges me before men, the Son of man also will acknowledge before the angels of God; 9. but he who denies me before men will be denied before the angels of God. 10. And every one who speaks a word against the Son of man will be forgiven; but he who blasphemes against the Holy Spirit will not be forgiven. 11. And when they bring you before the synagogues and the rulers and the authorities, do not be anxious how or what you are to answer or what you are to say; 12. for the Holy Spirit will teach you in that very hour what you ought to say."

The substance of Deuteronomy 12:1–14's prohibition of sacrifice on the traditional high places and restriction of worship to the (Jerusalem) Temple, finds no real echo in Luke, who waits to apply roughly parallel material to Deuteronomy 12:15–16, which allows for the preparation and eating of meat as a purely secular process at home. (*i.e.*, no longer must every eating of meat be part of a sacrifice, traditionally offered at home.) Here we read that clean and unclean alike may eat meat in this way, and Luke has seized on this rubric to introduce the Q material on the inability of the Pharisees to tell the real difference between clean and unclean (Luke 11:39–52//Matthew 23:4–7, 23–36, as well as Mark 7:1–5 (//Luke 11:37–38) and the Q material Matthew 10:26–35//Luke 12:2–9. The connection is merely that of catchwords (particular words used, often fortuitously, in both passages, regardless of context or even denotation) as proves also to be the case when we notice that the Q phrase "the blood of all the prophets shed" (Luke 11:50//Matthew 23:35, "all the righteous blood shed on earth") just barely recalls the Deuteronomic phrase, "you shall not eat the blood; you shall pour it out upon the earth" (12:16).

k. Inheritance (Deuteronomy 12:17–32; Luke 12:13–34)

Deuteronomy 12:17. You may not eat within your towns the tithe of your grain or of your wine or of your oil, or the firstlings of your herd or of your flock, or any of your votive offerings which you vow, or your freewill offerings, or the offering that you present; 18. but you shall eat them before the LORD your God in the place which the LORD your God will choose, you and your son and your daughter, your manservant and your maidservant, and the Levite who is within your towns; and you shall rejoice before the LORD your God in all that you undertake. 19. Take heed that you do not forsake the Levite as long as you live in your land. 20. "When the LORD your God enlarges your territory, as he has promised you, and you say, 'I will eat flesh,' because you crave flesh, you may eat as much flesh as you desire. 21. If the place which the LORD your God will choose to put his name there is too far from you, then you may kill any of your herd or your flock, which the LORD has given you, as I have commanded you; and you may eat within your towns as much as you desire. 22. Just as the gazelle or the hart is eaten, so you may eat of it; the unclean and the clean alike may eat of it. 23. Only be sure that you do not eat the blood; for the blood is the life, and you shall not eat the life with the flesh. 24. You shall not eat it; you shall pour it out upon the earth like water. 25. You shall not eat it; that all may go well with you and with your children after you, when you do what is right in the sight of the LORD. 26. But the holy things which are due from you, and your votive offerings, you shall take, and you shall go to the place which the LORD will choose, 27. and offer your burnt offerings, the flesh and the blood, on the altar of the LORD your God; the blood of your sacrifices shall be poured out on the altar of the LORD your God, but the flesh you may eat. 28. Be careful to heed all these words which I command you, that it may go well with you and with your children after you for ever, when you do what is good and right in the sight of the LORD your God. 29. "When the LORD your God cuts off before you the nations whom you go in to dispossess, and you dispossess them and dwell in their land, 30. take heed that you be not ensnared to follow them, after they have been destroyed before you, and that you do not inquire about their gods, saying, 'How did these nations serve their gods? — that I also may do likewise.' 31. You shall not do so to the LORD your God; for every abominable thing which the LORD hates they have done for their gods; for they even burn their sons and their daughters in the fire to their gods. 32. "Everything that I command you you shall be careful to do; you shall not add to it or take from it.

Luke 12:13. One of the multitude said to him, "Teacher, bid my brother divide the inheritance with me." 14. But he said to him, "Man, who made me a judge or divider over you?" 15. And he said to them, "Take heed, and beware of all covetousness; for a man's life does not consist in the abundance of his possessions." 16. And he told them a parable, saying, "The land of a rich man brought forth plentifully; 17. and he thought to himself, 'What shall I do, for I have nowhere to store my crops?' 18. And he said, 'I will do this: I will pull down my barns, and build larger ones; and there I will store all my grain and my goods. 19. And I will say to my soul, Soul, you have ample goods laid up for many years; take your ease, eat, drink, be merry.' 20. But God said to him, 'Fool! This night your soul is required of you; and the things you have prepared, whose will they be?' 21. So is he who lays up treasure for himself, and is not rich toward God." 22. And he said to his disciples, "Therefore I tell you, do not be anxious about your life, what you shall eat, nor about your body, what you shall put on. 23. For life is more than food, and the body more than clothing. 24. Consider the ravens: they neither sow nor reap, they have neither storehouse nor barn, and yet God feeds them. Of how much more value are you than the birds! 25. And which of you by being anxious can add a cubit to his span of life? 26. If then you are not able to do as small a thing as that, why are you anxious about the rest? 27. Consider the lilies, how they grow; they neither toil nor spin; yet I tell you, even Solomon in all his glory was not arrayed like one of these. 28. But if God so clothes the grass which is alive in the field today and tomorrow is thrown into the oven, how much more will he clothe you, O men of little faith! 29. And do not seek what you are to eat and what you are to drink, nor be of anxious mind. 30. For all the nations of the world seek these things; and your Father knows that you need them. 31. Instead, seek his kingdom, and these things shall be yours as well. 32. "Fear not, little flock, for it is your Father's good pleasure to give you the kingdom. 33. Sell your possessions, and give alms; provide yourselves with purses that do not grow old, with a treasure in the heavens that does not fail, where no thief approaches and no moth destroys. 34. For where your treasure is, there will your heart be also.

Approached by someone in the crowd who seeks to have Jesus adjudicate an inheritance dispute, Jesus refuses to play the role of arbiter, one commonly played by itinerant Near Eastern holy men (who, having no earthly connections or interests, the theory went, must be impartial as well as inspired). His retort, "Man, who made me a judge or divider over you?" (Luke 12:14), echoes and no doubt derives from Exodus 2:14a, "Who made you a prince and a judge over us?" Moses had sought to interfere in his people's worldly troubles, only to be rebuffed. Jesus' intervention is sought, but he rebuffs the request. Here is another Moses-Jesus antitype, at the expense of Moses, since one greater than Moses is ostensibly here.

The ensuing parable, Luke 12:16–21, seems to be based on Ecclesiastes/Qoheleth 6:–2, "a man to whom God gives wealth, possessions, and honor, so that he lacks nothing of all he desires, yet God does not give him the opportunity to enjoy them, but a stranger enjoys them." See also Ecclesiastes/Qoheleth 2:18–21.

l. Severe Punishments (Deuteronomy 13:1–11; Luke 12:35–53)

Deuteronomy 13:1. "If a prophet arises among you, or a dreamer of dreams, and gives you a sign or a wonder, 2. and the sign or wonder which he tells you comes to pass, and if he says, 'Let us go after other gods,' which you have not known, 'and let us serve them,' 3. you shall not listen to the words of that prophet or to that dreamer of dreams; for the LORD your God is testing you, to know whether you love the LORD your God with all your heart and with all your soul. 4. You shall walk after the LORD your God and fear him, and keep his commandments and obey his voice, and you shall serve him and cleave to him. 5. But that prophet or that dreamer of dreams shall be put to death, because he has taught rebellion against the LORD your God, who brought you out of the land of Egypt and redeemed you out of the house of bondage, to make you leave the way in which the LORD your God commanded you to walk. So you shall purge the evil from the midst of you. 6. "If your brother, the son of your mother, or your son, or your daughter, or the wife of your bosom, or your friend who is as your own soul, entices you secretly, saying, 'Let us go and serve other gods,' which neither you nor your fathers have known, 7. some of the gods of the peoples that are round about you, whether near you or far off from you, from the one end of the earth to the other, 8. you shall not yield to him or listen to him, nor shall your eye pity him, nor shall you spare him, nor shall you conceal him; 9. but you shall kill him; your hand shall be first against him to put him to death, and afterwards the hand of all the people. 10. You shall stone him to death with stones, because he sought to draw you away from the LORD your God, who brought you out of the land of Egypt, out of the house of bondage. 11. And all Israel shall hear, and fear, and never again do any such wickedness as this among you.

Luke 12:35. "Let your loins be girded and your lamps burning, 36. and be like men who are waiting for their master to come home from the marriage feast, so that they may open to him at once when he comes and knocks. 37. Blessed are those servants whom the master finds awake when he comes; truly, I say to you, he will gird himself and have them sit at table, and he will come and serve them. 38. If he comes in the second watch, or in the third, and finds them so, blessed are those servants! 39. But know this, that if the householder had known at what hour the thief was coming, he would not have left his house to be broken into. 40. You also must be ready; for the Son of man is coming at an unexpected hour." 41. Peter said, "Lord, are you telling this parable for us or for all?" 42. And the Lord said, "Who then is the faithful and wise steward, whom his master will set over his household, to give them their portion of food at the proper time? 43. Blessed is that servant whom his master when he comes will find so doing. 44. Truly, I say to you, he will set him over all his possessions. 45. But if that servant says to himself, 'My master is delayed in coming,' and begins to beat the menservants and the maidservants, and to eat and drink and get drunk, 46. the master of that servant will come on a day when he does not expect him and at an hour he does not know, and will punish him, and put him with the unfaithful. 47. And that servant who knew his master's will, but did not make ready or act according to his will, shall receive a severe beating. 48. But he who did not know, and did what deserved a beating, shall receive a light beating. Every one to whom much is given, of him will much be required; and of him to whom men commit much they will demand the more. 49. "I came to cast fire upon the earth; and would that it were already kindled! 50. I have a baptism to be baptized with; and how I am constrained until it is accomplished! 51. Do you think that I have come to give peace on earth? No, I tell you, but rather division; 52. for henceforth in one house there will be five divided, three against two and two against three; 53. they will be divided, father against son and son against father, mother against daughter and daughter against her mother, mother-in-law against her daughter-in-law and daughter-in-law against her mother-in-law."

Deuteronomy takes aim at false prophets, prophets of rival deities, warning Israel not to heed their seductions. It is God who has sent them, and not the deities whom they think themselves to be speaking for. God is in this way testing Israel's fidelity. To match this theme, Luke has chosen to use parable material based on the Markan Apocalypse (Mark 13:34–37); note Luke's expansion of Mark 13:37, "What I say to you I say to all: watch," into a dialogue between Jesus and Peter: "Peter said, 'Lord, are you telling this parable for us, or for all?'" (Luke 12:41 *ff.*). The Markan parable had the departing master set tasks for his servants; hence they functioned as tests to prove how well they would perform. For Luke, connecting the parable with Deuteronomy, the church's job while their Lord is away in heaven is to remain faithful to his name as against the blandishments of other saviors and prophets (Luke 21:8).

Since Deuteronomy does not exempt even family members who may have fallen under the spell of forbidden gods (13:6–11), Luke adds the Q saying Luke 51–53//Matthew 10:34–36, largely based on an unacknowledged quotation of Micah 7:6, "for the son treats the father with contempt, the daughter rises up against her mother, the daughter-in-law against her mother-in-law; a man's enemies are men of his own household."

m. Judgment on this People (Deuteronomy 13:12–18; Luke 12:54–13:5)

Deuteronomy 13:12. "If you hear in one of your cities, which the LORD your God gives you to dwell there, 13. that certain base fellows have gone out among you and have drawn away the inhabitants of the city, saying, 'Let us go and serve other gods,' which you have not known, 14. then you shall inquire and make search and ask diligently; and behold, if it be true and certain that such an abominable thing has been done among you, 15. you shall surely put the inhabitants of that city to the sword, destroying it utterly, all who are in it and its cattle, with the edge of the sword. 16. You shall gather all its spoil into the midst of its open square, and burn the city and all its spoil with fire, as a whole burnt offering to the LORD your God; it shall be a heap for ever, it shall not be built again. 17. If one of the devoted things shall cleave to your hand; that the LORD may turn from the fierceness of his anger, and show you mercy, and have compassion on you, and multiply you, as he swore to your fathers, 18. if you obey the voice of the LORD your God, keeping all his commandments which I command you this day, and doing what is right in the sight of the LORD your God.

Luke 12:54. He also said to the multitudes, "When you see a cloud rising in the west, you say at once, 'A shower is coming'; and so it happens. 55. And when you see the south wind blowing, you say, 'There will be scorching heat'; and it happens. 56. You hypocrites! You know how to interpret the appearance of earth and sky; but why do you not know how to interpret the present time? 57. "And why do you not judge for yourselves what is right? 58. As you go with your accuser before the magistrate, make an effort to settle with him on the way, lest he drag you to the judge, and the judge hand you over to the officer, and the officer put you in prison. 59. I tell you, you will never get out till you have paid the very last copper."

Luke 13:1. There were some present at that very time who told him of the Galileans whose blood Pilate had mingled with their sacrifices. 2. And he answered them, "Do you think that these Galileans were worse sinners than all the other Galileans, because they suffered thus? 3. I tell you, No; but unless you repent you will all likewise perish. 4. Or those eighteen upon whom the tower in Siloam fell and killed them, do you think that they were worse offenders than all the others who dwelt in Jerusalem? 5. I tell you, No; but unless you repent you will all likewise perish."

Whole cities lapsing into pagan apostasy are to be eliminated, destroyed, Deuteronomy mandates, with nothing ever to be rebuilt on the desolation, so seriously does Israel's God take spiritual infidelity. No less gravely does the Lukan Jesus take the lack of repentance on the part of Galileans and Jews. Past tragedies and atrocities will be seen as the mere beginning of the judgments to fall like the headsman's ax on an unrepentant people. Of course, the Lukan Jesus prophesies long after the fact, referring to the bloody triumph of Rome in Galilee and Judea culminating in 73 CE.

n. The Third Year (Deuteronomy 14:28; Luke 13:6–9)

Deuteronomy 14:28. At the end of every three years you shall bring forth all the tithe of your produce in the same year, and lay it up within your towns.

Luke 13:6. And he told this parable: "A man had a fig tree planted in his vineyard; and he came seeking fruit on it and found none. 7. And he said to the vinedresser, 'Lo, these three years I have come seeking fruit on this fig tree, and I find none. Cut it down; why should it use up the ground?' 8. And he answered him, 'Let it alone, sir, this year also, till I dig about it and put on manure. 19. And if it bears fruit next year, well and good; but if not, you can cut it down.'"

Luke has seen fit to skip Deuteronomy 14:1–31, a list of clean and unclean animals, and 14:22–27, which repeats 12:17–31.

Deuteronomy 14 stipulates a tithe of one's produce every three years. Luke uses the law as a springboard for a retrospective parable accounting for the Roman defeat of Judea and Galilee, continuing his discussion from the preceding pericopae. The people of God is like a barren fig tree which has disappointed its owner three years straight, yielding nothing to offer God. The vinedresser pleads for an extra year's grace period before the fruitless tree should be uprooted. Luke's point: don't say God didn't go the second mile before exacting judgment.

o. Release of the Bondslave (Deuteronomy 15:1–18; Luke 13:10–21)

Deuteronomy 15:1. "At the end of every seven years you shall grant a release. 2. And this is the manner of the release: every creditor shall release what he has lent to his neighbor; he shall not exact it of his neighbor, his brother, because the LORD's release has been proclaimed. 3. Of a foreigner you may exact it; but whatever of yours is with your brother your hand shall release. 4. But there will be no poor among you (for the LORD will bless you in the land which the LORD your God gives you for an inheritance to possess), 5. if only you will obey the voice of the LORD your God, being careful to do all this commandment which I command you this day. 6. For the LORD your God will bless you, as he promised you, and you shall lend to many nations, but you shall not borrow; and you shall rule over many nations, but they shall not rule over you. 7. "If there is among you a poor man, one of your brethren, in any of your towns within your land which the LORD your God gives you, you shall not harden your heart or shut your hand against your poor brother, 8. but you shall open your hand to him, and lend him sufficient for his need, whatever it may be. 9. Take heed lest there be a base thought in your heart, and you say, 'The seventh year, the year of release is near,' and your eye be hostile to your poor brother, and you give him nothing, and he cry to the LORD against you, and it be sin in you. 10. You shall give to him freely, and your heart shall not be grudging when you give to him; because for this the LORD your God will bless you in all your work and in all that you undertake. 11. For the poor will never cease out of the land; therefore I command you, You shall open wide your hand to your brother, to the needy and to the poor, in the land. 12. "If your brother, a Hebrew man, or a Hebrew woman, is sold to you, he shall serve you six years, and in the seventh year you shall let him go free from you. 13. And when you let him go free from you, you shall not let him go empty-handed; 14. you shall furnish him liberally out of your flock, out of your threshing floor, and out of your wine press; as the LORD your God has blessed you, you shall give to him. 15. You shall remember that you were a slave in the land of Egypt, and the LORD your God redeemed you; therefore I command you this today. 16. But if he says to you, 'I will not go out from you,' because he loves you and your household, since he fares well with you, 17. then you shall take an awl, and thrust it through his ear into the door, and he shall be your bondman for ever. And to your bondwoman you shall do likewise. 18. It shall not seem hard to you, when you let him go free from you; for at half the cost of a hired servant he has served you six years. So the LORD your God will bless you in all that you do.

Luke 13:10. Now he was teaching in one of the synagogues on the sabbath. 11. And there was a woman who had had a spirit of infirmity for eighteen years; she was bent over and could not fully straighten herself. 12. And when Jesus saw her, he called her and said to her, "Woman, you are freed from your infirmity." 13. And he laid his hands upon her, and immediately she was made straight, and she praised God. 14. But the ruler of the synagogue, indignant because Jesus had healed on the sabbath, said to the people, "There are six days on which work ought to be done; come on those days and be healed, and not on the sabbath day." 15. Then the Lord answered him, "You hypocrites! Does not each of you on the sabbath untie his ox or his ass from the manger, and lead it away to water it? 16. And ought not this woman, a daughter of Abraham whom Satan bound for eighteen years, be loosed from this bond on the sabbath day?" 17. As he said this, all his adversaries were put to shame; and all the people rejoiced at all the glorious things that were done by him. 18. He said therefore, "What is the kingdom of God like? And to what shall I compare it? 19. It is like a grain of mustard seed which a man took and sowed in his garden; and it grew and became a tree, and the birds of the air made nests in its branches." 20. And again he said, "To what shall I compare the kingdom of God? 21. It is like leaven which a woman took and hid in three measures of flour, till it was all leavened."

Deuteronomy calls for the cancellation of debts in the seventh year, a kind of release from bondage, as well as freedom for bondservants. The last case stipulated is that of the bondwoman (Deuteronomy 15:17). From this last, Luke has developed his story of a woman, a bondservant of Satan for eighteen years by virtue of a bent spine, being freed by Jesus.

Luke and Matthew, each using both Q and Mark, have inherited the Markan story of the man with the withered hand (Mark 3:1–6), a controversy about healing on the sabbath, and the Q saying "Which of you, having one sheep [Luke: "a son/ass or ox"] that falls into a pit [Luke: "well"] on the sabbath, will not lay hold of it and pull it out?" (Matthew 12:11//Luke 1414:5). Matthew inserted the Q saying into the Markan story, while Luke chose to duplicate Mark's story of the man with the withered hand as the healing of the man with dropsy (Luke 14:1–6) and to insert the Q saying into it at the equivalent spot. But he also created the story of the woman with the bent spine, basing it on a paraphrase of the same Q saying, adapted to the case suggested by Deuteronomy, the release from a bond, so that the parallel cited becomes *releasing* a farm animal from its *tether* on the sabbath.

p. Go to Jerusalem (Deuteronomy 16:1–17; 17:7; Luke 13:22–35)

Deuteronomy commands thrice-yearly pilgrimage to the Jerusalem Temple, and the Lukan Jesus declares nothing will deflect his inexorable progress to Jerusalem to die there as a prophet must. As the declaration presupposes the Lukan redactional agenda of the Central Section itself, as well as the distinctive Lukan prophet Christology, the saying is itself redactional.

Deuteronomy 16:1. "Observe the month of Abib, and keep the passover to the LORD your God; for in the month of Abib the LORD your God brought you out of Egypt by night. 2. And you shall offer the passover sacrifice to the LORD your God, from the flock or the herd, at the place which the LORD will choose, to make his name dwell there. 3. You shall eat no leavened bread with it; seven days you shall eat it with unleavened bread, the bread of affliction — for you came out of the land of Egypt in hurried flight — that all the days of your life you may remember the day when you came out of the land of Egypt. 4. No leaven shall be seen with you in all your territory for seven days; nor shall any of the flesh which you sacrifice on the evening of the first day remain all night until morning. 5. You may not offer the passover sacrifice within any of your towns which the LORD your God gives you; 6. but at the place which the LORD your God will choose, to make his name dwell in it, there you shall offer the passover sacrifice, in the evening at the going down of the sun, at the time you came out of Egypt. 7. And you shall boil it and eat it at the place which the LORD your God will choose; and in the morning you shall turn and go to your tents. 8. For six days you shall eat unleavened bread; and on the seventh day there shall be a solemn assembly to the LORD your God; you shall do no work on it. 9. "You shall count seven weeks; begin to count the seven weeks from the time you first put the sickle to the standing grain. 10.

Then you shall keep the feast of weeks to the LORD your God with the tribute of a freewill offering from your hand, which you shall give as the LORD your God blesses you; 11. and you shall rejoice before the LORD your God, you and your son and your daughter, your manservant and your maidservant, the Levite who is within your towns, the sojourner, the fatherless, and the widow who are among you, at the place which the LORD your God will choose, to make his name dwell there. 12. You shall remember that you were a slave in Egypt; and you shall be careful to observe these statutes. 13. "You shall keep the feast of booths seven days, when you make your ingathering from your threshing floor and your wine press; 14. you shall rejoice in your feast, you and your son and your daughter, your manservant and your maidservant, the Levite, the sojourner, the fatherless, and the widow who are within your towns. 15. For seven days you shall keep the feast to the LORD your God at the place which the LORD will choose; because the LORD your God will bless you in all your produce and in all the work of your hands, so that you will be altogether joyful. 16. "Three times a year all your males shall appear before the LORD your God at the place which he will choose: at the feast of unleavened bread, at the feast of weeks, and at the feast of booths. They shall not appear before the LORD empty-handed; 17. every man shall give as he is able, according to the blessing of the LORD your God which he has given you.

Deuteronomy 17:1. "You shall not sacrifice to the LORD your God an ox or a sheep in which is a blemish, any defect whatever; for that is an abomination to the LORD your God. 2. "If there is found among you, within any of your towns which the LORD your God gives you, a man or woman who does what is evil in the sight of the LORD your God, in transgressing his covenant, 3. and has gone and served other gods and worshiped them, or the sun or the moon or any of the host of heaven, which I have forbidden, 4. and it is told you and you hear of it; then you shall inquire diligently, and if it is true and certain that such an abominable thing has been done in Israel, 5. then you shall bring forth to your gates that man or woman who has done this evil thing, and you shall stone that man or woman to death with stones. 6. On the evidence of two witnesses or of three witnesses he that is to die shall be put to death; a person shall not be put to death on the evidence of one witness. 7. The hand of the witnesses shall be first against him to put him to death, and afterward the hand of all the people. So you shall purge the evil from the midst of you.

Luke 13:22. He went on his way through towns and villages, teaching, and journeying toward Jerusalem. 23. And some one said to him, "Lord, will those who are saved be few?" And he said to them, 24. "Strive to enter by the narrow door; for many, I tell you, will seek to enter and will not be able. 25. When once the householder has risen up and shut the door, you will begin to stand outside and to knock at the door, saying, 'Lord, open to us.' He will answer you, 'I do not know where you come from.' 26. Then you will begin to say, 'We ate and drank in your presence, and you taught in our streets.' 27. But he will say, 'I tell you, I do not know where you come from; depart from me, all you workers of iniquity!' 28. There you will weep and gnash your teeth, when you see Abraham and Isaac and Jacob and all the prophets in the kingdom of God and you yourselves thrust out. 29. And men will come from east and west, and from north and south, and sit at table in the kingdom of God. 30. And behold, some are last who will be first, and some are first who will be last." 31. At that very hour some Pharisees came, and said to him, "Get away from here, for Herod wants to kill you." 32. And he said to them, "Go and tell that fox, 'Behold, I cast out demons and perform cures today and tomorrow, and the third day I finish my course. 33. Nevertheless I must go on my way today and tomorrow and the day following; for it cannot be that a prophet should perish away from Jerusalem.' 34. O Jerusalem, Jerusalem, killing the prophets and stoning those who are sent to you! How often would I have gathered your children together as a hen gathers her brood under her wings, and you would not! 35. Behold, your house is forsaken. And I tell you, you will not see me until you say, 'Blessed is he who comes in the name of the Lord!'"

q. Righteous Judges; Remembering the Poor (Deuteronomy 16:18–20; 17:8–18; Luke 14:1–14)

Deuteronomy 16:18. "You shall appoint judges and officers in all your towns which the LORD your God gives you, according to your tribes; and they shall judge the people with righteous judgment. 19. You shall not pervert justice; you shall not show partiality; and you shall not take a bribe, for a bribe blinds the eyes of the wise and subverts the cause of the righteous. 20. Justice, and only justice, you shall follow, that you may live and inherit the land which the LORD your God gives you.

Deuteronomy 17:8. "If any case arises requiring decision between one kind of homicide and another, one kind of legal right and another, or one kind of assault and another, any case within your towns which is too difficult for you, then you shall arise and go up to the place which the LORD your God will choose, 9. and coming to the Levitical priests, and to the judge who is in office in those days, you shall consult them, and they shall declare to you the decision. 10. Then you shall do according to what they declare to you from that place which the LORD will choose; and you shall be careful to do according to all that they direct you; 11. according to the instructions which they give you, and according to the decision which they pronounce to you, you shall do; you shall not turn aside from the verdict which they declare to you, either to the right hand or to the left. 12. The man who acts presumptuously, by not obeying the priest who stands to minister there before the LORD your God, or the judge, that man shall die; so you shall purge the evil from Israel. 13. And all the people shall hear, and fear, and not act presumptuously again. 14. When you come to the land which the LORD your God gives you, and you possess it and dwell in it, and then say, 'I will set a king over me, like all the nations that are round about me'; 15. you may indeed set as king over you him whom the LORD your God will choose. One from among your brethren you shall set as king over you; you may not put a foreigner over you, who is not your brother. 16. Only he must not multiply horses for himself, or cause the people to return to Egypt in order to multiply horses, since the LORD has said to you, 'You shall never return that way again.' 17. And he shall not multiply wives for himself, lest his heart turn away; nor shall he greatly multiply for himself silver and gold. 18. "And when he sits on the throne of his kingdom, he shall write for himself in a book a copy of this law, from that which is in the charge of the Levitical priests;

Luke 14:1. One sabbath when he went to dine at the house of a ruler who belonged to the Pharisees, they were watching him. 2. And behold, there was a man before him who had dropsy. 3. And Jesus spoke to the lawyers and Pharisees, saying, "Is it lawful to heal on the sabbath, or not?" 4. But they were silent. Then he took him and healed him, and let him go. 5. And he said to them, "Which of you, having a son or an ox that has fallen into a well, will not immediately pull him out on a sabbath day?" 6. And they could not reply to this. 7. Now he told a parable to those who were invited, when he marked how they chose the places of honor, saying to them, 8. "When you are invited by any one to a marriage feast, do not sit down in a place of honor, lest a more eminent man than you be invited by him; 9. and he who invited you both will come and say to you, 'Give place to this man,' and then you will begin with shame to take the lowest place. 10. But when you are invited, go and sit in the lowest place, so that when your host comes he may say to you, 'Friend, go up higher'; then you will be honored in the presence of all who sit at table with you. 11. For every one who exalts himself will be humbled, and he who humbles himself will be exalted." 12. He said also to the man who had invited him, "When you give a dinner or a banquet, do not invite your friends or your brothers or your kinsmen or rich neighbors, lest they also invite you in return, and you be repaid. 13. But when you give a feast, invite the poor, the maimed, the lame, the blind, 14. and you will be blessed, because they cannot repay you. You will be repaid at the resurrection of the just."

The fit here is loose, but the connection is nonetheless evident. Deuteronomy is concerned with people accepting the oracular verdict of priests and judges, and with limiting the prerogatives of the king. Luke, apparently simply to secure the parallel, has set his scene in the house of a "ruler" and tells the story of the dropsical man to exalt Jesus' judgment over that of the scribes.

The rest of the Lukan passage refers back to the preceding Deuteronomic text, 16:14, whose ranking of various guests enables Luke to tack on a piece of table etiquette borrowed from Proverbs 25:6–7 ("Do not put yourself forward in the king's presence or stand in the place of the great; for it is better to be told, 'Come up here,' than to be put lower in the presence of the prince."). The specific inclusion of the widow and the sojourner in Deuteronomy 16:14 has inspired Luke's admonition to invite the poor, the maimed, the blind, and the lame instead of one's friends and relatives. While the Lukan version may seem a more radical suggestion than Deuteronomy's inclusion of the poor alongside one's family, it actually tends toward minimizing the discomfort of the situation: one can bask in playing the benefactor to one's poor clients without having to embarrass one's fellow sophisticates with the crude manners of the poor at the same table (though in 1 Corinthians 11:18–22 we learn some "solved" the problem by segregating the two groups at the same event!).

r. Excuses before Battle (Deuteronomy 20; Luke 14:15–35)

Deuteronomy 1:1. "When you go forth to war against your enemies, and see horses and chariots and an army larger than your own, you shall not be afraid of them; for the LORD your God is with you, who brought you up out of the land of Egypt. 2. And when you draw near to the battle, the priest shall come forward and speak to the people, 3. and shall say to them, 'Hear, O Israel, you draw near this day to battle against your enemies: let not your heart faint; do not fear, or tremble, or be in dread of them; 4. for the LORD your God is he that goes with you, to fight for you against your enemies, to give you the victory.' 5. Then the officers shall speak to the people, saying, 'What man is there that has built a new house and has not dedicated it? Let him go back to his house, lest he die in the battle and another man dedicate it. 6. And what man is there that has planted a vineyard and has not enjoyed its fruit? Let him go back to his house, lest he die in the battle and another man enjoy its fruit. 7. And what man is there that has betrothed a wife and has not taken her? Let him go back to his house, lest he die in the battle and another man take her.' 8. And the officers shall speak further to the people, and say, 'What man is there that is fearful and fainthearted? Let him go back to his house, lest the heart of his fellows melt as his heart.' 9. And when the officers have made an end of speaking to the people, then commanders shall be appointed at the head of the people. 10. "When you draw near to a city to fight against it, offer terms of peace to it. 11. And if its answer to you is peace and it opens to you, then all the people who are found in it shall do forced labor for you and shall serve you. 12. But if it makes no peace with you, but makes war against you, then you shall besiege it; 13. and when the LORD your God gives it into your hand you shall put all its males to the sword, 14. but the women and the little ones, the cattle, and everything else in the city, all its spoil, you shall take as booty for yourselves; and you shall enjoy the spoil of your enemies, which the LORD your God has given you. 15. Thus you shall do to all the cities which are very far from you, which are not cities of the nations here. 16. But in the cities of these peoples that the LORD your God gives you for an inheritance, you shall save alive nothing that breathes, 17. but you shall utterly destroy them, the Hittites and the Amorites, the Canaanites and the Perizzites, the Hivites and the Jebusites, as the LORD your God has commanded; 18. that they may not teach you to do according to all their abominable practices which they have done in the service of their gods, and so to sin against the LORD your God. 19. "When you besiege a city for a long time, making war against it in order to take it, you shall not destroy its trees by wielding an axe against them; for you may eat of them, but you shall not cut them down. Are the trees in the field men that they should be besieged by you? 20. Only the trees which you know are not trees for food you may destroy and cut down that you may build siegeworks against the city that makes war with you, until it falls.

Luke 14:15. When one of those who sat at table with him heard this, he said to him, "Blessed is he who shall eat bread in the kingdom of God!" 16. But he said to him, "A man once gave a great banquet, and invited many; 17. and at the time for the banquet he sent his servant to say to those who had been invited, 'Come; for all is now ready.' 18. But they all alike began to make excuses. The first said to him, 'I have bought a field, and I must go out and see it; I pray you, have me excused.' 19. And another said, 'I have bought five yoke of oxen, and I go to examine them; I pray you, have me excused.' 20. And another said, 'I have married a wife, and therefore I cannot come.' 21. So the servant came and reported this to his master. Then the householder in anger said to his servant, 'Go out quickly to the streets and lanes of the city, and bring in the poor and maimed and blind and lame.' 22. And the servant said, 'Sir, what you commanded has been done, and still there is room.' 23. And the master said to the servant, 'Go out to the highways and hedges, and compel people to come in, that my house may be filled. 24. For I tell you, none of those men who were invited shall taste my banquet'." 25. Now great multitudes accompanied him; and he turned and said to them, 26. "If any one comes to me and does not hate his own father and mother and wife and children and brothers and sisters, yes, and even his own life, he cannot be my disciple. 27. Whoever does not bear his own cross and come after me, cannot be my disciple. 28. For which of you, desiring to build a tower, does not first sit down and count the cost, whether he has enough to complete it? 29. Otherwise, when he has laid a foundation, and is not able to finish, all who see it begin to mock him, 30. saying, 'This man began to build, and was not able to finish.' 31. Or what king, going to encounter another king in war, will not sit down first and take counsel whether he is able with ten thousand to meet him who comes against him with twenty thousand? 32. And if not, while the other is yet a great way off, he sends an embassy and asks terms of peace. 33. So therefore, whoever of you does not renounce all that he has cannot be my disciple. 34. "Salt is good; but if salt has lost its taste, how shall its saltness be restored? 35. It is fit neither for the land nor for the dunghill; men throw it away. He who has ears to hear, let him hear."

219

Luke has omitted Deuteronomy 19's discussions of cities of refuge and of false witnesses.

Commentators commonly note the similarity between the excuses offered by those invited to the great supper in Q (Matthew 22:1–10//Luke 14:16–24), implicitly sneered at by the narrator, and those circumstances exempting an Israelite from serving in holy war in Deuteronomy 20, building a new house, planting a new vineyard, getting married. One can only suspect that Q represents a tightening up of what were considered by an enthusiastic sect to be too lax standards, just as the divorce rules were tightened by Christians. (Those standards were now seen to apply, no doubt, to the spiritual crusade of evangelism.)

The parable of the Great Supper is pre-Lukan, as it appears already in Q (Luke 14:16–24//Matthew 22:1–10 *ff.*) and the Gospel of Thomas, saying 64. It is very likely an adaptation of the rabbinic story of the tax-collector Bar-Majan, who sought to climb socially by inviting the respectable rich to a great feast. All, refusing to fall for the ploy, begged off, whereupon the tax-collector decided to share the food with the poor that it not go to waste. This act of charity did win him a stately funeral but was not enough to mitigate his punishment in hell (Jerusalem Talmud, *Hagigah*, II, 77d).

The rest of Luke 14:25–33 has perched here because of the treatment of warfare in the parallel section of Deuteronomy, though the connection is really only that of catchwords, as often in the Central Section.

s. Rights of the First-Born versus Wicked Sons (Deuteronomy 21:15–22:4; Luke 15)

Deuteronomy 21:15. "If a man has two wives, the one loved and the other disliked, and they have borne him children, both the loved and the disliked, and if the first-born son is hers that is disliked, 16. then on the day when he assigns his possessions as an inheritance to his sons, he may not treat the son of the loved as the first-born in preference to the son of the disliked, who is the first-born, 17. but he shall acknowledge the first-born, the son of the disliked, by giving him a double portion of all that he has, for he is the first issue of his strength; the right of the first-born is his. 18. "If a man has a stubborn and rebellious son, who will not obey the voice of his father or the voice of his mother, and, though they chastise him, will not give heed to them, 19. then his father and his mother shall take hold of him and bring him out to the elders of his city at the gate of the place where he lives, 20. and they shall say to the elders of his city, 'This our son is stubborn and rebellious, he will not obey our voice; he is a glutton and a drunkard.' 21. Then all the men of the city shall stone him to death with stones; so you shall purge the evil from your midst; and all Israel shall hear, and fear. 22. "And if a man has committed a crime punishable by death and he is put to death, and you hang him on a tree, 23. his body shall not remain all night upon the tree, but you shall bury him the same day, for a hanged man is accursed by God; you shall not defile your land which the LORD your God gives you for an inheritance.

Deuteronomy 22:1. "You shall not see your brother's ox or his sheep go astray, and withhold your help from them; you shall take them back to your brother. 2. And if he is not near you, or if you do not know him, you shall bring it home to your house, and it shall be with you until your brother seeks it; then you shall restore it to him. 3. And so you shall do with his ass; so you shall do with his garment; so you shall do with any lost thing of your brother's, which he loses and you find; you may not withhold your help. 4. You shall not see your brother's ass or his ox fallen down by the way, and withhold your help from them; you shall help him to lift them up again.

Luke 15:1. Now the tax collectors and sinners were all drawing near to hear him. 2. And the Pharisees and the scribes murmured, saying, "This man receives sinners and eats with them." 3. So he told them this parable: 4. "What man of you, having a hundred sheep, if he has lost one of them, does not leave the ninety-nine in the wilderness, and go after the one which is lost, until he finds it? 5. And when he has found it, he lays it on his shoulders, rejoicing. 6. And when he comes home, he calls together his friends and his neighbors, saying to them, 'Rejoice with me, for I have found my sheep which was lost.' 7. Just so, I tell you, there will be more joy in heaven over one sinner who repents than over ninety-nine righteous persons who need no repentance. 8. "Or what woman, having ten silver coins, if she loses one coin, does not light a lamp and sweep the house and seek diligently until she finds it? 9. And when she has found it, she calls together her friends and neighbors, saying, 'Rejoice with me, for I have found the coin which I had lost.' 10. Just so, I tell you, there is joy before the angels of God over one sinner who repents." 11. And he said, "There was a man who had two sons; 12. and the younger of them said to his father, 'Father, give me the share of property that falls to me.' And he divided his living between them. 13. Not many days later, the younger son gathered all he had and took his journey into a far country, and there he squandered his property in loose living. 14. And when he had spent everything, a great famine arose in that country, and he began to be in want. 15. So he went and joined himself to one of the citizens of that country, who sent him into his fields to feed swine. 16. And he would gladly have fed on the pods that the swine ate; and no one gave him anything. 17. But when he came to himself he said, 'How many of my father's hired servants have bread enough and to spare, but I perish here with hunger! 18. I will arise and go to my father, and I will say to him, "Father, I have sinned against heaven and before you; 19. I am no longer worthy to be called your son; treat me as one of your hired servants".' 20. And he arose and came to his father. But while he was yet at a distance, his father saw him and had compassion, and ran and embraced him and kissed him. 21. And the son said to him, 'Father, I have sinned against heaven and before you; I am no longer worthy to be called your son.' 22. But the father said to his servants, 'Bring quickly the best robe, and put it on him; and put a ring on his hand, and shoes on his feet; 23. and bring the fatted calf and kill it, and let us eat and make merry; 24. for this my son was dead, and is alive again; he was lost, and is found.' And they began to make merry. 25. "Now his elder son was in the field; and as he came and drew near to the house, he heard music and dancing. 26. And he called one of the servants and asked what this meant. 27. And he said to him, 'Your brother has come, and your father has killed the fatted calf, because he has received him safe and sound.' 28. But he was angry and refused to go in. His father came out and entreated him, 29. but he answered his father, 'Lo, these many years I have served you, and I never disobeyed your command; yet you never gave me a kid, that I might make merry with my friends. 30. But when this son of yours came, who has devoured your living with harlots, you killed for him the fatted calf!' 31. And he said to him, 'Son, you are always with me, and all that is mine is yours. 32. It was fitting to make merry and be glad, for this your brother was dead, and is alive; he was lost, and is found.'"

Luke leaves aside Deuteronomy 21:1–14, the treatment of corpses and female captives.

The great parable of the Prodigal Son is Luke's own creation, as is evident not only from its juxtaposition of two type-characters, but also from the uniquely Lukan device of character introspection in a tight spot: "What shall I do? I shall..." The Prodigal, having painted himself into a corner, reflects, "I will arise and go to my father, and I will say to him..." (15:18), just as the Unjust Judge, exasperated, "said to himself, 'I will vindicate her...'" (Luke 18:4–5). Similarly, the Dishonest Steward "said to himself, 'What shall I do? ... I have decided what to do...'" (16:3–4). And the Rich Fool "thought to himself, 'What shall I do...? I will do this...'" (12:17–18)

The parable's theme was suggested to him by the Deuteronomic treatment of sons and their inheritance in 21:15–21. Luke has combined the elements of division of property between a pair of sons, the possibility of favoring the wrong one, and the problem of a rebellious son who shames his family. But, typically, Luke replaces the sternness of the original legal provision (no doubt because he writes for a Diaspora audience for whom some of these laws can no longer apply) with an example of mercy. Here the rebellious son is accepted in love, not executed.

The Christ Myth Theory And Its Problems

Though the basic inspiration of the parable comes thus from Deuteronomy, Luke owes the building blocks to another source, the *Odyssey*. The character of the Prodigal was suggested by both the long-absent Odysseus himself and his son Telemachus who returns from his own long quest to find his father. Both the parable's elements of wandering far from home and of the father-son reunion stem from here. The cavorting of the Prodigal with loose women in far lands was suggested by Odysseus' dalliance with Calypso. But the motif of the Prodigal's having "devoured [his father's] estate with loose living" is based on the similar judgment passed more than once by Telemachus and Eumaeus on the "gang of profligates" infesting Odysseus' estate during his absence, the suitors.

The Prodigal's taking a job as a swine herder, a galling "transformation" for a Jew, may reflect the transformation of Odysseus' men into swine by Circe, especially since the hungry Prodigal would like to fill his stomach with the pods the pigs eat, *i.e.*, act like a pig. Then again, his working as a swineherd may stem from Eumaeus' having been one. The latter's frequent characterization as a "righteous swineherd" may have suggested the depiction of the Prodigal as a repentant swineherd. The return of the Prodigal was suggested by the return of Odysseus, but no less of Telemachus, who together share the same actantial role. The Prodigal hopes to enter his father's household as a mere slave, whereas the returning Odysseus actually disguises himself as a slave on his own estate. The glad reception afforded the Prodigal by his father recalls the reunion of Odysseus and Telemachus, also father and son, but even more the reunion of Telemachus and Eumaeus, his father's faithful servant: "The last words were not out of his mouth when his [Odysseus'] own son appeared in the gateway. Eumaeus jumped up in amazement, and the bowls in which he had been busy mixing the sparkling wine tumbled out of his grasp. He ran forward to meet his young master. He kissed his lovely eyes and then kissed his right hand and his left, while the tears streamed down his cheeks. Like a fond father welcoming his son after nine years abroad, his only son, the apple of his eye and the centre of all his anxious cares, the admirable swineherd threw his arms around Prince Telemachus and showered kisses on him as though he had just escaped from death."

Next, Luke splits Odysseus into two characters, the two brothers. The elder son also returns from being away, albeit only out in the field (the scene of conflict between another famous pair of brothers, Cain and Abel). Returning, he is dismayed, like Odysseus, to discover a feast in progress. (Here we must note also the echo of Exodus 32:18, "It is not the sound of shouting for victory, or the sound of the cry of defeat, but the sound of... *singing* that I hear!") It is a feast in honor of a profligate, as the elder brother is quick to point out, just like that of Penelope's suitors. And, just as their feast is predicated upon the assumption of Odysseus' death, the Prodigal's father explains to the elder son that they must feast since the Prodigal was dead and has now returned alive, as Odysseus is about to do.

Deuteronomy 22:1–4 stipulates all manner of lost objects which must be returned if found, just as Luke 15:3–7 and 8–10 provide examples of lost things zealously sought and found. The first of these is an appropriate Q parable, that of the Lost Sheep (see also Matthew 18:10–14), while the second, the parable of the Lost Coin, is presumably Luke's own creation, reminiscent of the uniquely Lukan parable of the Yeast (3:20–21) and his story of Martha (10:38–42), each with its busy housekeeper.

t. Masters, Slaves, Money, and Divorce (Deuteronomy 23:15–24:4; Luke 16:1–18)

Deuteronomy 23:15. "You shall not give up to his master a slave who has escaped from his master to you; 16. he shall dwell with you, in your midst, in the place which he shall choose within one of your towns, where it pleases him best; you shall not oppress him. 17. "There shall be no cult prostitute of the daughters of Israel, neither shall there be a cult prostitute of the sons of Israel. 18. You shall not bring the hire of a harlot, or the wages of a dog, into the house of the LORD your God in payment for any vow; for both of these are an abomination to the LORD your God. 19. "You shall not lend upon interest to your brother, interest on money, interest on victuals, interest on anything that is lent for interest. 20. To a foreigner you may lend upon interest, but to your brother you shall not lend upon interest; that the LORD your God may bless you in all that you undertake in the land which you are entering to take possession of it. 21. "When you make a vow to the LORD your God, you shall not be slack to pay it; for the LORD your God will surely require it of you, and it would be sin in you. 22. But if you refrain from vowing, it shall be no sin in you. 23. You shall be careful to perform what has passed your lips, for you have voluntarily vowed to the LORD your God what you have promised with your mouth. 24. "When you go into your neighbor's vineyard, you may eat your fill of grapes, as many as you wish, but you shall not put any in your vessel. 25. When you go into your neighbor's standing grain, you may pluck the ears with your hand, but you shall not put a sickle to your neighbor's standing grain.

Deuteronomy 24:1. "When a man takes a wife and marries her, if then she finds no favor in his eyes because he has found some indecency in her, and he writes her a bill of divorce and puts it in her hand and sends her out of his house, and she departs out of his house, 2. and if she goes and becomes another man's wife, 3. and the latter husband dislikes her and writes her a bill of divorce and puts it in her hand and sends her out of his house, or if the latter husband dies, who took her to be his wife, 4. then her former husband, who sent her away, may not take her again to be his wife, after she has been defiled; for that is an abomination before the LORD, and you shall not bring guilt upon the land which the LORD your God gives you for an inheritance.

Luke 16:1. He also said to the disciples, "There was a rich man who had a steward, and charges were brought to him that this man was wasting his goods. 2. And he called him and said to him, 'What is

this that I hear about you? Turn in the account of your stewardship, for you can no longer be steward.' 3. And the steward said
to himself, 'What shall I do, since my master is taking the stewardship away from me? I am not strong enough to dig, and I am
ashamed to beg. 4. I have decided what to do, so that people may
receive me into their houses when I am put out of the stewardship.'
5. So, summoning his master's debtors one by one, he said to the
first, 'How much do you owe my master?' 6. He said, 'A hundred
measures of oil.' And he said to him, 'Take your bill, and sit down
quickly and write fifty.' 7. Then he said to another, 'And how much
do you owe?' He said, 'A hundred measures of wheat.' He said to
him, 'Take your bill, and write eighty.' 8. The master commended
the dishonest steward for his shrewdness; for the sons of this world
are more shrewd in dealing with their own generation than the sons
of light. 9. And I tell you, make friends for yourselves by means of
unrighteous mammon, so that when it fails they may receive you
into the eternal habitations. 10. "He who is faithful in a very little
is faithful also in much; and he who is dishonest in a very little is
dishonest also in much. 11. If then you have not been faithful in the
unrighteous mammon, who will entrust to you the true riches? 12.
And if you have not been faithful in that which is another's, who
will give you that which is your own? 13. No servant can serve
two masters; for either he will hate the one and love the other, or he
will be devoted to the one and despise the other. You cannot serve
God and mammon." 14. The Pharisees, who were lovers of money,
heard all this, and they scoffed at him. 15. But he said to them, "You
are those who justify yourselves before men, but God knows your
hearts; for what is exalted among men is an abomination in the sight
of God. 16. "The law and the prophets were until John; since then
the good news of the kingdom of God is preached, and every one
enters it violently. 17. But it is easier for heaven and earth to pass
away, than for one dot of the law to become void. 18. "Every one
who divorces his wife and marries another commits adultery, and he
who marries a woman divorced from her husband commits adultery.

Luke skips Deuteronomy 22:5–23:14, a catch-all.

The Christ Myth Theory And Its Problems

Luke appears to have used the Deuteronomy 23 provision for the welcoming of an escaped slave to live in one's midst as the basis for his parable of the Dishonest Steward, who must soon leave his master's employ and so manipulates his master's accounts as to assure he will be welcomed into his grateful clients' midst after his dismissal.

Luke has nothing particular to say concerning cult prostitutes ("priestitutes," one might call them) and vows, but the Deuteronomic discussion of debts and usury inspires him to accuse the Pharisees of being "lovers of money." Greed like theirs is an "abomination" (βδελυγμα) before God, a word he has borrowed from the same Deuteronomic passage's condemnation of a man remarrying his divorced wife after a second man has also divorced her. On the question of divorce, Luke oddly juxtaposes against the Deuteronomic provision the diametrically opposite Markan rejection of divorce, even while adding that the Torah cannot change!

u. Vindication of the Poor, of Lepers; Fair Judges (Deuteronomy 24:6–25:3; Luke 16:19–18:8)

Deuteronomy 24:6. "No man shall take a mill or an upper millstone in pledge; for he would be taking a life in pledge. 7. "If a man is found stealing one of his brethren, the people of Israel, and if he treats him as a slave or sells him, then that thief shall die; so you shall purge the evil from the midst of you. 8. "Take heed, in an attack of leprosy, to be very careful to do according to all that the Levitical priests shall direct you; as I commanded them, so you shall be careful to do. 9. Remember what the LORD your God did to Miriam on the way as you came forth out of Egypt. 10. "When you make your neighbor a loan of any sort, you shall not go into his house to fetch his pledge. 11. You shall stand outside, and the man to whom you make the loan shall bring the pledge out to you. 12. And if he is a poor man, you shall not sleep in his pledge; 13. when the sun goes down, you shall restore to him the pledge that he may sleep in his cloak and bless you; and it shall be righteousness to you before the LORD your God. 14. "You shall not oppress a hired servant who is poor and needy, whether he is one of your brethren or one of the sojourners who are in your land within your towns; 15. you shall give him his hire on the day he earns it, before the sun goes down (for he is poor, and sets his heart upon it); lest he cry against you to the LORD, and it be sin in you. 16. "The fathers shall not be put to death for the children, nor shall the children be put to death for the fathers; every man shall be put to death for his own sin. 17. "You shall not pervert the justice due to the sojourner or to the fatherless, or take a widow's garment in pledge; 18. but you shall remember that you were a slave in Egypt and the LORD your God redeemed you from there; therefore I command you to do this. 19. "When you reap your harvest in your field, and have forgotten a sheaf in the field, you shall not go back to get it; it shall be for the sojourner, the fatherless, and the widow; that the LORD your God may bless you in all the work of your hands. 20. When you beat your olive trees, you shall not go over the boughs again; it shall be for the sojourner, the fatherless, and the widow. 21. When you gather the grapes of your vineyard, you shall not glean it afterward; it shall be for the sojourner, the fatherless, and the widow. 22. You shall remember that you were a slave in the land of Egypt; therefore I command you to do this.

Deuteronomy 25.1 "If there is a dispute between men, and they come into court, and the judges decide between them, acquitting the innocent and condemning the guilty, 2. then if the guilty man deserves to be beaten, the judge shall cause him to lie down and be beaten in his presence with a number of stripes in proportion to his offense. 3. Forty stripes may be given him, but not more; lest, if one should go on to beat him with more stripes than these, your brother be degraded in your sight.

Luke 16:19. "There was a rich man, who was clothed in purple and fine linen and who feasted sumptuously every day. 20. And at his gate lay a poor man named Lazarus, full of sores, 21. who desired to be fed with what fell from the rich man's table; moreover the dogs came and licked his sores. 22. The poor man died and was carried by the angels to Abraham's bosom. The rich man also died and was buried; 23. and in Hades, being in torment, he lifted up his eyes, and saw Abraham far off and Lazarus in his bosom. 24. And he called out, 'Father Abraham, have mercy upon me, and send Lazarus to dip the end of his finger in water and cool my tongue; for I am in anguish in this flame.' 25. But Abraham said, 'Son, remember that you in your lifetime received your good things, and Lazarus in like manner evil things; but now he is comforted here, and you are in anguish. 26. And besides all this, between us and you a great chasm has been fixed, in order that those who would pass from here to you may not be able, and none may cross from there to us.' 27. And he said, 'Then I beg you, father, to send him to my father's house, 28. for I have five brothers, so that he may warn them, lest they also come into this place of torment.' 29. But Abraham said, 'They have Moses and the prophets; let them hear them.' 30. And he said, 'No, father Abraham; but if some one goes to them from the dead, they will repent.' 31. He said to him, 'If they do not hear Moses and the prophets, neither will they be convinced if some one should rise from the dead'."

Luke 17:1. And he said to his disciples, "Temptations to sin are sure to come; but woe to him by whom they come! 2. It would be better for him if a millstone were hung round his neck and he were cast into the sea, than that he should cause one of these little ones to sin. 3. Take heed to yourselves; if your brother sins, rebuke him, and if he repents, forgive him; 4. and if he sins against you seven times in the day, and turns to you seven times, and says, 'I repent,' you must forgive him." 5. The apostles said to the Lord, "Increase our faith!" 6. And the Lord said, "If you had faith as a grain of mustard seed, you could say to this sycamine tree, 'Be rooted up, and be planted in the sea,' and it would obey you. 7. "Will any one of you, who has a servant plowing or keeping sheep, say to him when he has come in from the field, 'Come at once and sit down at table'? 8. Will he not rather say to him, 'Prepare supper for me, and gird yourself and serve me, till I eat and drink; and afterward you shall eat and drink'?

9. Does he thank the servant because he did what was commanded? 10. So you also, when you have done all that is commanded you, say, 'We are unworthy servants; we have only done what was our duty'." 11. On the way to Jerusalem he was passing along between Samaria and Galilee. 12. And as he entered a village, he was met by ten lepers, who stood at a distance 13. and lifted up their voices and said, "Jesus, Master, have mercy on us." 14. When he saw them he said to them, "Go and show yourselves to the priests." And as they went they were cleansed. 15. Then one of them, when he saw that he was healed, turned back, praising God with a loud voice; 16. and he fell on his face at Jesus' feet, giving him thanks. Now he was a Samaritan. 17. Then said Jesus, "Were not ten cleansed? Where are the nine? 18. Was no one found to return and give praise to God except this foreigner?" 19. And he said to him, "Rise and go your way; your faith has made you well." 20. Being asked by the Pharisees when the kingdom of God was coming, he answered them, "The kingdom of God is not coming with signs to be observed; 21. nor will they say, 'Lo, here it is!' or 'There!' for behold, the kingdom of God is in the midst of you." 22. And he said to the disciples, "The days are coming when you will desire to see one of the days of the Son of man, and you will not see it. 23. And they will say to you, 'Lo, there!' or 'Lo, here!' Do not go, do not follow them. 24. For as the lightning flashes and lights up the sky from one side to the other, so will the Son of man be in his day. 25. But first he must suffer many things and be rejected by this generation. 26. As it was in the days of Noah, so will it be in the days of the Son of man. 27. They ate, they drank, they married, they were given in marriage, until the day when Noah entered the ark, and the flood came and destroyed them all. 28. Likewise as it was in the days of Lot — they ate, they drank, they bought, they sold, they planted, they built, 29. but on the day when Lot went out from Sodom fire and sulphur rained from heaven and destroyed them all — 30. so will it be on the day when the Son of man is revealed. 31. On that day, let him who is on the housetop, with his goods in the house, not come down to take them away; and likewise let him who is in the field not turn back. 32. Remember Lot's wife. 33. Whoever seeks to gain his life will lose it, but whoever loses his

life will preserve it. 34. I tell you, in that night there will be two in one bed; one will be taken and the other left. 35. There will be two women grinding together; one will be taken and the other left." 36. Two men will be in the field; one will be taken and the other left. 37. And they said to him, "Where, Lord?" He said to them, "Where the body is, there the eagles will be gathered together."

Deuteronomy 18:1. And he told them a parable, to the effect that they ought always to pray and not lose heart. 2. He said, "In a certain city there was a judge who neither feared God nor regarded man; 3. and there was a widow in that city who kept coming to him and saying, 'Vindicate me against my adversary.' 4. For a while he refused; but afterward he said to himself, 'Though I neither fear God nor regard man, 5. yet because this widow bothers me, I will vindicate her, or she will wear me out by her continual coming'." 6. And the Lord said, "Hear what the unrighteous judge says. 7. And will not God vindicate his elect, who cry to him day and night? Will he delay long over them? 8. I tell you, he will vindicate them speedily. Nevertheless, when the Son of man comes, will he find faith on earth?"

Inspired by Deuteronomy's injunctions concerning fair treatment of the poor, Luke has created the parable of the Rich Man and Lazarus, probably basing it upon both the Egyptian Tale of the Two Brothers, where the postmortem fates of two men are disclosed as a lesson for the living, and the rabbinic parable of the tax-collector Bar-Majan (*Hagigah*, II, 77d), whose single act of charity (inviting the poor to a banquet when his invited guests, the respectable rich, did not show up) accounted karmically for his sumptuous funeral, but failed to mitigate his torments in hell afterward.

Luke places the Q saying about the millstone (Luke 17:1–2// Matthew18:6–7) to match the Deuteronomic mention of a millstone as the irreplaceable tool of one's trade (24:6), a mere catchword connection.

The provision for a leper's cure and certification (Deuteronomy 24:8–9) prompts Luke to create another pro-Samaritan story (with Deuteronomy 24:14's counsel to treat the sojourning foreigner fairly also in mind). It is the story of the nine Jewish lepers whom Jesus cures without thanks versus the single Samaritan who returns to thank Jesus. The centrality of the motif of praising/thanking God for a miracle, elsewhere Luke's redactional addition to older miracle stories, brands this one as completely Lukan.

Deuteronomy 24:17–18, 25:1–3 concern fair judgments rendered on behalf of the poor and fair treatment of widows. Luke required no more inspiration than this to create his parable of the Unjust Judge who delays vindicating a widow too poor to bribe him till she finally wears him out. This he uses to advocate patience in prayer: if even a corrupt judge will at length give in to a just petition, cannot the righteous God be expected to answer just prayers in his own time?

v. Confessing One's Righteousness (Deuteronomy 26; Luke 18:9–14)

Deuteronomy 26:1. "When you come into the land which the LORD your God gives you for an inheritance, and have taken possession of it, and live in it, 2. you shall take some of the first of all the fruit of the ground, which you harvest from your land that the LORD your God gives you, and you shall put it in a basket, and you shall go to the place which the LORD your God will choose, to make his name to dwell there. 3. And you shall go to the priest who is in office at that time, and say to him, 'I declare this day to the LORD your God that I have come into the land which the LORD swore to our fathers to give us.' 4. Then the priest shall take the basket from your hand, and set it down before the altar of the LORD your God. 5. "And you shall make response before the LORD your God, 'A wandering Aramean was my father; and he went down into Egypt and sojourned there, few in number; and there he became a nation, great, mighty, and populous. 6. And the Egyptians treated us harshly, and afflicted us, and laid upon us hard bondage. 7. Then we cried to the LORD the God of our fathers, and the LORD heard our voice, and saw our affliction, our toil, and our oppression; 8. and the

The Christ Myth Theory And Its Problems

LORD brought us out of Egypt with a mighty hand and an outstretched arm, with great terror, with signs and wonders; 9. and he brought us into this place and gave us this land, a land flowing with milk and honey. 10. And behold, now I bring the first of the fruit of the ground, which thou, O LORD, hast given me.' And you shall set it down before the LORD your God, and worship before the LORD your God; 11. and you shall rejoice in all the good which the LORD your God has given to you and to your house, you, and the Levite, and the sojourner who is among you. 12. "When you have finished paying all the tithe of your produce in the third year, which is the year of tithing, giving it to the Levite, the sojourner, the fatherless, and the widow, that they may eat within your towns and be filled, 13. then you shall say before the LORD your God, 'I have removed the sacred portion out of my house, and moreover I have given it to the Levite, the sojourner, the fatherless, and the widow, according to all thy commandment which thou hast commanded me; I have not transgressed any of thy commandments, neither have I forgotten them; 14. I have not eaten of the tithe while I was mourning, or removed any of it while I was unclean, or offered any of it to the dead; I have obeyed the voice of the LORD my God, I have done according to all that thou hast commanded me. 15. Look down from thy holy habitation, from heaven, and bless thy people Israel and the ground which thou hast given us, as thou didst swear to our fathers, a land flowing with milk and honey.' 16. "This day the LORD your God commands you to do these statutes and ordinances; you shall therefore be careful to do them with all your heart and with all your soul. 17. You have declared this day concerning the LORD that he is your God, and that you will walk in his ways, and keep his statutes and his commandments and his ordinances, and will obey his voice; 18. and the LORD has declared this day concerning you that you are a people for his own possession, as he has promised you, and that you are to keep all his commandments, 19. that he will set you high above all nations that he has made, in praise and in fame and in honor, and that you shall be a people holy to the LORD your God, as he has spoken."

Luke 18:9. He also told this parable to some who trusted in themselves that they were righteous and despised others: 10. "Two men went up into the temple to pray, one a Pharisee and the other a tax collector. 11. The Pharisee stood and prayed thus with himself, 'God, I thank thee that I am not like other men, extortioners, unjust, adulterers, or even like this tax collector. 12. I fast twice a week, I give tithes of all that I get.' 13. But the tax collector, standing far off, would not even lift up his eyes to heaven, but beat his breast, saying, 'God, be merciful to me a sinner!' 14. I tell you, this man went down to his house justified rather than the other; for every one who exalts himself will be humbled, but he who humbles himself will be exalted."

Luke skips Deuteronomy 25:4–19, about Levirate marriage, false weights, *etc.*

Deuteronomy 26:12–15 allows that one offering the firstfruits of his crops may confess his own perfect obedience to the commandments, provided one has done so, and thus may rightly claim God's blessing on the land. This must have struck Luke as pretentious and presumptuous, and he satirizes the section in his parable of the Pharisee (whose self-praise in the guise of prayer echoes that of Deuteronomy) and the Publican (counted righteous by virtue of his humble self-condemnation).

7. The Ascension (2 Kings 2:11; Luke 24:49–53)

2 Kings 2:11. And as they still went on and talked, behold, a chariot of fire and horses of fire separated the two of them. And Elijah went up by a whirlwind into heaven.

Luke 24:49. And behold, I send the promise of my Father upon you; but stay in the city, until you are clothed with power from on high." 50. Then he led them out as far as Bethany, and lifting up his hands he blessed them. 51. While he blessed them, he parted from them, and was carried up into heaven. 52. And they returned to Jerusalem with great joy, 53. and were continually in the temple blessing God.

Luke's ascension narrative (the only one in the gospels) is based primarily upon the account of Elijah's ascension in 2 Kings 2:11

The Christ Myth Theory And Its Problems

(Brodie, p. 254–264). He seems to have added elements of Josephus' story of Moses' ascension as well ("And as soon as they were come to the mountain called Abarim..., he was going to embrace Eleazar and Joshua, and was still discoursing with them, [when] a cloud stood over him on the sudden, and he disappeared in a certain valley" *Jewish Antiquities* V. 1. 48, Whiston trans.). (Interestingly, the phrase "and was carried up to heaven" is lacking in two of the most important New Testament manuscripts — *Codex Bezae* and the original reading of *Codex Sinaiticus* — in which Jesus simply "parted from them.")

In 2 Kings 2:9, Elijah and Elisha agree on the master's bequest to his disciple: Elisha is to receive a double share of Elijah's mighty spirit, *i.e.*, power. Likewise, just before his own ascension, Jesus announces to his disciples his own bequest: "the promise of my father" (Luke 24:49). It will be a "clothing" with power, recalling Elijah's miracle of parting the Jordan with his own rolled-up mantle (1 Kings 2:12). Both Elijah and Jesus are assumed into heaven (1 Kings 2:11; Luke 24:50–53: Acts 1:1–1), the former with the aid of Apollo's chariot, but both are pointedly separated from their disciples (2 Kings 2:11; Luke 24:51). After this, the promised spirit comes, empowering the disciples (2 Kings 2:15, "Now when the sons of the prophets who were at Jericho saw him over against them, they said, 'The spirit of Elijah rests on Elisha.' And they came to meet him, and bowed to the ground before him;" Acts 2:4, "And they were all filled with the Holy Spirit and began to speak in other tongues, as the Spirit gave them utterance."). Elijah's ascent is witnessed by disciples, whose search failed to turn up his body (2 Kings 2:16–18):

> 2 Kings 2:16. And they said to him, "Behold now, there are with your servants fifty strong men; pray, let them go, and seek your master; it may be that the Spirit of the LORD has caught him up and cast him upon some mountain or into some valley." And he said, "You shall

not send." 17. But when they urged him till he was ashamed, he said, "Send." They sent therefore fifty men; and for three days they sought him but did not find him. 18. And they came back to him, while he tarried at Jericho, and he said to them, "Did I not say to you, Do not go?"

Likewise, Jesus' disciples find only an empty tomb (Luke 24:2–3: "And they found the stone rolled away from the tomb, but when they went in they did not find the body."), then behold his ascent. "Then he led them out as far as Bethany, and lifting up his hands he blessed them. While he blessed them, he parted from them, and was carried up into heaven" (Luke 24:50–51).

> Acts 1:9. And when he had said this, as they were looking on, he was lifted up, and a cloud took him out of their sight. 10. And while they were gazing into heaven as he went, behold, two men stood by them in white robes, 11. and said, "Men of Galilee, why do you stand looking into heaven? This Jesus, who was taken up from you into heaven, will come in the same way as you saw him go into heaven. (Acts 1:9–11).

Notoriously, Luke's gospel has the ascension occur on Easter evening, while Acts has it happen forty days later. How to explain this, since Luke and Acts are usually held to be sequential works by the same author? We have already noted that the ascension is missing from two very important New Testament manuscripts. It would seem that Acts originally directly followed Luke's gospel, and the ascension occurred only in Acts. But when editors began to group the four gospels together, they separated Luke from Acts and might have felt the need to round off the gospel story with the ascension, thus bringing to conclusion Jesus' earthly existence, so they added the ascension on the very heels of the resurrection. Then why not also remove Acts 1:9–11 to smooth the whole thing out? For one thing, ancient scribes were usually more inclined to add "corrections" to the text than to remove problem texts. For another, the ascension could not be excised from the beginning of Acts without gutting the narrative, since too much else in the chapter depends upon it.

E. The Gospel of John

1. Nathanael (Genesis 28:17; John 1:43–51)

Genesis 28:11 And he came to a certain place, and stayed there that night, because the sun had set. Taking one of the stones of the place, he put it under his head and lay down in that place to sleep. 12. And he dreamed that there was a ladder set up on the earth, and the top of it reached to heaven; and behold, the angels of God were ascending and descending on it! 13. And behold, the LORD stood above it and said, "I am the LORD, the God of Abraham your father and the God of Isaac; the land on which you lie I will give to you and to your descendants; 14. and your descendants shall be like the dust of the earth, and you shall spread abroad to the west and to the east and to the north and to the south; and by you and your descendants shall all the families of the earth bless themselves. 15. Behold, I am with you and will keep you wherever you go, and will bring you back to this land; for I will not leave you until I have done that of which I have spoken to you." 16. Then Jacob awoke from his sleep and said, "Surely the LORD is in this place; and I did not know it." 17. And he was afraid, and said, "How awesome is this place! This is none other than the house of God, and this is the gate of heaven."

John 1:43. The next day Jesus decided to go to Galilee. And he found Philip and said to him, "Follow me." 44. Now Philip was from Bethsaida, the city of Andrew and Peter. 45. Philip found Nathanael, and said to him, "We have found him of whom Moses in the law and also the prophets wrote, Jesus of Nazareth, the son of Joseph." 46. Nathanael said to him, "Can anything good come out of Nazareth?" Philip said to him, "Come and see." 47. Jesus saw Nathanael coming to him, and said of him, "Behold, an Israelite indeed, in whom is no guile!" 48. Nathanael said to him, "How do you know me?" Jesus answered him, "Before Philip called you, when you were under the

fig tree, I saw you." 49. Nathanael answered him, "Rabbi, you are
the Son of God! You are the King of Israel!" 50. Jesus answered him,
"Because I said to you, I saw you under the fig tree, do you believe?
You shall see greater things than these." 51. And he said to him, "Tru-
ly, truly, I say to you, you will see heaven opened, and the angels of
God ascending and descending upon the Son of man."

As all commentators agree, this episode is based on Jacob's dream
of the ladder/stairway between heaven and earth, with angels going
up and down along it (Genesis 28:11–17 *ff*). Nathaniel is to be a
New Testament Jacob, lacking the shrewd worldliness of his prototype.

2. Water into Wine (1 Kings 17:8–24 LXX; John 2:1–11)

1 Kings 17:8. And the word of the Lord came to Eliu saying, 9.
Arise, and go to Sarepta of the Sidonian land: behold, I have there
commanded a widow-woman to maintain thee. 10. And he arose
and went to Sarepta, and came to the gate of the city: and, behold, a
widow-woman was there gathering sticks; and Eliu cried after her,
and said to her, Fetch me, I pray thee, a little water in a vessel that I
may drink. 11. And she went to fetch it; and Eliu cried after her, and
said, Bring me, I pray thee, a morsel of the bread that is in thy hand.
12. And the woman said, As the Lord thy God lives, I have not a
cake, but only a handful of meal in the pitcher, and a little oil in the
cruise, and, behold, I am going to gather two sticks, and I shall go in
and dress it for myself and my children, and we shall eat it and die.
13. And Eliu said to her, Be of good courage, go in and do according
to thy word: but make me thereof a little cake, and thou shalt bring it
out to me first, and thou shalt bring it out to me first, and thou shalt
make some for thyself and thy children last. 14. For thus saith the
Lord, The pitcher of meal shall not fail, and the cruse of oil shall
not diminish , until the day that the Lord gives rain upon the earth.
15. And the woman went and did so, and did eat, she, and he, and
her children. 16. And the pitcher of meal failed not, and the cruse of
oil was not diminished, according to the word of the Lord which he

spoke by the hand of Eliu. 17. And it came to pass afterward, that the son of the woman the mistress of the house was sick; and his sickness was very severe, until there was no breath left in him. 18. And she said to Eliu, What have I to do with thee, O man of God? hast thou come in to me to bring my sins to remembrance, and to slay my son? 19. And Eliu said to the woman, Give me thy son. And he took him out of her bosom, and took him up to the chamber in which he himself lodged, and laid him on the bed. 20. And Eliu cried aloud, and said, Alas, O Lord, the witness of the widow with whom I sojourn, thou hast wrought evil for her in slaying her son. 21. And he breathed on the child thrice, and called on the Lord, and said, O Lord my God, let, I pray thee, the soul of this child return to him. 22. And it was so, and the child cried out, 23. and he brought him down from the upper chamber into the house, and gave him to his mother; and Eliu said, See, thy son lives. 24. And the woman said to Eliu, Behold, I know that thou art a man of God, and the word of the Lord in thy mouth is true.

John 2:1. On the third day there was a marriage at Cana in Galilee, and the mother of Jesus was there; 2. Jesus also was invited to the marriage, with his disciples. 3. When the wine failed, the mother of Jesus said to him, "They have no wine." 4. And Jesus said to her, "O woman, what have you to do with me? My hour has not yet come." 5. His mother said to the servants, "Do whatever he tells you." 6. Now six stone jars were standing there, for the Jewish rites of purification, each holding twenty or thirty gallons. 7. Jesus said to them, "Fill the jars with water." And they filled them up to the brim. 8. He said to them, "Now draw some out, and take it to the steward of the feast." So they took it 9. When the steward of the feast tasted the water now become wine, and did not know where it came from (though the servants who had drawn the water knew), the steward of the feast called the bridegroom 10. and said to him, "Every man serves the good wine first; and when men have drunk freely, then the poor wine; but you have kept the good wine until now." 11. This, the first of his signs, Jesus did at Cana in Galilee, and manifested his glory; and his disciples believed in him.

Though the central feature of this miracle story, the transformation of one liquid into another, no doubt comes from the lore of Dionysus, the basic outline of the story owes much to the story of Elijah in 1 Kings 17:8–24 LXX (Helms, p. 86). The widow of Zarephath, whose son has just died, upbraids the prophet: "What have I to do with you, O man of God?" (Τι εμοι και σοι, 17:18). John has transferred this brusque address to the mouth of Jesus, rebuking his mother (2:4, Τι εμοι και σοι, γυναι). Jesus and Elijah both tell people in need of provisions to take empty pitchers (υδρια in 1 Kings 17:12, υδριαι in John 2:6–7), from which sustenance miraculously emerges. And just as this feat causes the woman to declare her faith in Elijah ("I know that you are a man of God," v. 24), so does Jesus' wine miracle cause his disciples to put their faith in him (v. 11).

3. The Samaritan Woman (Exodus 2:15–22; John 4:1–34)

Exodus 2:15. When Pharaoh heard of it, he sought to kill Moses. But Moses fled from Pharaoh, and stayed in the land of Midian; and he sat down by a well. 16. Now the priest of Midian had seven daughters; and they came and drew water, and filled the troughs to water their father's flock. 17. The shepherds came and drove them away; but Moses stood up and helped them, and watered their flock. 18. When they came to their father Reuel, he said, "How is it that you have come so soon today?" 19. They said, "An Egyptian delivered us out of the hand of the shepherds, and even drew water for us and watered the flock." 20. He said to his daughters, "And where is he? Why have you left the man? Call him, that he may eat bread." 21. And Moses was content to dwell with the man, and he gave Moses his daughter Zipporah. 22. She bore a son, and he called his name Gershom; for he said, "I have been a sojourner in a foreign land."

John 4:1. Now when the Lord knew that the Pharisees had heard that Jesus was making and baptizing more disciples than John 2. (although Jesus himself did not baptize, but only his disciples), 3. he left Judea and departed again to Galilee. 4. He had to pass through Samaria. 5. So he came to a city of Samaria, called Sychar, near the field that Jacob gave to his son Joseph. 6. Jacob's well was there, and so Jesus, wearied as he was with his journey, sat down beside the well. It was about the sixth hour. 7. There came a woman of Samaria to draw water. Jesus said to her, "Give me a drink." 8. For his disciples had gone away into the city to buy food. 9. The Samaritan woman said to him, "How is it that you, a Jew, ask a drink of me, a woman of Samaria?" For Jews have no dealings with Samaritans. 10. Jesus answered her, "If you knew the gift of God, and who it is that is saying to you, 'Give me a drink,' you would have asked him, and he would have given you living water." 11. The woman said to him, "Sir, you have nothing to draw with, and the well is deep; where do you get that living water? 12. Are you greater than our father Jacob, who gave us the well, and drank from it himself, and his sons, and his cattle?" 13. Jesus said to her, "Every one who drinks of this water will thirst again, 14. but whoever drinks of the water that I shall give him will never thirst; the water that I shall give him will become in him a spring of water welling up to eternal life." 15. The woman said to him, "Sir, give me this water, that I may not thirst, nor come here to draw." 16. Jesus said to her, "Go, call your husband, and come here." 17. The woman answered him, "I have no husband." Jesus said to her, "You are right in saying, 'I have no husband'; 18. for you have had five husbands, and he whom you now have is not your husband; this you said truly." 19. The woman said to him, "Sir, I perceive that you are a prophet. 20. Our fathers worshiped on this mountain; and you say that in Jerusalem is the place where men ought to worship." 21. Jesus said to her, "Woman, believe me, the hour is coming when neither on this mountain nor in Jerusalem will you worship the Father. 22. You worship what you do not know; we worship what we know, for salvation is from the Jews. 23. But the hour is coming, and now is, when the true worshipers will worship the Father in spirit and truth, for such the Father seeks to worship him. 24. God is spirit, and those who worship him must worship in spirit and truth." 25. The woman said to him, "I know that Messiah is coming (he who is called Christ); when he comes, he will show us all things." 26. Jesus said to her, "I who speak to you am he." 27. Just then his disciples came. They marveled that he was talking with a woman, but none said, "What do you wish?" or, "Why are you talking with her?" 28. So the woman left her water jar, and went away into the city, and said to the people, 29. "Come, see a man who told me all that I ever did. Can this be the Christ?" 30. They went out of the city and were coming to him. 31. Meanwhile the disciples besought him, saying, "Rabbi, eat." 32. But he said to them, "I have food to eat of which you do not know." 33. So the disciples said to one another, "Has any one brought him food?" 34. Jesus said to them, "My food is to do the will of him who sent me, and to accomplish his work.

As Robert Alter notes (p. 48), this scene is a variant of the "type scene" which frequently recurs in the Bible of a young man leaving home and coming to a well where he meets young women, one of whom he marries. Other instances and variants include Genesis 24 (Abraham's servant meets Rebecca), Genesis 29 (Jacob meets Rachel); Exodus 2 (Moses meets Zipporah): Ruth 2 (Ruth meets Boaz); and 1 Samuel 9 (Saul meets the maidens at Zuph). But Helms (pp. 89–90) adds 1 Kings 17, where, again, Elijah encounters the widow of Zarephath, and it is this story which seems to have supplied the immediate model for John 4. Elijah and Jesus alike leave home turf for foreign territory. Each is thirsty and meets a woman of whom he asks a drink of water. In both stories the woman departs from the pattern of the type scene because, though having no husband as in the type scene, she is mature and lacks a husband for other reasons. The woman of Zarephath is a widow, while the Samaritan woman has given up on marriage, having had five previous husbands, now dead or divorced, and is presently just cohabiting. In both stories it is really the woman who stands in need more than the prophet, and the latter offers the boon of a miraculously self-renewing supply of nourishment, Elijah that of physical food, Jesus that of the water of everlasting life. Just as the widow exclaims that Elijah must have come to disclose her past sins ("You have come to me to bring my sin to remembrance," 1 Kings 17:18), the Samaritan admits Jesus has the goods on her as well ("He told me all that I ever did," John 4:39).

The Christ Myth Theory And Its Problems

4. Jesus Appears to Mary Magdalene (Tobit 12:14–21; John 20:1, 11–17)

Tobit 12:14. "So now God set me to heal you and your daughter-in-law Sarah. 15. I am Raphael, one of the seven holy angels who present the prayers of the saints and enter into the presence of the glory of the Holy One." 16. They were both alarmed; and they fell upon their faces, for they were afraid. 17. But he said to them, "Do not be afraid; you will be safe. But praise God forever. 18. For I did not come as a favor on my part, but by the will of our God. Therefore praise him forever. 19. All these days I merely appeared to you and did not eat or drink, but you were seeing a vision. 20. And now give thanks to God, for I am ascending to him who sent me. Write in a book everything that has happened." 21. Then they stood up; but they saw him no more.

John 20:1. Now on the first day of the week Mary Magdalene came to the tomb early, while it was still dark, and saw that the stone had been taken away from the tomb. […] 11. But Mary stood weeping outside the tomb, and as she wept she stooped to look into the tomb; 12. and she saw two angels in white, sitting where the body of Jesus had lain, one at the head and one at the feet. 13. They said to her, "Woman, why are you weeping?" She said to them, "Because they have taken away my Lord, and I do not know where they have laid him." 14. Saying this, she turned round and saw Jesus standing, but she did not know that it was Jesus. 15. Jesus said to her, "Woman, why are you weeping? Whom do you seek?" Supposing him to be the gardener, she said to him, "Sir, if you have carried him away, tell me where you have laid him, and I will take him away." 16. Jesus said to her, "Mary." She turned and said to him in Hebrew, "Rabboni!" (which means Teacher). 17. Jesus said to her, "Do not hold me, for I have not yet ascended to the Father; but go to my brethren and say to them, I am ascending to my Father and your Father, to my God and your God."

This story owes much to the self-disclosure of the angel Raphael at the climax of the Book of Tobit (Helms, pp. 146–147). When

Tobias first saw Raphael, he "did not know" he was really an angel (Tobit 5:5), just as when Mary, weeping outside the tomb, first saw Jesus there, she "did not know" who he really was (20:14). Having delivered Sarah from her curse, Raphael reveals himself to Tobit and his son Tobias and announces, his work being done, that "I am ascending to him who sent me" (Tobit 12:20), just as Jesus tells Mary, "I am ascending to my father and your father, to my God and your God" (John 20:17). Why does the risen Jesus warn Mary "Touch/hold me not, for I have not yet ascended to the father" (20:17a)? This is probably an indication of docetism, that Jesus (at least the risen Jesus) cannot be touched, not having (any longer?) a fleshly body (the story was not originally followed by the Doubting Thomas story with its tactile proofs, hence need not be consistent with it; note that in 20:17b Jesus seems to anticipate not seeing the disciples again). The reason for seeing docetism here is the parallel it would complete between John 20 and the Raphael revelation/ascension scene, where the angel explains (Tobit 12:19), "All these days I merely appeared to you and did not eat or drink, but you were seeing a vision" (*i.e.*, a semblance).

F. Acts of the Apostles

1. Pentecost (Numbers 11:6–25; Acts 2:1–4 ff)

The whole scene comes, obviously, from the descent of the Mosaic spirit upon the seventy elders in Numbers 11:16–17, 24–25.

Numbers 11:16. And the LORD said to Moses, "Gather for me seventy men of the elders of Israel, whom you know to be the elders of the people and officers over them; and bring them to the tent of meeting, and let them take their stand there with you. 17. And I will come down and talk with you there; and I will take some of the spirit which is upon you and put it upon them; and they shall bear the burden of the people with you, that you may not bear it yourself alone

The Christ Myth Theory And Its Problems

[...] 24. So Moses went out and told the people the words of the LORD; and he gathered seventy men of the elders of the people, and placed them round about the tent. 25. Then the LORD came down in the cloud and spoke to him, and took some of the spirit that was upon him and put it upon the seventy elders; and when the spirit rested upon them, they prophesied. But they did so no more.
Acts 2:1. When the day of Pentecost had come, they were all together in one place. 2. And suddenly a sound came from heaven like the rush of a mighty wind, and it filled all the house where they were sitting. 3. And there appeared to them tongues as of fire, distributed and resting on each one of them. 4. And they were all filled with the Holy Spirit and began to speak in other tongues, as the Spirit gave them utterance.

There is also borrowing from Euripides' *The Bacchae*, where we read "Flames flickered in their curls and did not burn them" (757–758), just as tongues of fire blazed harmlessly above the heads of the apostles (Acts 2:3). Ecstatic speech caused some bystanders to question the sobriety of the disciples, but Peter defends them ("These are not drunk as you suppose" Acts 2:15a), as does Pentheus' messenger: "Not, as you think, drunk with wine" (686–687).

2. Ananias and Sapphira; the Martyrdom of Stephen (1 Kings 21:1–21; Joshua 7; Acts 5:1–11; 6:8–15)

1 Kings 21:1. Now Naboth the Jezreelite had a vineyard in Jezreel, beside the palace of Ahab king of Samaria. 2. And after this Ahab said to Naboth, "Give me your vineyard, that I may have it for a vegetable garden, because it is near my house; and I will give you a better vineyard for it; or, if it seems good to you, I will give you its value in money." 3. But Naboth said to Ahab, "The LORD forbid that I should give you the inheritance of my fathers." 4. And Ahab went into his house vexed and sullen because of what Naboth the Jezreelite had said to him; for he had said, "I will not give you the inheritance of my fathers." And he lay down on his bed, and turned away his face, and

would eat no food. 5. But Jezebel his wife came to him, and said to him, "Why is your spirit so vexed that you eat no food?" 6. And he said to her, "Because I spoke to Naboth the Jezreelite, and said to him, 'Give me your vineyard for money; or else, if it please you, I will give you another vineyard for it'; and he answered, 'I will not give you my vineyard'." 7. And Jezebel his wife said to him, "Do you now govern Israel? Arise, and eat bread, and let your heart be cheerful; I will give you the vineyard of Naboth the Jezreelite." 8. So she wrote letters in Ahab's name and sealed them with his seal, and she sent the letters to the elders and the nobles who dwelt with Naboth in his city. 9. And she wrote in the letters, "Proclaim a fast, and set Naboth on high among the people; 10. and set two base fellows opposite him, and let them bring a charge against him, saying, 'You have cursed God and the king.' Then take him out, and stone him to death." 11. And the men of his city, the elders and the nobles who dwelt in his city, did as Jezebel had sent word to them. As it was written in the letters which she had sent to them, 12. they proclaimed a fast, and set Naboth on high among the people. 13. And the two base fellows came in and sat opposite him; and the base fellows brought a charge against Naboth, in the presence of the people, saying, "Naboth cursed God and the king." So they took him outside the city, and stoned him to death with stones. 14. Then they sent to Jezebel, saying, "Naboth has been stoned; he is dead." 15. As soon as Jezebel heard that Naboth had been stoned and was dead, Jezebel said to Ahab, "Arise, take possession of the vineyard of Naboth the Jezreelite, which he refused to give you for money; for Naboth is not alive, but dead." 16. And as soon as Ahab heard that Naboth was dead, Ahab arose to go down to the vineyard of Naboth the Jezreelite, to take possession of it. 17. Then the word of the LORD came to Elijah the Tishbite, saying, 18. "Arise, go down to meet Ahab king of Israel, who is in Samaria; behold, he is in the vineyard of Naboth, where he has gone to take possession. 19. And you shall say to him, 'Thus says the LORD, "Have you killed, and also taken possession?" ' And you shall say to him, 'Thus says the LORD: "In the place where dogs licked up the blood of Naboth shall dogs lick your own blood".' " 20. Ahab said to Elijah, "Have you found me, O my enemy?" He answered, "I have found you, because you have sold yourself to do what is evil in the sight of the LORD. 21. Behold, I will bring evil upon you; I will utterly sweep you away, and will cut off from Ahab every male, bond or free, in Israel;

Joshua 7:1. But the people of Israel broke faith in regard to the devoted things; for Achan the son of Carmi, son of Zabdi, son of Zerah, of the tribe of Judah, took some of the devoted things; and the anger of the LORD burned against the people of Israel. 2. Joshua sent men from Jericho to Ai, which is near Beth-a'en, east of Bethel, and said to them, "Go up and spy out the land." And the men went up and spied out Ai. 3. And they returned to Joshua, and said to him, "Let not all the people go up, but let about two or three thousand men go up and attack Ai; do not make the whole people toil up there, for they are but few."4. So about three thousand went up there from the people; and they fled before the men of Ai, 5. and the men of Ai killed about thirty-six men of them, and chased them before the gate as far as Shebarim, and slew them at the descent. And the hearts of the people melted, and became as water. 6. Then Joshua rent his clothes, and fell to the earth upon his face before the ark of the LORD until the evening, he and the elders of Israel; and they put dust upon their heads.7. And Joshua said, "Alas, O Lord GOD, why hast thou brought this people over the Jordan at all, to give us into the hands of the Amorites, to destroy us? Would that we had been content to dwell beyond the Jordan! 8. O Lord, what can I say, when Israel has turned their backs before their enemies! 9. For the Canaanites and all the inhabitants of the land will hear of it, and will surround us, and cut off our name from the earth; and what wilt thou do for thy great name?" 10. The LORD said to Joshua, "Arise, why have you thus fallen upon your face? 11. Israel has sinned; they have transgressed my covenant which I commanded them; they have taken some of the devoted things; they have stolen, and lied, and put them among their own stuff. 12. Therefore the people of Israel cannot stand before their enemies; they turn their backs before their enemies, because they have become a thing for destruction. I will be with you no more, unless you destroy the devoted things from among you. 13. Up, sanctify the people, and say, 'Sanctify yourselves for tomorrow; for thus says the LORD, God of Israel, "There are devoted things in the midst of you, O Israel; you cannot stand before your enemies, until you take away the devoted things from among you." 14. In the morning therefore you shall be brought near by your tribes; and the tribe which the LORD takes shall come near by families; and the family which the LORD takes shall come near by households; and the household which the LORD takes shall come near man by man. 15. And he who is taken with the devoted things shall be burned with fire, he and all that he has, because he has transgressed the covenant of the LORD, and because he has done a shameful thing in Israel'.'" 16. So Joshua rose early in the morning, and brought Israel near tribe by tribe, and the tribe of Judah was taken; 17. and he brought near the families of Judah, and the family of the Zerahites was taken; and he brought near the family of the Zerahites man by man, and Zabdi was taken; 18. and he brought near his household man by man, and Achan the son of Carmi, son of Zabdi, son of Zerah, of the tribe of Judah, was taken. 19. Then Joshua said to Achan, "My son, give glory to the LORD God of Israel, and render praise to him; and tell me now what you have done; do not hide it from me." And Achan answered Joshua, "Of a truth I have sinned against the LORD God of Israel, and this is what I did: 21. when I saw among the spoil a beautiful mantle from Shinar, and two hundred shekels of silver, and a bar of gold weighing fifty shekels, then I coveted them, and took them; and behold, they are hidden in the earth inside my tent, with the silver underneath." 22. So Joshua sent messengers, and they ran to the tent; and behold, it was hidden in his tent with the silver underneath. 23. And they took them out of the tent and brought them to Joshua and all the people of Israel; and they laid them down before the LORD. 24. And Joshua and all Israel with him took Achan the son of Zerah, and the silver and the mantle and the bar of gold, and his sons and daughters, and his oxen and asses and sheep, and his tent, and all that he had; and they brought them up to the Valley of Achor. 25. And Joshua said, "Why did you bring trouble on us? The LORD brings trouble on you today." And all Israel stoned him with stones; they burned them with fire, and stoned them with stones. 26. And they raised over him a great heap of stones that remains to this day; then the LORD turned from his burning anger. Therefore to this day the name of that place is called the Valley of Achor.

Acts 5:1. But a man named Ananias with his wife Sapphira sold a piece of property, 2. and with his wife's knowledge he kept back some of the proceeds, and brought only a part and laid it at the apostles' feet. 3. But Peter said, "Ananias, why has Satan filled your heart to lie to the Holy Spirit and to keep back part of the proceeds of the land? 4. While it remained unsold, did it not remain your own? And after it was sold, was it not at your disposal? How is it that you have contrived this deed in your heart? You have not lied to men but to God." 5. When Ananias heard these words, he fell down and died. And great fear came upon all who heard of it. 6. The young men rose and wrapped him up and carried him out and buried him. 7. After an interval of about three hours his wife came in, not knowing what had happened. 8. And Peter said to her, "Tell me whether you sold the land for so much." And she said, "Yes, for so much." 9. But Peter said to her, "How is it that you have agreed together to tempt the Spirit of the Lord? Hark, the feet of those that have buried your husband are at the door, and they will carry you out." 10. Immediately she fell down at his feet and died. When the young men came in they found her dead, and they carried her out and buried her beside her husband. 11. And great fear came upon the whole church, and upon all who heard of these things.

Acts 6:8. And Stephen, full of grace and power, did great wonders and signs among the people. 9 Then some of those who belonged to the synagogue of the Freedmen (as it was called), and of the Cyrenians, and of the Alexandrians, and of those from Cilicia and Asia, arose and disputed with Stephen. 10. But they could not withstand the wisdom and the Spirit with which he spoke. 11. Then they secretly instigated men, who said, "We have heard him speak blasphemous words against Moses and God." 12. And they stirred up the people and the elders and the scribes, and they came upon him and seized him and brought him before the council, 13. and set up false witnesses who said, "This man never ceases to speak words against this holy place and the law; 14. for we have heard him say that this Jesus of Nazareth will destroy this place, and will change the customs which Moses delivered to us." 15. And gazing at him, all who sat in the council saw that his face was like the face of an angel.

The conspiracy of Ahab and Jezebel to cheat the pious Naboth out of his vineyard (1 Kings 21:1–21) has provided Luke the raw material for two of the most exciting episodes of Acts, those of Ananias and Sapphira and of Stephen (Brodie, pp. 271–275). Ahab finds himself obsessed with Naboth's vineyard, which seems more desirable to him, since he cannot possess it, than all his royal possessions. Jezebel advises him to take what he wants by devious means. Luke has punningly made Naboth into the righteous Bar*nab*as, and now it is the latter's donation (rather than possession) of a field that excites a wicked couple's jealousy. Ananias plays Ahab, Sapphira Jezebel. Only they do not conspire to murder anyone. That element Luke reserves for the martyrdom of Stephen.

The crime of Ananias and Sapphira is borrowed instead from that of Achan (Judges 7), who appropriated for himself treasure ear-marked for God. Ananias and Sapphira have sold a field (wanting to be admired like Barnabas), but they have kept back some of the money while claiming to have donated the full price. They have no business keeping the rest: it is rightfully God's since they have dedicated it as "devoted to the Lord."

Peter confronts Ananias and Sapphira, just as Joshua did Achan (Joshua 7:25) and as Elijah confronted Ahab (1 Kings 20:17–18). Luke takes the earlier note about Ahab's disturbance in spirit (20:4) and makes it into the charge that Ananias and Sapphira had lied to the Spirit of God (Acts 5:3b–4, 9b). Elijah and Peter pronounce death sentences on the guilty, and those of Ananias and Sapphira (like Achan's) transpire at once (Acts 5:5a, 10a), while those of Ahab and Jezebel delay for some time. Fear fell on all who heard of Ananias' and Sapphira's fate, recalling the fear of God sparked in poor indecisive Ahab by Elijah's doom oracle (1 Kings 20:27–29).

Not long after the Naboth incident we learn that the young men of Israel defeated the greedy Syrians (21:1–21), a tale which likely made Luke think of having the young men (never in evidence elsewhere in Acts) carry out and bury the bodies of the greedy couple (Acts 5:6, 10b).

Returning to the hapless Naboth, he has become Stephen, Acts' proto-martyr. Naboth was railroaded by the schemes of Jezebel. She directed the elders and *freemen* to set up Naboth, condemning him through lying witnesses. Stephen suffers the same at the hands of the Synagogue of *Freedmen*. Stephen, like Naboth, is accused of double blasphemy (Naboth: God and king; Stephen: Moses and God) Both are carried outside the city limits and stoned to death. When Ahab heard of the fruit of his desires, he tore his garments in remorse. Luke has carried this over into the detail that young Saul of Tarsus checked the coats of the stoning mob.

3. The Ethiopian Eunuch (2 Kings 5:1–14; Acts 8:26–39)

2 Kings 5:1. Naaman, commander of the army of the king of Syria, was a great man with his master and in high favor, because by him the LORD had given victory to Syria. He was a mighty man of valor, but he was a leper. 2. Now the Syrians on one of their raids had carried off a little maid from the land of Israel, and she waited on Naaman's wife. 3. She said to her mistress, "Would that my lord were with the prophet who is in Samaria! He would cure him of his leprosy." 4. So Naaman went in and told his lord, "Thus and so spoke the maiden from the land of Israel." 5. And the king of Syria said, "Go now, and I will send a letter to the king of Israel." So he went, taking with him ten talents of silver, six thousand shekels of gold, and ten festal garments. 6. And he brought the letter to the king of Israel, which read, "When this letter reaches you, know that

I have sent to you Naaman my servant, that you may cure him of his leprosy." 7. And when the king of Israel read the letter, he rent his clothes and said, "Am I God, to kill and to make alive, that this man sends word to me to cure a man of his leprosy? Only consider, and see how he is seeking a quarrel with me." 8. But when Elisha the man of God heard that the king of Israel had rent his clothes, he sent to the king, saying, "Why have you rent your clothes? Let him come now to me, that he may know that there is a prophet in Israel." 9. So Naaman came with his horses and chariots, and halted at the door of Elisha's house. 10. And Elisha sent a messenger to him, saying, "Go and wash in the Jordan seven times, and your flesh shall be restored, and you shall be clean." 11. But Naaman was angry, and went away, saying, "Behold, I thought that he would surely come out to me, and stand, and call on the name of the LORD his God, and wave his hand over the place, and cure the leper. 12. Are not Abana and Pharpar, the rivers of Damascus, better than all the waters of Israel? Could I not wash in them, and be clean?" So he turned and went away in a rage. 13. But his servants came near and said to him, "My father, if the prophet had commanded you to do some great thing, would you not have done it? How much rather, then, when he says to you, 'Wash, and be clean'?" 14. So he went down and dipped himself seven times in the Jordan, according to the word of the man of God; and his flesh was restored like the flesh of a little child, and he was clean.

Acts 8:26. But an angel of the Lord said to Philip, "Rise and go toward the south to the road that goes down from Jerusalem to Gaza." This is a desert road. 27. And he rose and went. And behold, an Ethiopian, a eunuch, a minister of Candace, queen of the Ethiopians, in charge of all her treasure, had come to Jerusalem to worship 28. and was returning; seated in his chariot, he was reading the prophet Isaiah. 29. And the Spirit said to Philip, "Go up and join this chariot." 30. So Philip ran to him, and heard him reading Isaiah the prophet, and asked, "Do you understand what you are reading?" 31. And he said, "How can I, unless some one guides me?" And he invited Philip to come up and sit with him. 32. Now the passage of the scripture which he was reading was this: "As a sheep led to the slaughter or a lamb before its shearer is dumb, so he opens not his mouth. 33. In his humiliation justice was denied him. Who can describe his generation? For his life is taken up from the earth." 34. And the eunuch said to Philip, "About whom, pray, does the prophet say this, about himself or about some one else?" 35. Then Philip opened his mouth, and beginning with this scripture he told him the good news of Jesus. 36. And as they went along the road they came to some water, and the eunuch said, "See, here is water! What is to prevent my being baptized?" 37. And Philip said, "If you believe with all your heart, you may." And he replied, "I believe that Jesus Christ is the Son of God." 38. And he commanded the chariot to stop, and they both went down into the water, Philip and the eunuch, and he baptized him. 39. And when they came up out of the water, the Spirit of the Lord caught up Philip; and the eunuch saw him no more, and went on his way rejoicing.

The story of the Ethiopian eunuch and of Philip the evangelist recalls several key features of the story of Elijah and Naaman the Syrian (2 Kings 5:1–14) (Brodie, pp. 316–327). The Elijah narrative depicts both healing (from leprosy) and conversion (from Syrian Rimmon-worship), while the Acts version tells only of conversion (from Godfearer to Christian). Luke was apparently reluctant to strain plausibility or good taste by having Philip physically restore a eunuch! Both Naaman and the Ethiopian are foreign officials of high status, both close to their monarchs (2 Kings 5:5; Acts 8:27c). Naaman came to Samaria to ask the king's help in contacting the prophet Elisha. The Ethiopian for his part had journeyed to Jerusalem to seek God in the Temple worship, but the need of his heart remained unmet. This he was to find satisfied on his way home (like those other Lukan characters, the Emmaus disciples, Luke 24:13*ff*). The Israelite king fails to grasp the meaning of the letter Naaman presents to him, but a word from the prophet supplies the lack, just as Luke has the Ethiopian fail to grasp the true import of the prophetic scroll he reads till the hitchhiking evangelist offers commentary. In both cases salvation is to be sought by immersion. Naaman initially balks, but his servant persuades him. Luke has this temporizing in mind when he has the Ethiopian ask rhetorically, "What prevents me from being baptized?" (Acts 8:36). Healing and/or conversion follow, though in both cases the official must return, alone in his faith, to his heathen court.

4. Paul's Conversion (2 Maccabees 3; Acts 9:1–21)

2 Maccabees 3:1. While the holy city was inhabited in unbroken peace and the laws were very well observed because of the piety of the high priest Onias and his hatred of wickedness, 2. it came about that the kings themselves honored the place and glorified the temple with the finest presents, 3. so that even Seleucus, the king of Asia, defrayed from his own revenues all the expenses connected with the service of the sacrifices. 4. But a man named Simon, of the tribe of Benjamin, who had been made captain of the temple, had a disagreement with the high priest about the administration of the city market; 5. and when he could not prevail over Onias he went to Apollonius of Tarsus, who at that time was governor of Coelesyria and Phoenicia. 6. He reported to him that the treasury in Jerusalem was full of untold sums of money, so that the amount of the funds could not be reckoned, and that they did not belong to the account of the sacrifices, but that it was possible for them to fall under the control of the king. 7. When Apollonius met the king, he told him of the money about which he had been informed. The king chose Heliodorus, who was in charge of his affairs, and sent him with commands to effect the removal of the aforesaid money. 8. Heliodorus at once set out on his journey, ostensibly to make a tour of inspection of the cities of Coelesyria and Phoenicia, but in fact to carry out the king's purpose. 9. When he had arrived at Jerusalem and had been kindly welcomed by the high priest of the city, he told about the disclosure that had been made and stated why he had come, and he inquired whether this really was the situation. 10. The high priest explained that there were some deposits belonging to widows and orphans, 11. and also some money of Hyrcanus, son of Tobias, a

man of very prominent position, and that it totaled in all four hundred talents of silver and two hundred of gold. To such an extent the impious Simon had misrepresented the facts. 12. And he said that it was utterly impossible that wrong should be done to those people who had trusted in the holiness of the place and in the sanctity and inviolability of the temple which is honored throughout the whole world. 13. But Heliodorus, because of the king's commands which he had, said that this money must in any case be confiscated for the king's treasury. 14. So he set a day and went in to direct the inspection of these funds. There was no little distress throughout the whole city. 15. The priests prostrated themselves before the altar in their priestly garments and called toward heaven upon him who had given the law about deposits, that he should keep them safe for those who had deposited them. 16. To see the appearance of the high priest was to be wounded at heart, for his face and the change in his color disclosed the anguish of his soul. 17. For terror and bodily trembling had come over the man, which plainly showed to those who looked at him the pain lodged in his heart. 18. People also hurried out of their houses in crowds to make a general supplication because the holy place was about to be brought into contempt. 19. Women, girded with sackcloth under their breasts, thronged the streets. Some of the maidens who were kept indoors ran together to the gates, and some to the walls, while others peered out of the windows. 20. And holding up their hands to heaven, they all made entreaty. 21. There was something pitiable in the prostration of the whole populace and the anxiety of the high priest in his great anguish. 22. While they were calling upon the Almighty Lord that he would keep what had been entrusted safe and secure for those who had entrusted it, 23. Heliodorus went on with what had been decided. 24. But when he arrived at the treasury with his bodyguard, then and there the Sovereign of spirits and of all authority caused so great a manifestation that all who had been so bold as to accompany him were astounded by the power of God, and became faint with terror. 25. For there appeared to them a magnificently caparisoned horse, with a rider of frightening mien, and it rushed furiously at Heliodorus and struck at him with its front hoofs. Its rider was seen to have armor and weapons of gold. 26. Two young men also appeared to him, remark-ably strong, gloriously beautiful and splendidly dressed, who stood on each side of him and scourged him continuously, inflicting many blows on him. 27. When he suddenly fell to the ground and deep darkness came over him, his men took him up and put him on a stretcher 28. and carried him away, this man who had just entered the aforesaid treasury with a great retinue and all his bodyguard but was now unable to help himself; and they recognized clearly the sovereign power of God. 29. While he lay prostrate, speech-less because of the divine intervention and deprived of any hope of recovery, 30. they praised the Lord who had acted marvelously for his own place. And the temple, which a little while before was full of fear and disturbance, was filled with joy and gladness, now that the Almighty Lord had appeared. 31. Quickly some of Heliodorus' friends asked Onias to call upon the Most High and to grant life to one who was lying quite at his last breath. 32. And the high priest, fearing that the king might get the notion that some foul play had been perpetrated by the Jews with regard to Heliodorus, offered sac-rifice for the man's recovery. 33. While the high priest was making the offering of atonement, the same young men appeared again to Heliodorus dressed in the same clothing, and they stood and said, "Be very grateful to Onias the high priest, since for his sake the Lord has granted you your life. 34. And see that you, who have been scourged by heaven, report to all men the majestic power of God." Having said this they vanished. 35. Then Heliodorus offered sacri-fice to the Lord and made very great vows to the Savior of his life, and having bidden Onias farewell, he marched off with his forces to the king. 36. And he bore testimony to all men of the deeds of the supreme God, which he had seen with his own eyes. 37. When the king asked Heliodorus what sort of person would be suitable to send on another mission to Jerusalem, he replied, 38. "If you have any enemy or plotter against your government, send him there, for you will get him back thoroughly scourged, if he escapes at all, for there certainly is about the place some power of God. 39. For he who has his dwelling in heaven watches over that place himself and brings it aid, and he strikes and destroys those who come to do it injury." 40.

The Christ Myth Theory And Its Problems

This was the outcome of the episode of Heliodorus and the protection of the treasury.

Acts 9:1. But Saul, still breathing threats and murder against the disciples of the Lord, went to the high priest 2. and asked him for letters to the synagogues at Damascus, so that if he found any belonging to the Way, men or women, he might bring them bound to Jerusalem. 3. Now as he journeyed he approached Damascus, and suddenly a light from heaven flashed about him. 4. And he fell to the ground and heard a voice saying to him, "Saul, Saul, why do you persecute me?" 5. And he said, "Who are you, Lord?" And he said, "I am Jesus, whom you are persecuting; 6. but rise and enter the city, and you will be told what you are to do." 7. The men who were traveling with him stood speechless, hearing the voice but seeing no one. 8. Saul arose from the ground; and when his eyes were opened, he could see nothing; so they led him by the hand and brought him into Damascus. 9. And for three days he was without sight, and neither ate nor drank. 10. Now there was a disciple at Damascus named Ananias. The Lord said to him in a vision, "Ananias." And he said, "Here I am, Lord." 11. And the Lord said to him, "Rise and go to the street called Straight, and inquire in the house of Judas for a man of Tarsus named Saul; for behold, he is praying, 12. and he has seen a man named Ananias come in and lay his hands on him so that he might regain his sight." 13. But Ananias answered, "Lord, I have heard from many about this man, how much evil he has done to thy saints at Jerusalem; 14. and here he has authority from the chief priests to bind all who call upon thy name." 15. But the Lord said to him, "Go, for he is a chosen instrument of mine to carry my name before the Gentiles and kings and the sons of Israel; 16. for I will show him how much he must suffer for the sake of my name." 17. So Ananias departed and entered the house. And laying his hands on him he said, "Brother Saul, the Lord Jesus who appeared to you on the road by which you came, has sent me that you may regain your sight and be filled with the Holy Spirit." 18. And immediately something like scales fell from his eyes and he regained his sight. Then he rose and was baptized, 19. and took food and was strengthened.

For several days he was with the disciples at Damascus. 20. And in the synagogues immediately he proclaimed Jesus, saying, "He is the Son of God." 21. And all who heard him were amazed, and said, "Is not this the man who made havoc in Jerusalem of those who called on this name? And he has come here for this purpose, to bring them bound before the chief priests."

As the great Tübingen critics already saw, the story of Paul's visionary encounter with the risen Jesus not only has no real basis in the Pauline epistles but has been derived by Luke more or less directly from 2 Maccabees 3's story of Heliodorus. In it one Benjaminite named Simon (3:4) tells Apollonius of Tarsus, governor of Coele-Syria and Phoenicia (3:5), that the Jerusalem Temple houses unimaginable wealth that the Seleucid king might want to appropriate for himself. Once the king learns of this, he sends his agent Heliodorus to confiscate the loot. The prospect of such a violation of the Temple causes universal wailing and praying among the Jews. But Heliodorus is miraculously turned back when a shining warrior angel appears on horseback. The stallion's hooves knock Heliodorus to the ground, where two more angels lash him with whips (25–26). He is blinded and is unable to help himself, carried to safety on a stretcher. Pious Jews pray for his recovery, lest the people be held responsible for his condition. The angels reappear to Heliodorus, in answer to these prayers, and they announce God's grace to him: Heliodorus will live and must henceforth proclaim the majesty of the true God. Heliodorus offers sacrifice to his Saviour (3:35) and departs again for Syria, where he reports all this to the king.

In Acts the plunder of the Temple has become the persecution of the church by Saul (also called Paulus, an abbreviated form of *Apollonius*), a *Benjaminite* from *Tarsus*. Heliodorus' appointed journey to Jerusalem from Syria has become Saul's journey from Jerusalem to Syria. Saul is stopped in his tracks by a heavenly visitant, goes blind and must be taken into the city, where the prayers of his former enemies avail to raise him up. Just as Heliodorus offers sacrifice, Saul undergoes baptism. Then he is told henceforth to proclaim the risen Christ, which he does.

Luke has again added details from Euripides. In *The Bacchae*, in a sequence Luke has elsewhere rewritten into the story of Paul in Philippi (Portefaix, pp. 170), Dionysus has appeared in Thebes as an apparently mortal missionary for his own sect. He runs afoul of his cousin, King Pentheus who wants the licentious cult (as he views it) to be driven out of the country. He arrests and threatens Dionysus, only to find him freed from prison by an earthquake. Dionysus determines revenge against the proud and foolish king by magically compelling Pentheus to undergo conversion to faith in him ("Though hostile formerly, he now declares a truce and goes with us. You see what you could not when you were blind," 922–924) and sending Pentheus, in woman's guise, to spy upon the Maenads, his female revelers. He does so, is discovered, and is torn limb from limb by the women, led by his own mother. As the hapless Pentheus leaves, unwittingly, to meet his doom, Dionysus comments, "Punish this man. But first distract his wits; bewilder him with madness... After those threats with which he was so fierce, I want him made the laughingstock of Thebes" (850–851, 854–855). "He shall come to know Dionysus, son of Zeus, consummate god, most terrible, and yet most gentle, to mankind" (859–861). Pentheus must be made an example, as must poor Saul, despite himself. His conversion is a punishment, meting out to the persecutor his own medicine. Do we not detect a hint of ironic malice in Christ's words to Ananias about Saul? "I will show him how much *he* must suffer for the sake of my name" (Acts 9:16).

5. Peter's Vision (Acts 10:9–16)

Acts 10:9. The next day, as they were on their journey and coming near the city, Peter went up on the housetop to pray, about the sixth hour. 10. And he became hungry and desired something to eat; but while they were preparing it, he fell into a trance 11. and saw the heaven opened, and something descending, like a great sheet, let down by four corners upon the earth. 12. In it were all kinds of animals and reptiles and birds of the air. 13. And there came a voice to him, "Rise, Peter; kill and eat." 14. But Peter said, "No, Lord; for I have never eaten anything that is common or unclean." 15. And the voice came to him again a second time, "What God has cleansed, you must not call common." 16. This happened three times, and the thing was taken up at once to heaven.

To prime the reluctant apostle for his visit to the dwelling of the Roman Cornelius, God sends Peter a vision, one recycled from the early chapters of Ezekiel (Helms, pp. 20–21). First Peter beholds the heavens open (τον ουρανον ανεωγμενον, 10:11), just like Ezekiel did (ηνοιχθησαν οι ουρανοι, Ezekiel 1:1 LXX, "Now it came to pass in the thirtieth year, in the fourth month, on the fifth day of the month, that I was in the midst of the captivity by the river of Chobar; and the heavens were opened, and I saw visions of God."). Peter sees a vast sheet of sailcloth containing every kind of animal, ritually clean and unclean, and the heavenly voice commands him, "Eat!" (Φαγε, Acts 10:13), just as Ezekiel is shown a scroll and told to "Eat!" (Φαγε, Ezekiel 2:8c LXX, "open thy mouth, and eat what I give thee."). Peter is not eager to violate kosher laws and so balks at the command. "By no means, Lord!" (Μηδαμως, Κυριε, Acts 10:14), echoing Ezekiel verbatim, Μηδαμως, Κυριε (Ezekiel 4:14a LXX, "Then I said, Not so, Lord God of Israel."), when the latter is commanded to cook his food over a dung fire. Peter protests that he has never eaten anything unclean (ακαθαρτον) before (10:14), nor has Ezekiel (ακαθαρσια, 4:14b LXX, "Surely my soul has not been defiled with uncleanness; nor have I eaten that which died of itself or was torn of beasts from my birth until now; neither has any corrupt flesh entered into my mouth.").

WORKS NOTED

Robert Alter, *The Art of Biblical Narrative*. (New York: Basic Books, 1981).

John Bowman, *The Gospel of Mark: The New Christian Jewish Passover Haggadah*. (Studia Post-Biblica 8. Leiden: E.J. Brill, 1965).

Thomas L. Brodie, "Luke the Literary Interpreter: Luke — Acts as a Systematic Rewriting and Updating of the Elijah-Elisha Narrative in 1 and 2 Kings." Ph.D. (dissertation presented to Pontifical University of St. Thomas Aquinas, Rome. 1988).

John Dominic Crossan, *The Cross That Spoke: The Origins of the Passion Narrative* (San Francisco: Harper & Row, Publishers, 1988).

J. Duncan M. Derrett, *The Making of Mark: The Scriptural Bases of the Earliest Gospel*. Volumes 1 and 2. (Shipston-on-Stour, Warwickshire: P. Drinkwater, 1985).

Earl Doherty, *The Jesus Puzzle: Did Christianity Begin with a Mythical Christ?* (Ottawa: Canadian Humanist Publications, 1999).

C.F. Evans, "The Central Section of St. Luke's Gospel." In D.E. Nineham (ed.), *Studies in the Gospels: Essays in Memory of R.H. Lightfoot*. (Oxford: Basil Blackwell, 1967, pp. 37–53).

Randel Helms, *Gospel Fictions*. (Buffalo: Prometheus Books, 1989).

Frank Kermode, *The Genesis of Secrecy: On the Interpretation of Narrative*. The Charles Eliot Norton Lectures 1977–1978. (Cambridge: Harvard University Press, 1979).

Dennis R. MacDonald, *The Homeric Epics and the Gospel of Mark*. (New Haven: Yale University Press, 2000).

Dale Miller and Patricia Miller. *The Gospel of Mark as Midrash on Earlier Jewish and New Testament Literature*. Studies in the Bible and Early Christianity 21. (Lewiston/Queenston/Lampeter: Edwin Mellen Press 1990).

Lilian Portefaix, *Sisters Rejoice: Paul's Letter to the Philippians and Luke-Acts as Seen by First-Century Philippian Women*. Coniectanea biblica. New Testament series, 20. (Stockholm: Almqvist & Wicksell, 1988).

Wolfgang Roth, *Hebrew Gospel: Cracking the Code of Mark*. (Oak Park: Meyer-Stone Books, 1988).

William R. Stegner, "The Baptism of Jesus: A Story Modeled on the Binding of Isaac." In Herschel Shanks (ed.), *Abraham & Family: New Insights into the Patriarchal Narratives*. (Washington, D.C.: Biblical Archaeology Society, 2001).

Rikki E. Watts, *Isaiah's New Exodus and Mark*. Wissenschaftliche Untersuchungen zum Neuen Testament 2. Reihe 88. (Tübingen: Mohr Siebeck, 1997).

Dubious Database
Second Thoughts on the Red and Pink Materials of the Jesus Seminar

I have been privileged to participate in the deliberations and the voting of the Jesus Seminar. We voted on each gospel pericope (individual unit), color-coding them red (surely authentic), pink (probably authentic), gray (probably not), and black (definitely not). This procedure was adapted from that of the United Bible Societies' committee on textual criticism, who consider the authenticity of variant readings in the New Testament manuscripts and rate them A, B, C, or D, depending on the likelihood of their originally having formed part of the autographs. The procedure obviously presupposes a range of opinions among the Fellows of the Seminar, or there would be no need for a vote.[1] I always found myself on the left, most skeptical end of the spectrum in our discussions. I find the 18% authenticity judged of both sayings and stories to be too optimistic. This skepticism stems, I like to think, not from any adolescent stubbornness, but rather from a more rigorous adherence to the methodology of the Higher Critics of the nineteenth century (*e.g.*, D.F. Strauss) and the great form and redaction critics of the twentieth (especially Bultmann). Simply put, again and again I found myself shaking my head and musing how Strauss and Bultmann would never make the judgments on the texts that we were making by majority vote. In what follows, I would like to illustrate two things by a sustained scrutiny of a collection of the red and pink materials as compiled in *The Gospel of Jesus according to the Jesus Seminar*.[2] First, I seek to highlight what I believe to be thorough-going critical methodology for sifting through the Jesus tradition, by indicating where I believe the Seminar neglected it. Second, I want to show that, just as the Seminar Fellows themselves have often suggested, the work needs to be done again and with new eyes. Nor will such an attempt by the new Jesus Project be the last.

1. *Prologue: Birth, childhood & family of Jesus*

"Jesus was a descendant of Abraham." Are we that sure there *was* a historical Abraham? There is significant room for doubting it. The most optimistic of the viable scholarly views of the Abraham character in modern Old Testament criticism is that of Albrecht Alt whose "Gods of the Fathers" hypothesis[3] allows that the "Abraham" implied in the phrase "the God of Abraham" might reflect some archaic clan patriarch whose remote descendants allied themselves with similar clans venerating "the Fear of Isaac" and "the Mighty One of Jacob." The seniority of the clans was reflected in the order of the fictive genealogy thus produced. The Abraham figurehead might have been a historical individual. But then Ignaz Goldziher long ago made a powerful case that Abraham, the father of a multitude, began as a moon god whose innumerable progeny were not *like* unto the stars of heaven but *were* those stars themselves.[4] If the existence of Jesus is doubtful, the existence of Abraham is more so.

"Jesus' parents were named Joseph and Mary." According to the stories of Matthew and Luke, yes, they were. And according to Homer's *Odyssey*, Odysseus' son was named Telemachus. Hercules' father was named Zeus. But was the historical father of an ostensible historical Jesus named Joseph? We must not pass by the serious question, raised by some scholars, of whether Jesus' epithet "son of Joseph" does not stem from some identifying him as the Northern counterpart to the Scion of David, namely the Messiah ben Joseph. Remember, Jesus is shown in Mark 12:35–37 repudiating the whole notion of a Davidic messiah.

Mark 12:35. And as Jesus taught in the temple, he said, "How can the scribes say that the Christ is the son of David? 36. David himself, inspired by the Holy Spirit, declared, 'The Lord said to my Lord, Sit at my right hand, till I put thy enemies under thy feet.' 37. David himself calls him Lord; so how is he his son?"

This passage may represent Galilean Christianity and Christology. So may the title "Son of Joseph."

"Jesus was born when Herod was king." Can we be so sure of this when Luke's synchronism ("In the fifteenth year of the reign of Tiberius Caesar, Pontius Pilate being governor of Judea, and Herod being tetrarch of Galilee, and his brother Philip tetrarch of the region of Ituraea and Trachonitis, and Lysanias tetrarch of Abilene, in the high-priesthood of Annas and Caiaphas, the word of God came to John the son of Zechariah in the wilderness," Luke 1:1–2) is riddled with contradictions, and Matthew's Jesus nativity is based on Josephus' Moses nativity (see "New Testament Narrative as Old Testament Midrash," in the present volume, section on Matthew's Nativity, Matthew 1:18–2:23), which required a plausible Pharaoh analogue? The "evidence" here is a set of rotten boards that may not bear the weight of this assertion. As Strauss warned us, we have no business dismissing the story as a whole as tendentious and then trying to retain this or that incidental detail of it as accurate.[5]

The Seminar says Jesus had likely worked as a local carpenter, as his neighbors subsequently recalled (Mark 6:3: "Is this not the carpenter, the son of Mary and brother of James and Joses and Judas and Simon, and are his sisters not here with us?"). But no: Geza Vermes showed that the reference denotes the acclamation of Jesus by the congregation as an able exponent of scripture, which he has just expounded in the course of synagogue preaching. The maxim was "Not even a carpenter, the son of a carpenter, could explain so-and-so."[6]

Jesus, we are told, haled from Nazareth. But there is serious doubt as to whether there was such a town in that century. Though between them Josephus and the Mishnah mention dozens of Galilean towns, neither mentions Nazareth. And there is a ready-made alternative. Again, as many scholars have suggested, "Jesus the Nazorean" is too suspiciously close to the sect-designation of the Nazoreans or Mandeans, mentioned even in ancient times as a sect of devout Jews. The epithet may have denoted "Jesus the sectarian."[7] Of course, our gospels have begun to take it as denoting Jesus' hometown, but that may be a historicizing evasion of the later-distasteful notion of the divine savior being anyone else's disciple. It is a wide-open question.

The Gospel of Jesus avers that Jesus had brothers named James, Judas, and Simon, and that, of these, at least James later became a leader of the movement (see Acts 15:13–20, "After they finished speaking, James replied, "Brethren, listen to me. […] Therefore my judgment is that we should not trouble those of the Gentiles who turn to God, but should write to them to abstain from the pollutions of idols and from unchastity and from what is strangled and from blood.") and received a resurrection appearance (1 Corinthians 15:7a, "Then he appeared to James, then to all the apostles.").

Is any of that probable? G.A. Wells[8] and others have reminded us that early Christian itinerants were called Jesus' brethren, and that a group of missionaries called "the Lord's brothers" is mentioned in 1 Corinthians 9:5 ("Do we not have the right to be accompanied by a sister as wife, as the other apostles and the brothers of the Lord and Cephas?") with no suggestion of a blood relation to Jesus. The list of Jesus' brothers in Mark 6:3 may reflect notables in this order, mistakenly "naturalized" as blood relatives once the original significance had been forgotten. Besides, James is called "*the Lord's* brother" (Besides Peter, "I saw none of the other apostles except James the Lord's brother."), not "the brother of *Jesus*," which may well denote something like spiritual kinship (or twinship) between Jesus and the spiritual adept, *à la* Thomas 13 ("I am not your master, because you have drunk, you have become filled, from the bubbling spring which

268

I have measured out.") Also, John the Baptist being Jesus' cousin (Luke 1:35–36, "And the angel said to her, "The Holy Spirit will come upon you, and the power of the Most High will overshadow you; therefore the child to be born will be called holy, the Son of God. And behold, your kinswoman Elizabeth in her old age has also conceived a son; and this is the sixth month with her who was called barren.") is clearly a Lukan fiction meant to ally the sects of which Jesus and the Baptizer served as figureheads. We cannot be sure that James, Jude, and Simeon were not equally fictive relations serving similar purposes.

Did Jesus' kinfolk try to seize him for his own good, thinking him mad? (See also # 11, ***Jesus' relatives think him mad***.) I doubt it. The scene in Mark 3:21–35 ("And when his family heard it, they went out to seize him, for they were saying, 'He is beside himself.' [...] And his mother and his brothers came; and standing outside they sent to him and called him. And a crowd was sitting about him; and they said to him, 'Your mother and your brothers are outside, asking for you.' And he replied, 'Who are my mother and my brothers?' And looking around on those who sat about him, he said, 'Here are my mother and my brothers! Whoever does the will of God is my brother, and sister, and mother'.") may very well be a polemic against a leadership group ("the Heirs" or the Pillars, Galatians 2:9, "James [the Just] and Cephas [Simeon bar Cleophas?] and John, who were reputed to be pillars") who claimed dynastic succession from Jesus, as many scholars believe. (Would this not fly in the face of the aforementioned suspicion that "the brothers of the Lord" were not supposed to be Jesus' actual siblings? Yes, but that doesn't matter. I am not setting forth and defending a consistent alternative position here, only listing alternative options that *might* well be true, undermining the supposed certainty of the positions voted by the Seminar Fellows.)

Besides, the scene is transparently based on Exodus 18 (see again "New Testament Narrative as Old Testament Midrash," under "Choosing the Disciples" in Mark), where Moses is told his relatives mean to call on him: they do, and Jethro, seeing Moses' workload, fears the constant demands will prove too much for him and suggests he appoint some assistants. Mark has very likely reworked a retelling of this story in which Jesus received his visiting family and heeded their advice to get some help lest he go mad, issuing in the appointment of the Twelve to share the workload. Mark has divided the story and made the appointment of the Twelve Jesus' own idea, getting it out of the way just before his family arrives — to no purpose. Again, we see factional polemics as well as a literary basis, not a historical one.

Are we red-letter confident that Jesus rose from the dead, much less appeared to James? All we can say on the basis of 1 Corinthians 15:7 is that some faction claimed the honor of a resurrection vision for James because it was a pre-requisite for exercising the apostolic office (1 Cor. 9:1, "Am I not an apostle? Have I not seen Jesus our Lord?"). Was the claim true? What's your favorite color?

2.   *John the Baptist & Jesus*

It is not hard to believe in a historical John the Baptist, though some (*e.g.*, Robert Eisler, noting the similarity to mythical Oannes, the divine sage who emerged from the sea to teach wisdom) have doubted it. The Seminar allows that John gave the crowds instructions to flesh out his demands for repentance, found in Luke 3:7–14.

> He said therefore to the multitudes that came out to be baptized by him, "You brood of vipers! Who warned you to flee from the wrath to come? Bear fruits that befit repentance, and do not begin to say to yourselves, 'We have Abraham as our father'; for I tell you, God is able from these stones to raise up children to Abraham. Even now the axe is laid to the root of the trees; every tree therefore that does not bear good fruit is cut down and thrown into the fire." And the multi-

tudes asked him, "What then shall we do?" And he answered them, "He who has two coats, let him share with him who has none; and he who has food, let him do likewise." Tax collectors also came to be baptized, and said to him, "Teacher, what shall we do?" And he said to them, "Collect no more than is appointed you." Soldiers also asked him, "And we, what shall we do?" And he said to them, "Rob no one by violence or by false accusation, and be content with your wages."

Only Luke has such sayings, and Conzelmann[9] urged their incompatibility with John's otherwise-attested apocalyptic urgency: what is he doing outlining a new ethic for an ongoing life in the world? That is so stamped with the Lukan *Tendenz* (to remove apocalyptic urgency) as to cast grave doubt on the authenticity of the sayings. (But the Seminar Fellows thought so, too.[10] They voted these sayings gray. What are they doing in this collection?)

John punctures the hopes of the crowd that he might be the messiah (Luke 3:15–17, "As the people were in expectation, and all men questioned in their hearts concerning John, whether perhaps he were the Christ, John answered them all, 'I baptize you with water; but he who is mightier than I is coming, the thong of whose sandals I am not worthy to untie; he will baptize you with the Holy Spirit and with fire. His winnowing fork is in his hand, to clear his threshing floor, and to gather the wheat into his granary, but the chaff he will burn with unquenchable fire."). But this is blatant redactional fabrication. By making the famous "One greater than me is coming after me" saying into an answer to a question that only Luke raises ("Could John be the Messiah?"), Luke puts a spin on the punch line, one that has everything to do with his agenda (on display in his parallel nativities of John and Jesus) to rebut the messianic claims of John's surviving sect. The implied dialogue is as fictional as the fetus John leaping in the womb when the pregnant Mary enters the room.

Surely Jesus was immersed by John, no?

John the baptizer appeared in the wilderness, preaching a baptism of repentance for the forgiveness of sins. And there went out to him all the country of Judea, and all the people of Jerusalem; and they were baptized by him in the river Jordan, confessing their sins. [...] In those days Jesus came from Nazareth of Galilee and was baptized by John in the Jordan." (Mark 1:4–9)

Maybe not. Since Mark obviously saw nothing embarrassing in the story or he wouldn't have told it, we cannot defend it with the "criterion of embarrassment," *i.e.*, no Christian would have invented it, given the stumbling-block it became.[12] What offended a later generation did not necessarily offend the more naïve Christology of its predecessor. In fact, as we will see, *the criterion of embarrassment is utterly worthless. The chief axiom of form criticism is that nothing could have survived that was not useful, at least to begin with.* As Guignebert and others have suggested,[11] the scene may have been created as a ritual etiology, giving baptism candidates Jesus' example to follow.

3. *Jesus is baptized (Mark 1:9)*

"In those days Jesus came from Nazareth of Galilee and was baptized by John in the Jordan."

The Jesus Seminar cuts all the visionary features from the baptism of Jesus, but that is, again, to forget Strauss' caveat: *we have no business trying to make bad evidence into good by stripping away the very features of the story for the sake of which it was told in the first place, and then seeing if we can salvage a couple of incidental details.*[13]

Moreover, there is another reason to reject the message of this verse. There is good reason to think that this verse is a later interpolation in the text of Mark. This is the only place in that gospel where the place-name *Nazareth* occurs, and the town does not figure in that gospel's account of the career of Jesus. Moreover, the name *Jesus* here is lacking the definite article, in contrast with the almost universal Markan usage employing the article. Mark does not speak of "Jesus," but rather of "the Jesus" — as though the name be treated according to its meaning, "the Savior."

4.   *Jesus is tested (Matthew 4:1–11//Luke 4:1–13)*

Matthew 4:1. Jesus was led up by the Spirit into the wilderness to be tempted by the devil. 2. And he fasted forty days and forty nights, and afterward he was hungry. 3. And the tempter came and said to him, "If you are the Son of God, command these stones to become loaves of bread." 4. But he answered, "It is written, 'Man shall not live by bread alone, but by every word that proceeds from the mouth of God'." 5. Then the devil took him to the holy city, and set him on the pinnacle of the temple, 6. and said to him, "If you are the Son of God, throw yourself down; for it is written, 'He will give his angels charge of you,' and 'On their hands they will bear you up, lest you strike your foot against a stone'." 7. Jesus said to him, "Again it is written, 'You shall not tempt the Lord your God'." 8. Again, the devil took him to a very high mountain, and showed him all the kingdoms of the world and the glory of them; 9. and he said to him, "All these I will give you, if you will fall down and worship me." 10. Then Jesus said to him, "Begone, Satan! for it is written, 'You shall worship the Lord your God and him only shall you serve'." 11. Then the devil left him, and behold, angels came and ministered to him.

We know we are in trouble, that criticism is in jeopardy, when we read that the Fellows saw fit to include the desert temptations of Jesus as authentic material. This is really astonishing. Satan coming on stage? We must not disregard Dibelius' "law of biographical analogy,"[14] *the axiom that the religious imagination everywhere and in every age resorts to the mythic hero archetype and starts telling the same tales about analogous heroes, saints, and founders.* For exactly analogous temptation stories are told featuring Abraham, Zoroaster, and the Buddha.[15] Zoroaster's temptations by the evil Ahriman ensue upon Zoroaster's stepping onto the river bank after a ritual immersion. The archangel Vohu Mana descends from heaven to reveal to him his prophetic mission, whereupon the arch-fiend attempts to dissuade him. Sound familiar? If we write off the slaughter of the innocents and the Bethlehem star as common my-themes, we must cut Jesus' temptations just as quickly.

Again, the Seminar discounts the story as fictive, but it owes its inclusion in *The Gospel of Jesus* to the fact that, as a piece of fiction, it nonetheless correctly sums up something about Jesus' character. But this is to renounce the task of historical-critical re-construction: "What the heck; close enough!"

Some of the Fellows believed the Temptation story might have been based on a visionary experience of Jesus, but this is to multiply explanations. As per Strauss,[16] once we have recognized the nature of the story as stock piece of hagiography, it is absolute-ly gratuitous to posit some earlier, less extravagant half-version. And what evidence do we have of Jesus having had such a vision? Clearly, someone here is looking for some vestige to hang onto.

5.   *Jesus announces the good news*

5.a.   *Children in God's domain (Mark 10:13–16)*

Mark 10:13. And they were bringing children to him, that he might touch them; and the disciples rebuked them. 14. But when Jesus saw it he was indignant, and said to them, "Let the children come to me, do not hinder them; for to such belongs the kingdom of God. 15. Truly, I say to you, whoever does not receive the kingdom of God like a child shall not enter it." 16. And he took them in his arms and blessed them, laying his hands upon them.

Did Jesus rebuke his disciples for turning away parents requesting Jesus kiss their babies? I doubt it, for two reasons. Form-critically, the story hinges on the "why wait?" or "who forbids?" motif com-mon to ancient baptism stories. As Oscar Cullmann[17] pointed out, that marks this pericope as a piece of infant baptism liturgy from the early church, not a scene from Jesus' life. All the more since the story seems to owe its only real action to the story of Elisha rebuking his disciple Gehazi for trying to turn away the weeping Shunnamite who has come for his help ("And when she came to the mountain to the man of God, she caught hold of his feet. And Gehazi came to thrust her away. But the man of God said, 'Let her alone, for she is in bitter distress; and the LORD has hidden it from me, and has not told me.'" 2 Kings 4:27). We cannot be too easy on the material or ourselves, trying to have our cake and eat it, too, as scholars do when they admit the literary parallel or the form-critical usefulness of a story and then say it could also have happened that way. *That is multiplying explanations, and Occam's Razor forbids.*

5.b.   *Kingdom banquet (Luke 14:16–24)*

Luke 14:16. But he said to him, "A man once gave a great banquet, and invited many, 17. and at the time for the banquet he sent his servant to say to those who had been invited, 'Come; for all is now ready.' 18. But they all alike began to make excuses. The first said to him, 'I have bought a field, and I must go out and see it; I pray you, have me excused.' 19. And another said, 'I have bought five yoke of oxen, and I go to examine them; I pray you, have me excused.' 20. And another said, 'I have married a wife, and therefore I cannot come.' 21. So the servant came and reported this to his master. Then the householder in anger said to his servant, 'Go out quickly to the streets and lanes of the city, and bring in the poor and maimed and blind and lame.' 22. And the servant said, 'Sir, what you command-ed has been done, and still there is room.' 23. And the master said to the servant, 'Go out to the highways and hedges, and compel people to come in, that my house may be filled. 24. For I tell you, none of those men who were invited shall taste my banquet.'"

The Christ Myth Theory And Its Problems

The Seminar accepts the most modest version, Luke's. The parallel version of the story found in Matthew 22:1–14 is longer and seems to bear more Matthean fingerprints:

> Matthew 22:1. And again Jesus spoke to them in parables, saying, 2. "The kingdom of heaven may be compared to a king who gave a marriage feast for his son, 3. and sent his servants to call those who were invited to the marriage feast; but they would not come. 4. Again he sent other servants, saying, 'Tell those who are invited, Behold, I have made ready my dinner, my oxen and my fat calves are killed, and everything is ready; come to the marriage feast.' 5. But they made light of it and went off, one to his farm, another to his business, 6. while the rest seized his servants, treated them shamefully, and killed them. 7. The king was angry, and he sent his troops and destroyed those murderers and burned their city. 8. Then he said to his servants, 'The wedding is ready, but those invited were not worthy. 9. Go therefore to the thoroughfares, and invite to the marriage feast as many as you find.' 10. And those servants went out into the streets and gathered all whom they found, both bad and good; so the wedding hall was filled with guests. 11. "But when the king came in to look at the guests, he saw there a man who had no wedding garment; 12. and he said to him, 'Friend, how did you get in here without a wedding garment?' And he was speechless. 13. Then the king said to the attendants, 'Bind him hand and foot, and cast him into the outer darkness; there men will weep and gnash their teeth.' 14. For many are called, but few are chosen."

But, as Joachim Jeremias[18] argued long ago, even the seemingly earlier Lukan version reads like half of the rabbinical parable of the tax-collector Bar-Ma'jan, who tried to enhance his reputation by inviting the local gentry to a feast, only to be chagrined when no one showed up, then giving the food to the beggars. This single act of charity resulted in God rewarding him with a well-attended funeral, though with nothing in the afterlife. Jeremias envisioned Jesus using the story as it was already circulating. But Jeremias forgot what Bultmann[19] remembered: *who remembers the great man quoting somebody else?* If it is found elsewhere, with a different attribution, then the attribution to Jesus here (as to anyone else elsewhere) is arbitrary. "Sounds good! Jesus must have said it!"

5.c. *Mustard Seed (Thomas 20:1–4//Mark 4:30–32//Matthew 13:31–32)*

Thomas 20. The disciples say to Jesus, "Tell us what the kingdom of heaven is like." He says to them, "It is like a mustard seed, smaller than all the rest of the seeds. But when it falls on the tilled earth, it produces a large branch and becomes lodging for the birds of the sky."

Mark 4:30. And he said, "With what can we compare the kingdom of God, or what parable shall we use for it? 31. It is like a grain of mustard seed, which, when sown upon the ground, is the smallest of all the seeds on earth; 32. yet when it is sown it grows up and becomes the greatest of all shrubs, and puts forth large branches, so that the birds of the air can make nests in its shade."

Matthew 13:31. Another parable he put before them, saying, "The kingdom of heaven is like a grain of mustard seed which a man took and sowed in his field; 32. it is the smallest of all seeds, but when it has grown it is the greatest of shrubs and becomes a tree, so that the birds of the air come and make nests in its branches."

5.d. *Leaven (Luke 13:20–21//Matthew 13:33//Thomas 96)*

Luke 13:20. And again he said, "To what shall I compare the kingdom of God? 21. It is like leaven which a woman took and hid in three measures of flour, till it was all leavened."

Matthew 13:33. He told them another parable. "The kingdom of heaven is like leaven which a woman took and hid in three measures of flour, till it was all leavened."

The Christ Myth Theory And Its Problems

> Thomas 96. Jesus says, "The kingdom of the Father is like a woman who has taken a pinch of leaven and hidden it in the dough, and has made large loaves from it. Whoever has ears, let him hear!"

Whether one understands the point to be the rapid or the gradual growth of the kingdom of God, James Breech[20] is right: it is retrospective, presupposing that the Christian movement has already made such great strides that to look back on its humble origins is amazing. The parable is therefore a *vaticinium ex eventu*. The same very definitely goes for the twin parable of the leaven, only there we may raise the additional suspicion of it looking like a *secondary homologous formation*: creating a new parable on the basis of an old one, as when Thomas 47 adds to the impossibility of serving two masters ("No one can serve two masters; for either he will hate the one and love the other, or he will be devoted to the one and despise the other. You cannot serve God and mammon." Matthew 6:24) that of riding two horses and shooting two arrows in different directions at the same time (Thomas 47, Jesus says, "It is impossible for a man to mount two horses at once and to stretch two bows, and it is impossible for a servant to serve two masters. If he tries, he will inevitably find himself honoring the one and, by the same act, offending the other").

6.   *Disciples & Discipleship*

6.a.   *First disciples*
Simon Peter and Andrew, James and John (Mark 1:16–20)

Mark 1:16. And passing along by the Sea of Galilee, he saw Simon and Andrew the brother of Simon casting a net in the sea; for they were fishermen. 17. And Jesus said to them, "Follow me and I will make you become fishers of men." 18. And immediately they left their nets and followed him. 19. And going on a little farther, he saw James the son of Zebedee and John his brother, who were in their boat mending the nets.

20. And immediately he called them; and they left their father Zebedee in the boat with the hired servants, and followed him.

6.b.　Levi (Mark 2:14)

And as he passed on, he saw Levi the son of Alphaeus sitting at the tax office, and he said to him, "Follow me." And he rose and followed him.

Mark's stories of Peter, Andrew, James, and John, and then Levi, abandoning their livelihoods and families to follow Jesus at his merest word of command, are very powerful. The decisiveness illustrated here almost counts as a miracle in its own right. In fact, subsequent evangelists felt compelled to supply psychological motivation for such a radical break. Luke added the miraculous catch of fish as the "clincher," while the Preaching of John (incorporated into the Acts of John) posited that James and John followed Jesus hoping for a solution to the puzzle of how they had seen him beckoning in changing and contradictory forms as he stood on shore. John's gospel is the most modest: the Mark/Matthew version was not what it seemed since these men had already been associated with Jesus through a prior adherence to John the Baptist's sect. But ultimately these discipleship paradigms must be simple rewrites of Elijah recruiting Elisha in 1 Kings 19:19–21.

1 Kings 19:19. So he departed from there, and found Elisha the son of Shaphat, who was plowing, with twelve yoke of oxen before him, and he was with the twelfth. Elijah passed by him and cast his mantle upon him. 20. And he left the oxen, and ran after Elijah, and said, "Let me kiss my father and my mother, and then I will follow you." And he said to him, "Go back again; for what have I done to you?" 21. And he returned from following him, and took the yoke of oxen, and slew them, and boiled their flesh with the yokes of the oxen, and gave it to the people, and they ate. Then he arose and went after Elijah, and ministered to him.

The Christ Myth Theory And Its Problems

But couldn't history have repeated itself in the case of Jesus and his disciples? Sure, but as F.C. Baur cautioned, *while anything may be admitted as **possible**, the critic must ask what is **probable**.*

The odd thing is that, once again, the Seminar cannot credit Mark's story either, but it is included in *The Gospel of Jesus* anyway, apparently as a place-holder for whatever the real circumstances of their recruitment may have been.[21]

6.c.   *Women companions of Jesus (Luke 8:1–3)*

Luke 8:1. Soon afterward he went on through cities and villages, preaching and bringing the good news of the kingdom of God. And the twelve were with him, 2. and also some women who had been healed of evil spirits and infirmities: Mary, called Magdalene, from whom seven demons had gone out, 3. and Joanna, the wife of Chuza, Herod's steward, and Susanna, and many others, who provided for them out of their means.

This list of some women supporters of Jesus does not go so far as to make them disciples as some today wish it had. Instead, they are said to be patronesses, paying the bills for the itinerant mendicants. While such an arrangement has no apparent parallels in Judaism, there are plenty in the Hellenistic cults of the day such as Juvenal satirizes, and this means the scenario envisioned by Luke seems out of context for a Palestinian Jesus. That is one question mark to be raised beside this unit. Another is the plainly legendary feature of Jesus having cast precisely seven demons out of Mary Magdalene. For her simply to have been a recovered demoniac poses no problem; the principle of analogy reminds us that exorcisms still occur today, whatever you want to make of them. The problem is the magic number seven, or indeed any number at all. How could anyone have known how many demons possessed her? Some manner of "ecto-meter" borrowed from the Ghostbusters?

But, again, we are told the Fellows painted this one gray. My guess is that Political Correctness forbade excluding the sole mention of Jesus having anything like female disciples. Including this passage in *The Gospel of Jesus* is like the chastened RSV editors putting the Long Ending of Mark

16:9. Now when he rose early on the first day of the week, he appeared first to Mary Magdalene, from whom he had cast out seven demons. 10. She went and told those who had been with him, as they mourned and wept. 11. But when they heard that he was alive and had been seen by her, they would not believe it. 12. After this he appeared in another form to two of them, as they were walking into the country. 13. And they went back and told the rest, but they did not believe them. 14. Afterward he appeared to the eleven themselves as they sat at table; and he upbraided them for their unbelief and hardness of heart, because they had not believed those who saw him after he had risen. 15. And he said to them, "Go into all the world and preach the gospel to the whole creation. 16. He who believes and is baptized will be saved; but he who does not believe will be condemned. 17. And these signs will accompany those who believe: in my name they will cast out demons; they will speak in new tongues; 18. they will pick up serpents, and if they drink any deadly thing, it will not hurt them; they will lay their hands on the sick, and they will recover." 19. So then the Lord Jesus, after he had spoken to them, was taken up into heaven, and sat down at the right hand of God. 20. And they went forth and preached everywhere, while the Lord worked with them and confirmed the message by the signs that attended it. Amen.

and the Adulteress pericope

John 7:53. They went each to his own house, 8:1. but Jesus went to the Mount of olives. 2. early in the morning he came again to the temple; all the people came to him, and he sat down and taught them. 3. The scribes and the Pharisees brought a woman who had been caught in adultery, and placing her in the midst 4. They said to him, "Teacher, this woman has been caught in the act of adultery. 5. Now in the law Moses commanded us to stone such. What do you say about her?" 6. This they said to test him, that they might have some charge to bring against him. Jesus bent down and wrote with his finger on the ground. 7. And as they continued to ask him, he stood up and said to them, "Let him who is without sin among you be the first to throw a stone at her." 8. And once more he bent down and wrote with his finger on the ground. 9. But when they heard it, they went away, one by one, beginning with the eldest, and Jesus was left alone with the woman standing before him. 10. Jesus looked up and said to her, "Woman, where are they? Has no one condemned you?" 11. She said, "No one, Lord." And Jesus said, "Neither do I condemn you; go, and do not sin again."

back in the text, restored from the footnote status to which they had been relegated in the first edition.

7. Teaching with authority
In the synagogue at Capernaum (Mark 1:21–22)

Mark 1:21. And they went into Capernaum; and immediately on the sabbath he entered the synagogue and taught. 22. And they were astonished at his teaching, for he taught them as one who had authority, and not as the scribes.

All that survives, in the Jesus Seminar gospel, of Mark 1:21–27 is the lead-in, where we are told that Jesus taught with the ring of authority, unlike the judicious scribes. But the Jesus Seminarists thus eviscerate the Markan original, which appeals in the crudest fashion to an immediately ensuing exorcism as miraculous proof of whatever the exorcist teaches. Rather than leap Lessing's ugly ditch, they tried instead to fill it in with manure. The notion that Jesus simply spoke dogmatically is garnered from Matthew's similar rewrite in Matthew 7:28–29 ("And when Jesus finished these sayings, the crowds were astonished at his teaching, for he taught them as one who had authority, and not as their scribes"), where it is no exorcism but rather the Sermon on the Mount that prompts the comment about speaking with authority. But that is secondary rationalizing, even demythologizing, on Matthew's part. The Seminar has mistaken superstructure for substructure.

8. *Vineyard laborers (Matthew 20:1–15)*

Matthew 20:1. For the kingdom of heaven is like a householder who went out early in the morning to hire laborers for his vineyard. 2. After agreeing with the laborers for a denarius a day, he sent them into his vineyard. 3. And going out about the third hour he saw others standing idle in the market place; 4. and to them he said, 'You go into the vineyard too, and whatever is right I will give you.' So they went. 5. Going out again about the sixth hour and the ninth hour, he did the same. 6. And about the eleventh hour he went out and found others standing; and he said to them, 'Why do you stand here idle all day?' 7. They said to him, 'Because no one has hired us.' He said to them, 'You go into the vineyard too.' 8. And when evening came, the owner of the vineyard said to his steward, 'Call the laborers and pay them their wages, beginning with the last, up to the first.' 9. And when those hired about the eleventh hour came, each of them received a denarius. 10. Now when the first came, they thought they would receive more; but each of them also received a denarius. 11. And on receiving it they grumbled at the householder, 12. saying, 'These last worked only one hour, and you have made them equal to us who have borne the burden of the day and the scorching heat.' 13. But he replied to one of them, 'Friend, I am doing you no wrong; did you not agree with me for a denarius? 14. Take what belongs to you, and go; I choose to give to this last as I give to you. 15. Am I not allowed to do what I choose with what belongs to me? Or do you begrudge my generosity?'

This parable is, among the gospels, unique to Matthew, a gospel that shares a number of features in common with the emerging rabbinic Judaism with which the Matthean community seems to have been struggling for dominance. This parable is so strongly reminiscent of the eulogy parable for Rabbi Bun bar Hijjah (where, however, the reversal of workers' expectations makes more sense) that we must hold open the possibility of Matthew having borrowed it from his rival rabbis.[22] It is not that Jesus couldn't or wouldn't have shared lore with colleagues, but rather that we have no business assuming it was so. We ought, to be on the safe side, to view the parable as one of Neusner's "wandering sayings" that has snagged here and there on different names in the wider tradition.[23] *That is the point of the famous criterion of dissimilarity: if a "Jesus" saying echoes something in contemporary Judaism, we have to assume the "worst," that it has been borrowed from that quarter because there is no particular reason to think otherwise.*[24] If we recognize the inherent uncertainty of the attribution but decide to ascribe it to Jesus anyhow, we ourselves are doing the very thing we admit the gospel tradents did, deciding: "Jesus might as well have said it, so let's say he did."

9. *Demons by the finger of God*
Jesus tours Galilee (Mark 1:35–39)

> Mark 1:35. And in the morning, a great while before day, he rose and went out to a lonely place, and there he prayed. 36. And Simon and those who were with him pursued him, 37. and they found him and said to him, "Every one is searching for you." 38. And he said to them, "Let us go on to the next towns, that I may preach there also; for that is why I came out." 39. And he went throughout all Galilee, preaching in their synagogues and casting out demons.

Well, why shouldn't he? The problem with this text is that it appears to be a bit of redactional connective tissue, presupposing the exorcisms and healings of the previous chapter and preparing for the activity of Jesus in the next. It is nothing to remember by itself and thus not a piece of genuine tradition. Also, the passage ends with a summarizing generalization, another mark of redaction. I believe the Fellows were not unaware of this, but the editor included it in *The Gospel of Jesus* because some transition was better than none. But then we are in the business of gospel-building, not of sifting evidence.

10. Unclean demon (Mark 1:23–28)

Mark 1:23. And immediately there was in their synagogue a man with an unclean spirit; 24. and he cried out, "What have you to do with us, Jesus of Nazareth? Have you come to destroy us? I know who you are, the Holy One of God." 25. But Jesus rebuked him, saying, "Be silent, and come out of him!" 26. And the unclean spirit, convulsing him and crying with a loud voice, came out of him. 27. And they were all amazed, so that they questioned among themselves, saying, "What is this? A new teaching! With authority he commands even the unclean spirits, and they obey him." 28. And at once his fame spread everywhere throughout all the surrounding region of Galilee.

As opposed to those spic-n'-span demons, one supposes. In any case, here is the rest of Mark's episode in the Capernaum synagogue. But there seem to have been no Galilean synagogues in the ostensible time of Jesus, save for a couple of Hellenized Herodian enclaves so as to make Diaspora Jews feel welcome in a "home away from their home away from home." Thus the whole premise here is anachronistic. Besides this, there is the fictional touch, presupposing the whole (redactional) "messianic secret" motif as well as the idea of the demon being privy to secrets loose on the astral plane and threatening to divulge them to mortals. Jesus may, as Bultmann said, have believed himself to be an exorcist, but this story is not an historical incident. Finally, the heckling of the local demoniac, "What have we to do with you, Jesus of Nazareth? Have you come to destroy us? I know who you are — the Holy

One of God!," comes directly from the defensive alarm of the Zarephath widow in 1 Kings 17:18: "What have you against me, O man of God? You have come to me to bring my sin to remembrance, and to cause the death of my son!"[25]

The notes[26] to *The Gospel of Jesus* inform us that the Fellows voted all individual exorcism stories as gray or black, but that they felt sure Jesus was actually an exorcist. But that seems an odd conclusion, a chain made altogether of weak links (which may be how the Gadarene demoniac snapped them). *If the evidence will not withstand scrutiny, why do we accept the proposition?*

11. Beelzebul controversy (Luke 11:15–19)
Demons by the finger of God (Luke 11:20)
Powerful Man (Mark 3:27)

Luke 11:15. But some of them said, "He casts out demons by Beelzebul, the prince of demons"; 16. while others, to test him, sought from him a sign from heaven. 17. But he, knowing their thoughts, said to them, "Every kingdom divided against itself is laid waste, and a divided household falls. 18. And if Satan also is divided against himself, how will his kingdom stand? For you say that I cast out demons by Beel-zebul. 19. And if I cast out demons by Beel-zebul, by whom do your sons cast them out? Therefore they shall be your judges. 20. But if it is by the finger of God that I cast out demons, then the kingdom of God has come upon you.

Mark 3:27. But no one can enter a strong man's house and plunder his goods, unless he first binds the strong man; then indeed he may plunder his house.

Can anyone miss the obviously midrashic character of this material? Jesus plays the role of Moses in the Exodus contest with Pharaoh's magician-priests who finally fail to duplicate his miracles and confess: "This is the finger of God!" (Exodus 8:19). The "sons" of the scribes correspond to the Egyptian magicians who could dispel the scribes' charge against Jesus if they would.

It appears, though, that all this about the supposed absurdity of Satan casting out his own flunkies is a later addition to mask the import of an original core in which Jesus was shown defending the practice of "binding" the strong man Satan so as to force him to banish his subordinates, making him yield up his possessions. Maybe, then, the historical Jesus was a magician like Morton Smith said. But, alas, even this portion looks to have been spun out of scripture: Isaiah 49:24: "Can the prey be taken from the mighty, or the captives of a tyrant be rescued? Surely thus says the LORD: Even the captives of the mighty shall be taken, and the prey of the tyrant be rescued, for I will contend with those who contend with you, and I will save your children."[27] And, again, as Bultmann said, who remembers the great man quoting somebody else? *Whenever what is offered us as a saying of Jesus* de novo *can be traced back to the Old Testament, we have to assume that someone has merely misattributed (or reattributed) a favorite quote.*

12. *Greek woman's daughter (Mark 7:24–30)*

Mark 7:24. And from there he arose and went away to the region of Tyre and Sidon. And he entered a house, and would not have any one know it; yet he could not be hid. 25. But immediately a woman, whose little daughter was possessed by an unclean spirit, heard of him, and came and fell down at his feet. 26. Now the woman was a Greek, a Syrophoenician by birth. And she begged him to cast the demon out of her daughter. 27. And he said to her, "Let the children first be fed, for it is not right to take the children's bread and throw it to the dogs." 28. But she answered him, "Yes, Lord; yet even the dogs under the table eat the children's crumbs." 29. And he said to her, "For this saying you may go your way; the demon has left your daughter." 30. And she went home, and found the child lying in bed, and the demon gone.

This story appears to be one of several gospel rewrites of Elijah and the widow of Sidonian Zarephath (1 Kings 17:8–16). There the prophet encounters the foreigner and does a miracle for her and her son. In both cases the miracle is preceded by a tense interchange between the prophet and the woman: the prophet thus raises the bar to gauge the woman's faith. The Syrophoenician parries Jesus' initial dismissal with a clever comeback; the widow of Zarephath is bidden to take her remaining meal and to cook it up for Elijah first, whereupon the meal is indefinitely multiplied.[28] Why call the woman and her daughter dogs? Mark has taken it from 2 Kings 8:7–15, where Elisha tells Hazael (a Syrian, like the woman in Mark), that he will succeed Ben-Hadad to the throne of Aram. He replies, "What is your servant, the dog, that he should accomplish this great thing?" In Mark, the question is whether the great deed shall be done *for* the "dog."[29] Now let us ask ourselves: which is more probable: that a man performed an exorcism by remote control? Or that another man simply rewrote a familiar miracle story?

Besides this, there is the heavy tendentiousness of the story, which makes the same point and by the same means as the story of healing the absent servant/child of the Centurion. In both, the *distance in space* between Jesus and the sufferer stands for the *distance in time* between Jesus and the Gentile mission. Thus each story seeks to invoke Jesus' *imprimatur* on the Gentile Mission.[30] Later still, someone thought of just scripting the Great Commission for Jesus to settle the issue.

13. Herod beheads John the Baptist (Mark 6:14–29)

Mark 6:14. King Herod heard of it; for Jesus' name had become known. Some said, "John the baptizer has been raised from the dead; that is why these powers are at work in him." 15. But others said, "It is Elijah." And others said, "It is a prophet, like one of the prophets of old." 16. But when Herod heard of it he said, "John, whom I beheaded, has been raised." 17. For Herod had sent and seized John, and bound him in prison for the sake of Herodias, his brother Philip's wife; because he had married her. 18. For John said

288

to Herod, "It is not lawful for you to have your brother's wife." 19. And Herodias had a grudge against him, and wanted to kill him. But she could not, 20. for Herod feared John, knowing that he was a righteous and holy man, and kept him safe. When he heard him, he was much perplexed; and yet he heard him gladly. 21. But an opportunity came when Herod on his birthday gave a banquet for his courtiers and officers and the leading men of Galilee. 22. For when Herodias' daughter came in and danced, she pleased Herod and his guests; and the king said to the girl, "Ask me for whatever you wish, and I will grant it." 23. And he vowed to her, "Whatever you ask me, I will give you, even half of my kingdom." 24. And she went out, and said to her mother, "What shall I ask?" And she said, "The head of John the baptizer." 25. And she came in immediately with haste to the king, and asked, saying, "I want you to give me at once the head of John the Baptist on a platter." 26. And the king was exceedingly sorry; but because of his oaths and his guests he did not want to break his word to her. 27. And immediately the king sent a soldier of the guard and gave orders to bring his head. He went and beheaded him in the prison, 28. and brought his head on a platter, and gave it to the girl; and the girl gave it to her mother. 29. When his disciples heard of it, they came and took his body, and laid it in a tomb.

MacDonald [31] shows how this story closely parallels the *Odyssey*'s story of the murder of Agamemnon (3:254–308: 4:512–547; 11:404–434). Both are even recounted as flashbacks. Herodias is made into another Queen Clytemnestra, who left her husband, preferring his cousin: Antipas in the one case, Aegisthus in the other. This tryst was threatened, in Clytemnestra's case, by the return of her husband from the Trojan War, in Herodias', by the denunciations of John. In both versions, the wicked adulteress plots the death of the nuisance. Aegisthus hosted a banquet to celebrate Agamemnon's return, just as Herod hosts a feast. During the revelry Agamemnon is slain, falling amid the dinner plates, and the Baptizer's head is severed and displayed on a serving platter. Homer uses the story to foreshadow the peril awaiting the returning Odysseus, while Mark uses John's martyrdom to adumbrate Jesus' own. The more impressive we find these parallels, the less likely we will be to accept Mark's version as history.

14. *Love & forgiveness*
The first stone (John 8:3–11)

John 8:3. 3. The scribes and the Pharisees brought a woman who had been caught in adultery, and placing her in the midst 4. They said to him, "Teacher, this woman has been caught in the act of adultery. 5. Now in the law Moses commanded us to stone such. What do you say about her?" 6. This they said to test him, that they might have some charge to bring against him. Jesus bent down and wrote with his finger on the ground. 7. And as they continued to ask him, he stood up and said to them, "Let him who is without sin among you be the first to throw a stone at her." 8. And once more he bent down and wrote with his finger on the ground. 9. But when they heard it, they went away, one by one, beginning with the eldest, and Jesus was left alone with the woman standing before him. 10. Jesus looked up and said to her, "Woman, where are they? Has no one condemned you?" 11. She said, "No one, Lord." And Jesus said, "Neither do I condemn you; go, and do not sin again."

The story is anachronistic, making Jesus' contemporaries view him already as the supposed equal of Moses, ushering in a new, Christian dispensation in which the Torah may no longer apply. Otherwise, why ask the question of whether Jesus approves of Moses' stipulation that adulterers be executed? It is almost as anachronistic as Thomas 53, where Jews ask Jesus if he endorses circumcision!

Apologists might suggest that the issue is whether Jesus, who is assumed to accept the provisions of Moses, will insist sentence be carried out even though Romans deny the Sanhedrin such powers. But that will not help. Surely the situation had arisen numerous times, and there must already have been some procedure they followed in such cases.

15. *Jesus at the table*
Dining with sinners (Mark 2:15–17)

Mark 2:15. And as he sat at table in his house, many tax collectors and sinners were sitting with Jesus and his disciples; for there were many who followed him. 16. And the scribes of the Pharisees, when they saw that he was eating with sinners and tax collectors, said to his disciples, "Why does he eat with tax collectors and sinners?" 17. And when Jesus heard it, he said to them, "Those who are well have no need of a physician, but those who are sick; I came not to call the righteous, but sinners."

The story is a *chreia* or apophthegm, told as a way of interpreting the culminating saying (the punch line). This means the story is an imaginary reconstruction, supplying an occasion to lend the saying meaning. The ideal (fictive) character of the lead-in is evident from the narrative improbabilities entailed if we take it as a piece of history.[32] How did the blue-nosed critics of Jesus know where Jesus kept company in the first place — unless they were doing the same thing themselves? How do the deacons know Pastor Smith is renting porn videos unless they spot him from across the aisle?

It is puzzling that *The Gospel of Jesus* includes these lead-in stories even though the notes admit their artificiality.[33] This may be because Funk and others believed, oddly to my way of thinking, that the most reliable evidence of what Jesus actually did was to be found in the generalizing summaries contained in these fictive lead-ins, rather than in the individual events described in specific stories. In any case, all such stories are what Gerard Genette calls "pseudo-iterations," offering distinctive events as if typical and repeated.[34]

16. *Question of fasting (Mark 2:18–19)*

Mark 2:18. Now John's disciples and the Pharisees were fasting; and people came and said to him, "Why do John's disciples and the disciples of the Pharisees fast, but your disciples do not fast?"

19. And Jesus said to them, "Can the wedding guests fast while the bridegroom is with them? As long as they have the bridegroom with them, they cannot fast. [No one sews a piece of unshrunk cloth on an old garment; if he does, the patch tears away from it, the new from the old, and a worse tear is made.]

17. *Aged wine (Thomas 47//Luke 5:37–39//Mark 2:22//Matthew 9:17)*

Thomas 47b. No one drinks old wine and immediately desires to drink new wine. And they avoid putting new wine into old wineskins, so as not to burst them; nor do they put old wine into new wineskins, to avoid spoiling it. They do not sew an old patch on a new garment, because it would result in a new tear."

Luke 5:37. And no one puts new wine into old wineskins; if he does, the new wine will burst the skins and it will be spilled, and the skins will be destroyed. 58. But new wine must be put into fresh wineskins. 59. And no one after drinking old wine desires new; for he says, 'The old is good.'."

Mark 2:22. And no one puts new wine into old wineskins; if he does, the wine will burst the skins, and the wine is lost, and so are the skins; but new wine is for fresh skins."

Matthew 9:17. Neither is new wine put into old wineskins; if it is, the skins burst, and the wine is spilled, and the skins are destroyed; but new wine is put into fresh wineskins, and so both are preserved."

Bultmann disallowed these sayings for the simple reason that, *like several others, the question explored is that of the practice, not of Jesus himself, but of his disciples, implying that early Christian ethics are in view here, not the behavior of Jesus himself.*[35] Otherwise, why not have the critics ask, "Why do *you* not fast like John the Baptist?" The *Sitz-im-Leben Kirche* is hardly veiled at all. Not only

so, but the most natural context for such a debate and the develop-
ments presupposed by it would seem to be the Gentile Mission:

> Romans 14:5. One man esteems one day as better than another,
> while another man esteems all days alike. Let every one be fully
> convinced in his own mind. 6. He who observes the day, observes
> it in honor of the Lord. He also who eats, eats in honor of the Lord,
> since he gives thanks to God; while he who abstains, abstains in
> honor of the Lord and gives thanks to God. 7. None of us lives to
> himself, and none of us dies to himself. 8. If we live, we live to the
> Lord, and if we die, we die to the Lord; so then, whether we live or
> whether we die, we are the Lord's. 8. For to this end Christ died and
> lived again, that he might be Lord both of the dead and of the living.

> Colossians 2:16. Therefore let no one pass judgment on you in ques-
> tions of food and drink or with regard to a festival or a new moon or
> a sabbath. 17. These are only a shadow of what is to come; but the
> substance belongs to Christ. 18. Let no one disqualify you, insist-
> ing on self-abasement and worship of angels, taking his stand on
> visions, puffed up without reason by his sensuous mind, 19. and not
> holding fast to the Head, from whom the whole body, nourished and
> knit together through its joints and ligaments, grows with a growth
> that is from God. 20. If with Christ you died to the elemental spir-
> its of the universe, why do you live as if you still belonged to the
> world? Why do you submit to regulations, 21. Do not handle, Do not
> taste, Do not touch" 22. (referring to things which all perish as they
> are used), according to human precepts and doctrines? 23. These
> have indeed an appearance of wisdom in promoting rigor of devo-
> tion and self-abasement and severity to the body, but they are of no
> value in checking the indulgence of the flesh.

The issue is whether or not to patch old garments with old cloth,
or to fill old skins with new wine is whether Gentiles brought to
faith in Christ need to embrace the alien cultural mores of Judaism. The transition from the old to the new is that brought by Jesus
Christ when he paved the way for Gentiles to join the people of

God, but on their own terms, not as Jewish proselytes. And this is all Pauline, post-Jesus, theology.

18. Celebration
Children in the marketplace (Luke 7:31–35//Matthew 11:16–19)

> Luke 7:31. "To what then shall I compare the men of this genera-
> tion, and what are they like? 32. They are like children sitting in the
> market place and calling to one another, 'We piped to you, and you
> did not dance; we wailed, and you did not weep.' 33. For John the
> Baptist has come eating no bread and drinking no wine; and you
> say, 'He has a demon.' 34. The Son of man has come eating and
> drinking; and you say, 'Behold, a glutton and a drunkard, a friend
> of tax collectors and sinners!' 35. Yet wisdom is justified by all her
> children."

> Matthew 11:16. "But to what shall I compare this generation? It is
> like children sitting in the market places and calling to their play-
> mates, 17. 'We piped to you, and you did not dance; we wailed, and
> you did not mourn.' 18. For John came neither eating nor drinking,
> and they say, 'He has a demon'; 19. the Son of man came eating and
> drinking, and they say, 'Behold, a glutton and a drunkard, a friend
> of tax collectors and sinners!' Yet wisdom is justified by her deeds."

As with all retrospective sayings, looking back on the coming of Jesus ("I / the Son of Man came to…"), this one is anachronistic. Bultmann knew it,[36] but the Seminar is less rigorous. The missions of the Baptist and Jesus are over, and now we may compare public reaction to both.

Frank Zindler has called attention to a phrase from this saying shared with one of Aesop's Fables, that of "The Fisherman Pip-ing," raising the possibility that the gospel parable might be based on the ancient fable, though they have little else in common.

> A fisherman skilled in music took his flute and his nets to the sea-
> shore. Standing on a projecting rock, he played several tunes in the

294

hope that the fish, attracted by his melody, would of their own accord dance into his net, which he had placed below. At last, having long waited in vain, he laid aside his flute, and casting his net into the sea, made an excellent haul of fish. When he saw them leaping about in the net upon the rock he said: "O you most perverse creatures, when I piped you would not dance, but now that I have ceased you do so merrily."

19.   *The lost sheep (Luke 15:4–6//Matthew 18:12–13//Thomas 107)*

Luke 15:4. "What man of you, having a hundred sheep, if he has lost one of them, does not leave the ninety-nine in the wilderness, and go after the one which is lost, until he finds it? 5. And when he has found it, he lays it on his shoulders, rejoicing. 6. And when he comes home, he calls together his friends and his neighbors, saying to them, 'Rejoice with me, for I have found my sheep which was lost.' "

Matthew 18:12. What do you think? If a man has a hundred sheep, and one of them has gone astray, does he not leave the ninety-nine on the mountains and go in search of the one that went astray? 13. And if he finds it, truly, I say to you, he rejoices over it more than over the ninety-nine that never went astray.

Thomas 107. Jesus says, "The kingdom is like a shepherd with a flock of a hundred sheep. One of them, the largest, wandered off. He left the ninety-nine to themselves while he went in search of the one, till he found it. He was exhausted, but he said to the sheep, 'I love you more than ninety-nine!'"

Several recent scholars claim this parable for the historical Jesus and then make him either a Jewish Zen master or just a wiseacre, describing nonsensical behavior in which no real shepherd would ever engage. Leave *ninety-nine* sheep to the predations of lions and wolves so you can find the single *one* that wandered off? Are you crazy? To hear some trendy exegetes tell it, Jesus must have been trying to awaken *Satori* in hearers by describing such improbable scenarios. More likely, the story was told by someone who knew nothing about the work of a shepherd, to an audience who could not be expected to know any better.[37] Most readers, equally ignorant, have never seen anything amiss here. And this all points to the story arising in an urban setting in which the shepherd's life was romanticized more than understood. It doesn't go back to Jesus.

20. Prodigal (Luke 15:11–32)

Luke 15:11. And he said, "There was a man who had two sons; 12. and the younger of them said to his father, 'Father, give me the share of property that falls to me.' And he divided his living between them. 13. Not many days later, the younger son gathered all he had and took his journey into a far country, and there he squandered his property in loose living. 14. And when he had spent everything, a great famine arose in that country, and he began to be in want. 15. So he went and joined himself to one of the citizens of that country, who sent him into his fields to feed swine. 16. And he would gladly have fed on the pods that the swine ate; and no one gave him anything. 17. But when he came to himself he said, 'How many of my father's hired servants have bread enough and to spare, but I perish here with hunger! 18. I will arise and go to my father, and I will say to him, "Father, I have sinned against heaven and before you; 19. I am no longer worthy to be called your son; treat me as one of your hired servants."' 20. And he arose and came to his father. But while he was yet at a distance, his father saw him and had compassion, and ran and embraced him and kissed him. 21. And the son said to him, 'Father, I have sinned against heaven and before you; I am no longer worthy to be called your son.' 22. But the father said to his servants, 'Bring quickly the best robe, and put it on him; and put a ring on his hand, and shoes on his feet; 23. and bring the fatted calf and kill it, and let us eat and make merry; 24. for this my son was dead, and is alive again; he was lost, and is found.' And they began to make merry. 25. "Now his elder son was in the field; and as he came and drew near to the house, he heard music and dancing. 26. And he called one of the servants and asked what this meant. 27. And he said to him, 'Your brother has come, and your father has killed the fatted calf, because he has received him safe and sound.' 28. But he was angry and refused to go in. His father came out and entreated him, 29. but he answered his father, 'Lo, these many years I have served you, and I never disobeyed your command; yet you never gave me a kid, that I might make merry with my friends. 30. But when this son of yours came, who has devoured your living with harlots, you killed for him the fatted calf!' 31. And he said to him, 'Son, you are always with me, and all that is mine is yours. 32. It was fitting to make merry and be glad, for this your brother was dead, and is alive; he was lost, and is found.'"

The Seminar is wrong because Alfred Loisy[38] was right: *all the long Lukan parables (especially the ones featuring a character's introspective "What shall I do? I shall...") are inauthentic and Lukan.* Arguing that such parables go back to Jesus is like ascribing the Johannine "I am" discourses to him. Forget it.

21. Sabbath observance

21.a. Lord of the Sabbath (Mark 2:23–24, 27–28)

Mark 2:23. One sabbath he was going through the grainfields; and as they made their way his disciples began to pluck heads of grain. 24. And the Pharisees said to him, "Look, why are they doing what is not lawful on the sabbath?" [...] 27. And he said to them, "The sabbath was made for man, not man for the sabbath; 28. so the Son of man is lord even of the sabbath."

Again, it is the conduct of the disciples that is in question, not that of Jesus himself. The story stems from early church deliberations.

21.b. Man with crippled hand (Mark 3:1–5)

Mark 3:1. Again he entered the synagogue, and a man was there who had a withered hand. 2. And they watched him, to see whether he would heal him on the sabbath, so that they might accuse him. 3. And he said to the man who had the withered hand, "Come here." 4. And he said to them, "Is it lawful on the sabbath to do good or to do harm, to save life or to kill?" But they were silent. 5. And he looked around at them with anger, grieved at their hardness of heart, and said to the man, "Stretch out your hand." He stretched it out, and his hand was restored.

As per Randel Helms,[39] Mark has rewritten this episode from the miracle of the Judean prophet of 1 Kings 13:1–7 *ff*. The prophet confronts King Jeroboam in the Bethel temple and predicts King Josiah's destruction of the rival altar. Jeroboam orders his arrest, but, as "the king stretched forth his hand (εξετεινεν... την χειρα αυτου) from the altar, saying, 'Take hold of him!' ... his hand which he stretched forth against him withered (εξηρανθη), and he could not draw it back to himself" (v.4). In Mark's scene, also laid in a house of worship, the man's hand is already withered (εξηραμμενην) when Jesus bids him, " 'Stretch out your hand!' He stretched it out (την χειρα... εξετεινεν), and his hand was restored" (Mark 3:5). The Judean prophet, too, heals the sufferer: "And King Jeroboam said to the man of God, 'Entreat the Lord your God, and let my hand be restored to me.' And the man of God entreated the Lord, and he restored the king's hand to him, and it became as before" (1 Kings 13:6 LXX). The withering and healing were the aftermath of the villains' attempt to arrest the prophet in 1 Kings, but Mark makes the healing prompt the agents of another "king," Herod, to plan his arrest (Mark 3:6).

Besides, the case envisioned seems arbitrary: the sufferer's life was in no danger, so whence the emergency? And in any case, from what we know, the scribes only forbade the paid services of medical professionals on the Sabbath, not healings "by a word."

22. Kinship in the kingdom

22.a. True relatives (Mark 3:20b–21, 31–35)

Mark 3:20. And the crowd came together again, so that they could not even eat. 21. And when his family heard it, they went out to seize him, for people were saying, "He is beside himself." […] 31. And his mother and his brothers came; and standing outside they sent to him and called him. 32. And a crowd was sitting about him; and they said to him, "Your mother and your brothers are outside, asking for you." 33. And he replied, "Who are my mother and my brothers?" 34. And looking around on those who sat about him, he said, "Here are my mother and my brothers! 35. Whoever does the will of God is my brother, and sister, and mother."

The story can be so readily understood as factional polemic aimed at the Heirs or Pillars in a succession dispute (which would, needless to say, be grossly anachronistic for the historical Jesus) that we would require some good reason to deem it anything else.

22.b. Hating father and mother (Luke 14:25–26//Matthew 10:37//Thomas 55, 101)

Luke 14:25. Now great multitudes accompanied him; and he turned and said to them, 26. "If any one comes to me and does not hate his own father and mother and wife and children and brothers and sisters, yes, and even his own life, he cannot be my disciple.

Matthew 10:37. He who loves father or mother more than me is not worthy of me; and he who loves son or daughter more than me is not worthy of me;

Thomas 55. Jesus says, "Whoever does not hate his father and his mother will not be able to qualify as my disciple; and whoever does not hate his brothers and his sisters and does not pick up his cross in my wake, will not prove worthy of me."

> Thomas 101. "Whoever does not hate his father and his mother following in my way will not be able to be a disciple of mine. My natural mother gave me death, but my true Mother gave me the Life."

The crisis choice between religious allegiance and family ties depicted here presupposes that Jesus-loyalty has taken on the proportions of an outlaw sect, wholly anachronistic for the career of Jesus. Surely this represents the controversies of the early church, once Christian practice and belief have developed in a "heretical" direction, much like the case of the Lubavitcher Hasidim following the death of Rebbe Menachem Mendel Schneerson.

22.c. No respect at home (Mark 6:1–6)

> Mark 6:1. He went away from there and came to his own country; and his disciples followed him. 2. And on the sabbath he began to teach in the synagogue; and many who heard him were astonished, saying, "Where did this man get all this? What is the wisdom given to him? What mighty works are wrought by his hands! 3. Is not this the carpenter, the son of Mary and brother of James and Joses and Judas and Simon, and are not his sisters here with us?" And they took offense at him. 4. And Jesus said to them, "A prophet is not without honor, except in his own country, and among his own kin, and in his own house." 5. And he could do no mighty work there, except that he laid his hands upon a few sick people and healed them. 6. And he marveled because of their unbelief. And he went about among the villages teaching.

The story of Jesus' rejection in his home town is very likely based on that of the disdain of Saul's countrymen in 1 Samuel 10:1–27: "What has come over Kish's son? Is Saul, too, now to be counted a prophet?" There is the sarcasm about the native son being a prophet, and even the reference to whose son he is.[40]

As for Mark's note that Jesus was surprised to find himself striking out in healing on that occasion, must we take this as historical on the basis of the criterion of embarrassment? Not at all.

Matthew, to be sure, found it distressing and changed it, but obviously Mark did not, or he wouldn't have included it. He probably thought the embarrassment belonged not to Jesus but to the faithless people. It is Deuteronomic theology/theodicy. And, insofar as the scene anticipates wholesale Jewish rejection of Jesus, we are certainly dealing with something long after the apostolic period, since such a total turning away cannot have become clear till some time in the second century (an anachronism in Acts and Romans 11, too).

23. In parables

23.a. Shrewd manager (Luke 16:1–8)

Luke 16:1. He also said to the disciples, "There was a rich man who had a steward, and charges were brought to him that this man was wasting his goods. 2. And he called him and said to him, 'What is this that I hear about you? Turn in the account of your stewardship, for you can no longer be steward.' 3. And the steward said to himself, 'What shall I do, since my master is taking the stewardship away from me? I am not strong enough to dig, and I am ashamed to beg. 4. I have decided what to do, so that people may receive me into their houses when I am put out of the stewardship.' 5. So, summoning his master's debtors one by one, he said to the first, 'How much do you owe my master?' 6. He said, 'A hundred measures of oil.' And he said to him, 'Take your bill, and sit down quickly and write fifty.' 7. Then he said to another, 'And how much do you owe?' He said, 'A hundred measures of wheat.' He said to him, 'Take your bill, and write eighty.' 8. master commended the dishonest steward for his shrewdness; for the sons of this world are more shrewd in dealing with their own generation than the sons of light.

23.b. Corrupt judge (Luke 18:1–8)

Luke 18:1. And he told them a parable, to the effect that they ought always to pray and not lose heart. 2. He said, "In a certain city there was a judge who neither feared God nor regarded man; 3. and there was a widow in that city who kept coming to him and saying, 'Vindicate me against my adversary.' 4. For a while he refused; but afterward he said to himself, 'Though I neither fear God nor regard man, 5. yet because this widow bothers me, I will vindicate her, or she will wear me out by her continual coming.'" 6. And the Lord said, "Hear what the unrighteous judge says. 7. And will not God vindicate his elect, who cry to him day and night? Will he delay long over them? 8. I tell you, he will vindicate them speedily. Nevertheless, when the Son of man comes, will he find faith on earth?"

Sorry, but these are two more of those character-driven, introspective Lukan originals, not parables of the historical Jesus.

23.c. *Leased vineyard (Thomas 65//Mark 12:1–8)*

Thomas 65. 65 He says, "A good man had a vineyard. He entrusted it to sharecroppers to work it, and he would receive his share of its fruit from them. When the time came he sent his servant for them to give him his share of the produce of the vineyard. They grabbed his servant and beat him. They stopped just short of killing him. The servant returned and told his master. His master said, 'They must not have recognized him!' So he sent another servant, but the sharecroppers beat him, too. Finally the owner sent his son, thinking, 'Surely they will respect my son!' But since those sharecroppers were well aware this one was the heir of the vineyard, they grabbed him and killed him. Whoever has ears to hear, let him hear!"

Mark 12:1. And he began to speak to them in parables. "A man planted a vineyard, and set a hedge around it, and dug a pit for the wine press, and built a tower, and let it out to tenants, and went into another country. 2. When the time came, he sent a servant to the tenants, to get from them some of the fruit of the vineyard. 3. And they took him and beat him, and sent him away empty-handed. 4. Again he sent to them another servant, and they wounded him in the head, and treated him shamefully. 5. And he sent another, and him they killed; and so with many others, some they beat and some they killed. 6. He had still one other, a beloved son; finally he sent him to them, saying, 'They will respect my son.' 7. But those tenants said to one another, 'This is the heir; come, let us kill him, and the inheritance will be ours.' 8. And they took him and killed him, and cast him out of the vineyard."

Despite the whittling away of the most obviously allegorical elements, the Seminarists cannot hide the fact, any more than Jeremias could, that the story is a transparent allegory of salvation history from a Christian perspective. When Jeremias[41] rationalized that the final focus on the son of the owner was simply part of the window-dressing, explaining how the share-croppers thought they would be in position to inherit the vineyard, it is all special pleading, a desperate attempt to salvage the parable for Jesus. All he has shown is that the introduction of "the son" into the story was not arbitrary. It fits the story as a story. He has by no means shown that the story is not irresistibly to be read as a Christological allegory. We have to be stubbornly obtuse not to see it.

MacDonald[42] identifies the source of the parable in the *Odyssey*, another tale of an absentee owner having left servants in charge of his estate while he is away on a long trip. The servants are not wicked, but the suitors are, the men who, assuming the long-absent Odysseus is dead, flock to his palace to woo his "widow" Penelope, eating her out of house and home for years. Their complete domination of the estates of Odysseus is threatened by the succession of Prince Telemachus, Odysseus' only son. They plot to kill him and so remove the last obstacle to their squatter's possession. He eludes their scheme. The caution of the Jewish leaders in the face of the veiled threat of the parable comes from the note in the *Odyssey* that the suitors had to tread lightly lest their brazenness finally push the people of Ithaca, Odysseus' subjects, too far and spark their wrath. Mark's result is a hybrid which applies Isaiah's judgment oracle not to the whole people but to their imagined usurping leaders and introduces the plot element of the rejected son.

24. Public & private piety
Pharisee and toll collector (Luke 18:9–14)

Luke 18:9. He also told this parable to some who trusted in themselves that they were righteous and despised others: 10. "Two men went up into the temple to pray, one a Pharisee and the other a tax collector. 11. The Pharisee stood and prayed thus with himself, 'God, I thank thee that I am not like other men, extortioners, unjust, adulterers, or even like this tax collector. 12. I fast twice a week, I give tithes of all that I get.' 13. But the tax collector, standing far off, would not even lift up his eyes to heaven, but beat his breast, saying, 'God, be merciful to me a sinner!' 14. I tell you, this man went down to his house justified rather than the other; for every one who exalts himself will be humbled, but he who humbles himself will be exalted."

Why not assign it to Luke? It seems to belong to the same set with the Prodigal Son, the Dishonest Steward, *etc.* It occurs only in Luke, it features a whole story, albeit short, and its pivotal character engages in introspection on the way to a decision that will save his skin.

25. Jesus & purity

25.a. Eating with defiled hands (Mark 7:1–5)

Mark 7:1. Now when the Pharisees gathered together to him, with some of the scribes, who had come from Jerusalem, 2. they saw that some of his disciples ate with hands defiled, that is, unwashed. 3. (For the Pharisees, and all the Jews, do not eat unless they wash their hands, observing the tradition of the elders; 4. and when they come from the market place, they do not eat unless they purify themselves; and there are many other traditions which they observe, the washing of cups and pots and vessels of bronze.) 5. And the Pharisees and the scribes asked him, "Why do your disciples not live according to the tradition of the elders, but eat with hands defiled?"

Conveniently, the Seminar snips out the Septuagint citations Jesus makes to condemn scribal traditionalism, since the historical Jesus could hardly be envisioned quoting the Greek Bible to Palestinian scribes! The use of the LXX is not merely part of translating the tradition into Greek, for the crucial point of the quote, without which it is irrelevant, is made only in the Greek. So the story originated in Greek. And the amused note concerning the ostensibly neurotic scruples of "those comical Jews" mistakenly imagines Jews in the Holy Land following the customs relevant only to the Diaspora.

25.b. *What goes in (Mark 7:14–16)*

Mark 7:14. And he called the people to him again, and said to them, "Hear me, all of you, and understand: 15. there is nothing outside a man which by going into him can defile him; but the things which come out of a man are what defile him. 16. "If any man has ears to hear, let him hear."

When Mark has Jesus summon the crowd and denounce the teaching of the scribes, he has based the scene on 1 Kings 18, when, competing with the prophets of Baal, "Elijah said to all the people, 'Come near to me'." (v. 30) "How long will you go limping with two different opinions? If Yahweh is God follow him; but if Baal, then follow him" (v. 21). Even so, Mark's Jesus calls the people to choose once and for all between his teaching and the tradition of the scribes, which he sees as just as much a man-made idol as Baal.

26. *Five cures*

26.a. *Peter's mother-in-law (Mark 1:29–31)*

Mark 1:29. And immediately he left the synagogue, and entered the house of Simon and Andrew, with James and John. 30. Now Simon's mother-in-law lay sick with a fever, and immediately they told him of her. 31. And he came and took her by the hand and lifted her up, and the fever left her; and she served them.

Mark appears to have reshuffled elements from 1 Kings 17:8–16 and 2 Kings 4. In the first, Elijah meets a widow of Zarephath and her son, and he delivers them from imminent starvation. As a result, she serves the man of God. In the second, Elisha raises from the dead the son of the Shunammite woman, who had served him. In Mark, it is the old woman herself who is raised up from her illness, not her son, who is nonetheless important to the story (Peter), and she serves the man of God, Jesus.[43] What is more likely, a miraculous healing, or a rewrite of well-known stories? Beyond this, the story is a piece of comedy: the hero expects service from the lady of the house. She is ill-disposed? Well, let's take care of that! Presto! She's well enough to get back in the kitchen!

26.b. Paralytic and four (Mark 213–12)

Mark 2:1–12. And when he returned to Capernaum after some days, it was reported that he was at home. 2. And many were gathered together, so that there was no longer room for them, not even about the door; and he was preaching the word to them. 3. And they came, bringing to him a paralytic carried by four men. 4. And when they could not get near him because of the crowd, they removed the roof above him; and when they had made an opening, they let down the pallet on which the paralytic lay. 5. And when Jesus saw their faith, he said to the paralytic, "My son, your sins are forgiven." 6. Now some of the scribes were sitting there, questioning in their hearts, 7. "Why does this man speak thus? It is blasphemy! Who can forgive sins but God alone?" 8. And immediately Jesus, perceiving in his spirit that they thus questioned within themselves, said to them, "Why do you question thus in your hearts? 9. Which is easier, to say to the paralytic, 'Your sins are forgiven,' or to say, 'Rise, take up your pallet and walk'? 10. But that you may know that the Son of man has authority on earth to forgive sins" — he said to the paralytic — 11. "I say to you, rise, take up your pallet and go home."

12. And he rose, and immediately took up the pallet and went out before them all; so that they were all amazed and glorified God, saying, "We never saw anything like this!"

There are four strikes against this one. First, the historian can factor in the probability only of psychosomatic healing. A report of a miraculous suspension of physics will always be more probably considered a legend. This one is a legend because it is not the man's own faith that issues in his recovery (as in attested cases of "mind-cure"), but that of his friends, which Jesus rewards by his godlike sovereignty. Second, it is difficult to imagine the scene. Did no one notice the men dismantling the roof above them until they dropped the man on the stretcher down in front of Jesus? If they did, would they not have tried to stop them? Where did they get the rope, etc? Third, Jesus is depicted as a superman or demigod who reads the minds of mere mortals. Do we have to believe the historical Jesus had ESP?

Fourth, the story looks to be based on 2 Kings 1:2–17a, where King Ahaziah gains his affliction by falling from his roof through the lattice and languishes in bed. Mark's sufferer is already afflicted when he descends through the roof on his bed (pallet). He rises from his bed because whatever sin of his had earned him the divine judgment of paralysis was now pronounced forgiven on account of his friends' faith, though nothing is said of his own. King Ahaziah is pointedly *not* healed of his affliction, because of his own pronounced lack of faith in the God of Israel: he had sent to the priests of the Philistine oracle god Baal-zebub to inquire as to his prospects. Elijah tells him he is doomed because of unbelief, a dismal situation reversed by Mark, who has Jesus grant forgiveness and salvation because of faith. Mark has preserved the Baal-zebub element for use in a later story (3:22).[44]

26.c. *Woman with a vaginal hemorrhage (Mark 5:24–34)*

Mark 5:24. And he went with him. And a great crowd followed him and thronged about him. 25. And there was a woman who had had a flow of blood for twelve years, 26. and who had suffered much un-der many physicians, and had spent all that she had, and was no bet-ter but rather grew worse. 27. She had heard the reports about Jesus, and came up behind him in the crowd and touched his garment. 28. For she said, "If I touch even his garments, I shall be made well." 29. And immediately the hemorrhage ceased; and she felt in her body that she was healed of her disease. 30. And Jesus, perceiving in himself that power had gone forth from him, immediately turned about in the crowd, and said, "Who touched my garments?" 31. And his disciples said to him, "You see the crowd pressing around you, and yet you say, 'Who touched me?' " 32. And he looked around to see who had done it. 32. But the woman, knowing what had been done to her, came in fear and trembling and fell down before him, and told him the whole truth. 34. And he said to her, "Daughter, your faith has made you well; go in peace, and be healed of your disease."

Here the Seminar Fellows have arbitrarily made a bad text into a good one, simply cutting the overtly legendary features of Mark's story: the woman had experienced a nonstop flow of blood for *twelve years* — until the Fellows cured her by redactional surgery. This is the sort of extravagance we find on the votive tablets of Epidaurus. Plus, Jesus is depicted as a human dynamo who feels it when someone sneaks up and plugs in, drawing off healing *mana* without so much as asking him. We are in the realm of legend here.

The notes in *The Gospel of Jesus* admit that most of this story is fiction,[46] but it gratuitously posits that some genuine healing ac-count lay at the basis of the legend. This is pure Euhemerism, not critical methodology.

26.d. Blind man of Bethsaida (Mark 8:22–24)

Again, the Fellows just cut off a part of the story they didn't like, where Jesus finishes the healing by a second application of imitative magic. But even in the portion that remains, we have to suspect that the story in some way embodies a midrash on the

Sodom story of Genesis 19. Else why is the blindness element (reflecting the angels blinding the Sodom mob) connected with Jesus' leading the man out of the city (as the angel led Lot)? Are we to understand that Bethsaida was ripe for judgment (like Sodom) as in Matthew 11:21–34?

27. *Hospitality*
Hospitable Samaritan (Luke 10:30–35)

Luke 10:30. Jesus replied, "A man was going down from Jerusalem to Jericho, and he fell among robbers, who stripped him and beat him, and departed, leaving him half dead. 31. Now by chance a priest was going down that road; and when he saw him he passed by on the other side. 32. So likewise a Levite, when he came to the place and saw him, passed by on the other side. 33. But a Samaritan, as he journeyed, came to where he was; and when he saw him, he had compassion, 34. and went to him and bound up his wounds, pouring on oil and wine; then he set him on his own beast and brought him to an inn, and took care of him. 35. And the next day he took out two denarii and gave them to the innkeeper, saying, 'Take care of him; and whatever more you spend, I will repay you when I come back.'

Another from the Lukan parable canon, his creation, not Jesus'.

28. *Sight & light*
Blind Bartimaeus (Mark 10:46–52)

Mark 10:46. And they came to Jericho; and as he was leaving Jericho with his disciples and a great multitude, Bartimaeus, a blind beggar, the son of Timaeus, was sitting by the roadside. 47. And when he heard that it was Jesus of Nazareth, he began to cry out and say, "Jesus, Son of David, have mercy on me!" 48. And many rebuked him, telling him to be silent; but he cried out all the more, "Son of David, have mercy on me!" 49. And Jesus stopped and said, "Call him." And they called the blind man, saying to him, "Take heart; rise, he is calling you." 50. And throwing off his mantle he sprang up and came to Jesus. 51. And Jesus said to him, "What do you want me to do for you?" And the blind man said to him, "Master, let me receive my sight." 52. And Jesus said to him, "Go your way; your faith has made you well." And immediately he received his sight and followed him on the way.."

This story is a narrative version of LXX Isaiah 35:5a, 6a, 8a: "Then the eyes of the blind shall be opened... then shall the lame man leap like a hart... And a highway shall be there, and it shall be called the holy way." This is why Bar-Timaeus leaps up, is given his sight, and follows Jesus on the way.[47] He is a "narrative-man" (Tzvetan Todorv),[48] a "character" who is no more than his narrative function and is named for it, a beggar named *Bar-teymah*, Aramaic for "son of poverty."[49] What is more probable: that someone healed blindness, or that someone turned a scripture text into a miracle story?

29. *In Jerusalem*

29.a. *Temple incident (Mark 11:15, 17)*

Mark 11:15. And they came to Jerusalem. And he entered the temple and began to drive out those who sold and those who bought in the temple, and he overturned the tables of the money-changers and the seats of those who sold pigeons; [...] and he would not allow any one to carry anything through the temple. 17. And he taught, and said to them, "Is it not written, 'My house shall be called a house of prayer for all the nations'? But you have made it a den of robbers."

There is hardly any story here at all. Jesus says nothing but a pair of scripture texts. Mark seems ignorant of the vast size of the temple court[50] and of the fact that any such action would have brought the temple guards down on Jesus' head then and there. It remains possible that, as S.G.F. Brandon suggested,[51] what we have here is Mark's sanitized account of what was originally and historically a large-scale, armed assault on the temple led by Jesus. But if this is true, then what we are reading is still fiction, as it is completely distorted.

29.b. Paralytic by the pool (John 5:2–3, 5–9)

John 5:2. Now there is in Jerusalem by the Sheep Gate a pool, in Hebrew called Beth-zatha, which has five porticoes. 3. In these lay a multitude of invalids, blind, lame, paralyzed. [...] 5. One man was there, who had been ill for thirty-eight years. 6. When Jesus saw him and knew that he had been lying there a long time, he said to him, "Do you want to be healed?" 7. The sick man answered him, "Sir, I have no man to put me into the pool when the water is troubled, and while I am going another steps down before me." 8. Jesus said to him, "Rise, take up your pallet, and walk." 9. And at once the man was healed, and he took up his pallet and walked. Now that day was the sabbath.

This is a particular kind of miracle story designed to make a traditional source of healing look bad by comparison to the new religion's savior. In the same way, Philostratus tells us that the healing god Asclepius, unable to cure a chronic drunkard, referred him to Apollonius of Tyana. The woman with a hemorrhage had wasted years and all her money on conventional medicine, but was healed by Jesus. Here, too, the famous healing shrine of Bethesda pales in comparison to Jesus. It is a kind of advertisement, not a report of anything.

Very little remains of the Passion narrative, just the essential points of a summary: his arrest in a garden, his flogging, crucifixion at Pilate's command, period.

The Christ Myth Theory And Its Problems

30. Somebody *Said Them: Vote Red*

I have left unmolested most of the teachings of Jesus included as genuine items in *The Gospel of Jesus*. Many of them come from the Q source, a collection of proverbs to which someone, somewhere, assigned Jesus' name, just as people used to tack the name Solomon on any wise sayings. I see nothing specific demanding some other author than Jesus. But that does not prove it was he who said them. There is no particular reason to deny these words to a historical Jesus, but where does that leave us? Can we henceforth simply assume that these sayings have passed the test and can be replied upon as authentic Jesus sayings? That seems to be the point of coloring them red (or pink). But I wonder if this is not one of those places where agnosticism is called for, and what we get instead is fideism. The historian cannot proceed by the axiom "innocent until proven guilty." If we were content to assume blithely that the sayings we could not manage to falsify were therefore reliable, then we would have retreated to the posture of "scissors-and-paste" historians as described by R.G. Collingwood. [52] It is inconsistent to be critical enough to peel away some of the material but then to cling to what is left in the same credulous way we used to regard *all* the material in pre-critical times. Our stance toward even what survives the sifting can never be what it was.

Jesus may perhaps have said these remaining sayings, or maybe it was somebody else. Solomon may have actually coined this or that proverb attributed to him in the three "Solomonic" collections of the Book of Proverbs. But no scholar simply assumes he did. The fictive and inauthentic element is so pervasive of the gospel tradition that finally we can afford to lift none of it above doubt. Inauthentic sayings may have been coined without tell-tale clues to their inauthenticity. Obviously, we have no right to declare all the sayings ascribed to Jesus to be *in*-authentic, either. We can never know. Thus, while some gospel passages deserve a black or a gray vote, none deserves a red or pink vote. The Gospel of Philip has Jesus enter the dye-works of Levi and pour all the color dyes into one large vat. By a miracle, they all come out white. I think that perhaps that is the final fate of the sayings ascribed to Jesus. To paraphrase a famous rhyme: red and black and pink and gray, they're all precious in their way. But authentic?

31. Dead End Doorway

I have more than once drawn attention to D.F. Strauss's critical axiom that, once we expose the mythical *Tendenz* of a gospel story, we have no right to try to salvage specifics, secondary details, from it. That is just a lame attempt to try to make bad evidence into good, and it partakes of a kind of Euhemerism, arbitrarily positing a more modest, possibly original version underlying that which we can in good conscience no longer accept. If we can no longer affirm as historians that Jesus walked on water, we cannot pretend that the story in which he did is still good as evidence that knew where the stepping stones were. There is no reason to insist that secondary details, there just to background or advance the story, have an independent historicity when the main story dissolves under critical scrutiny.

I will ask no one to follow me here, but I cannot deny that the question weighs more and more on my critical conscience whether the same thinking ought not apply to the mythos of Jesus Christ as a whole. I mean, the story of Jesus which we have, in every form, remains a redemption myth constructed along the lines of the universal Mythic Hero Archetype, with no "secular," biographical material left over.[53] When we are done dismantling the records and we begin ghoulishly picking through the scanty remains for clues to an underlying "historical Jesus," like people scavenging gold from the teeth and fingers of the battlefield dead, are we perhaps engaging in Euhemerism? I have assumed throughout the

313

present chapter that we could picture a forceful itinerant preacher in a first-century Jewish context. But, based on that paradigm, the Jesus Seminar found precious little data fitting the model, and I have found even less. Is this because we have been trying to interpret the data against their intent? The story wants to preach to us a divine savior who entered this world from heaven and shortly returned there, betrayed, repudiated, martyred, but vindicated. We are having none of that. We can tell that is myth, pure and simple. So we ask what bits would make sense if we abstracted them from their familiar context and made them mean something else, as if the Atheist should take the Psalm verse out of context, stripping away the introduction, "The fool has said in his heart," then triumphantly quoting what is left: "There is no God!"

NOTES

1. This means, of course, that any Fellow of the Jesus Seminar could write the kind of critical review I am undertaking here, arguing for more (or less!) skeptical results on the questions on which he or she voted differently from the majority. I am not so conceited as to imagine this essay is any more definitive a comment on the work of the Jesus Seminar than any other private account of it would be.

2. Robert W. Funk and the Jesus Seminar, *The Gospel of Jesus according to the Jesus Seminar* (Santa Rosa: Polebridge Press, 1999).

3. Albrecht Alt, "The God of the Fathers," In Alt, *Essays on Old Testament History and Religion*. Trans. R.A. Wilson (Garden City: Doubleday Anchor, 1968), pp. 1–100.

4. Ignaz Goldziher, *Mythology Among the Hebrews and Its Historical Development*. Trans. Russell Martineau (1877; rpt. NY: Cooper Square Publishers, 1967), pp. 32, 45–47.

5. David Friedrich Strauss, *The Life of Jesus Critically Examined*. Trans. George Eliot. Ed. Peter C. Hodgson. Fortress Lives of Jesus Series (Philadelphia: Fortress Press, 1972), pp. 55, 90.

6. Geza Vermes, *Jesus the Jew: A Historian's Reading of the Gospels* (London: Fontana/Collins, 1976), pp. 21–22

7. Charles Guignebert, *Jesus*. Trans. S.H. Hooke (New Hyde Park: University Books, 1956), pp. 86–89. Noting that some make it a sect tag, Guignebert himself breaks it down as equivalent to "Holy One of God."

8. G.A. Wells, *The Historical Evidence for Jesus* (Buffalo: Prometheus Books, 1988), pp. 167–168.

9. Hans Conzelmann, *The Theology of St. Luke*. Trans. Geoffrey Buswell (NY: Harper & Row, 1961), p. 102.

10. *Gospel of Jesus*, p. 91.

11. Guignebert, pp. 147–148; *cf.* Rudolf Bultmann, *History of the Synoptic Tradition*. Trans. John Marsh (NY: Harper & Row, rev. ed., 1968), p. 253, who says Luke has shaped the story, as Jesus prays after immersion, according to liturgical patterns.

12. See the summary in John P. Meier, *A Marginal Jew: Rethinking the Historical Jesus*, (Garden City: Doubleday: 1991) vol 1: p. 168–171. The idea seems to go back to Paul W. Schmiedel, "Gospels," in *Encyclopedia Biblica*, 2:1761–1898, ed. T. K. Cheyne and J. Sutherland Black (New York: Macmillan, 1901), 1881.

13. Strauss, *Ibid*.

14. Martin Dibelius, *From Tradition to Gospel*. Trans. Bertram Lee Woolf (NY: Charles Scriber's Sons, nd), 108–109.

15. Bultmann, p. 253, on the Temptation parallels.

16. Strauss, *Ibid.*

17. Oscar Cullmann, *Baptism in the New Testament*. Trans. J.K.S. Reid. Studies in Biblical Theology No. 1 (London: SCM Press, 1950), pp.78–79.

18. Joachim Jeremias, *The Parables of Jesus*. Trans. S.H. Hooke. (NY: Charles Scriber's Sons, 2nd Rev. ed. 1972), pp. 178–179.

19. Bultmann, pp. 49, 101.

20. James Breech, *The Silence of Jesus: The Authentic Voice of the Historical Man* (Philadelphia: Fortress Press, 1983), p. 72.

21. *Gospel of Jesus*, p. 92.

22. Jeremias, pp. 138–139.

23. Jacob Neusner, *The Peripatetic Saying: The Problem of the Thrice-Told Tale in Talmudic Literature*. Brown Judaic Studies 89 (Chico: Scholars Press, 1985).

24. Norman Perrin, *Rediscovering the Teaching of Jesus* (NY: Harper & Row, 1976), pp. 39–40; Bultmann, p. 205.

25. Dale Miller and Patricia Miller. *The Gospel of Mark as Midrash on Earlier Jewish and New Testament Literature*. Studies in the Bible and Early Christianity 21. (Lewiston/Queenston/Lampeter: Edwin Mellen Press, 1990), p. 76.

26. *Gospel of Jesus*, p. 94.

27. Rikki E. Watts, *Isaiah's New Exodus and Mark*. Wissenschaftliche Untersuchungen zum Neuen Testament 2. Reihe 88 (Tübingen: Mohr Siebeck, 1997), pp. 148–149.

28. Wolfgang Roth, *Hebrew Gospel: Cracking the Code of Mark* (Oak Park: Meyer-Stone Books, 1988), pp. 51–52; Miller and Miller, pp. 196–197.

29. Roth, p. 44.

30. Bultmann, pp. 38–39.

31. Dennis R. MacDonald, *The Homeric Epics and the Gospel of Mark* (New Haven: Yale University Press, 2000), pp. 80–81, 176.

32. Bultmann, pp. 39–40.

33. *Gospel of Jesus*, p. 93.

34. Gerard Genette, *Narrative Discourse: An Essay in Method.* Trans. Jane E. Lewin (Ithaca: Cornell University Press, 1980), p. 121–122.

35. Bultmann, pp. 15–16, 19, 48–49.

36. *Ibid.*, p. 155–156.

37. C.H. Dodd, *The Epistle of Paul to the Romans* (London: Collins/Fontana, 1959), p. 189, makes the same point about the Romans 11:17–24 olive tree allegory. It is just ill-informed, not "radical" or "subversive."

38. Alfred Loisy, *The Birth of the Christian Religion.* Trans. L.P. Jacks (London: George Allen & Unwin, 1948), p. 49; Bultmann, p. 191.

39. Randel Helms, *Gospel Fictions* (Buffalo: Prometheus Books, 1989), pp. 90–91.

40. Miller and Miller, p. 167.

41. Jeremias, pp. 72–73.

42. MacDonald, p. 37.

43. Miller and Miller, p. 79.

44. Roth, p. 56.

45. Helms, p. 66.

46. *Gospel of Jesus*, p. 101.

47. John Bowman, *The Gospel of Mark: The New Christian Jewish Passover Haggadah*. Studia Post-Biblica 8 (Leiden: E.J. Brill, 1965), p. 172.

48. Tzvetan Todorov, "Narrative-Men." In Todorov, *The Poetics of Prose*. Trans. Richard Howard (Ithaca: Cornell University Press, 1977), pp. 66–79.

49. J. Duncan M. Derrett, *The Making of Mark: The Scriptural Bases of the Earliest Gospel*. Volumes 1 and 2. (Shipston-on-Stour, Warwickshire: P. Drinkwater, 1985), p. 185.

50. Robert W. Funk and the Jesus Seminar, *The Acts of Jesus: What Did Jesus Really Do?* (San Francisco: HarperSanFrancisco / Santa Rosa: Polebridge Press, 1998), p. 121.

51. S.G.F. Brandon, *The Fall of Jerusalem and the Christian Church: A Study of the Effects of the Jewish Overthrow of A.D. 70 on Christianity* (London: SPCK, 1951), pp. 103–104; Brandon, *Jesus and the Zealots: A Study of the Political Factor in Primitive* Christianty (NY: Charles Scribner's Sons, 1967), pp. 330–336.

52. R.G. Collingwood, *The Idea of History* (NY: Oxford University Press Galaxy Books, 1956), pp. 238–239, 248–249, 260–261, 268–269, 280–281.

53. Alan Dundes, "The Hero Pattern and the Life of Jesus," in Robert A. Segal, ed., *In Quest of the Hero* (Princeton: Princeton University Press, 1990, pp. 179–223.

The Abhorrent Void
The Rapid Attribution of Fictive Sayings and Stories to a Mythic Jesus

"Nature abhors a vacuum." — Jesus Christ
(at least you can't prove he *didn't* say it!)

Out of Nothing Something Comes

It seems to conservative scholars, to apologists, and to rank and file gospel readers quite implausible, indeed outlandish, when critics write off the majority of sayings and stories of Jesus in the gospels as secondary and inauthentic. Even if one grants the likelihood that false attribution, secondary embellishments, may occasionally have occurred, does it not seem like skeptical axe-grinding for scholars to dismiss most of the tradition as spurious? C.H. Dodd, no fundamentalist, sought to rein in such skepticism.

> When Mark was writing, there must have been many people about who were in their prime under Pontius Pilate, and they must have remembered the stirring and tragic events of that time at least as vividly as we [in 1949] remember 1914. If anyone had tried to put over an entirely imaginary or fictitious account of them, there would have been middle-aged or elderly people who would have said (as you or I might say) 'You are wasting your breath: I remember it as if it were yesterday!'*

Is it my imagination? Or is this argument not hopelessly circular? It makes a lot of sense provided we know in advance that the events involving Jesus and Pilate were indeed as the grumpy old-timers claimed to remember them. Otherwise, we cannot know whose version of the story was imaginary and fictitious. Dodd

---

* C.H. Dodd, *About the Gospels* (radio broadcast, 1949, quoted in F.F. Bruce, *Tradition: Old and New* (Grand Rapids: Zondervan, 1970), p. 41).

already sides with the old hecklers and assumes we do, too. It behooves us to observe, too, that Dodd's appeal to a solid historical bottom against which traditions may be sounded is gratuitous if we do not take for granted that a historical Jesus was born when the gospels imply, between 4 and 6 BCE. If, as some of us think, such dating is insecure, as is the very existence of a single historical founder of Christianity, then spurious traditions (myths, legends, rumors) will have had all the time in the world to grow and evolve.

Everett F. Harrison, more of a conservative than Dodd, still seems to utter only common sense when he voices his skepticism *re* skepticism.

> All will agree that, according to the gospels, teaching was one of the major activities of the Master and that His teaching made a profound impression on those who heard it (Mk. 1:22;[*] cf. Jn. 7:46).[†] To have a tradition *that* Jesus taught, without a tradition of *what* He taught, would be strange indeed and quite incomprehensible, since the tradition *that* He taught includes the report of the impact of his words. It would be strange also, on the assumption that the church rather than Jesus had authored or doctored the greater part of the corpus of instruction in the gospels, that the statement of His uniqueness in this area should be retained, "You are not to be called rabbi, for you have one teacher" (Mt. 23:8, RSV; cf. Mk. 1:27).[‡]

But Harrison had not yet grasped the full extent of the insidious character of the critical mind. Should it not be obvious that, if

---

[*]   "And they were astonished at his teaching, for he taught them as one who had authority, and not as the scribes."

[†]   "The officers answered, 'No man ever spoke like this man!'"

[‡]   Everett F. Harrison, "Tradition of the Sayings of Jesus: A Crux Interpretum," in Clark H. Pinnock and David F. Wells, eds., *Towards a Theology of the Future* (Carol Stream: Creation House, 1971), p. 44. Mark 1:27, "And they were all amazed, so that they questioned among themselves, saying, "What is this? A new teaching! With authority he commands even the unclean spirits, and they obey him."

there had been no teacher, no Rabbi Jesus (Paul knows of no such character, nor of a thaumaturge Jesus), the subsequent attempt to claim his divine authority for one's own teachings would make it advisable to posit that Jesus had been a great teacher? One is thus feathering one's own nest, providing increased clout for whatever one intends to ascribe to Jesus. It is not strange at all. It would be like claiming Jesus had been a carpenter so that one could sell off one's own bedroom and dining room sets as Jesus' work!§

We have three models, proposed analogies, to help us understand how plausible it is to posit that a wholesale and rapid growth of a vast body of inauthentic Jesus traditions, even that it might have been expected. And this will be the case whether we believe in a Jesus who was, however (like fellow messiah Sabbatai Sevi), not much of a teacher, or whether we think there was no Jesus Christ. In other words, such things as "skeptical" critics posit in the case of the gospel traditions have famously happened before in historically analogous cases.

Kid Stuff

First we may recall that many or most early Christians came to believe that Jesus had initially appeared (or been adopted) as a deity in adult form. Picture it either way you prefer. Perhaps Jesus grew up in obscurity, entering public life only once he received John's baptism. When this happened, many early Christians, presumably including Mark the evangelist, believed Jesus had been divinely anointed as God's Son. He could not have laid claim to that honor at any previous time. Others held, as Marcion did, that this Jesus deity appeared out of thin air upon our earth one day, but in adult form, like Adam created as an adult — with a belly button he had never needed. In either case, stories of Jesus would have depicted him as an adult gifted with divine power. Later on, Christians came to believe that Jesus, having been born

---

§   As Don Imus's character the Reverend Billy Saul Hargis once tried to do!

from a miraculous conception, was the Son of God from day one. Christian curiosity rapidly went to work filling the newly apparent gap. What would an infant or a child god have been doing in the years before tradition made him appear on the public scene? There was an immediate flood of stories. The ample results are contained in the Infancy Gospels of Thomas, Matthew, and James, and the Arabic Infancy Gospel. The canonical Gospels of Luke and John each contain one example of such stories: Luke 2:41–51[*] and John 2:1–10.[†]

---

[*] "Now his parents went to Jerusalem every year at the feast of the Passover. And when he was twelve years old, they went up according to custom; and when the feast was ended, as they were returning, the boy Jesus stayed behind in Jerusalem. His parents did not know it, but supposing him to be in the company they went a day's journey, and they sought him among their kinsfolk and acquaintances; and when they did not find him, they returned to Jerusalem, seeking him. After three days they found him in the temple, sitting among the teachers, listening to them and asking them questions; and all who heard him were amazed at his understanding and his answers. And when they saw him they were astonished; and his mother said to him, 'Son, why have you treated us so? Behold, your father and I have been looking for you anxiously.' And he said to them, 'How is it that you sought me? Did you not know that I must be in my Father's house?' And they did not understand the saying which he spoke to them. And he went down with them and came to Nazareth, and was obedient to them; and his mother kept all these things in her heart. And Jesus increased in wisdom and in stature, and in favor with God and man."

[†] "On the third day there was a marriage at Cana in Galilee, and the mother of Jesus was there; Jesus also was invited to the marriage, [with his disciples]. When the wine failed, the mother of Jesus said to him, 'They have no wine.' And Jesus said to her, 'O woman, what have you to do with me? My hour has not yet come.' His mother said to the servants, 'Do whatever he tells you.' Now six stone jars were standing there, for the Jewish rites of purification, each holding twenty or thirty gallons. Jesus said to them, 'Fill the jars with water.' And they filled them up to the brim. He said to them, 'Now draw some out, and take it to the steward of the feast.' So they took it. When the steward of the feast tasted the water now become wine, and did not know where it came from (though the servants who had drawn the water knew), the steward of the feast called the bridegroom and said to him, 'Every man serves the good wine first; and when men have drunk freely, then the poor wine; but you have kept the good wine until now.'"

As Raymond E. Brown[‡] argued, the Cana story must have had a prehistory as a story of Jesus the divine prodigy. As in practically all such stories, Jesus' miracles and precocious insights are magnified against the stupidity and incompetence of adults. Same here: they have run out of wine. And, contra the redactional frame, where the water-into-wine miracle is explicitly said to be his first, mother Mary knows Jesus will give in and bail out the adults with a handy miracle as he always does ("Do whatever he tells you.").

Well, in precisely the same way, the Christ-Myth theory reasons that, once an adult, mortal-seeming Jesus was said to have come to earth in recent history, Christian imagination went to work supplying what he must have been doing and saying. These stories and sayings now fill the familiar gospels. It does not sound so odd that, *e.g.*, the Jesus Seminar was able to authenticate only 18 per cent of the material. And I consider that way too optimistic.

Some might dispute the aptness of the analogy, pointing out that the Infancy Gospel stories are comical compared to the stories of the adult Jesus, which, despite their miraculous extravagance, do not seem ridiculous. But I would suggest the reason for the difference is simply the comedy inherent in stories of a child prodigy with miraculous powers. Jesus the Menace. I am not saying the idea is not silly. Indeed it is. But can one take all the canonical stories completely seriously? Cursing the fig tree? Sending demoniac pigs into a lake? Healing Peter's mother-in-law so she can cook dinner for Jesus? My point is simply that fictions featuring Jesus the god-man as an adult might be equally extravagant as stories featuring him as a child but would be less comical since they would not involve the inevitably comedic element of a child displaying adult behavior.

[‡]   Raymond E. Brown, *The Gospel of John: Introduction, Translation, and Notes*. Anchor Bible 29 (Garden City: Doubleday, 1966), Vol. 1, comments on John 2:1–11.

The Christ Myth Theory And Its Problems

The (Growing) Beard of the Prophet

The second analogy/model for a rapid accretion of spurious Jesus traditions lies ready to hand in the explosion of (universally spurious) hadith, traditions of what the Prophet Muhammad had said and done, providing precedents and teachings for devout Muslims, thus supplementing the Koran. And just as some Muslim hadith reflect Rabbinical and New Testament sources,[*] it is no surprise that the gospels should be filled to the brim with echoes of Rabbinical, Cynic, and Stoic materials, as well as maxims first offered in the epistles with no claim that they originated with an historical Jesus.[†]

Consider how the reasons for the fabrication of "traditional" stories and sayings of Muhammad correspond precisely to those suggested for gospel traditions by the form critics.

> The Prophet's authority was invoked by every group for every idea it evolved: for legal precepts couched in the form of tradition, as well as for maxims and teachings of an ethical or simply edificatory nature. Through solid chains of tradition, all such matters acquired an unbroken tie to the "Companions" who had heard these pronouncements and statutes from the Prophet or had seen him act in pertinent ways. It took no extraordinary discernment on the part of Muslim critics to suspect the authenticity of much of this material: some reports were betrayed by anachronisms or other dubious features, some contradicted others. Moreover, certain people are named outright who fabricated and spread abroad traditions to support one trend or another. Not a few pious persons admitted, as the end of life neared, how great their contribution to the body of fictive

---

[*]   Ignaz Goldziher, *Hadith and the New Testament* (London: SPCK, 1902).

[†]   Paul-Louis Couchoud, *The Creation of Christ: An Outline of the Beginnings of Christianity*. Trans. C. Bradlaugh Bonner (London: Watts, 1939), p. 182. Of course, many non-Mythicist gospel critics recognize the same thing, but they do not seem to notice the oddity that the Christ-Mythicist Couchoud noticed: why would such a wholesale borrowing be necessary if there really had been a great teacher at the start of the thing?

hadiths had been. To fabricate hadith was hardly considered dishonorable if the resulting fictions served the cause of the good. A man honorable in all other respects could be discredited as a traditionist without having his religious reputation tarnished or his honor as a member of society called into question. It was, of course, possible to assert, on the Prophet's authority, that the bottomless pit awaited those who fraudulently ascribed to Muhammad utterances that he never made. But one could also try to save the situation by vindicatory maxims, in which the Prophet had supposedly recognized such fictions in advance as his own spiritual property: "After my death more and more sayings will be ascribed to me, just as many sayings have been ascribed to previous prophets (without their having really said them). When a saying is reported and attributed to me, compare it with God's book. Whatever is in accordance with that book is from me, whether I really said it or no."‡ Further: "Whatever is rightly spoken was spoken by me."§

The fabricators of tradition, as we see, laid their cards on the table. "Muhammad said" in such cases merely means "it is right, it is religiously unassailable, it is even desirable, and the Prophet himself would applaud it."¶

Even if one prefers to reckon according to a historical Jesus who was born in Herod the Great's reign and perished in that of Pontius Pilate,** there is plenty of time available in which to picture

‡   *Cf.* John 14:26; 16:12–15.
§   *Cf.* Luke 10:16; 21:14–15.
¶   Ignaz Goldziher, *Introduction to Islamic Theology and Law.* Modern Classics in Near Eastern Studies. Trans. Andras and Ruth Hamori (Princeton: Princeton University Press, 1981), pp. 43–44.
**   The Herod story, that of the slaughter of the Innocents, is most easily explained as copied from Josephus' account of Moses' nativity, while the link with the historical Pilate is ruined by the gross improbability of the ruthless Roman bending over backwards to free Jesus, even letting a known killer of Romans go free in his place. It is just not believable as history. See S.G.F. Brandon, *Jesus and the Zealots: A Study of the Political Factor in Primitive Christianity* (NY: Scribner's, 1967), pp. 3–5.

the eruption of false Jesus hadith. It certainly seems not to have taken very long in the case of Islam.

> All the Islamic authorities agree that an enormous amount of forgery was committed in the *hadith* literature... The Victorian writer William Muir thought that it began during the caliphate of Uthman. It is more likely, however, that it originated during the lifetime of the Prophet himself. His opponents would not have missed the opportunity to forge and attribute words and deeds to him for which he was not responsible, in order to rouse the Arab tribes against his teaching*... During the caliphate of Abu Bakr, too, when apostasy had raised its head, it is not unlikely that some of the apostates should have forged such traditions as suited their purpose... During the caliphate of Uthman, this kind of dishonesty became more common. Some members of the factions into which the community was then divided forged traditions in order to advance their faction's interests.† During the first century of Islam, and also thereafter, the various political parties, the heretics, the professional preachers, and even a number of sincere Muslims, all made their contributions to the growing rubbish-heap of false traditions.‡

Sectarian leaders as well as popular edifying story-tellers both forged plenty as they addressed the people following morning and evening prayers.§

Compared to the volume of hadith generated in the name of Muhammad by interested and imaginative parties, the scope of invention when it comes to Jesus is quite modest.

---

*   *Cf.* Rom. 3:8

†   See the stories in which Jesus repudiates his relatives, a polemic against the leadership of the Heirs, *e.g.*, Mark 3:20–21,31–35; John 7:5, or endorses them, Mark 6:3's official list of his caliph-successors; *cf.* Thomas saying 12. Pro-Paul in Mark 9:38–40; anti-Paul in Matt. 5:17–19; 7:21–23.

‡   Muhammad Zubayr Siddiqi, *Hadith Literature: Its Origin, Development & Special Features* (Cambridge: Islamic Texts Society, 1993), p. 32.

§   *Ibid*, 33–34.

Spurious traditions were coming into being, drowning the genuine ones. There were motives at play behind this development. Some of these new traditions were merely pious frauds, worked up in order to promote what the fabricators thought were elements of a pious life,¶ or what they thought were the right theological views**...Spurious traditions also arose in order to promote factional interests. Soon after Muhammad's death, there were cutthroat struggles for power between several factions, particularly the Alids, the Ummayads, and later on the Abassides. In this struggle, great passions were generated, and under their influence, new traditions were concocted, and old ones usefully edited.

The pious and hero-worshipping mind also added many miracles around the life of Muhammad, so that the man tended to be lost in the myth.

Under these circumstances, a serious effort was made to collect and sift all the current traditions, rejecting the spurious ones and committing the correct ones to writing. [The need for this work was recognized about a century after the Prophet's death, but it took another century for the process to get started.]

[Muhammad Ismail al-] Bukhari [810–870 CE] laid down elaborate canons of authenticity and applied them with a ruthless hand. It is said that he collected 600,000 traditions but accepted only 7,000 of them as authentic.††

But even the remainder of Muhammadan hadith seems excessive. Apparently what Bukhari and the others did was merely to catalogue those hadith that were not debunked by their criteria, not that this vindicated them. The same error attaches to the decisions of New Testament critics who nominate as authentically dominical the sayings that are not obviously disqualified by their criteria of dissimilarity, multiple attestation, coherence, *etc.* Any or all of

---

¶   *E.g.*, pro-fasting in Matt. 6:16–17; Mark 2:20; Thomas saying 27; anti-fasting in Mark 2:21–22; Thomas saying 14.

**   *E.g.*, mission only to Jews in Matt. 10:5, or to all nations in Matt. 28:19.

††   Ram Swarup, *Understanding the Hadith: The Sacred Traditions of Islam* (Amherst: Prometheus Books, 2002), pp. 6–7.

them still might be spurious; they just haven't been "caught in the act." ("I know of nothing against myself, but I am not thereby acquitted." 1 Cor. 4:4). Just so, there is no particular reason to regard *any* of the hadith of Muhammad as definitely authentic.

> We must… abandon the gratuitous assumptions that there existed originally an authentic core of information going back to the time of the Prophet, that spurious and tendentious additions were made to it in every generation, that many of these were eliminated by the criticism of isnads [chains of attestors] as practiced by the Muhammadan scholars, that other spurious traditions escaped rejection, but that the genuine core was not completely overlaid by later accretions. If we shed these prejudices we become free to consider the Islamic traditions objectively in their historical context, within the framework of the development of the problems to which they refer, and this enables us to find a number of criteria for establishing the relative and even the absolute chronology of a great many traditions.[*]

Indeed, why not consider the Koran itself as hadith? It appears to be a collection of contradictory and redundant materials on various topics, all ascribed to Muhammad (and thence to Gabriel) in order to secure prophetic authority.

When I see how conservatives[†] flock to the suggestion of Harald Riesenfeld and Birger Gerhardsson[‡] (admittedly very great

---

[*]   Joseph Schacht, "A Reevaluation of Islamic Traditions," in Ibn Warraq, trans. and ed., *The Quest for the Historical Muhammad* (Amherst: Prometheus Books, 2000), p. 361.

[†]   *E.g.*, I. Howard Marshall, *I Believe in the Historical Jesus.* I Believe Series No. 5 (Grand Rapids Eerdmans, 1977), p. 195–196.

[‡]   Harald Riesenfeld, *The Gospel Tradition.* Trans. Margaret Rowley and Robert Kraft (Philadelphia: Fortress Press, 1970); Birger Gerhardsson, *Memory and Manuscript: Oral Tradition and Written Transmission in Rabbinic Judaism and Early Christianity.* Acts Seminarii Neotestamentici Upsaliensis XXII. Trans. Eric J. Sharpe (Lund & Copenhagen: C.W.K. Gleerup & Ejnar Munksgaard, 1961); Gerhardsson, *The Reliability of the Gospel Tradition* (Peabody: Hendrickson, 2001).

scholars) that the canonical gospel traditions be read on analogy with strictly memorized, authorized Rabbinical traditions simply because conceivably the early disciples *might possibly* have followed such practices, it becomes clear to me we are dealing again with apologetics. Why not consider the analogy of the Muhammadan hadith? The diversity, anachronism, and tendentiousness of the gospel material would seem to me to make the hadith analogy the better fit. (However, we ought to keep in mind Jacob Neusner's demonstration[§] that Rabbinical sayings-ascriptions are no likelier to be authentic anyway!)

From Muhammad to Nag Hammadi

In her fascinating treatise *Jesus in the Nag Hammadi Writings*, Majella Franzmann[¶] points out the theological agenda that has excluded the Egyptian Gnostic texts from serious consideration as possible sources for the historical Jesus and for early Christology. She does not argue, as does Margaret Barker,[**] that the Nag Hammadi texts provide substantial material for a reconstruction of the Jesus of history. No, her point is rather that few bother even to look — outside the canon. The same blind spot occurs among the apologists.

Indeed, the evidence is that the early Christians were careful to distinguish between sayings of Jesus and their own inferences and judgments. Paul, for example, when discussing the vexed questions of marriage and divorce in I Corinthians vii, is careful to make this distinction between his own advice on the subject and the Lord's decisive ruling: 'I, not the Lord,' and again, 'Not I, but the Lord.'[††]

[§]   Jacob Neusner, *The Peripatetic Saying: The Problem of the Thrice-Told Tale in Talmudic Literature*. Brown Judaic Studies 89 (Chico: Scholars Press, 1985).

[¶]   Majella Franzmann, *Jesus in the Nag Hammadi Writings* (Edinburgh: T. & T. Clark, 1996), pp. 1–18.

[**]   Margaret Barker, *The Risen Lord: The Jesus of History as the Christ of Faith* (Trinity Press International, 1996), pp. 98–110.

[††]   F.F. Bruce, *The New Testament Documents: Are They Reliable?* 5th ed.

The Christ Myth Theory And Its Problems

On the one hand, it is far from clear that, in these instances, Paul means to say he has on record a quoted statement from Jesus of Nazareth. In light of 1 Corinthians 14:37,[*] it seems much more likely that he merely distinguishes between his own sage advice and revelations he has received in a mantic state ("prophesying"). On the other, it is obvious to us, as it was not to the orthodox Bruce, great scholar though he was, that "the evidence" is not to be found only in the canon. (He doesn't even seem to consider the letters to the seven churches in Revelation chapters 1 through 3.)

I should say the evidence as to whether "the early Christians were careful to distinguish between sayings of Jesus and their own inferences and judgments" must include the voluminous, if deadly boring, Gnostic texts (Nag Hammadi and Berlin Codices) and the Epistle of the Apostles. Granted, Ron Cameron and others have sought to dredge up some authentic words of Jesus from *The Dialogue of the Savior* and *The Apocryphon of James*, and Thomas' gospel is a special case. But most of these attempts to find a needle in a haystack are exceptions that amply prove the rule: the early Christians who composed these texts had no thought of segregating their own words from those of a historical Jesus Christ. Indeed, they did not even think it was a good idea. The very existence of works like *Pistis Sophia*, *The Books of Jeu*, *The Dialogue of the Savior*, *The Gospel of Mary*, *The Sophia of Jesus Christ*[†], and so on make it simply ridiculous to urge that early Christians would never have dared put Jesus' name on their own fabrications,

---

(London: Inter-Varsity Fellowship, 1960), p. 33, quoted in John Warwick Montgomery, *History & Christianity* (Downers Grove: InterVarsity Press, 1974), p. 39.

    *   "If any one thinks that he is a prophet, or spiritual, he should acknowledge that what I am writing to you is a command of the Lord."

    †   In the Nag Hammadi codices, *The Sophia of Jesus Christ* follows the philosophical work *Theognostos the Blessed*. *The Sophia* is cast in the form of a dialogue in which material from *Theognostos* is placed in the mouth of Jesus and is represented as his teaching.

any more than Elizabeth Claire Prophet[‡] and Helen Schucman[§] do today. Why does anyone fail to see this? Because, for most, the "real" early Christians are New Testament characters. Whoever wrote *Pistis Sophia* was one of those Gnostic heretics, in short, spurious "early Christians" who weren't really Christians at all, any more than today's Protestant fundamentalist is willing to admit that Roman Catholics are genuine Christians. But this is not a judgment fit for historians. It is no judgment at all, but only a prejudice. And the same prejudice makes it falsely obvious to conservatives that the canonical gospels could not be the result of wholesale fabrication by well-meaning Christians. There is just no reason Christian writers could not have composed the Sermon on the Mount if they created *The Dialogue of the Savior*. If they could have fabricated *Pistis Sophia*, they could much more easily have fabricated the Gospel of John. Whether they did is another matter, the discussion of which starts here, not stops.

[‡]   Elizabeth Claire Prophet (as Jesus Christ), *Watch with Me* (Gardiner, Montana: Summit Lighthouse, 1965).

[§]   Helen Schucman, *A Course in Miracles* (Glen Ellen, CA: Foundation for Inner Peace, 1975).

James the Just:
Achilles Heel of the Christ Myth Theory?

You Don't Mess Around With Jim

The most powerful argument against the Christ-Myth theory, in my judgment, is the plausibility of what Ethelbert Stauffer called "the Caliphate of James."[*] It is not merely that Galatians 1:19[†] refers to "James the Lord's brother," though that is powerful evidence that Jesus was a recent historical figure. It is not just that Mark 6:3[‡] lists James and three more brothers and at least two sisters of a historical Jesus. One can also assemble divers hints from Galatians, Acts chapters 15 and 21,[§] and the Pseudo-Clementines to imply that James was viewed in some manner as Jesus' vicar or vice-regent on earth, a successor to a deceased or occulted Messiah. Accordingly, the various gospel texts that seem to be taking trouble to show the brothers of the Lord in either favorable[¶] or unfavorable[**] light would appear to be polemical shots between

---

[*] Ethelbert Stauffer, "The Caliphate of James." Trans. by Darrell J. Doughty. *Journal of Higher Criticism* 4/2 (Fall 1997), pp. 120–143

[†] "But I saw none of the other apostles except James the Lord's brother."

[‡] "Is not this the carpenter, the son of Mary and brother of James and Joses and Judas and Simon, and are not his sisters here with us?"

[§] Galatians 2:12, "For before certain men came from James, he ate with the Gentiles; but when they came he drew back and separated himself, fearing the circumcision party." Acts 15:13, 19, "After they finished speaking, James replied, "Brethren, listen to me. [...] 'My judgment is that...'" Acts 21:25, "But as for the Gentiles who have believed, we have sent a letter with our judgment that they should abstain from what has been sacrificed to idols and from blood and from what is strangled and from unchastity."

[¶] Luke 8:20–21, And he was told, "Your mother and your brothers are standing outside, desiring to see you." But he said to them, "My mother and my brothers are those who hear the word of God and do it."

[**] Mark 3:21, 31–35, "And when his family heard it, they went out to seize him, for people were saying, 'He is beside himself.' [...] And his mother and his brothers came; and standing outside they sent to him and called him.

one leadership faction (the Pillars* or Heirs of Jesus) and another (the Twelve). Such succession disputes may almost be expected upon the death of a great leader, as witness the split of Mormonism into the Church of Jesus Christ of Latter-day Saints, following the quorum of apostles, and the Reorganized Church of Jesus Christ of Latter-day Saints, following Joseph Smith, Jr. Or think of the schism in the Bab'i Faith upon the martyrdom of their master, Ali Muhammad (the Bab): some followed his designated caretaker *and brother*, Subh-i-Azal, while most rallied to Hussein Ali (Baha'u'llah). But the most famous case is that of Islam after Muhammad's passing. His cousin and adopted son Ali stepped aside for the Prophet's early Companion (and uncle) Abu-Bekr, followed by 'Umar, then 'Uthman. Once given the nod, Ali served as Caliph until deposed in a war of succession. The Shi'ite community, which favored Ali, was no stranger to succession disputes, either, as another led to the split between the Ismail'is (Seveners) and the Twelver sect dominant in Iran today.

As historians of ancient religion trying to figure out just what went on in early Christianity, we work by the Principle of Analogy, seeking historical parallels to either reported ancient claims or modern reconstructions based on ancient evidence. If an ancient account bears no analogy to experiences observed and verified today, but is analogous to what all today agree are legends, then we class the account among the latter, not the former. And if we must reconstruct what happened in some situation, our hypothesis will be deemed the more probable insofar as we can find actual,

---

And a crowd was sitting about him; and they said to him, 'Your mother and your brothers are outside, asking for you.' And he replied, 'Who are my mother and my brothers?' And looking around on those who sat about him, he said, 'Here are my mother and my brothers! Whoever does the will of God is my brother, and sister, and mother'." John 7:5, "For even his brothers did not believe in him."

*   Galatians 2:9, "James and Cephas and John, who were reputed to be pillars, gave to me and Barnabas the right hand of fellowship, that we should go to the Gentiles and they to the circumcised."

documented cases analogous to the reconstruction we are positing. And with regard to the historical Jesus question, we cannot
overlook a very powerful analogy of the latter sort at this point:
the succession dispute we seem to glimpse in the New Testament
between the Companions of Jesus (his ostensible disciples) and
the Pillars, or relatives of Jesus (Ali's immediate kin were also
called the Pillars) seems to ring true as a plausible historical scenario. And such a scenario presupposes a historical founder who
has died or disappeared.

The hypothesis of a Caliphate of James is itself not lacking
in radical implications, as witness the work of Robert Eisenman.[†]
But it functions as a thorn in the flesh for the Christ Myth theory,
since the Christ Myth Jesus admits of no historical entanglements.
James the Just places Christ Myth theorists in a situation ironically quite similar to that of the Roman Catholics who used to
agonize over James' relationship to Jesus on the one hand, and his
possible identification, on the other, with James son of Zebedee
or James of Alphaeus among the Twelve. Since Roman Catholic
dogma affirmed the perpetual virginity of Mary, she can have had
no other children, Mark 6:3's list notwithstanding. So who must
these people be? One theory (proposed by Helvidius) made these
siblings the children of widower Joseph who had married young
Mary simply for the sake of legal appearances, the result being
that James and the rest were Jesus' step brothers and sisters, like
the brothers and sisters on *The Brady Bunch*. Another theory (that
of Epiphanius) made them the half brothers and sisters of Jesus,
Jesus being the son of Mary and the Spirit, while James and the
others were the offspring of Joseph and Mary. Finally, yet another
schema (Jerome's) makes the "brothers and sisters" cousins.[‡] At

---

[†]   Robert Eisenman, *James the Brother of Jesus: The Key to Unlocking
the Secrets of Early Christianity and the Dead Sea Scrolls* (NY: Viking, 1996).
[‡]   John McHugh, *The Mother of Jesus in the New Testament* (Garden
City: Doubleday, 1975), pp. 200–233.

The Christ Myth Theory And Its Problems

least the first and third, if not all three, are obviously desperate expedients, harmonizations begotten of the incongruity between the plain sense of New Testament texts and a theory imposed upon them. I say that the same texts pose the same problem and create the same embarrassment for the Christ Myth theory, which is likewise obliged to deny that Jesus had genuine siblings, though for a completely different reason. When I find myself considering the relative merits of harmonization strategies, I know I am in familiar territory. I spent a lot of time there as a fundamentalist and an apologist. I do not like the place and do not want to be there.

In what follows I want to survey three ways of understanding James' epithet "brother of the Lord" that would not entail physical relationship to a historical Jesus. First is the possibility that James was understood, like Thomas, to be the earthly, physical counterpart to a heavenly Jesus. Second is that James was prominent among the missionaries known as "brothers of the Lord." Third is that his fraternal connection is fictive and presupposes the historicization of a heavenly Jesus and seeks retrospectively to co-opt the James sect by subordinating its figurehead to Jesus as his brother. I want to evaluate each one as impartially and inductively as I can. I do not want to engage in special pleading on behalf of a pet theory. It must not count in favor of any of these hypotheses that, if true, it would make the case for the Christ Myth theory easier. If they end up sounding like text-twisting harmonizations, we must say so and reject them. I feel no need to pretend that 100% of the evidence falls in the column of one theory, with none at all in the other column. Thus the Christ Myth theory does not stand or fall with this datum, but it seems worthwhile to see how serious a difficulty it may pose.

Image of the Invisible God

In the Apocryphal Acts of the Apostles, specifically the so-called Leucian Acts of Paul, of Peter, of Thomas, of Andrew, and of John, we find the vestiges of the original Gnostic concept of apostleship as reconstructed by Walter Schmithals, namely that the Christ or Primal Man of Light had entered the world to bring enlightenment to the pneumatic elect, but not incarnate in an individual body. Rather, the "Redeemed Redeemer" was awakened collectively among the first individuals to discover enlightenment. They shared this identity among them, and they thenceforth carried the gnosis to their fellows in the role of apostles. The Christ appeared upon earth physically only in their person.[*] Later on this Redeemer was associated with the Christian Jesus, whether by appropriating a Jewish messiah named Jesus or by concretizing the Gnostic Redeemer as a single, mythical-symbolic character named Jesus ("Savior"). The Apocryphal Acts, though their narratives presuppose a recent earthly ministry of Jesus, retain definite traces of this earlier Christology/Soteriology in a set of scenes that occur like clockwork in every one of the five writings.[†] First there is a scene or scenes in which the Risen/Ascended Christ appears on earth in the physical semblance of the apostle. He does so for different reasons and at different junctures, but it always happens. Here is an example from the Acts of Thomas:

> The king requested the groomsmen to leave the bridal chamber. When all had left, and the doors were shut, the bridegroom raised the curtain of the bridal chamber, that he might bring the bride to himself. And he saw the Lord Jesus talking with the bride. He had the appearance of Judas Thomas, the apostle, who shortly before had blessed them and departed; and he said to him, "Did you not go out before them all? And how is it that you are here now?" And the Lord said to him, "I am not Judas Thomas, I am his brother." (Acts of Thomas 11)[‡]

---

[*]   Walter Schmithals, *The Office of Apostle in the Early Church.* Trans. John E. Steely (NY: Abingdon Press, 1969), pp. 114–230.

[†]   Robert M. Price, "Docetic Epiphanies: A Structuralist Analysis of the Apocryphal Acts." *Journal of Higher Criticism* 5/2 (Fall 1998), pp. 163–187.

[‡]   J.K. Elliott, *The Apocryphal New Testament* (NY: Oxford University

The Christ Myth Theory And Its Problems

Then there is a series of scenes in each Acts which portray the apostle virtually as a Christ in his own right, sometimes extending even to resurrection appearances after his martyrdom. In other words, the apostle is implicitly the real Christ, the Acts his gospel; and the Heavenly Redeemer appears on earth only in the form of these human apostles.

As we have just seen, the Acts of Thomas calls Jesus and Thomas brothers in precisely this context, opening up the possibility that "brother of the Lord" (*not* "brother of Jesus," if that makes any difference) implies that one, an enlightened mortal, is the earthly counterpart of the other, a heavenly being. One is the visible twin of the other, who remains invisible to mortal eyes. The Apostle Mani claimed that he had received his revelation from his heavenly twin, the Living Paraclete or Holy Spirit.[*] Had he called himself the brother of the Lord, no one would have thought he meant he was the blood brother of a man named Jesus.

Then think about the Taiping Messiah Hong Xiuquan, a nineteenth-century revolutionary leader in China: he proclaimed himself "the Little Brother of Jesus." Obviously he didn't mean he was a blood relative of the ancient Jesus of Nazareth. No doubt Hong Xiuquan believed in a historical Jesus, but what he had in mind was that he was the incarnation of a second heavenly Son-hypostasis of God.[†] I believe this is a powerful possible parallel to James the Lord's brother. Whether "brother of the Lord" seems more naturally to refer to a deceased earthly master or a hidden heavenly one really depends on which theological context in which one places the title. And that is just the point at issue. If we had reason to believe that early Christians worshipped a heavenly savior who had never come to earth, James' epithet would be easily understood as parallel to that of Hong Xuiquan.

Press, 1993), p. 452.

[*]   See Geo Widengren, *Mani and Manichaeism*. History of Religions Series. Trans. Charles Kessler (NY: Holt, Rinehart and Wilson, 1965), pp. 26–27.

[†]   Jonathan D. Spence, *God's Chinese Son: The Taiping Heavenly Kingdom of Hong Xiuquan* (NY: W.W. Norton & Company, 1996), pp. 46–49, 64–65.

Returning to Thomas, widely referred to in ancient writings as Jesus' twin brother, we have just seen that his fraternal connection to Jesus occurs in a context suggesting spiritual kinship with a heavenly being. But the case is not clear, since, though the document preserves an underlying Gnostic concept of a heavenly Redeemer "incarnate" only in the form of earthly apostles, it now occurs in a Christianized text in which Jesus is believed to have once lived upon the earth in some form or another. But do any other ancient references to Thomas as Jesus' twin imply anything about the nature of the kinship?

> The savior said, "Brother Thomas… since it has been said that you are my twin and true companion, examine yourself and learn who you are, in what way you exist, and how you will come to be. Since you will be called my brother, it is not fitting that you be ignorant of yourself." (The Book of Thomas the Contender 138:4, 7–12) ‡

Jesus says that Thomas is destined to be "called" his brother, implying he will have achieved the designation as an honorific designation, not as a simple fact of birth. How did he merit such a title? As at several other points, The Book of Thomas seems to be commenting upon the earlier Gospel of Thomas. This passage seems to presuppose the Gospel of Thomas 13:

> Jesus says to his disciples, "Compare me and tell me what I am like." Simon Peter says to him, "You are like a righteous angel." Matthew says to him, "You are like a philosopher possessed of understanding." Thomas says to him, "Master, my mouth can scarcely frame the words of what you are like!" Jesus says, "I am not your master, because you have drunk, you have become filled, from the bubbling spring which I have measured out." He took him aside privately and said three things to him. So when Thomas rejoined his companions, they pressed him, saying, "What did Jesus say to you?" Thomas said to them, "If I tell you even one of the things he said

---

‡   Trans. John D. Turner. In James M. Robinson, ed., *The Nag Hammadi Library*. (San Francisco: Harper & Row, Rev. ed. 1988), p. 201.

to me, you will pick up stones and hurl them at me — and fire will
erupt from the stones and consume you!" (Gospel of Thomas 13)[*]

It is, then, by virtue of spiritual insight that Thomas has attained
spiritual equality, "twin brotherhood," with Jesus. It hardly seems
particularly unnatural for us to take James' status as "the Lord's
brother" as equivalent in meaning. We find something similar in 1
Apocalypse of James:

> It is the Lord who spoke with me: "See now the completion of my re-
> demption. I have given you a sign of these things, James, my brother.
> For not without reason have I called you my brother, although you are
> not my brother materially." (1 Apocalypse of James 24:10–16)[†]

I must admit, though, that the phrase "although you are not my brother
materially" might sound like an attempt to discount a prior tradition
whereby James and Jesus *were* blood brothers. The point of this text
might be to affirm that James was not merely hanging on the coattails
of his famous brother, but that he deserved his prominence on account
of his own holiness. The Caliph Ali had the same problem to deal
with. His partisans held that the office of Caliph ought to have been
kept within the Prophetic bloodline, but his opponents said there is no
such thing as a Prophetic bloodline. One does not inherit spirituality or
spiritual authority, as it is of God, not of the flesh. Thus Ali's supporters were obliged to point to the spiritual virtues of their Imam to show
he would make a good Caliph in any case. It is easy to imagine the
same in the case of James: physical relation, initially a strategic boon,
eventually proved insufficient, so James' followers might have shifted
the emphasis, redefining "brother of the Lord." We may even see this
process in motion in a pair of passages from 2 Apocalypse of James:

---

[*]   Trans. Robert M. Price, *The Pre-Nicene New Testament* (Salt Lake
City: Signature Books, 2006), p.975.

[†]   Trans. Douglas M. Parrott, In James M. Robinson, ed., *The Nag Hammadi Library*. (San Francisco: Harper & Row, Rev. ed. 1988) p. 262.

> Once when I was sitting deliberating, [he] opened [the] door. That one whom you hated and persecuted came in to me. He said to me, "Hail, my brother; my brother, hail." As I raised my [face] to stare at him, (my) mother said to me, "Do not be frightened, my son, because he said, 'My brother' to you. For you [both] were nourished with the same milk. Because of this he calls me, 'My mother.' For he is not a stranger to us. He is your [half-brother...]." Jesus said to James, "Your father is not my father, but my father has become a father to you." (2 Apocalypse of James 50:6–23; 51:19–22)[‡]

First we have the half-brother solution to the conundrum of Mary having other children. Jesus and James share Mary as their mother. This implies a physical Jesus and a physical James. But a bit later Jesus tells James that he deserves to be called his brother (at least that seems to be the point) because, though they do not share a common earthly father, they are equally sons of a Heavenly Father. Again, there is a mitigation of their fraternal link, a tendency to redefine it, presupposing a prior literalistic understanding. And, sure enough, the passage appears to be based upon the following, better known, scene from the Gospel according to the Hebrews:

> Now the Lord, when he had given the linen cloth to the servant of the priest, went to James and appeared to him, for James had sworn that he would not eat bread from that hour wherein he had drunk the Lord's cup until he should see him risen again from among those who sleep. And he said to him, "Hail!" And he called to the servants, who were greatly amazed. "Bring," said the Lord, "a table and bread." He took bread and blessed and broke and gave it to James the Just and said to him, "My brother, eat your bread, for the man has risen from those who sleep."[§]

The 2 Apocalypse of James passage implies the Jesus-James encounter follows the suffering and crucifixion of Jesus, mentioned

---

[‡]   Trans. Douglas M. Parrott, In James M. Robinson, ed., *The Nag Hammadi Library*. (San Francisco: Harper & Row, Rev. ed. 1988) pp. 271–272.

[§]   Trans. Robert M. Price, *The Pre-Nicene New Testament* (Salt Lake City: Signature Books, 2006), p. 225.

in the immediate context, and that James is startled at seeing Jesus because the last he knew, Jesus was dead. Likewise, we may wonder if his "deliberation" was not over what to do next, now that his world had come crashing down. The passage has been rewritten as a gloss upon the Gospel according to the Hebrews' note that the Risen Jesus addressed James as "my brother." Mary explains the relationship of the two "brothers" in a manner acceptable to later dogma.

But it seems possible to trace a change in the meaning of these terms in the opposite way, too! Richard Bauckham detects certain polemical innuendoes that may possess wider implications than he means to suggest. "James is also called 'our Lord's brother according to the flesh' in Didascalia 24... (*cf.* Ap[ostolic] Const[itutions] 8:35:1: 'the brother of Christ according to the flesh'... In [such] phrases 'according to the flesh' designates the realm of merely physical relationships, by contrast with relationships 'according to the Spirit' (*cf.* Rom 1:3–4; Gal 3:23, 29; Philem 16). So, whereas 'the Lord's brother' might indicate a special relationship with Jesus not shared by other Christian leaders, 'the Lord's brother *according to the flesh*' relativizes that relationship as *only* a natural relationship."* Let me make clear that I am going well beyond the point Bauckham means to make, but it occurs to me that the same logic might imply something quite different: might an attempt to highlight the physicality of the fraternal relation to Jesus denote an orthodox apologetical attempt to concretize an *originally spiritual* fraternity with Jesus *into* a blood relation? The attempt would be exactly analogous to that discerned in the Synoptic resurrection narratives' stress on the physical tangibility of the risen body of Jesus: to defeat and co-opt Gnostic theologoumena. I readily admit that texts which try to "clarify" for the reader that, despite appearances, the fraternity of Jesus and James is only spiritual and abstract are naturally (though not inevitably) read as "docetizing" an originally

---

* Richard Bauckham, *Jude and the Relatives of Jesus in the Early Church* (Edinburgh: T&T Clark, 1990), pp. 127–128.

physical conception that needs to be reconceived for a Gnostic context. But here we may see evidence of the opposite tendency. And then it is pretty much up for grabs which tendency (and therefore which conception of James' brotherhood with Jesus) was first.

Big Brother Is Watching You

G.A Wells, following J.M. Robertson, has long held that James as "the brother of the Lord" might simply denote his role as a leading missionary, since there are indications in the New Testament that such traveling preachers were called "brothers" or even "the Lord's brethren."[†] The famous depiction of the Final Judgment in Matthew 25:31–46[‡] focuses on the class of Christian missionaries

---

[†]   G.A. Wells, *The Historical Evidence for Jesus* (Buffalo: Prometheus Books, 1988), pp. 167–168.

[‡]   Matthew 25:31. "When the Son of man comes in his glory, and all the angels with him, then he will sit on his glorious throne. 32. Before him will be gathered all the nations, and he will separate them one from another as a shepherd separates the sheep from the goats, 33. and he will place the sheep at his right hand, but the goats at the left. 34. Then the King will say to those at his right hand, 'Come, O blessed of my Father, inherit the kingdom prepared for you from the foundation of the world; 35. for I was hungry and you gave me food, I was thirsty and you gave me drink, I was a stranger and you welcomed me, 36. I was naked and you clothed me, I was sick and you visited me, I was in prison and you came to me.' 37. Then the righteous will answer him, 'Lord, when did we see thee hungry and feed thee, or thirsty and give thee drink? 38. And when did we see thee a stranger and welcome thee, or naked and clothe thee? 39. And when did we see thee sick or in prison and visit thee?' 40. And the King will answer them, 'Truly, I say to you, as you did it to one of the least of these my brethren, you did it to me.' 41. Then he will say to those at his left hand, 'Depart from me, you cursed, into the eternal fire prepared for the devil and his angels; 42. for I was hungry and you gave me no food, I was thirsty and you gave me no drink, 43. I was a stranger and you did not welcome me, naked and you did not clothe me, sick and in prison and you did not visit me.' 44. Then they also will answer, 'Lord, when did we see thee hungry or thirsty or a stranger or naked or sick or in prison, and did not minister to thee?' 45. Then he will answer them, 'Truly, I say to you, as you did it not to one of the least of these, you did it not to me.' 46. And they will go away into eternal punishment, but the righteous into eternal life."

The Christ Myth Theory And Its Problems

for whose sake the book was written, the Jewish-Christian (Nazarene) preachers to the nations (Matthew 28:19–20)*: "my brothers" (Matthew 25:40). It is they who are envisioned as hungry, thirsty, strangers newly arrived with no place to lay their heads, naked, even in prison. These are the pitfalls to which the wandering missionaries are heirs, as we see in Matthew 6:31–33† (needing food and drink), Matthew 8:20;‡ 10:11§ (needing shelter in new towns), Matthew 10:10¶ (no back-up garment in case the first is lost, Matthew 5:40**; 6:28–30)†† and 24:9‡‡ (persecution, *i.e.*, imprisonment). Jesus had promised God would supply all such necessities, but he would do so through the generosity of the preachers' hearers (Matthew 10:40–42).§§ Thus if these fail in their duty, there will be

---

* "Go therefore and make disciples of all nations, baptizing them in the name of the Father and of the Son and of the Holy Spirit, teaching them to observe all that I have commanded you; and lo, I am with you always, to the close of the age."

† "Therefore do not be anxious, saying, 'What shall we eat?' or 'What shall we drink?' or 'What shall we wear?' For the Gentiles seek all these things; and your heavenly Father knows that you need them all. But seek first his kingdom and his righteousness, and all these things shall be yours as well."

‡ "Foxes have holes, and birds of the air have nests; but the Son of man has nowhere to lay his head.".

§ "And whatever town or village you enter, find out who is worthy in it, and stay with him until you depart."

¶ Take "no bag for your journey, nor two tunics, nor sandals, nor a staff; for the laborer deserves his food."

** "If any one would sue you and take your coat, let him have your cloak as well."

†† "And why are you anxious about clothing? Consider the lilies of the field, how they grow; they neither toil nor spin; yet I tell you, even Solomon in all his glory was not arrayed like one of these. But if God so clothes the grass of the field, which today is alive and tomorrow is thrown into the oven, will he not much more clothe you, O men of little faith?"

‡‡ "Then they will deliver you up to tribulation, and put you to death; and you will be hated by all nations for my name's sake."

§§ "He who receives you receives me, and he who receives me receives him who sent me. He who receives a prophet because he is a prophet shall receive a prophet's reward, and he who receives a righteous man because he is a

hell to pay (Matthew 10:14–15).¶¶

3 John 5–7 describes the wing-and-a prayer existence of the itinerant brothers: "Beloved, you are acting faithfully in whatever you accomplish for the brethren, and especially when they are strangers, and they have testified to your love before the church. You will do well to send them on their way in a manner worthy of God. For they went out for the sake of the Name, accepting nothing from the Gentiles. Therefore we ought to support such men, so that we may be fellow workers with the truth."

1 Corinthians 8:4–5 enumerates some of the privileges of itinerant preachers: "Do we not have a right to eat and drink? Do we not have a right to take along a sister as wife even as the rest of the apostles and the brothers of the Lord and Cephas?" There is no particular reason to think that Paul refers here, out of the blue, to the blood relatives of Jesus. Where do we catch any hint that they were all missionaries? Or that *any* were? In this verse the term would more naturally seem to denote a particular group of missionaries analogous to "the apostles," the brotherhood of the Lord.*** The title need imply that they were brothers to Jesus or God no more than the phrase "God's fellow workers," applied to Paul, Apollos, and Cephas in 1 Corinthians 3:9,††† means to picture the apostles working alongside God on the same task. Rather, it means, co-laborers (with one another) employed by God, as in Matthew 20:1–16,‡‡‡ where a landowner hires harvesters. See also

---

righteous man shall receive a righteous man's reward. And whoever gives to one of these little ones even a cup of cold water because he is a disciple, truly, I say to you, he shall not lose his reward."

¶¶   "And if any one will not receive you or listen to your words, shake off the dust from your feet as you leave that house or town. Truly, I say to you, it shall be more tolerable on the day of judgment for the land of Sodom and Gomorrah than for that town."

***   G.A. Wells, *The Jesus of the Early Christians* (London: Pemberton Books, 1971), p. 142.

†††   "For we are God's fellow workers; you are God's field, God's building."

‡‡‡   "For the kingdom of heaven is like a householder who went out early

The Christ Myth Theory And Its Problems

Matthew 9:37–38;* John 4:35–38.† They are God's servants, not his colleagues, if we can even imagine such a thing. So with James: one of those who are brothers among themselves, sharing a common heavenly Father, precisely as in 2 Apocalypse of James 51:19–22.

2 Corinthians 8:18 and 22 single out one individual in particular. Some think his name has dropped out, but as the chapter seems originally to have circulated as a fund-raising letter, there may have been a blank into which the bearer's name would have been inserted. In any case he is called "the brother" and "our brother," and to single out James as "the Lord's brother" might denote the same thing as here: "the brother whose fame in the gospel has

---

in the morning to hire laborers for his vineyard. After agreeing with the laborers for a denarius a day, he sent them into his vineyard. And going out about the third hour he saw others standing idle in the market place; and to them he said, 'You go into the vineyard too, and whatever is right I will give you.' So they went. Going out again about the sixth hour and the ninth hour, he did the same. And about the eleventh hour he went out and found others standing; and he said to them, 'Why do you stand here idle all day?' They said to him, 'Because no one has hired us.' He said to them, 'You go into the vineyard too.' And when evening came, the owner of the vineyard said to his steward, 'Call the laborers and pay them their wages, beginning with the last, up to the first.' And when those hired about the eleventh hour came, each of them received a denarius. Now when the first came, they thought they would receive more; but each of them also received a denarius. And on receiving it they grumbled at the householder, saying, 'These last worked only one hour, and you have made them equal to us who have borne the burden of the day and the scorching heat.' But he replied to one of them, 'Friend, I am doing you no wrong; did you not agree with me for a denarius? Take what belongs to you, and go; I choose to give to this last as I give to you. Am I not allowed to do what I choose with what belongs to me? Or do you begrudge my generosity?' So the last will be first, and the first last."

*   "Then he said to his disciples, 'The harvest is plentiful, but the laborers are few; pray therefore the Lord of the harvest to send out laborers into his harvest."

†   "Do you not say, 'There are yet four months, then comes the harvest'? I tell you, lift up your eyes, and see how the fields are already white for harvest. He who reaps receives wages, and gathers fruit for eternal life, so that sower and reaper may rejoice together. For here the saying holds true, 'One sows and another reaps.' I sent you to reap that for which you did not labor; others have labored, and you have entered into their labor.'"

spread through all the churches" (2 Corinthians 8:18). Thomas 12 ("Wherever you have come from you will go report to James the Just, for whom heaven and earth were prepared.") has Jesus tell his disciples that, following their future missionary journeys, they must report to James, implying that he should be considered *the* brother of the Lord, even if the term intended only missionaries.

Grafted into the Family Tree

Hermann Gunkel long ago showed[‡] how a number of stories and notes in Genesis made most sense when understood as what he called "ethnological (or ethnographical) myths," stories typifying clans and nations in the fictive personae of their (sometimes) eponymous ancestors. Such stories sought to account for historic patterns of relations (war or peace, independence or servitude) by establishing the same relations among their progenitors, with the ostensible result that these relations were "in the blood" and would continue on in perpetuity. Thus Jacob/Israel, the father of the Israelite tribes, and Esau, father of the Edomite tribes,[§] are described as ethnic stereotypes of the groups they represent rather in the manner of today's political cartoons. Why don't they get

---

[‡]   Hermann Gunkel, *Genesis*. Mercer Library of Biblical Studies. Trans. Mark E. Biddle (Macon: Mercer University Press, 1997), pp. xiv–xviii.

[§]   Why is the mythical progenitor of the Edomites not called "Edom"? I cannot help thinking that he *was*, and that the Edomites believed their national ancestor to be the first man created. The Israelites borrowed this bit of creation mythology, for some reason displacing their own, home-grown, primordial man, Enosh, whose name means "man," in favor of the Edomite version, Edom, or with different vowel pointing, *Adam*. Enosh was shunted to the side (though the Mandaeans would remember his original status). Once the Israelites became fierce competitors with their kinsmen of Edom, they could scarcely say their rivals were the direct offspring of the first man, so they posited a demoted version of the sun-god Esau as the Edomites' proximate ancestor. Esau had been the personification of the setting sun, red with great rays, and this made him a good match for the Edomites with their red and bushy hair, hair often symbolizing sun rays, as with Samson's locks.

along? What do you expect? It's in the blood! They've always been that way!

A variation on this theme was the use of genealogical links as a fictive, narrative way of cementing political, economic, or military alliances, or simply to explain geographical proximity. This is why Isaac and Ishmael are both made sons of Abraham, to seal the deal between Israelites and Arab tribes at some point in their history. When Abraham is said to have married Keturah (Genesis 25:1–4)* it is strictly for the sake of sealing a late alliance between the Israelite tribes and the other cities and tribes there said to spring from the marriage. The largest-scale case of such alliance-through-expanding-the-genealogy is the connection of the twelve Israelite tribes as blood brothers, the offspring of twelve sons of one father. We can tell that the various tribal patriarchs are artificial characters because some of their names were originally not personal names at all. "Ephraim" meant "those who live on Mount Ephrath." "Issachar" meant "migrant workers." "*Benjamin*" denoted "Sons of the Right Hand," *i.e.*, Southerners, as in Yemen today. Other tribes bore the names of favorite gods, such as Asher, Zebulun, and Gad. These twelve tribes got together (as many groups of twelve did, all over the ancient Mediterranean) and formed a tribal league centered about shared, rotating care for a central shrine (Shiloh), one tribe having a turn each month. They sealed the alliance by making themselves the progeny of a single fictive ancestor, Jacob/Israel.

I believe something similar still went on in New Testament times. It is clear to scholars, for instance, that the idea of John the Baptist being the cousin of Jesus is a Lukan invention aimed at co-opting members of the John the Baptist sect which had continued

---

*   "Abraham took another wife, whose name was Keturah. She bore him Zimran, Jokshan, Medan, Midian, Ishbak, and Shuah. Jokshan was the father of Sheba and Dedan. The sons of Dedan were Asshurim, Letushim, and Leummim. The sons of Midian were Ephah, Epher, Hanoch, Abida, and Eldaah. All these were the children of Keturah."

as a rival alongside of Christianity.[†] This is absolutely clear in Luke 1:41–44, when, upon the pregnant Mary's entrance, her pregnant cousin Elizabeth feels her fetus, John the Baptist, not merely kicking but leaping for joy in the womb. Matthew did not think of this, so he has John recognize Jesus' messianic identity as soon as he sees him at the Jordan and humbly protest his unworthiness to baptize his superior. John's gospel has John the Baptist telling his own followers to abandon him and to follow Jesus instead of him. So for Luke to make John the Baptist into the cousin of Jesus is to link the two sects together, establishing Jesus' superiority to John. After all, it is baby John who rejoices at Jesus' arrival, not the other way around.

In precisely the same manner, I suggest, early Christian tradition seized upon the figure of James the Just, the head of his own sect (perhaps that of the Dead Sea Scrolls), and made him the "brother of the Lord" (long after the fact) in order to absorb and yet honor both the sect and its figurehead, while maintaining the centrality of Jesus (who by this late date had already been historicized). This would certainly help account for the otherwise-puzzling rivalry between partisans of the Twelve and those of the Pillars (led by James), both groups being patently Jewish Torah-Christians. We can understand why shots would be fired between Law-free Paulinists and Petrine *or* Jamesian Torah Christians. But why the rivalry between two Jewish groups? One plausible reason would be the subordination of the survivors of the sect of James the Righteous Teacher to that of Peter and the Twelve. It would

---

[†]   David Friedrich Strauss, *The Life of Jesus Critically Examined.* Trans. George Eliot. Lives of Jesus Series (4th ed., 1840, rpt. Philadelphia: Fortress Press, 19772, pp. 151, 226–228; Charles Guignebert, *Jesus.* Trans. S.H. Hooke (New Hyde Park: University Books, 1956), p. 156; Robert M. Price, *The Incredible Shrinking Son of Man: How Reliable is the Gospel Tradition?* (Amherst: Prometheus Books, 2003), pp. 111–113.

have been political, not theological. In that case, the clout of the James group need have had *nothing to do with advancing one's case in a succession dispute.*

The evidence Eisenman puts together concerning James also suggests he functioned as an unorthodox High Priest for his sect, and that he was finally arrested for his would-be priestly ministrations in the Holies of Holies on the Day of Atonement (by his calendar), which the temple police viewed as trespassing and blasphemy.[*] This is also quite consistent with James having his own reasons for being venerated, and not merely as the blood brother of Jesus. After all, a literal brother of Jesus might have been no more than a first-century Billy Carter or Roger Clinton. James as a fictive brother of Jesus would be exactly like John the Baptist, figurehead of a rival sect, who had to be tied in with the Jesus story, albeit tangentially, so as to leave intact most of the figure's own, already established, story. Here I think we have an entirely natural way of understanding "brother of the Lord" in a way that presupposes not a real historical Jesus but only a historicized Jesus, to whom James might usefully and fictively be connected in order to make transition into the Jesus movement easier. So, yes, it would mean James was understood as Jesus' physical brother, but it would be a fiction and thus no real evidence for a historical Jesus.

Josephus and James

Josephus *Antiquities* 20:200–202 mentions Jesus as it leads into the story of James the Just's martyrdom. Ananus "assembled the sanhedrim of the judges, and brought before them the brother of Jesus, who was called Christ, whose name was James, and some others, and when he had formed an accusation against them as breakers of the law, he delivered them to be stoned." Henry Chadwick, S.G.F.

---

[*] Robert M. Price, "Eisenman's Gospel of James the Just: A Review." In Bruce Chilton and Jacob Neusner, eds., *The Brother of Jesus: James the Just and his Mission* (Louisville: Westminster/John Knox Press, 2011, p. 194.

Brandon, Emil Schürer, and G.A. Wells all considered this passage another interpolation, a summary of the more elaborate account of the martyrdom in the Jewish-Christian historian Hegesippus, which gives the execution of James as the reason God gave Jerusalem over to the Roman sword ("And so he suffered martyrdom… and at once Vespasian began to besiege them."). Partly this is because Origen tells us that Josephus, "though he did not believe in Jesus as Christ, sought for the cause of the fall of Jerusalem and the destruction of the temple. He ought to have said that the plot against Jesus was the reason why these catastrophes came upon the people, because they had killed the prophesied Christ; however, though unconscious of it, he is not far from the truth when he says that these disasters befell the Jews to avenge James the Just, who was a brother of Jesus, him called Christ." (*Against Celsus* 1:47) Origen was not reading what we are reading in our copies of Josephus, and we must wonder if his contained the story of the martyrdom of John the Baptist and Herod Antipas' subsequent defeat by Aretas IV as a divine punishment for it. The two accounts would seem to be alternative versions of the same legend, perhaps both interpolations, and this possibility is enough to remove the reference to "James the brother of Jesus called Christ" from consideration.

But in any case, a mythic Jesus would have been historicized by Josephus' time, and if his writing presupposed a human Jesus who had a brother, that should not surprise us. The amalgamation of the James and Jesus sects would already have been accomplished, and the characters fictively associated in the manner just suggested.

Stranger in Paradigm

So the notion of James as the Lord's brother may denote his membership or leadership in a missionary circle. For James' fraternal connection to have denoted his status as the visible twin of an invisible Christ is plausible but equivocal, since one may as easily see the transformation going the other way: a natural brother being theologically "docetized." And yet I must say I find the possible parallel to the case of Hong Xiuquan, the Taiping Messiah, the Younger Son of God, to be, almost by itself, proof that James' being "the Lord's brother" need not prove a recent historical Jesus. We know it didn't in the one case, so we cannot be sure it did in the other. And the option of James' connection to a historical Jesus being a fictive link (like that of the twelve tribes to Jacob) seems to me by itself sufficient to obviate the whole problem.

And yet others may find none of the available options satisfactory. I should be quite willing to admit that the reconstruction of the Caliphate of James remains the strongest evidence that Jesus was not a mythic character subsequently historicized. What I will not say is that it is the Achilles' Heel of the Christ-Myth theory. I do not grant that it is fatal to the theory. Remember, we are not fundamentalists trying to settle arguments with authoritative prooftexts. Instead, we are scientific students of scripture, seeking to shape an interpretive paradigm and to lay it over the text to try it on for size. If there are numerous points where the paradigm strikingly illuminates the data, the paradigm is not overthrown by the stubborn persistence of bits of anomalous data. The history of the progression of explanatory paradigms in science would rather suggest that sooner or later someone will come along who can expand a useful paradigm, making room for the hitherto-ill-fitting data alongside the rest.[*] What we must guard against is a hell-bent adherence to a hobbyhorse of a theory. We must maintain only a tentative and provisional acceptance of any proposed paradigm (including the Christ Myth theory) until something better, maybe a better version of it, comes along. We only want to know what happened, not to know that a certain thing happened — or didn't.

---

[*] Thomas S. Kuhn, *The Structure of Scientific Revolutions* (Chicago: University of Chicago Press, 1962).

Does the Christ Myth Theory Require an Early Date for the Pauline Epistles?

Epistles versus Gospels

One of the pillar arguments of the Christ Myth Theory as usually put forth today is the absence from the Pauline Epistles of any gospel-like teaching ascribed to Jesus. If the gospels' Jesus Christ, Jesus of Nazareth, the itinerant sage and thaumaturge, was well known, at least among Christians, it would stand to reason that such a Jesus would meet us throughout the apostolic letters by way of quotations and anecdotes. But we find no such material. Suddenly, however, such a Jesus portrait appears in the gospels, written after the epistles, and the explanation for this discrepancy, according to Mythicists, is that, between the composition of epistles on the one hand and gospels on the other, the popular Christian imagination (as well as the inventiveness of Christian scribes) "historicized" the originally suprahistorical, spiritual (mythical) savior of whom Paul and the rest had earlier written so much of a dogmatic, but none of an historical-biographical nature. For various reasons it had become desirable in some quarters to posit a recent historical Jesus of Nazareth to whom one could trace oneself and one's institutional claims of authority. And in this window of time between epistles and gospels, various unnamed prophets (and borrowers and tall-tale-tellers) supplied the many things this Jesus would have, *must* have, done and said. Such a figure had not existed as far as the epistolarians knew, and so of course there was no such material with which to lard their epistles. But now that the newly-minted material was available, it found the epistle genre altogether too confining and called for a more appropriate format, that of the Hellenistic hero or saint biography, and so the gospels were born.

Parenthetically, it is worth pointing out that we possess two striking analogies for the rapid generation of "filler" sayings and stories.

The Christ Myth Theory And Its Problems

Think of the imaginative fabrication of episodes of the child Jesus preserved in the well-known apocryphal infancy gospels (attributed to Thomas, Matthew, James, and others); as soon as Christians came to believe that Jesus had not merely been adopted (as an adult) as God's Son, but that he had been born divine, they went to work filling in the imagined gap: what super-deeds must the divine child have been doing during those years? Secondly, after the promulgation of the Koran, a swelling flood of spurious hadith, stories of the words and deeds of the Prophet Muhammad, burst the levees of historical probability to correct and supplement the teaching of scripture. It is by no means far-fetched to suggest, then, that all the gospel stories of a mortal Jesus walking the earth swiftly arose to fill the newly discerned gap once such a Jesus was posited. It is no stretch to imagine Christian scribes and prophets supplying what their new earthly Jesus would have said, either. If it sounded good, Jesus said it.

This understanding of the epistles as preceding the gospels grounds the arguments of the two greatest Christ Myth theorists of our day, George A. Wells and Earl Doherty. Their views differ significantly at many points, but they agree here. Let me quote the venerable Wells.

> It is generally agreed that the NT epistles addressed to the Romans, Corinthians, Galatians, Ephesians, Philippians, Colossians and Thessalonians were written before the gospels... These early epistles exhibit such complete ignorance of the events which were later recorded in the gospels as to suggest that these events were not known to Paul or whoever it was who wrote the epistles.[*]

Doherty agrees:

> The story told [initially] in the Gospel of Mark first begins to surface toward the end of the first century CE. Yet the curious fact is that

---

[*] G.A. Wells, *The Jesus of the Early Christians: A Study in Christian Origins* (London: Pemberton Books, 1971), p. 131.

when we search for that story in all the non-Gospel documents written before that time, it is nowhere to be found... If we had to rely on the letters of the earliest Christians, such as Paul and those who wrote most of the other New Testament epistles, we would be hard pressed to find anything resembling the details of the gospel story. If we did not read Gospel associations into what Paul and the others say about their Christ Jesus, we could not even tell that this figure, the object of their worship, was a man who had recently lived in Palestine and had been executed by the Roman authorities with the help of a hostile Jewish establishment.[†]

Wells goes on: "Orthodox writers sometimes claim that [Paul] omitted references to Jesus' views and behaviour because they were irrelevant to the matters discussed in his letters... But this is hardly plausible." Paul everywhere proclaims the stultification of the Torah. Would none of the gospel Sabbath controversies have been relevant? Not even the Matthean antitheses?[‡] "In II Cor. viii, 9[§], in order to induce the Corinthians to contribute liberally to the collection for the poor in Palestine, he mentions Jesus as an example of liberality," but it is an appeal only to the doctrine of the Son's descent from heavenly glory to share the rude lot of mortals: nothing truly biographical. And why no citation of the uncomfortably many admonitions of the gospel Jesus to sell one's possessions and turn the proceeds over to the poor (*e.g.*, Luke 18:22)?[¶]

[†]   Earl Doherty, *The Jesus Puzzle: Did Christianity Begin with a Mythical Christ?* (Ottowa, Canadian Humanist Publications, 1990), p. 2.

[‡]   Matthew 5:21–39, *e.g.*, "You have heard that it was said to the men of old, 'You shall not kill; and whoever kills shall be liable to judgment.' But I say to you that every one who is angry with his brother shall be liable to judgment; whoever insults his brother shall be liable to the council, and whoever says, 'You fool!' shall be liable to the hell of fire."

[§]   2 Corinthians 8:9, "For you know the grace of our Lord Jesus Christ, that though he was rich, yet for your sake he became poor, so that by his poverty you might become rich."

[¶]   Wells, *Jesus of the Early Christians*, p. 147. Luke 18:22, "And when Jesus heard it, he said to him, 'One thing you still lack. Sell all that you have and

The Christ Myth Theory And Its Problems

When Paul recommends celibacy (1 Cor. 7:7–8),* why doesn't he quote Matthew 19:10–12?† When he urges Christians, though citizens of heaven, not to evade Roman taxes (Rom. 13:1–6),‡ why does he not reinforce the point with a citation of the now-famous "Render unto Caesar" logion (Mark 12:15–17)?§ Had the vexing business of dietary laws arisen (Rom. 14:1–4; 1 Corinthians 8; Colossians 2:20–21)?¶

distribute to the poor, and you will have treasure in heaven; and come, follow me.'"

* "I wish that all were as I myself am. But each has his own special gift from God, one of one kind and one of another. To the unmarried and the widows I say that it is well for them to remain single as I do."

† Wells, *Did Jesus Exist?* (London: Elek/Pemberton, 1975), p. 19. Matthew 19:10–12, "The disciples said to him, 'If such is the case of a man with his wife, it is not expedient to marry.' But he said to them, 'Not all men can receive this saying, but only those to whom it is given. For there are eunuchs who have been so from birth, and there are eunuchs who have been made eunuchs by men, and there are eunuchs who have made themselves eunuchs for the sake of the kingdom of heaven. He who is able to receive this, let him receive it.'"

‡ Romans 13:1–6, *e.g.*, "For the same reason you also pay taxes, for the authorities are ministers of God, attending to this very thing."

§ Wells, *Jesus of the Early Christians*, p. 147. Mark 12:14–17, "And they came and said to him, 'Teacher, we know that you are true, and care for no man; for you do not regard the position of men, but truly teach the way of God. Is it lawful to pay taxes to Caesar, or not? Should we pay them, or should we not?' But knowing their hypocrisy, he said to them, 'Why put me to the test? Bring me a coin, and let me look at it.' And they brought one. And he said to them, 'Whose likeness and inscription is this?' They said to him, 'Caesar's.' Jesus said to them, 'Render to Caesar the things that are Caesar's, and to God the things that are God's.' And they were amazed at him."

¶ Romans 14:3, "Let not him who eats despise him who abstains, and let not him who abstains pass judgment on him who eats; for God has welcomed him." 1 Corinthians 8:8–10, "Food will not commend us to God. We are no worse off if we do not eat, and no better off if we do. Only take care lest this liberty of yours somehow become a stumbling block to the weak. For if any one sees you, a man of knowledge, at table in an idol's temple, might he not be encouraged, if his conscience is weak, to eat food offered to idols?" Colossians 2:20–21, "If with Christ you died to the elemental spirits of the universe, why do you live as if you still belonged to the world? Why do you submit to regulations, "Do not handle, Do not taste, Do not touch" (referring to things which all perish as they are used), according to human precepts and doctrines? These have indeed an appearance of

Quoting Mark 7:15** would have made short work of that one. Was there controversy over circumcision? There was in Romans 3:1 and Galatians 5:1–12,†† but Paul never thinks to cite Thomas 53,‡‡ which would have closed the book on that one fast. "Precisely where the author of Romans might be expected to invoke the authority of Jesus, he does not."§§

But suppose there were originally no dominical sayings to settle these questions; it is not hard to imagine that soon people would be coining them — or attaching Jesus' name to a saying they already liked, to make it authoritative.

Wells deftly parries one of the predictable thrusts against his argument: "It is often alleged that Paul would not specify details with which his readers were already familiar. Yet he repeatedly specifies the incarnation, death and resurrection with which they were, in the terms of the case, familiar."¶¶ Not only that; see 1 Corinthians 2:1–5*** and 15:1, 15††† (recollection of his initial preaching); 5:9–11‡‡‡

---

wisdom in promoting rigor of devotion and self-abasement and severity to the body, but they are of no value in checking the indulgence of the flesh."

**   Mark 7:15, "There is nothing outside a man which by going into him can defile him; but the things which come out of a man are what defile him."

††   Romans 3:1, "Then what advantage has the Jew? Or what is the value of circumcision?" Galatians 5:2, "Now I, Paul, say to you that if you receive circumcision, Christ will be of no advantage to you."

‡‡   Gospel of Thomas 53, "His disciples say to him, 'Is circumcision worthwhile or not?' He says to them, 'If it were, men would be born that way automatically. But the true circumcision in spirit has become completely worthwhile.'"

§§   Wells, *Jesus of the Early Christians*, p. 133.

¶¶   Wells, *Jesus of the Early Christians*, p. 147.

***   1 Corinthians 2:1–2, "When I came to you, brethren, I did not come proclaiming to you the testimony of God in lofty words or wisdom. For I decided to know nothing among you except Jesus Christ and him crucified."

†††   1 Corinthians 15:1, "Now I would remind you, brethren, in what terms I preached to you the gospel, which you received, in which you stand."

‡‡‡   1 Corinthians 5:9–11, "I wrote to you in my letter not to associate with immoral men; not at all meaning the immoral of this world, or the greedy and robbers, or idolaters, since then you would need to go out of the world. But rather

The Christ Myth Theory And Its Problems

(shunning backsliders); 6:3* (the chaste will one day judge the fallen Sons of God); 2 Corinthians 2:1–4† (his previously announced travel plans); 13:2‡ (former disciplinary warnings); Galatians 1:13–14§ (his pre-Christian life); 3:1¶ (their first graphic encounter with the Christian Mystery); 4:13–15** (their kind reception of him in his hour of suffering); 5:21†† (a familiar list of mortal sins); Ephesians 4:20‡‡ (their first catechism); Philippians 3:1 §§ (on repeating what he has previously written them); 3:18¶¶ (his old rivals); Colossians

---

I wrote to you not to associate with any one who bears the name of brother if he is guilty of immorality or greed, or is an idolater, reviler, drunkard, or robber — not even to eat with such a one."

 *   1 Corinthians 6:3, "Do you not know that we are to judge angels? How much more, matters pertaining to this life!"

 †   2 Corinthians 2:3–4, "And I wrote as I did, so that when I came I might not suffer pain from those who should have made me rejoice, for I felt sure of all of you, that my joy would be the joy of you all. For I wrote you out of much affliction and anguish of heart and with many tears, not to cause you pain but to let you know the abundant love that I have for you."

 ‡   2 Corinthians 13:2, "I warned those who sinned before and all the others, and I warn them now while absent, as I did when present on my second visit, that if I come again I will not spare them."

 §   Galatians 1:13–14, "For you have heard of my former life in Judaism, how I persecuted the church of God violently and tried to destroy it; and I advanced in Judaism beyond many of my own age among my people, so extremely zealous was I for the traditions of my fathers."

 ¶   Galatians 3:1, "O foolish Galatians! Who has bewitched you, before whose eyes Jesus Christ was publicly portrayed as crucified?"

 **   Galatians 4:13–15, "you know it was because of a bodily ailment that I preached the gospel to you at first; and though my condition was a trial to you, you did not scorn or despise me, but received me as an angel of God, as Christ Jesus. What has become of the satisfaction you felt? For I bear you witness that, if possible, you would have plucked out your eyes and given them to me."

 ††   Galatians 5:21b, "I warn you, as I warned you before, that those who do such things shall not inherit the kingdom of God."

 ‡‡   Ephesians 4:20, "You did not so learn Christ!"

 §§   Philippians 3:1b, "To write the same things to you is not irksome to me, and is safe for you."

 ¶¶   Philippians 3:18, "For many, of whom I have often told you and now

1:5–6*** (the well-known spread of the gospel); 2:7††† (their roots in Christ); 1 Thessalonians 1:5;‡‡‡ 2:5–12§§§ (his solid reputation among them); 4:1–2¶¶¶ (the pattern of Christian living); 5:1–3**** (eschatology of which they should require no reminder, *but do*). So the Paul of the epistles had no compunction about repeating himself and his teaching. There is no reason to believe that, had he initially laid a foundation of gospel-style materials about Jesus that he would

tell you even with tears, live as enemies of the cross of Christ."

*** Colossians 1:5b–6, "Of this you have heard before in the word of the truth, the gospel which has come to you, as indeed in the whole world it is bearing fruit and growing — so among yourselves, from the day you heard and understood the grace of God in truth."

††† Colossians 2:6–7, "As therefore you received Christ Jesus the Lord, so live in him, rooted and built up in him and established in the faith, just as you were taught, abounding in thanksgiving."

‡‡‡ 1 Thessalonians 1:5, "for our gospel came to you not only in word, but also in power and in the Holy Spirit and with full conviction. You know what kind of men we proved to be among you for your sake."

§§§ 1 Thessalonians 2:5–12, "For we never used either words of flattery, as you know, or a cloak for greed, as God is witness; nor did we seek glory from men, whether from you or from others, though we might have made demands as apostles of Christ. But we were gentle among you, like a nurse taking care of her children. So, being affectionately desirous of you, we were ready to share with you not only the gospel of God but also our own selves, because you had become very dear to us. For you remember our labor and toil, brethren; we worked night and day, that we might not burden any of you, while we preached to you the gospel of God. You are witnesses, and God also, how holy and righteous and blameless was our behavior to you believers; for you know how, like a father with his children, we exhorted each one of you and encouraged you and charged you to lead a life worthy of God, who calls you into his own kingdom and glory."

¶¶¶ 1 Thessalonians 4:1, "Finally, brethren, we beseech and exhort you in the Lord Jesus, that as you learned from us how you ought to live and to please God, just as you are doing, you do so more and more. For you know what instructions we gave you through the Lord Jesus."

**** 1 Thessalonians 5:1–3, "But as to the times and the seasons, brethren, you have no need to have anything written to you. For you yourselves know well that the day of the Lord will come like a thief in the night. When people say, "There is peace and security," then sudden destruction will come upon them as travail comes upon a woman with child, and there will be no escape."

not have had ample occasion to revisit it, any more than a modern preacher does.

Some say that the epistles display extensive awareness of the gospel teachings of Jesus but paraphrase them without indicating that Jesus first said them. Romans 12 and the Epistle of James are full of such logia. James D.G. Dunn,[*] maintains that Paul and James intended the reader to sniff out the dominical origin (and authority) in these cases, but left them as allusions for those who had ears to hear ("wink, wink, nudge, nudge"). But this is one of those arguments no one would offer if he were not trying to climb out of a tight spot. Think about it: if you want to settle a question by appealing to the words of Jesus, you're going to make sure the reader understands that they are indeed words of Jesus, and that by saying so. It seems quite reasonable to suggest that in the epistles we find early Christian sayings just *before* they were ascribed to Jesus.

But does Paul not derive at least the Lord's Supper pericope from Synoptic tradition? No, he says he received it immediately, by direct revelation from the Lord himself.[†] In the same way, it is utterly gratuitous for apologists to point to Paul's "commands of the Lord" as representing a Q-like list of dominical maxims.

> To the married, I give charge (not I but the Lord), that the wife should not separate from the husband, but if she does, let her remain single or else be reconciled to her husband, and that the husband should not divorce his wife. To the rest, I say, not the Lord, that if any brother has a wife who is an unbeliever, and she consents to live with him, he should not divorce her. (1 Cor. 7:10–12).
>
> Now concerning the unmarried, I have no command of the Lord, but I give my opinion as one who by the Lord's mercy is trustworthy. (1 Cor. 7:25)

---

[*] James D.G. Dunn, "Jesus Tradition in Paul," in Bruce Chilton and Craig A. Evans (eds.), *Studying the Historical Jesus* (Leiden: E.J. Brill, 1994), pp. 177–178.

[†] Wells, *Jesus of the Early Christians* p. 273: *cf.* Hyam Maccoby, *Paul and Hellenism* (Philadelphia: Trinity Press International, 1991), chapter 4, "Paul and the Eucharist," pp. 90–128..

Robert M. Price   Early Date for the Pauline Epistles?

But in my judgment she is happier if she remains as she is. And I think I have the Spirit of God. (1 Cor. 7:40)

The Lord commanded that those who proclaim the gospel should get their living by the gospel. (1 Cor. 9:14)

If anyone thinks he is a prophet or a pneumatic, he should acknowledge that what I am writing to you is a command of the Lord. 1 Cor. 14:37

Especially in view of the last of these snippets, it becomes obvious that the first, fourth, and fifth have originated in prophetic bulletins, "words of knowledge" or "words of wisdom" vouchsafed to Christian prophets, oracles of the Risen Christ, probably to the writer himself. This becomes especially clear in light of the second and third statements, which define the "commands of the Lord" by contrast. It is not that the "commands" have some origin elsewhere than Paul; it is only that they have not emerged from a prophetic state as the "commands" did. It seems gross over-interpretation even to hold open the possibility that in his "commands of the Lord" the writer should be referring to sayings of the historical Jesus. What we are seeing is a Christian rebirth of the Old Testament practice of the priests "giving Torah" via oracular judgments on matters brought to them. The result is what Noth[‡] called "apodictic" law as opposed to casuistic or circumstantial law. Again, they would be what Käsemann[§] dubbed "sentences of holy law."

There are other, perhaps equally important, foundations of today's Christ Myth Theory, such as the absence of extra-canonical witnesses to Jesus' historical existence, as well as the striking parallels between Jesus and the purely mythic dying and rising god

---

[‡]   Martin Noth, *The Laws in the Pentateuch and Other Studies*. D.R. Ap-Thomas (London: SCM Press, 1984), pp. 7, 243.

[§]   Ernst Käsemann, "Sentences of Holy Law," in Käsemann, *New Testament Questions of Today*. Trans. W.J. Montague (Philadelphia: Fortress Press, 1979), pp. 66–81.

The Christ Myth Theory And Its Problems

cults, whose divine heroes and saviors had never existed as historical characters. But these do not concern us here.

Yesteryear and Beyond

The scholars of a past generation used many of the same arguments as their successors do today, but there are many differences as well. Our business here is to compare the way in which the date of the Pauline Epistles figured into the Christ Myth Theory as it used to be argued. It will have been noted that Wells and Doherty uphold the traditional dates and (for the most part) authorship ascriptions of the epistles. Wells and Doherty are willing, indeed eager, to take for granted traditional claims for assigning age and authorship. This makes them admirably early and leaves plenty of time for gospel story-tellers to have done their subsequent work, historicizing Jesus and pillaging the epistles for sayings to reattribute to Jesus. One feels that things would begin to blur if the gospels and epistles had to be placed as more or less contemporary. That condition would open up the possibility or need to find another solution for the lack of gospel-type tradition in the epistles.

In the estimation of Paul-Louis Couchoud[*] the Pauline Epistles, at least in their shorter, Marcionite editions, are genuine. This means leaving out more than a third of Romans as Catholicizing padding.[†] But Marcion, Couchoud believed, added 2 Thessalonians as a corrective to 1 Thessalonians' apocalyptic urgency and penned Laodiceans (=Ephesians) as a commentary on Colossians.[‡] In addition, "Marcion is probably the author of a life of St. Paul which was to form the framework of the Acts of the Apostles."[§]

---

[*]   P.L. Couchoud, *The Creation of Christ: An Outline of the Beginnings of Christianity*. Trans. C. Bradlaugh Bonner (London: Watts, 1939).

[†]   Couchoud, *Creation of Christ*, p. 65.

[‡]   Couchoud, *Creation of Christ*, p. 125.

[§]   Couchoud, *Creation of Christ*, p. 126.

362

That is, the itinerary. Shortly before Marcion, and under pagan influence, Jesus was historicized in popular belief. Christians began to believe Christ had lived on earth, among humanity, in the recent past. His death had been a mundane, political execution, though occurring according to divine Providence. Marcion's gospel (of which Couchoud speaks as if Marcion himself wrote it) was the first literary embodiment of the new notion. The notion came in handy because it fit Marcion's idea of Jesus having *recently* revealed his *new God*.

Marcion's gospel reflects the Bar Kochba revolt and stems from *ca.* 133.[¶] Mark (*ca.* 133–134, or shortly after 135) abridged Marcion's gospel at some points, expanding it at others. Only a few years later (140), Matthew did the same. Marcion lived to read the four gospels, all dependent upon his. Couchoud's thinking raises a crucial point he seems not to have recognized, but with which we absolutely must come to terms: on Couchoud's reading, Marcion would have been the author of at least two of the "Pauline" epistles as well as a gospel, and this means that one might indeed be familiar with the teaching of the gospel Jesus, ascribed to Jesus, and yet have reasons for omitting any of it in one's epistles. *If Marcion could have known gospel tradition and yet mentioned none of it in his epistles, so could Paul.*

To be fair, Couchoud has characterized Marcion's hypothetical epistolary efforts in such a way as not to entail gospel-quoting: Ephesians as a mere commentary upon Colossians, a writing ignorant of Jesus-attributed teachings, need hardly introduce any of them. And if the goal of 2 Thessalonians was only to correct the hot-head eschatology of 1 Thessalonians, all Marcion need have done was to write what looks like a second version of 1 Thessalonians, differing only in this matter of de-apocalypticizing. As

---

[¶]   A view newly upheld in Hermann Detering, "The Synoptic Apocalypse (Mark 13 par): A Document from the Time of Bar Kochba" in *The Journal of Higher Criticism* 7/2 (Fall, 2000), pp. 161–210.

he intended to stick as close to the look and feel of the original, almost to the point of replacing it, in penning 2 Thessalonians Marcion might have had added reason to avoid any ostensible Jesus-teachings he might have known, since including them would make 2 Thessalonians seem needlessly different from its model, 1 Thessalonians. But we will see that there are other reasons to posit Marcionite authorship of still more "Pauline" material, and the same solution will not suffice.

Edouard Dujardin[*] sees the same epistle-to-gospel discrepancy, though his view of a Pauline historical Jesus is a bit different. He has Paul envisioning a Jesus who descended to earth only very briefly, and not in a fleshly body. "It can be shown that the Jesus of St. Paul is a god who took the appearance, and only the appearance, of a man during the few days that the sacred drama lasted."[†]

We find nothing in these epistles except the abstract affirmation that Jesus was crucified. The only precise indication is contained in the First Epistle to the Corinthians, ii. 8, in which we read that Jesus was crucified by the demons.[‡] St. Paul speaks unceasingly in all the pages of his epistles of the crucifixion of Jesus, and never directly or indirectly refers to the actors who play their parts in the gospel drama; never refers to the intervention of the Jews or Romans; never for an instant conjures up any of the episodes of the Passion. St. Paul knew that Jesus was crucified, but was wholly unaware that he was arrested, that he was arraigned before one or several tribunals, that he was condemned, and that his death took the form of a judicial crucifixion.[§]

Arthur Drews[¶] first dismisses the question of authenticity (did Paul actually write the letters bearing his name?) as irrelevant

[*]   Edouard Dujardin, *Ancient History of the God Jesus*. Abridged and trans. A. Brodie Sanders (London: Watts, 1938).
[†]   Dujardin, p. 23; *cf.* 62–63.
[‡]   Dujardin, p. 32.
[§]   Dujardin, p. 33.
[¶]   Arthur Drews, *The Christ Myth*. Trans. C. DeLisle Burns. Westminster College-Oxford: Classics in Religious Studies (1910; rpt: Amherst: Prometheus Books, 1998).

since impossible to solve. He thus anticipates Derrida's metaphor of "the Postcard," a literary object whose detachment from any knowledge of origin and authorial intention becomes integral to its character and interpretation.[**] Drews says:

> Let us leave completely on one side the question of the authenticity of the Pauline epistles, a question absolute agreement on which will probably never be attained, for the simple reason that we lack any certain basis for its decision. Instead of this let us turn rather to what we learn from these epistles concerning the historical Jesus.[††] [T]he Jesus painted by Paul is not a man, but a purely divine personality, a heavenly spirit without flesh and blood, an unindividual superhuman phantom.[‡‡] Christ, as the principle of redemption, is for Paul only an allegorical or symbolical personality and not a real one.[§§] Christ's life and death are for Paul neither the moral achievement of a man nor in any way historical facts, but something super-historical, events in the supra-sensual world.[¶¶]

Date, it seems, is not so irrelevant as authorship. Drews continues:

> It must be considered that, if the Pauline epistles stood in the edition of the New Testament where they really belong — that is, before the gospels — hardly any one would think that Jesus, as he there meets him, was a real man and had wandered on the earth in flesh and blood; but he would in all probability find therein the detailed development of the "suffering servant of God," and would conclude that it was an irruption of heathen ideas into Jewish religious thought.[***]

But even the question of authorship/authenticity creeps back in, having been ejected too soon.

[**]   Jacques Derrida, *The Post Card: From Socrates to Freud and Beyond.* Trans.Alan Bass (Chicago: University of Chicago Press, 1987)

[††]   Drews, *Christ Myth*, pp. 168–169.

[‡‡]   Drews, *Christ Myth*, p. 180.

[§§]   Drews, *Christ Myth*, p. 204.

[¶¶]   Drews, *Christ Myth*, p. 206.

[***]   Drews, *Christ Myth*, p. 208.

The Christ Myth Theory And Its Problems

If Paul refers in his Epistles to an historical Jesus, these Epistles, bearing his name, cannot possibly have been written by the apostle who was changed from Saul to Paul by the Damascus vision. For it is inconceivable that an historical individual should, so soon after his death, be elevated by the apostle to the dignity of a second God, a co-worker in the creation and redemption of the world.[*]

If the Epistles were really written by Paul, the Jesus Christ who is a central figure in them cannot be an historical personality. The way in which the supposed Jew Paul speaks of him is contrary to all psychological and historical experience. *Either the Pauline Epistles are genuine, and in that case Jesus is not an historical personality; or he is an historical personality, and in that case the Pauline Epistles are not genuine, but written at a much later period.* This later period would have no difficulty in raising to the sphere of deity a man of former times who was known to it only by a vague tradition.[†]

But if they are that late, late enough for the facts to have passed from collective memory, are the epistles still to be dated later than the gospels? Why would the spurious traditions collected in the gospels have waited *this* long to rear their heads? Would hagiographic embellishments have begun only in order to replace a complete loss of remembered facts? That is not unnatural. After all, we hypothesize that a number of myths have attached themselves to rituals in order to provide some sort of an explanation long after the original reason for the ritual has been forgotten. A total eclipse of an historical Jesus and a subsequent substitution with mythology would not be that different.

---

[*]   Drews, *Christ* Myth, p. 116.

[†]   Arthur Drews, *The Witnesses to the Historicity of Jesus*. Trans. Joseph McCabe (Chicago: Open Court, n.d.), p. 117.

Robert M. Price   **Early Date for the Pauline Epistles?**

Mythology versus Methodology

Another consideration: remember that Bultmann[‡] suggested that originally many sayings ascribed to Jesus circulated with no narrative introduction, with the result that it was anybody's guess what the sayings were about. We still have trouble being sure what was meant by "Take care not to cast your pearls before swine or holy things to dogs, lest they trample them underfoot and turn on you to maul you." Bultmann posited that at first many such isolated sayings made the rounds, and that people supplied hypothetical contexts to lend them some meaning. "The sound have no need of a physician, but only the sick. I came not to call the righteous but sinners." "The son of man is lord even of the Sabbath." "The son of man came to save human lives, not to destroy them." Once narrative introductions were added, such enigmatic aphorisms became "pronouncement stories." This means sayings were prior to stories. And it is not hard to picture the sayings originating (*à la* Wells and Doherty) as comments by the epistle writers and only subsequently picking up added *meaning* by a supplied narrative context and added *authority* by a connection to Jesus. We require no absolute dates here. It is simply the logic of the process, and it implies that epistle material is earlier than gospel material, whatever the actual date of any of it.

Yet another criterion from gospel criticism may come to our aid. In any case where we entertain two versions of a story (or two rival stories) and one is more spectacular than the other, the historian must reject the more spectacular as the more likely to have been made up to enhance the story's hero.[§] If the more spectacular version were first known, what would motivate anyone to fabricate the less impressive? But if an original, more modest story

---

[‡]   Rudolf Bultmann, *History of the Synoptic Tradition*. Trans. John Marsh (NY: Harper & Row, 1968), pp. 39–40, 47–50, 57, 61–62.

[§]   David Friedrich Strauss, *The Life of Jesus Critically Examined*. Trans. George Eliot [Mary Ann Evans]. Lives of Jesus Series (Philadelphia: Fortress Press, 1972), p. 229.

had failed to impress, it is easy to imagine that someone might want to replace it with something more impressive. For example, Mark tells us both that the prophecy of Elijah's return was fulfilled figuratively in John the Baptist (9:12–13),[*] *and* that Elijah himself returned, along with Moses, on the Mount of Transfiguration (9:4).[†] Clearly, the figurative John the Baptist version was first, but anyone could see how lame it was: no proof of anything, a reinterpretation of evidence in light of faith, not something to create faith. So they invented a way in which they could swear up and down that Elijah himself, his footprints matching those at Mann's Chinese Theatre, did appear before witnesses! Ah, too bad you weren't there, but what are you going to do? If the tradition had begun with the Transfiguration version, who would have bothered for a split second with the Baptist figurative version? No one, that's who.[‡]

Well, that is the way it is in the case of epistle material versus gospel material. Claims of spiritual upheavals in unseen worlds are as old as the hills, and admittedly unverifiable. On the other hand, a bag full of stories of virgin births, angelic interventions, demon exorcisms, nature miracles, and a resurrection from the dead! Well, that is more spectacular, hands down. One might protest that an ostensible war in heaven, or a contest in which the Light-Man defeated the Principalities and Powers in the lower heavens, is pretty spectacular! But really it is like the difference between claiming that Uncle Frank has died and gone to heaven and claiming that Uncle Frank ascended into heaven in plain sight of many witnesses. By this criterion, then, as I think Drews implies, the vaguer epistolary version still trumps the gospel version as the earlier. And this remains true no matter when each text was first written down.

---

[*]   Mark 9:12–13, "But I tell you that Elijah has come, and they did to him whatever they pleased, as it is written of him."

[†]   Mark 9:4, "And there appeared to them Elijah with Moses; and they were talking to Jesus."

[‡]   Strauss, p. 543.

Robert M. Price   Early Date for the Pauline Epistles?

It is interesting that, no matter the date of the underlying document, Drews reasons that 1 Corinthians 11:23 *ff*, the Last Supper
episode, must be an interpolation,[§] presumably because it stands out
like a sore thumb: epistles just do not include such materials except
as barnacles on the hull. Here an historical accident (epistles lack
Jesus narratives because, at the time, none existed) becomes a genre
convention (epistles *do* not, *i.e.*, *can*-not contain Jesus-narratives).

William Benjamin Smith is equally willing to grant an early
date to the epistles, as long as one allows for interpolations. Even
if the epistles on the whole predate the gospels, it can be shown
(and he argues the point in great detail) that the two historicizing
passages in 1 Cor (11:23–27 and 15:1–11) do not.[¶] As we have
seen, Wells is even more conservative than this, as he is willing
to allow the Last Supper passage to stand as authentically Pauline as long as we realize that the scene came to him in a vision,
presumably like those breaking upon Anna Katherine Emmerich,
compiled in her *The Dolorous Passion of our Lord Jesus Christ*.

John M. Robertson sees things in much the same terms as
Arthur Drews, like him, entertaining a much more radical estimate
of the date and integrity of the epistles than our recent Christ Myth
advocates, Wells and Doherty.

> The fact is that the higher criticism of the New Testament has thus
> far missed the way… by taking for granted the general truth of the
> tradition. [footnote at this point: "An emphatic exception, certainly,
> must be made as regards the Pauline epistles, which by the late Pro-
> fessor van Manen and others are rejected as entirely spurious.]…
> it clings to the conception of a preaching and cult-founding Jesus,
> when an intelligent perusal of the epistles of Paul can suffice to
> show that the preaching was created after they were written.[**]

§   Drews, *Christ Myth*, p. 175.
¶   William Benjamin Smith, *Ecce Deus: Studies of Primitive Christian-
ity* (London: Watts, 1912), pp. 146–157.
**   John M. Robertson, *Pagan Christs: Studies in Comparative Mythol-*

The Christ Myth Theory And Its Problems

The implication, if not the main point at issue, is that even if the epistles are quite late, as Bruno Bauer and the Dutch radicals made them, the gospels may be dated still later, as per some of the same critics. And in this case, we would still have the same relative dating: earlier epistles without Jesus-narratives, followed by later gospels complete with Jesus-narratives, a spirit-Jesus having been historicized in the meantime. In all this Robertson is echoed by Georg Brandes: "as far as it is possible to tell, the gradually constructed and repeatedly edited compilations known as the Synoptic Gospels must be at least fifty years younger than the genuine parts of the epistles ascribed to Paul."[*]

> The epistles which bear his name, genuine or not, are far older than the Gospels. The author of these epistles had never seen Jesus, and he neither knows nor communicates anything at all about the real life of Jesus. The man called Paul has a purely theological conception of Jesus.[†] The likelihood seems to be that only the epistles to the Galatians, the Romans, and parts of the first one to the Corinthians can be held genuine. [But] Even if they should be older than the gospels, the Pauline writings may be antedated. [Referring to the work of Van Manen, implying a 2nd century date.][‡]
>
> At the same time, Rylands anticipates the conclusion of Maccoby and others that even a Jesus-narrative like that occurring in 1 Corinthians 11:23–25[§] is pure dogma, not history. It is a piece of a cult legend, not biographical information.

---

ogy (London: Watts, 2nd rev. ed., 1911), p. 237.

[*] Georg Brandes, *Jesus a Myth*. Trans. Edwin Björkman (NY: Albert & Charles Boni, 1926), p. 42.

[†] Brandes, p. 44.

[‡] Brandes, p. 45.

[§] 1 Corinthians 11:23–25, "For I received from the Lord what I also delivered to you, that the Lord Jesus on the night when he was betrayed took bread, and when he had given thanks, he broke it, and said, 'This is my body which is for you. Do this in remembrance of me.' In the same way also the cup, after supper, saying, 'This cup is the new covenant in my blood. Do this, as often as you drink it, in remembrance of me.'"

Robert M. Price   Early Date for the Pauline Epistles?

The Pauline writers are interested only in the death and resurrection of Jesus. The writer of Galatians, whom theologians, except those of the Dutch radical school, believe to have been Paul, says not only that he had not learnt what he taught upon this subject from men, but that he did not wish to obtain from men any information with regard to it. A sufficient proof that what he taught was pure dogma.[¶]

Not only in the Pauline Epistles, but in all the Epistles, there is not the faintest trace of any impression that had been made by any human personality. If the supposed impression had been made, the experiences through which the disciples had lived in the company of Jesus would have been handed down and the thought of early Christians would have been full of them. But these early Christian writers never reinforce their arguments by anything they had heard that Jesus had done. He is never set before those to whom these Epistles are addressed as an example which they should follow in any human relationship, by pointing to his behaviour on some particular occasion. For the writers of these Epistles Jesus is not a man whose example other men could follow. He is the "Son of God's love, in whom we have our redemption, the image of the invisible God, the firstborn of all creation."[**]

Robertson avers:

The question of the general genuineness of "the four" epistles [the so-called *Hauptbriefe*, or principle epistles which F.C. Baur considered largely authentic: Romans, Galatians, 1 and 2 Corinthians] I have left open, while leaning more and more, though always with some reserves, to Van Manen's conclusions. But my case was and is that, whether the epistles to the Corinthians be genuine or spurious, they betray a general ignorance of the purport of the gospel narratives. As thus: (a) the passage 1 Cor. xv, 3–9[††] cannot well have been current

---

[¶]   L. Gordon Rylands, *Did Jesus Ever Live?* (London: Watts, 1935), p. 23.

[**]   Rylands, *Did Jesus Ever Live?*, p. 26.

[††]   1 Corinthians 15:3–8, "For I delivered to you as of first importance what I also received, that Christ died for our sins in accordance with the scrip-

as it stands before the gospels, else they would surely have given the "five hundred" story;[*] [though] (b) verse 5 must have been written before the Judas story was added to the gospels, since it speaks of Jesus as appearing to the whole "twelve," where the synoptics say "the eleven";[†] (c) the non-mention of the women also [implies] the ignorance of the gospel story; (d) the specification of "all the apostles" tells of an interpolation either of that phrase or of "the twelve"; and (e) the specification of James is again independent of the gospel story... If the writer of the epistle knew the facts, and if the gospels give the facts, how came he to ignore the central role of Judas? If he drew on a current report concerning the "five hundred," how came the gospels to ignore that? ... Be the epistle genuine or spurious, how can it be held to show knowledge of the gospel story?[‡]

Robertson is especially close to Drews when he defines the alternatives this way:

It does not indeed follow that Paul's period was what the tradition represents. The reasonable inference from his doctrine is that his Jesus was either a mythic construction or a mere tradition, a remote figure said to have been crucified, but no longer historically traceable. If Paul's Jesus, as is conceivable, be merely a nominal memory

---

tures, that he was buried, that he was raised on the third day in accordance with the scriptures, and that he appeared to Cephas, then to the twelve. Then he appeared to more than five hundred brethren at one time, most of whom are still alive, though some have fallen asleep. Then he appeared to James, then to all the apostles. Last of all, as to one untimely born, he appeared also to me."

[*]   It is thus a later interpolation, as I argue in "Apocryphal Apparitions: 1 Corinthians 15:3–11" in Price and Jeffrey Jay Lowder, eds., *The Empty Tomb: Jesus beyond the* Grave (Amherst: Prometheus Books, 2005), pp. 69–104.

[†]   See Alfred Loisy, *The Birth of the Christian Religion.* Trans. L.P. Jacks (London: George Allen & Unwin, 1948), p.82; Loisy, *The Origins of the New Testament.* Trans. L.P. Jacks (London: George Allen & Unwin, 1950), p. 100; Frank Kermode, *The Genesis of Secrecy* (Cambridge: Harvard University Press, 1979), pp. 84–88; Hyam Maccoby, *Judas Iscariot and the Myth of Jewish Evil* (NY: Free Press, 1992).

[‡]   Robertson, p. 399.

of the slain Jesus ben Pandira of the Talmud (about 100 B.C.),[§] Paul himself may belong to an earlier period than that traditionally assigned to him. Certainly the most genuine-looking epistles in themselves give no decisive chronological clue. But such a shifting of his date would not finally help the case for "Jesus of Nazareth." Escape the argument from the silence of Paul by putting Paul a generation or more earlier, and you are faced by the fresh incredibility of a second crucified Jesus, a second sacrificed Son of God, vouched for by records for the most part visibly false, and containing but a fraction of plausible narrative. The only conclusion open is that the teaching Jesus of the gospels is wholly a construction of the propagandists of the cult, even as is [Jesus] the wonder-working God.[¶]

Myths versus Legends

But Robertson shows signs of a very different argument he might have employed when he notes that "the bulk of the cumulative argument of the examination of 'The Gospel Myths' in *Christianity and Mythology* remains to be dealt with even if the problem of the Pauline Epistles be put aside... The acceptance of the tradition by 'Paul' would not establish the historicity of the tradition."[**] Robertson refers to his comparative-mythology analysis of the gospel stories in an earlier work. Even if all of these stories were to be found verbatim in the epistles, even if the epistles should all prove to be authentically Pauline, we would still be dealing with the (rapid) accumulation of stock, predictable hagiographic legends. We would still have to offer some pretty compelling reason for an impartial historian to accept the gospel versions as historically true

---

[§]   Alvar Ellegård argued something like this in his *Jesus One Hundred Years before Christ: A Study in Creative Mythology* (London: Century, 1999): the gospel Jesus is a fiction though there is, dimly discernable behind the epistolary references, the Essene Teacher of Righteousness. Wells moves to a similar position in *The Jesus Myth* (Chicago: Open Court, 1999), pp. 102–103.

[¶]   Robertson, p. 237.

[**]   Robertson, p. 398.

The Christ Myth Theory And Its Problems

while rejecting medieval, classical, Buddhist, or Hindu parallels as false. That is what the principle of analogy is all about.

One might put this valuable insight of Robertson's a bit differently. Suppose one concluded that the gospels were not so late as the epistles after all, making both products of the late-first, early-second century. Suppose the late gospels were even *earlier* than the epistles. That alone would still mean little. How shall we describe what we find in the gospels? Would one call it sober biographical and historical data, even by ancient standards? Or would we not recognize it rather easily as a set of barely historicized hero myths? Consider the major features of the *Mythic Hero Archetype* compiled from the hero myths (both Indo-European and Semitic) and delineated by Lord Raglan, Otto Rank, Alan Dundes[*] and others,. Here are the twenty-two recurrent features, *highlighting* those appearing in the gospel story of Jesus. They make it pretty clear that it is not merely the death-and-resurrection complex in which the Jesus story parallels myth more than history.

1. *mother is a royal virgin*
2. *father is a king*
3. father related to mother
4. *unusual conception*
5. *hero reputed to be son of god*
6. *attempt to kill hero*
7. *hero spirited away*
8. reared *by foster parents* in a far country
9. *no details of childhood*
10. *goes to future kingdom*
11. is victor over king
12. marries a princess (often daughter of predecessor)
13. *becomes king*

---

[*] Alan Dundes, "The Hero Pattern in the Life of Jesus," in Robert A. Segal, ed., *In Quest of the Hero*. Princeton: Princeton University Press, 1990. The late Professor Dundes also discusses the relevance of the Mythic Hero Archetype to the gospel Jesus in an interview on the DVD *The God Who Wasn't There*.

14. *for a time he reigns uneventfully*
15. *he prescribes laws*
16. *later loses favor with* gods or *his subjects*
17. *driven from throne and city*
18. *meets with mysterious death*
19. *often at the top of a hill*
20. his children, if any, do not succeed him [*i.e., does not found a dynasty*]
21. *his body is not buried*
22. *nonetheless has one or more holy sepulchers*

Jesus' mother Mary is indeed a virgin, though she is not of royal blood (though later apocrypha, as if to fill the lack, do make Mary Davidic). Joseph is "of the house of David," though he does not sit on the throne; but of course the point is that his heir, the true Davidic king, is *coming*. Mary and Joseph are not blood relatives. Jesus' conception certainly qualifies as unusual, being virginal and miraculous. Jesus is the Son of God, and more and more people begin to recognize it. He is at once persecuted by the reigning monarch, Herod the Great. In most of these hero tales, the persecutor is also the hero's father who fears, like Kronos did, that his son will one day overthrow him. This role is divided between Joseph, a royal heir but not king, and Herod, who occupies Joseph's rightful throne. Escaping persecution, our hero disappears into distant Egypt. Mary is not a foster parent, though Joseph is. The story supplies no details about Jesus' childhood or upbringing. (The one apparent exception, Jesus visiting the temple as a youth, Luke 2:41–52, is itself a notable hero theme: the child prodigy.) Sure enough, eventually Jesus goes to Jerusalem to be acclaimed as king, though rejecting political power. But he comes into conflict with the rulers anyway. He does not marry (though, again, as if to fill the gap, pious speculation has always believed he married Mary Magdalene). Does Jesus have a peaceful reign, issuing decrees? Not exactly. But he does enjoy brief popular favor as King of

The Christ Myth Theory And Its Problems

the Jews and holds court in the temple, giving teachings and moral commands. All of a sudden his once-loyal followers turn on him, demanding his death. They hound Jesus outside the city, where he is crucified on Golgotha's crest. Temporarily buried, his tomb winds up empty, and later various sites were nominated as his burial place. He has no children, except in modern legends which make him the progenitor of the Merovingian dynasty of medieval France.

In other words, there is a lot less difference between the Jesus story of the gospels and the Christ myth of the epistles than we usually assume. Neither is the stuff of history. What is the difference between myth and legend?

> Myth operates by bringing a sacred (and hence essentially and paradoxically "timeless") past to bear preemptively on the present and inferentially on the future ("as it was in the beginning, is now, and ever shall be"). Yet in the course of human events societies pass and religious systems change; the historical landscape gets littered with the husks of desiccated myths. These are valuable nonmaterial fossils of mankind's recorded history, especially if still embedded in layers of embalmed religion, as part of a stratum of religion complete with cult, liturgy and ritual. Yet equally important is the next level of transmission, in which the sacred narrative has already been secularized, myth has been turned into saga, sacred time into heroic past, gods into heroes, and mythical action into "historical" plot.[*]

> Myth can be transmitted either in its immediate shape, as sacred narrative anchored in theology and interlaced with liturgy and ritual, or in transmuted form, as past narrative that has severed its ties to sacred time and instead functions as an account of purportedly secular, albeit extraordinary happenings... This transposition of myth to heroic saga is a notable mechanism in ancient Indo-European traditions, wherever a certain cultic system has been supplanted in living religion and the superannuated former apparatus falls prey to literary manipulation.[†]

---

[*] Jaan Puhvel, *Comparative Mythology* (Baltimore: Johns Hopkins University Press, 1987), p. 2.

[†] Puhvel, p. 39.

The logic of development from pure myth, accounts of gods pure and simple, taking place in the heavens or primordial times, to quasi-historical legend, featuring super-powered demigods on earth in the past, only reinforces the conclusion that the epistolary version of the myth-god Christ is prior to the Jesus hero version found in the gospels. While it is conceivable that the latter managed to take literary form before the former, the former must still be judged the earlier version. If it did reach written form only later, that would probably indicate that a community maintaining the original mythic version survived alongside that which cherished the newer, more evolved version, uncontaminated by it. We would have a particularly clear case of this in Philippians 2:6–11. Suppose the epistle as a whole is historically posterior to the gospels. Even so, as virtually all scholars agree, it preserves an older hymn fragment, crystallizing a form of Christ-faith that had otherwise perhaps been forgotten:

> Who, though he was in the form of God,
> Did not count equality with God a thing to be grasped,
> But emptied himself, taking the form of a slave,
> Being born in the likeness of men.
> And being found in human form, he humbled himself
> And became obedient unto death [even death on a cross].
> Therefore God has highly exalted him,
> And bestowed on him the *name* that is above every name,
> That at the *name* of Jesus, every knee should bow,
> In heaven and on earth, and under the earth,
> And every tongue confess that Jesus Christ is Lord
> To the glory of God the Father.

The hymn text is based ultimately on Isa. 45:22–23:

> Turn to me and be saved,
> All the ends of the earth!
> For I am God, and there is no other.

The Christ Myth Theory And Its Problems

> By myself I have sworn,
> From my mouth has gone forth in righteousness
> A word that shall not return:
> "To me every knee shall bow,
> Every tongue shall swear."

The Philippians hymn thus depicts the divine enthronement of the vindicated Christ. But scholars traditionally read the text as if God had bestowed the divine title *Kurios*, "Lord" (equivalent to Adonai in the Old Testament, often substituted in Jewish liturgy for the divine name Yahweh) — on someone already named Jesus. Couchoud noticed that this is not quite what the text says. Instead, what we read is that, because of his humiliating self-sacrifice, an unnamed heavenly being has been granted a mighty name which henceforth should call forth confessions of fealty from all beings in the cosmos. At the name "Jesus" every knee should bow, every tongue acknowledging his Lordship. And, Couchould[*] reasoned with relentless logic, does not this piece of early Christian tradition presuppose a theology of a savior who received the name Jesus only *after* his death struggle, even as Jacob received the honorific name Israel only after wrestling with God (Gen. 32:24–28)?[†] In that case, there can have been no Galilean adventures of an itinerant teacher and healer named Jesus. The antique myth/Christology had managed to survive even after most readers no longer knew how to understand it, what to make of it. And in the same way, even if the Christ myth version were textually attested only later (*e.g.*, if the

---

[*]   Couchoud, *Creation of Christ*, p. 438.

[†]   Genesis 32:24–28, "And Jacob was left alone; and a man wrestled with him until the breaking of the day. When the man saw that he did not prevail against Jacob, he touched the hollow of his thigh; and Jacob's thigh was put out of joint as he wrestled with him. Then he said, "Let me go, for the day is breaking." But Jacob said, "I will not let you go, unless you bless me." And he said to him, "What is your name?" And he said, "Jacob." Then he said, "Your name shall no more be called Jacob, but Israel, for you have striven with God and with men, and have prevailed."

378

epistles should turn out to have been written later than the gospels), the nature of the thing can still be recognized in contrast with the hero legend of Jesus, even if the former be embedded in the latter.

Had the partisans of the pure Christ myth heard of the demigod Jesus and his adventures they might have rejected it all as degrading heresy, just as some Ebionites rejected the virginal conception Nativity which other Ebionites had embraced. The only way we happen to know that some Ebionites rejected the Virgin Birth is that a heresiologist mentions the to-him strange fact in the course of discussing the doctrine, so for us the non-Virgin Birth version is attested only subsequently to the Virgin Birth version. Yet if we compare the inherent logic of the two positions, anyone can see that the later-attested version (the natural birth version) must be the earlier version. Legends grow; they do not shrink.

Marcion and the Gospel Story

Once again: what if Marcion was one of the authors of the Pauline Epistles? If he also knew a version of Luke's gospel, as we usually assume, does that not prove that someone might well be familiar with gospel traditions yet avoid mentioning them (for whatever reason) when writing epistles? Let us pause to take stock of what we believe we know about the content of Marcion's own canon, as opposed to that of the Marcionite church, in case there may have been a difference.

We always read that Marcion came to the theological fray armed with a sheaf of Pauline letters plus a single gospel, a shorter version of canonical Luke. Church apologists said Marcion's version was shorter than Luke because Marcion abbreviated it, removing what he deemed "false pericopes." Others believe Marcion possessed an original, shorter gospel, with which he tampered only minimally, an Ur-Lukas. Paul-Louis Couchoud‡ argued forcefully that Marcion's

---

‡   Paul-Louis Couchoud, "Was Marcion's Gospel One of the Synop-

gospel was very nearly what B.F. Streeter and Vincent Taylor called Proto-Luke,[*] though with just a bit of other Synoptic material. G.R.S. Mead hypothesized that Marcion had no actual gospel text but rather only a collection of sayings, something like the hypothetical Q.[†] This diversity of opinion translates into the uncertainty as to whether we are dealing with Marcion's own canon or whether we are hearing, in this or that secondary source, of the canon of subsequent Marcionites. Harnack observed: "his pupils constantly made alterations in the texts — sometimes more radical than his own, sometimes more conservative — perhaps under his very eyes, but certainly after his death."[‡] We know they were not exactly hidebound traditionalists. It is my opinion, for two reasons to be explained directly, that Marcion's scripture contained only epistles, with no gospel. His followers added Proto-Luke (or Ur-Lukas, or something) later on.

First, it appears to me both that Marcion is responsible for significant portions of the epistolary text and that the epistles are quite innocent of the gospel tradition of sayings and deeds by an earthly Jesus. Therefore, Marcion not only possessed no gospel but knew nothing of our Jesus tradition.

The second reason for doubting that Marcion knew any written gospel is the astonishing phenomenon of the near-total dependence of the gospel stories upon corresponding Old Testament passages. A raft of scholars including Randel Helms, Thomas L. Brodie, John Dominic Crossan, *etc.*,[§] have shown again and again

---

tics?" *Hibbert Journal* XXXIV/2, pp. 265–277.

    [*]   B.F. Streeter, *The Four Gospels: A Study of Origins* (London: Macmillan, 1924; rev. ed. 1939), Chapter VIII, "Proto-Luke," pp. 199–222; Vincent Taylor, *Behind the Third Gospel: A Study of the Proto-Luke Hypothesis* (Oxford at the Clarendon Press, 1926).

    [†]   G.R.S. Mead, *Fragments of a Faith Forgotten: The Gnostics: A Contribution to the Study of the Origins of Christianity* (New Hyde Park: University Books, n.d.), p. 244.

    [‡]   Adolf von Harnack, *Marcion: The Gospel of the Alien God*. Trans. John E. Steely and Lyle Bierma (1924; rpt: Durham: Labyrinth Press, 1990), p. 30.

    [§]   John Bowman, *The Gospel of Mark: The New Christian Jewish Pass-*

Robert M. Price   **Early Date for the Pauline Epistles?**

how this and that gospel passage likely originated as a Christian rewrite of this or that Old Testament passage. What one testament had Moses do, the other had Jesus do. Fill in the name. What did David do? Joshua? Elijah? Elisha? Turns out Jesus did it, too, and even in the same descriptive words! When one assembles the best and most convincing of these studies¶ the results are startling indeed: one can make a compelling argument for virtually every gospel story's derivation from Old Testament sources. How do we account for this? Why the sudden interest in rewriting the Jewish scripture as a book about Jesus?

The Catholic policy was to retain the Old Testament but to reread it as a book about (predicting) Jesus and Christianity. If this procedure were cut off, as Marcion did, what remained? One had to *rewrite* the Old Testament to make it *explicitly* about Jesus! In this way, even the Old Testament of the Jews became, as Martin Luther would say, *"was Christum triebt."*

---

over Haggadah. Studia Post-Biblica 8 (Leiden: E.J. Brill, 1965); Thomas L. Brodie, "Luke the Literary Interpreter: Luke — Acts as a Systematic Rewriting and Updating of the Elijah-Elisha Narrative in 1 and 2 Kings." Ph.D. dissertation presented to Pontifical University of St. Thomas Aquinas, Rome. 1988; John Dominic Crossan, *The Cross That Spoke: The Origins of the Passion Narrative* (San Francisco: Harper & Row, Publishers, 1988); J. Duncan M. Derrett, *The Making of Mark: The Scriptural Bases of the Earliest Gospel.* Volumes 1 and 2. (Shipston-on-Stour, Warwickshire: P. Drinkwater, 1985); Randel Helms, *Gospel Fictions* (Buffalo: Prometheus Books, 1989); Dale Miller and Patricia Miller. *The Gospel of Mark as Midrash on Earlier Jewish and New Testament Literature.* Studies in the Bible and Early Christianity 21 (Lewiston/Queenston/Lampeter: Edwin Mellen Press, 1990; Wolfgang Roth, *Hebrew Gospel: Cracking the Code of Mark* (Oak Park: Meyer-Stone Books, 1988); William R. Stegner, "The Baptism of Jesus: A Story Modeled on the Binding of Isaac." In Herschel Shanks (ed.), *Abraham & Family: New Insights into the Patriarchal Narratives.* Washington, D.C.: Biblical Archaeology Society, 2001; Rikki E. Watts, *Isaiah's New Exodus and Mark.* Wissenschaftliche Untersuchungen zum Neuen Testament 2. Reihe 88 (Tübingen: Mohr Siebeck, 1997).

¶   Robert M. Price, "New Testament Narrative as Old Testament Midrash," in Jacob Neusner and Alan J. Avery-Peck, eds., *Encyclopedia of Midrash: Biblical Interpretation in Formative Judaism* (E.J. Brill, 2005), Volume One, pp. 534–573.

The Christ Myth Theory And Its Problems

But this had not happened by Marcion's time. Marcion would never have used the Old Testament in this way, given his antipathy for the book. Such rewriting must have seemed too close to the allegorical Christianizing of Catholics (of which it was, after all, but another version, creating antitypes to justify typology!). As we will see, Marcionites joined the game once they saw others playing it, but this would have been a retrenching move, like Lutherans who could not bring themselves to go the whole way with Martin Luther and relegate James and Jude to a quasi-canonical limbo. By fabricating new scripture (gospel traditions) they could co-opt what they still (guiltily) liked of the old. So there were yet no gospels for Marcion himself to include in his new scripture, only epistles which show no sign of acquaintance with any gospels. But soon there was Marcionite involvement in the production of gospels.

Mark's gospel, for instance, holds what can hardly be called other than a Marcionite view of the buffoonish twelve disciples and a Gnostic view of secret teaching which, despite their privileged position, the twelve simply do not grasp. Or think of the Transfiguration (Mark 9:1–8)*: how can one miss the Marcionite implications of Mark's setting up Jesus, Moses (the Torah), and Elijah (the Prophets) as in a police line-up, followed by the Father's urging that, of the three, Jesus alone is to be heard and heeded? And Mark, of course, refers to Jesus giving his life a ransom for many (Mark 10:45).† Though

---

* Mark 9:1–8, "And he said to them, 'Truly, I say to you, there are some standing here who will not taste death before they see that the kingdom of God has come with power.' And after six days Jesus took with him Peter and James and John, and led them up a high mountain apart by themselves; and he was transfigured before them, and his garments became glistening, intensely white, as no fuller on earth could bleach them. And there appeared to them Elijah with Moses; and they were talking to Jesus. And Peter said to Jesus, 'Master, it is well that we are here; let us make three booths, one for you and one for Moses and one for Elijah.' For he did not know what to say, for they were exceedingly afraid. And a cloud overshadowed them, and a voice came out of the cloud, "This is my beloved Son; listen to him." And suddenly looking around they no longer saw any one with them but Jesus only."

† Mark 10:45, "For the Son of man also came not to be served but to serve, and to give his life as a ransom for many."

Mark fails to tell us to whom Jesus would be paying this ransom, Marcion tells us. He paid it to the Creator, and no non-Marcionite theologian has produced a better candidate.

One wonders if even the name of the Gospel of Mark reflects awareness of the fundamentally (though not completely) Marcionite character of the book. Mark the secretary of Peter (as Papias makes him), the John Mark of Acts, would be too early for us to identify with Marcion, but it is quite possible that Mark the secretary of Peter is an unhistorical character, a "safe" version of Marcion to have authored the gospel, much as Eusebius posited a "John the Elder" as the author of Revelation once he no longer wanted to ascribe that book to John son of Zebedee.

The Gospel of John is heavily Marcionite: Moses and his Jews knew nothing of God. Despite all that Deuteronomy says about Moses seeing God face to face,[‡] John denies that any mortal has ever seen the true God (John 1:18).[§] Jesus' Father is not the same God the Jews worship (8:54–55).[¶] All who came to the Jews before Jesus, presumably the Old Testament prophets, were mere despoilers (10:8).[**] The Father is unknown to the world (17:25).[††] The Torah had nothing to do with grace and truth (1:17).[‡‡] Jesus raised himself from the dead (10:17–18).[§§]

[‡]   Deuteronomy 34:10, "And there has not arisen a prophet since in Israel like Moses, whom the LORD knew face to face."

[§]   John 1:18, "No one has ever seen God; the only Son, who is in the bosom of the Father, he has made him known. "

[¶]   John 8:54–55, "Jesus answered, "If I glorify myself, my glory is nothing; it is my Father who glorifies me, of whom you say that he is your God. But you have not known him; I know him. If I said, I do not know him, I should be a liar like you; but I do know him and I keep his word."

[**]   John 10:8, "All who came before me are thieves and robbers; but the sheep did not heed them."

[††]   John 17:25, "O righteous Father, the world has not known thee, but I have known thee; and these know that thou hast sent me."

[‡‡]   John 1:17, "For the law was given through Moses; grace and truth came through Jesus Christ."

[§§]   John 10:17–18, "For this reason the Father loves me, because I lay

The Christ Myth Theory And Its Problems

The Q Document has Jesus exclaim that no one knows his Father but him (Matt. 11:27//Lk.10:22). What? Not Israel? Not Moses? Not John the Baptist? It would take quite a lot of ingenuity to come up with some other interpretation of this one. "No one knows the Father except for the Son and any to whom the Son may deign to reveal him." That's straight Marcionism. Isn't it?

Thomas 52 has "His disciples say to him, 'Twenty-four prophets spoke in Israel, and every one of them predicted you!' He said to them, 'You have disregarded the Living, who is right in front of you, to prattle on about the dead!'" Augustine found the second half of the saying, Jesus' reply, quoted in an explicitly Marcionite pamphlet handed him on the street in Carthage. The first half of the saying, the set-up remark of the disciples, was unknown till 1945 when the Gospel of Thomas was discovered. Looking at the truncated version, Joachim Jeremias* surmised that, while Marcionites must have taken "the dead" to refer to the prophets, Jesus was really refuting rabbinic arguments that the messiah to come would be a returned Old Testament personality, perhaps Joshua or Hezekiah. No, here he is right in front of you! Have you forgotten? Jeremias' theory must be judged an extreme harmonization, an attempt to preserve an attractive saying by scrubbing away the Marcionite tint. And the discovery of Thomas proved him wrong. Or rather, he was right the first time, about the Marcionite reading. The Marcionites were right, and they were only reading what was before them, while Jeremias was prating on about the dead.

So the composition of gospels, being rewrites of the Old Testament, was a counterblast to the Marcionite rejection of the Old Testament. Once the trend began, Marcionites made their own

---

down my life, that I may take it again. No one takes it from me, but I lay it down of my own accord. I have power to lay it down, and I have power to take it again; this charge I have received from my Father."

    *   Joachim Jeremias, *Unknown Sayings of Jesus*. Trans. Reginald H. Fuller (NY: Macmillan, 1957), pp. 74–77. All discussion of the saying has vanished from the 1964 edition of the book.

contributions to it, and thus to the process of historicizing an originally mythic Jesus. Marcion himself, then, had no gospel. It must have been subsequent Marcionites who ascribed the choice of one to him.

Conclusion

Though today's leading proponents of the Christ Myth theory tend to hold to a conventional, mid-first-century dating of the epistles, a good twenty to forty years before the (conventional) dates assigned the gospels, one suspects this is almost a circumstantial *ad hominem* fallacy, accepting conventional dates mainly for the sake of argument in order to embarrass the orthodox who hold to these dates for apologetical reasons. Christ Myth theorists are not above pursuing an apologetical agenda of their own, which may explain their reluctance to apply the same ruthless skepticism to the Pauline Epistles as they do to the gospels. If they did (like their nineteenth-century forbears did), they would find the picture becoming a bit fuzzier, true, but there might also be significant gains. In a brief survey of remarks on the age and integrity of the Pauline Epistles by Robertson, Couchoud, Smith, and others, we have detected pregnant hints of arguments for the historical priority of the Christ Myth as attested in the epistles over the Jesus-epic met with in the gospels, and this regardless of either the relative or absolute dates of the gospels and epistles.

The "Pre-Christian Jesus" Revisited

The common cavil directed against the majority critical theory on the life of Jesus and the process by which he came to be worshipped as a god is that there was not enough time for such claims to be made gratuitously about the deceased rabbi between his death and his mythologizing deification. The alternative urged by apologists is that Jesus himself outlined an orthodox Christology, right out of the starting gate, and so we need envision no process of development at all. The recent case of the Lubavitcher Rebbe Menachem Mendel Schneerson has shown that no time at all is required for such Christological transformation.[*] Rabbi Schneerson, after all, though he predicted the imminent arrival of King Messiah, made absolutely no claims about a messianic role for himself, but hours or days after his passing, his eager followers proclaimed him both Messiah and God Incarnate.[†]

At any rate, the Christ Myth theory does not have any such constraints to deal with, as there is no beginning point close to the time of writing of the gospels. There is available all the time in the world, since this theory envisions the slow evolution of already ancient mythemes and beliefs into a new form emerging in the first or second century CE. Some god or hero or other superhuman entity must already have existed as the alternative to a historical Christian sect founder. For even if we trace Christianity back to Jesus ben Pandera or an Essene Teacher of Righteousness[‡] in the first century BCE, we

---

[*]   David Berger, *The Rebbe, the Messiah, and the Scandal of Orthodox Indifference* (London & Portland OR: Littman Library of Jewish Civilization, 2001), pp. 82–83.

[†]   An apologist might want to reply that a full-blown notion of divine messiahship lay ready to hand for the Lubavitchers to borrow from Christianity. But if one imagines such borrowing as a likely option for ultra-conservative Hassidic Jews, then one had best give up the claim that the early disciples, as Jews, could never have thought of borrowing savior-god concepts from neighboring pagan religions, because that would be the closest analogy.

[‡]   Alvar Ellegård, *Jesus One Hundred Years before Christ: A Study in*

still have a historical Jesus. The Christ Myth theory maintains that the Christian Jesus was originally a god who eventually became flesh in the imaginations of believers. Of what sort would this god, this pre-Christian Jesus, have been? There have been various answers, supplying a handful of similar and related pre-Christian Jesuses. I want to survey some of these, then narrow the focus to the version seemingly most popular among historic Christ Myth theorists: that of a "Joshua cult" based on the Old Testament hero Joshua, himself the fictive transformation of an originally mythical deity.

Ancient Israel not Monotheistic

Christ Myth scholars have long understood that an argument for a pre-Christian Jesus/Joshua cult cannot get started at all until we realize that the religion of ancient Israel was by no means monotheistic until pretty late times. Even among the ranks of the Hasmonean freedom fighters who gave their very lives in battle against the Seleucid pagans one found (ineffective!) amulets depicting the gods of Yavneh (2 Maccabees 12:40).* It is obvious from even a surface reading of the Old Testament that Israelites worshipped a pantheon of divinities even under the roof of Solomon's temple: Yahweh, Asherah, Zedek, Shalman, Shahar, Nehushtan, *etc.* The Deuteronomic and Priestly redactors would have us think that the people who worshipped other gods than Yahweh were syncretists, picking the forbidden fruits of Canaanite pantheons; but modern research has shown that these redactors were only reshaping the past in accord with their own theological preferences: in their view Israel and Judah should always have been monotheistic, so in retrospect, they are believed to have known that standard, albeit constantly falling away from it. Likewise, our picture of Judaism in New Testament times has until very recently been under the control of Rabbinical

Creative Mythology (London: Century, 1999).
　　* 　"Then under the tunic of every one of the dead they found sacred tokens of the idols of Jamnia, which the law forbids the Jews to wear."

apologetics. It was in the interest of the Jewish faction prevailing after the destruction of Jerusalem by the Romans to appeal, as a credential, to an imaginary past in which their own ideological for-bears constituted the mainstream, the basic stock, of a unified Judaism. Accordingly, everyone took for granted that something very like Rabbinical Judaism prevailed before 70 C.E. Now we realize that the Judaism at the dawn of the Common Era was multiform and many-headed. Many streams of Hebrew faith must have survived the centuries, on the ground, among the common people, stubborn-ly resistant to the high-handed demands of monotheistic orthodoxy. Old ideas and beliefs and mythemes continued to survive, even past the time of the circumstances in which they first made sense. Even when monotheism prevailed, vestiges of the old order survived in-cognito, as in the Song of Solomon, where the love songs of Ishtar Shalmith and Tammuz have been assigned instead to Solomon and a foreign princess.

We are accustomed to look upon the Jewish religion as strictly monotheistic. In truth, it never was, even in the Mosaic times, until after the return from Exile. And this is clear, in spite of the effort the composers of the so-called historic[al] books of the Old Testament have taken to work up the traditions in a monotheistic sense and to obliterate the traces of the early Jewish polytheism, by transform-ing the ancient gods into patriarchs, heroes, angels, and servants of Jahve.[†] (Arthur Drews)

On the surrounding people Judaism imposed its god Jahveh and its law, the Mosaic law. Some of the ancient religions of Palestine disappeared, others persisted in the form of obscure and illicit sur-vivals, which were amalgamated in Judaism and were themselves more or less Judaized... Where Judaism fully succeeded, the ancient Baals of Palestine were transformed into heroic servants of Jahveh;

[†]   Arthur Drews, *The Christ Myth*. Trans. C. DeLisle Burns. Westminster College-Oxford: Classics in Religious Studies (1910; rpt: Amherst: Prometheus Books, 1998), p. 55; see also p. 265.

where it gained only partial victory they became secondary gods. The result was that some of them were subjected to both treatments simultaneously, and became in orthodox circles heroes in the cause of Jahveh, and in heretical circles the second god. Such was the case of the god whose history we are studying.* (Edouard Dujardin)

The first Christians were therefore descendants of men who had been Judaized by compulsion, and who preserved in secret their old beliefs and practices. Such 'double belief' is a well-known phenomenon and would permit an old Pre-Canaanite religion, successively contaminated by Canaanite, Israelite, Syrian, and finally Jewish elements, to exist within the framework of Judaism.† (Edouard Dujardin)

It would mean that those who had not experienced or accepted the reformulations of the exilic prophet and the Deuteronomists would have retained the older belief in El and Yahweh as separate deities, perhaps as a Father figure and a Son figure, which is what the Ugaritic texts lead us to suppose and what Deut. 32.8‡ (in the Qumran version) actually says. Yahweh received Israel for his portion when El Elyon divided the nations among the sons of God.§ (Margaret Barker)

Drews nonetheless seems to have envisioned only a marginal existence for partisans of the old faiths: "we are dealing with a secret cult, the existence of which we can decide upon only by indirect means."¶ He seems, in other words, to have supposed that the Jesus-cult persisted on the sly like Gnosticism did once Constantine came to the throne. But the truth is most likely to be that, as he also anticipates

---

* Edouard Dujardin, *Ancient History of the God Jesus*. Abridged and trans. A. Brodie Sanders (London: Watts, 1938), p. 46, 47.

† Dujardin p. 128.

‡ Deuteronomy 32:8–9, "When the Most High gave to the nations their inheritance, when he separated the sons of men, he fixed the bounds of the peoples according to the number of the sons of God. For the LORD's portion is his people, Jacob his allotted heritage."

§ Margaret Barker, *The Great Angel: A Study of Israel's Second God* (Louisville: Westminster/John Knox, 1992), p. 21.

¶ Drews, p. 22.

("in spite of the effort the composers of the so-called historic[al] books of the Old Testament have taken to work up the traditions in a monotheistic sense and to obliterate the traces of the early Jewish polytheism"),[**] that, while the "heresies" continued with vigor, only scanty remains of them survive for our scrutiny after the largely successful, later orthodox attempt to suppress and destroy their rivals.

This may all prove to have been a red herring of sorts, as we will see, but it is important in that it nullifies one of the most frequently heard apologetical arguments against tracing Jesus to the dying-and-rising savior deities, that monotheistic Jews would never have adopted gods and myths from unwashed pagans.[††] If ancient Israel had never been even ostensibly monotheistic, if ancient Jews had already worshipped Tammuz, for instance, as one of their own deities (as in Ezekiel 8:14),[‡‡] we need not strain imagination picturing them importing alien deities.

Let us briefly walk through the exhibit of Ideal Types of the pre-Christian Jesus. Not surprisingly, the various scholars tended to combine elements from various of these icons, or to hover somewhere between them, with more or less clarity. Nor is that a criticism of their work, since they knew well that they were trying to restore the lost outlines of a theological creature likely possessed of quirky and ungainly form: a theoretical model with no comeliness that we should desire it.

Apocalyptic Son of Man

According to P.L. Couchoud,[§§] the pre-Christian savior is Enoch's Son of Man fused with the Second Isaiah's Suffering Servant.[¶] From

---

[**]   *Ibid.*

[††]   C.S. Lewis, *Mere Christianity* (NY: Macmillan, 1960), p. 56.

[‡‡]   "Then he brought me to the entrance of the north gate of the house of the LORD; and behold, there sat women weeping for Tammuz."

[§§]   Paul-Louis Couchoud, *The Creation of Christ: An Outline of the Beginnings of Christianity.* Trans. C. Bradlaugh Bonner (London: Watts, 1939), pp. 18–21.

[¶]   *Ibid.*, p. 34

the latter, specifically Second Isaiah 61:1,[*] he derives the title "Christ," the one anointed to save and succor.[†] He is said to have a mighty and secret name, which turns out to be Jesus/Joshua.[‡] His death at the hands of cosmic archons (1 Cor.2:8[§] and Col. 2:15)[¶] occurred before the creation (Rev. 5:6;[**] 13:8).[††] He had lately been seen in a series of visions by the Twelve and the Pillars and Paul,[‡‡] but there was no earthly advent, though one was expected in the very near future. The Baptizer had proclaimed his advent, but the claim that he had actually appeared to a select few before the time set the new Christian sect apart in a schism.[§§]

> Jesus is of heaven, heavenly, and he is yet to come. He has nought as yet to do with the earth or with history, and is manifested in visions alone.... He is at once the officiating priest and the sacrifice for all eternity, the redemption given by God. He has had no earthly existence. But he will take on such an existence to last a thousand years, when he will leap down from heaven on a snowy horse, draped in a cloak red with dripping blood.[¶¶]

---

[*] "The Spirit of the Lord GOD is upon me, because the LORD has anointed me to bring good tidings to the afflicted; he has sent me to bind up the brokenhearted, to proclaim liberty to the captives, and the opening of the prison to those who are bound."

[†] *Ibid.,* p. 32.

[‡] *Ibid.,* p. 32.

[§] "None of the rulers of this age understood this; for if they had, they would not have crucified the Lord of glory."

[¶] "He disarmed the principalities and powers and made a public example of them, triumphing over them in him."

[**] "And between the throne and the four living creatures and among the elders, I saw a Lamb standing, as though it had been slain, with seven horns and with seven eyes, which are the seven spirits of God sent out into all the earth."

[††] "And all who dwell on earth will worship it, every one whose name has not been written in the book of life of the Lamb that was slain before the foundation of the world."

[‡‡] *Ibid.,* p.p. 36–37.

[§§] *Ibid.,* p. 38.

[¶¶] *Ibid.,* p. 105.

What Couchoud envisions, the creation of the pre-Christian Jesus through the process of scribal exegetical conflation, should have a ring of familiarity about it. He was suggesting that the ancient "creative community" followed pretty much the same thought process to the same results as twentieth-century scholars, including Rudolf Otto,[***] Joachim Jeremias,[†††] and Hugh J. Schonfield,[‡‡‡] all of whom argued that New Testament Christology was the alchemical product of an ingenious religious mind mixing together the apocalyptic Son of Man of Daniel and 1 Enoch with 2 Isaiah's Suffering Servant. The only difference, admittedly a significant one, is that, for the mainstream scholars, the one who hybridized the two theological strains was Jesus of Nazareth. It was he who had thus combined these passages and seen in them the path before him. Armed with this new theological chimera, a highly artificial construct never spelled out explicitly anywhere in either the Old or the New Testament, scholar after scholar preceded to apply it as a key to unlock this and that gospel passage, as if this were what Jesus must have had in mind. It was perhaps the classic case of the "Kittel mentality" flagged by James Barr.[§§§] Once theologians (posing humbly as mere descriptive exegetes) had built up the theologoumenon from simple pieces (scattered verses, each mentioning a son of man or a sufferer), they gratuitously assumed they had restored an effaced original mosaic from a few colored stones, and they proceeded as if, every time any contributing piece occurred in any text, it was the tip of the underlying iceberg of the "Suffering Son of Man"

[***]   Rudolf Otto, *The Kingdom of God and the Son of Man: A Study in the History of Religion*. Trans. Floyd V. Filson and Bertram Lee-Woolf (rev. ed., Boston: Starr King Press, 1957), pp. 249–255.

[†††]   Joachim Jeremias, *New Testament Theology, Volume One: The Proclamation of Jesus*. Trans. John Bowden (London: SCM Press, 1971), pp. 275–276, 286–287.

[‡‡‡]   Hugh J. Schonfield, *The Passover Plot:New Light on the History of Jesus* (NY: Bernard Geis Associates, 1965), pp. 215–227.

[§§§]   James Barr, *The Semantics of Biblical Language* (London: Oxford University Press, 1961).

complex. How marvelously dialectical it seemed! And what a shell game! Such was the synthesizing genius of the old "Biblical Theology" movement, whose accent was really on the theology more than the "biblical" aspect. Like all theologians before them, they were systematizers who claimed they had merely excavated their new constructs from the mine of the text. In this case, the result was a theological Jesus, an integer in a theological formula called "salvation history." He was an abstraction posing as an historical rediscovery. And what was different in Couchoud's proposed scenario? He, too, envisioned scribes distilling a Jesus Christ abstraction out of a handful of texts hybridized in a new way.

And eventually, like Jeremias, Otto, and the rest, Couchoud's second group of ancient exegetes finally decided this Suffering Son of Man must have come, that is, already, in the past. Once one has decided this, well, the exegetical maneuvers entailed will come as no surprise to anyone familiar with Wrede and the Messianic Secret.[*] One would begin to read that, though the Son of Man Jesus had in fact recently arrived, it is possible for us to have missed it since he hushed up those whom he healed and exorcized, told witnesses of his Transfiguration to keep it under their turbans *till later*, warned them not to circulate news of his messiahship, and finally entrusted the big disclosure to frightened women who failed to tell the news. If we may imagine the puzzlement of the first who read Mark's newly-minted empty tomb account ("Why didn't I ever heard these things before? Oh, I see…"), we may as easily picture the reaction of those who had expected the Suffering Son of Man upon first hearing the secret unveiled: he has already appeared! It would be no different from the Diaspora synagogue attendees whom Acts pictures learning from Paul and Barnabas that the long-awaited Messiah has already come — and gone! Again, I think of the first time I heard of the Baha'i Faith. Seals

---

[*] Wilhelm Wrede, *The Messianic Secret in Mark*. Trans. J.C.G. Greig. Library of Theological Translations. (London: James Clarke, 1971).

and Crofts were performing on *The Mike Douglas Show* and mentioned their faith in Baha'ullah. Christians, they quietly averred, were still waiting for the Second Coming, but what if he had already appeared? Again, "His disciples say to him, 'When will the repose of the dead begin? And when will the new world come?' He says to them, 'What you look for has already come, but you fail to recognize it'" (Gospel of Thomas, saying 51). Couchoud is by no means asking us to believe in a mental maneuver no one was likely to have navigated. It is by no means hard to imagine.

And how, pray tell, does Couchoud know the sacred, secret name was "Joshua"? I must infer that, again, he made the same sort of move that Jeremias[†] did, identifying the vindicated sufferer of Philippians 2:6–11[‡] with the Servant of Isaiah 53.[§] If it is a true

---

[†]   Jeremias's view is discussed in Ralph P. Martin, *Carmen Christi: Philippians 2:5–11 in Recent Interpretation and in the Setting of Early Christian Worship* (rev. ed., Grand Rapids: Eerdmans, 1983), pp. 182–190.

[‡]   "who, though he was in the form of God, did not count equality with God a thing to be grasped, but emptied himself, taking the form of a servant, being born in the likeness of men. And being found in human form he humbled himself and became obedient unto death, even death on a cross. Therefore God has highly exalted him and bestowed on him the name which is above every name, that at the name of Jesus every knee should bow, in heaven and on earth and under the earth, and every tongue confess that Jesus Christ is Lord, to the glory of God the Father."

[§]   "Who has believed what we have heard? And to whom has the arm of the LORD been revealed? For he grew up before him like a young plant, and like a root out of dry ground; he had no form or comeliness that we should look at him, and no beauty that we should desire him. He was despised and rejected by men; a man of sorrows, and acquainted with grief; and as one from whom men hide their faces he was despised, and we esteemed him not. Surely he has borne our griefs and carried our sorrows; yet we esteemed him stricken, smitten by God, and afflicted. But he was wounded for our transgressions, he was bruised for our iniquities; upon him was the chastisement that made us whole, and with his stripes we are healed. All we like sheep have gone astray; we have turned every one to his own way; and the LORD has laid on him the iniquity of us all. He was oppressed, and he was afflicted, yet he opened not his mouth; like a lamb that is led to the slaughter, and like a sheep that before its shearers is dumb, so he opened not his mouth. By oppression and judgment he was taken away; and

match, then the name above all names bestowed upon him was "Jesus," the name at which all knees, angelic, mortal, or demonic, shall bow, like it or not, the name to which all tongues, whether of flesh or of fire, shall swear fealty. There is no wealth of data here, but when is it ever otherwise when one seeks to reconstruct the dimming past?

Wisdom

There is a natural link, at least potentially, between the Son of Man expectation and the speculation about personified Wisdom (or the Logos), in that both were favorite concerns of the scribes. Accordingly, some of our pre-Christian Jesus models tend to overlap at this point. But here let us focus on Dame Wisdom, whom Philo changed into the male Logos. G.A. Wells, a recent Christ Myth theorist who is willing to cut loose many of the speculations of his forbears, nominates Dame Wisdom as the prototype for the incarnate savior, rejected by sinful mortals, and received again into heavenly glory.

Proverbs 3:19* and 8:22–36† represent Wisdom as a supernatural

as for his generation, who considered that he was cut off out of the land of the living, stricken for the transgression of my people? And they made his grave with the wicked and with a rich man in his death, although he had done no violence, and there was no deceit in his mouth. Yet it was the will of the LORD to bruise him; he has put him to grief; when he makes himself an offering for sin, he shall see his offspring, he shall prolong his days; the will of the LORD shall prosper in his hand; he shall see the fruit of the travail of his soul and be satisfied; by his knowledge shall the righteous one, my servant, make many to be accounted righteous; and he shall bear their iniquities. Therefore I will divide him a portion with the great, and he shall divide the spoil with the strong; because he poured out his soul to death, and was numbered with the transgressors; yet he bore the sin of many, and made intercession for the transgressors."

*   "The LORD by wisdom founded the earth; by understanding he established the heavens."

†   Proverbs 8:22–30, "The LORD created me at the beginning of his work, the first of his acts of old. Ages ago I was set up, at the first, before the beginning of the earth. When there were no depths I was brought forth, when there were no springs abounding with water. Before the mountains had been shaped, before the

396

personage, created by God before he created heaven or earth, mediating in this creation and leading man into the path of truth. In the Wisdom of Solomon… Wisdom is the sustainer and governor of the universe (Wisd. of Sol. 8:1;[‡] 9:9–14)[§] who comes to dwell among men and bestows her gifts on them. Most of them reject her. First Enoch tells that after being humiliated on earth, Wisdom returned to heaven.[¶] It is thus obvious that the humiliation on earth and exaltation to heaven of a supernatural personage, as preached by Paul and other early Christian writers, could have been thus derived.[**]

The parallels with Philo are much more extensive as well as specific. It is hard not to wonder if Philo was not in fact the direct source for most New Testament Christological speculations. Consider the similarities. Philo says the divine Logos whereby God made and upholds the world ("I sustained the universe to rest firm and sure

---

hills, I was brought forth; before he had made the earth with its fields, or the first of the dust of the world. When he established the heavens, I was there, when he drew a circle on the face of the deep, when he made firm the skies above, when he established the fountains of the deep, when he assigned to the sea its limit, so that the waters might not transgress his command, when he marked out the foundations of the earth, then I was beside him, like a master workman; and I was daily his delight, rejoicing before him always."

‡   "She [wisdom] reaches mightily from one end of the earth to the other, and she orders all things well."

§   Wisdom of Solomon 9:9–10a, "With thee is wisdom, who knows thy works and was present when thou didst make the world, and who understands what is pleasing in thy sight and what is right according to thy commandments. Send her forth from the holy heavens, and from the throne of thy glory send her."

¶   1 Enoch XLII:1–2, "Wisdom found no place where she might dwell; then a dwelling-place was assigned her in the heavens. Wisdom went forth to make her dwelling among the children of men, and found no dwelling-place: wisdom returned to her place and took her seat among the angels." *The Book of* Enoch. Trans. R.H. Charles (Translations of Early Documents (London: SPCK Press, 1917), p. 61.

**   G.A. Wells, "The Historicity of Jesus," in R. Joseph Hoffmann and Gerald Larue, eds., *Jesus in History and Myth* (Buffalo: Prometheus Books, 1986), 36–37; *cf.*, Wells, *Did Jesus Exist?* (London: Elek/Pemberton, 1975), pp. 38–39, 116–117.

The Christ Myth Theory And Its Problems

upon the mighty Logos who is my viceroy." *On Dreams* I.241) is symbolized in scripture by Aaron and the high priests. "For there are, as is evident, two temples of God: one of them this universe in which there is also as High Priest his First-born, the Divine Logos, and the other the rational soul, whose priest is the real Man" (*On Dreams* I. 215). "God's Man, the Logos of the Eternal" (*On the Confusion of Tongues* 41, 146). "This same Logos, his Archangel, ... both pleads with the immortal as suppliant for afflicted mortality, and acts as ambassador of the ruler to the subject" (*Who Is the Heir?* 205) — just as Jesus as heavenly high priest intercedes for his own.

Both the high priest's vestments and the veil of the Holy of Holies, says Philo, are symbols of the physical universe, and just as the priest enters the Holy of Holies through the veil and returns through it, this symbolizes the entry of the creative Logos of God through the veil separating heaven and earth. On the one hand the Logos is the veil; on the other, he clothes himself in the vestments of the material world to appear here, *i.e.*, presumably in the creation:

> And the oldest Logos of God has put on the universe as a garment... "He does not tear his garments" for the Logos of God is the bond of all things... and holds together all parts, and prevents them by its constriction from breaking apart and becoming separated. (*On Flight,* 112)

In like manner, Hebrews 10:19–20[*] speaks of Christ passing through the veil of his own torn flesh to enter the heavenly Tabernacle where he intercedes for us.

Philo even speaks of the divine Logos as a "second God."

> Nothing mortal can be made in the likeness of the Most High One and Father of the Universe, but only in that of the second God, who is his Logos... the Head of all things. (*Quaest. Ex.* 2, 117) The heavenly Man, being the eternal archetype of mankind, is therefore the Logos,

---

[*]   "Therefore, brethren, since we have confidence to enter the sanctuary by the blood of Jesus, by the new and living way which he opened for us through the curtain, that is, through his flesh."

and as such the First-born Son of God. [He is] neither uncreated as God, nor created as you, but midway between the two extremes, a surety to both sides. (*Who Is the Heir?* 205f.)

Note here that we seem to have a ready-made cluster of Christological associations which may have passed directly over into the New Testament: Heavenly Adam, First-born Son, Logos, High Priest. This remains equally likely whether we imagine an historical Jesus who was quickly robed in available theological fabrics, or a mythic Jesus who was fictively made man.

And if this is true, Philo would seem to weight Logos Christology in an Arian direction:

> And do not fail to mark the language used, but carefully enquire whether there are two Gods; for we read 'I am the God that appeared to thee,' not 'in my place,' but 'in the place of God,' as though it were another's. What then are we to say? He that is truly God is One, but those that are improperly so called are more than one. Accordingly, the holy word in the present instance has indicated him who truly is God by means of the articles, saying 'I am the God,' while it omits the article when mentioning him who is improperly so called, saying 'Who appeared to thee in the place' not 'of the God' but simply 'of God.' Here it gives the title 'God' to his chief Logos, not from any superstitious nicety in applying names, but with one aim before him, to use words to express facts. (*On Dreams* I.228)

But what, in Wells's view, would have led early Christians to conclude that this being, this Logos Son of God, had recently appeared on earth? There is no great mystery to it. Some simply took seriously, literally, the perfect and past tenses of passages like Proverbs 9:1, "Wisdom has built her house." The result? "And the Word became flesh and pitched his tent among us" (John 1:14). Not much of a stretch, I'd say. Of a piece with the early (and modern!) Christian tendency to write up the Jesus story from Old Testament details taken out of context. Just as Dispensationalist prophecy buffs scour the scripture for details to flesh out their scenario for the second advent of Christ, Wells depicts the first Christians gleaning leftover exegetical stubble to enhance their scenario of the equally hypothetical first advent.

Gnostic Primal Man

For L. Gordon Rylands,[*] the name Joshua/Jesus was already the name of divinity, applied to the Christian Jesus among others. Gnostics, who divinized other Old Testament patriarchs as angels and saviors (Abel, Seth, Abraham, Jacob, Moses, *etc.*) would have/must have seen Joshua, too, as an embodiment of the Logos. We know of one sect, the Naassenes, who identified the Christian Jesus with the Son of Man, that is, son of a god named Adamas. He was an entity, spread abroad, symbolically, in the hearts of all men. He was suffering by virtue of his incarnation in the bodies of the whole human race. Salvation of initiated individuals would free and reunite this Son of Man. His captivity in the body constituted his own tutelary suffering. This is all recognizable as another version of the doctrine of the Primal Man, the heavenly Adam, as the *guph*, or storehouse of all human souls. Thus the Son of Adamas (Man) is another form of the Primal Man.

Arthur Drews explores some of the same possibilities. Two Vedic deities, Agni (also called, as creator, Visvakarman) and Purusha, are said to sacrifice themselves at the beginning in order to create the world. (Even Mithras may be interpreted this way.) In Zoroastrian myth, Gayomard, a Humpty-Dumpty like figure, is the Primal Man, originally sufficient unto himself, but split into two procreating halves by the foolish assault of Ahriman who thus only multiplied his troubles. Here is another version of the Primal Man who sacrifices himself at the dawn of time in order to create (or save) the human race. It is the ancient son of man mytheme. Even "the anointed" may refer to the anointing of Agni.[†]

---

[*]   L. Gordon Rylands, *The Beginnings of Gnostic Christianity* (London: Watts, 1940), pp. 156–160.

[†]   Drews, pp. 130–131.

Drews says Pauline Christianity derives from Mandaeanism and Gnosticism in general,[‡] but he omits the Redeemed Redeemer idea, which I regard as the lynchpin: the supramundane crucifixion of the Light-Man was *before the creation* and allowed the human race to flourish, albeit in a condition of suffering from which Christ's revelatory teaching would later free them. The missing link toward which Drews and Rylands were groping is the mysterious unity of the Light-Man and the Christ-Aion. Originally the sacrifice was pre-historical, even pre-cosmic. It took place at the hands of the supramundane archons, Ahriman, *etc.* The subsequent revealer, redeemer, Christ-Aion, Saoshyans, was a doublet of the Light-Man. His appearance on earth would have been an anticipatory symbol of the reassembling of the sundered Light-Man in a final harvesting of salvation which would reintegrate the Light-Man and doom the murky wreck of the material world. At some point, it came to someone by revelation that the reintegration was about to come to consummation, no doubt because the esoteric spirituality seemed to be gaining ground. "It can't be long now!" The original Gnostic apostles (described so well by Walter Schmithals[§]) were appearing. They would have been itinerate bodhisattvas who had a larger share of the pleromatic photons in them. They were the vanguard of the resurrected Primal Man, heralding and preparing his way, the way to the revelation of all the sons of God.

Dying and Rising Savior Joshua

There is a direct link between the Mystery Cult saviors, with their deaths and resurrections on the one hand, and the Gnostic Redeemers on the other. Gnosticism obviously was a kind of Mystery (or initiation) Religion, though perhaps of a more abstract,

---

[‡]   Drews 273–282),

[§]   Walter Schmithals, *The Office of Apostle in the Early Church*. Trans. John E. Steely (NY: Abingdon Press, 1969), pp. 114–191.

pseudo-philosophical type. I believe they share the following connection. The Mystery Religions were at first agricultural in nature, representing the performative celebrations by which ancient peoples assured that the seasons would continue to follow one another, bringing a return of vegetation, or of the strength of the sun. There was in all such societies also a set of initiation rites, or rites of passage, but these were separate. Rites of passage punctuated each human life, giving it signification as each person progressed from one category, one social matrix, to another. The most important was the passage into adulthood. At this time the adolescent would be vouchsafed the tribe's secrets of sex, death, and the sacred. These elements also occurred in the seasonal rites since these involved the death of nature as well as its fertilization, and the whole thing was a sacred drama. In the Hellenistic period, which witnessed an unprecedented cosmopolitanism, cultures and religions traveled with merchants, missionaries, slaves, and soldiers. Pockets of immigrants, say, from Phrygia who wound up in Rome gathered with fellow Phrygian transplants in local religious fellowships. These were, of course, their old national/tribal faiths, only, in their new urban settings, the faiths' myths and rites required retooling. The agricultural element fell away, and initiation became instead a new and advanced degree of life passage.[*] One could seek out a rebirth, above and beyond the adult competency imparted by the familiar and universal puberty rite. Thus other-worldly salvation and enlightenment became new concerns in these old but transformed religions. Many of the ritual elements were familiar: sacred marriage with Isis, death and resurrection with Sarapis. The (indigenous, exoteric) Mystery Religions thus became the (transplanted, esoteric) Mystery Cults.

Another important ingredient in the transformation was democratization. What was happening to the common initiate had once been restricted to the king. It was only he who had shared

---

[*]   Dujardin, p. 56.

the death and resurrection ordeal of the creator god (Marduk, Yahweh, Baal, *etc.*), with the result that he was himself the Son of God on earth, sacrificing himself for the world and his people. But once the great Western empires did away with these monarchies and their royal ideologies, the common people took on both the sacramental roles and the hopes for immortal divinity that their long-lost monarchs had once enjoyed.

It is the ancient royal ideology of the king as the vicar and embodiment of the dying and rising creator and savior which forms the basis of the doctrine of the Gnostic Primal Man, whose release from fleshly degradation means salvation for all those united with him, either by nature or by initiation (which amounts to the same thing, since initiation is self-realization). It is just that, by the time we reach Gnosticism (or Sufism, for that matter, for it, too, preserved the Primal Man doctrine), it has been completely abstracted: no more reference to nature, to vegetation, to kings or dragons (though even that element will pop up again in the Manicheaean version). Again, the importance of this underlying relation/identification is that it makes it difficult and, ultimately, almost moot to distinguish which surviving version of this many-headed hydra of a doctrine was the immediate womb of the Christian Jesus figure. This helps explain how Arthur Drews, for instance, could switch back and forth between a Gnostic pre-Christian Jesus and a Mystery Savior Jesus. You say, "to-*may*-to," and I say, "to-*mah*-to."

Robertson states the case well:

> The grounds for surmising a pre-Christian cult of a Jesus or Joshua may here be noted. The first is the fact that the Joshua (Jesus) of the [Old Testament] book so named is quite certainly unhistorical, and that the narrative concerning him is a late fabrication. We can but derive from it that, having several attributes of the Sun-God, he is like Samson and Moses an ancient deity, latterly reduced to human status... That he... should be credited with the miracle of staying

The Christ Myth Theory And Its Problems

the course of the sun and moon — a prodigy beyond any ascribed to Moses — it is not to be explained except on the view that he held divine status in the previous myth. As his name was held in special reverence among the Samaritans,... the probability is that he was an Ephraimite deity, analogous to Joseph, whose legend has such close resemblances to the myth of Tammuz-Adonis.[*]

We have seen how Arthur Drews recognizes Gnostic elements, but here he explains how the Mystery precursor to the Christian Jesus was a Mystery rite savior identified with the Hexateuchal Joshua.

Joshua himself is apparently an ancient Ephraimite God of the Sun and Fruitfulness.[†] But the Ephraimitic Joshua too must have been a kind of Tammuz or Adonis. His name (Joshua, Syrian, Jeshu) characterizes him as savior and deliverer.[‡] When Joshua dies at Timnath-heres, the place of the eclipse of the Sun (*i.e.*, at the time of the summer solstice, at which the death of the Sun-God was celebrated [Judges 2:9]),[§] he appears again as a kind of Tammuz, while the 'lamentation' of his death alludes possibly to the lamentation at the death of the Sun-God.[¶] We are compelled to suppose that in the case of all the Gods of this nature the idea of the dying away of vegetation during the heat of the year and its revival had become intertwined and commingled with that of the declining and reviving strength of the sun.[**] Joshua too, the Jesus of the Old Testament, whom we have learnt to recognize as an ancient Ephraimtic God of the Sun and Fruitfulness, was accompanied in his passage of the Jordan by twelve assistants, one from each tribe.[††]

Dujardin is pretty consistent in seeing Jesus as a direct survival of a Palestinian Jewish Mystery Religion of Joshua. Joshua

---

[*] Robertson, *Pagan Christs*, p. 163.
[†] Drews, p. 57.
[‡] Drews, p. 83.
[§] "And they buried him within the bounds of his inheritance in Timnath-heres, in the hill country of Ephraim, north of the mountain of Gaash."
[¶] Drews, p. 84
[**] Drews, p. 94.
[††] Drews, p. 135.

was associated with Gilgal, which is simply a variant version of the name Golgotha. And there is no Golgotha near Jerusalem. The crucifixion story preserves the sacrificial ritual of a stand-in for the god Joshua on the ancient "high places," adorned with menhirs, or stone circles, which is what "Golgotha" means.‡‡

For Dujardin, Jesus was a classic Mystery Cult deity, whose sacrifice first stood for the renewal of nature, then changed to spiritual salvation. He asks, quite reasonably, whether it is best deemed mere coincidence that the gospel Jesus story parallels all the main outlines of the Mystery pattern as seen in the cases of other gods and their cults. Why should one insist that in this particular case it all actually happened?§§ John M. Robertson,¶¶ perhaps the greatest of the old Christ-Mythicists, understood the gospel drama as based on a Mystery rite. (No wonder the Passion lends itself so well to Oberammergau-type adaptations!) Here Robertson draws into the drama theory the odd detail of the name "Jesus Bar-Abbas" from Old Latin manuscripts of Matthew 27:17.

> The natural inference from the Barabbas story is that it was customary to give up to the people about the time of the Passover a prisoner, who was made to play a part in some rite under the name Barabbas, "Son of the Father"; and the reading "Jesus Barabbas" suggests that the full name of the bearer of this art included that of "Jesus" — a detail very likely to be suppressed by copyists as an error. Is not the proper presumption, then, this: that the preservation of the name "Jesus Barabbas" tells of the common association of those names in some such rite as must be held to underlie the Gospel myth — that, in short, a "Jesus the Son of the Father" was a figure in an old Semitic ritual of sacrifice before the Christian era? The Syrian form of the name, Yeschu, closely resembles the Hebrew name Yishak,

---

‡‡   Dujardin, pp. 57–58. Rylands, (*Gnostic Christianity*, p. 171) too, argues for the original crucifixion site in Galilee.

§§   Dujardin p. 56.

¶¶   John M. Robertson, *Pagan Christs: Studies in Comparative Mythology* (London: Watts, 2nd rev. ed., 1911).

which we read Isaac; and that Isaac was in earlier myth sacrificed by his father is a fair presumption.[*]

The equating of the names Yishak (Yitzakh) and Yeshua seems far-fetched, but the rest of it makes sense, especially in light of the odd item in Philo about a mock king charade starring one called "Carabbas."

> There was a certain madman named Carabbas..., the sport of idle children and wanton youths; and they, driving the poor wretch as far as the public gymnasium, and setting him up there on high that he might be seen by everybody, flattened out a leaf of papyrus and put it on his head instead of a diadem, and clothed the rest of his body with a common door mat instead of a cloak, and instead of a sceptre they put in his hand a small stick of... papyrus... and when he had been adorned like a king, the young men bearing sticks on their shoulders stood on each side of him instead of spear bearers..., and then others came up, some as if to salute him, and others as though they wished to plead their causes before him... Then from the multitude... there arose a... shout of men calling out '*Maris!*' And this is the name by which it is said that they call the kings among the Syrians; for they knew that Agrippa was by birth a Syrian, and also that he was possessed of a great district of Syria of which he was the sovereign. (*Against Flaccus*, VI, 36–39)[†]

What are we to make of this? It can't be simple coincidence. The one story is unlikely to be a retelling of the other. It is at least as plausible to posit two accounts of a similar mock-king ritual such as had once been commonly associated with the yearly ritual death of a surrogate for the king who would understandably prefer to keep his head on his shoulders. It was no longer practiced for real in the time of Philo or Mark or Matthew, but it had formed part of

---

[*] Robertson, *Pagan Christs,* p. 162.

[†] C.D. Yonge, trans., *The Works of Philo* (Peabody: Hendrickson, 1993), p. 728.

the Mystery passion, dating from a much earlier time, when such things were current. Hence the evangelists and Philo don't quite know what to do with it.

Drews explains that in the passion drama, the death was that of a Passover Lamb, albeit a heavenly one, as in Revelation 4, but that this feature was eventually transformed into the crucifixion. "'The Revelation of John.'… appears to be a Christian redaction of an original Jewish work which in all likelihood belonged to a pre-Christian cult of Jesus. The god Jesus which appears in it has nothing to do with the Christian Jesus."[‡] Robertson says the same: Revelation seems to be pre-Christian and identifies the Lamb and the Logos with some Jesus.[§]

How did the alternate metaphor of crucifixion of a human gain currency and even eclipse the Passover Lamb notion? Though there may be more involved, I think we find more than a sufficient answer in Jaan Puhvel's description of the process by which raw myth is reinterpreted as epic legend, gods and demons reduced to mighty men and epic heroes.

Myth operates by bringing a sacred (and hence essentially and para-doxically "timeless") past to bear preemptively on the present and inferentially on the future ("as it was in the beginning, is now, and ever shall be"). Yet in the course of human events societies pass and religious systems change; the historical landscape gets littered with the husks of desiccated myths. These are valuable nonmaterial fossils of mankind's recorded history, especially if still embedded in layers of embalmed religion, as part of a stratum of religion complete with cult, liturgy and ritual. Yet equally important is the next level of trans-mission, in which the sacred narrative has already been secularized, myth has been turned into saga, sacred time into heroic past, gods into heroes, and mythical action into "historical" plot.[¶] (Jaan Puhvel)

---

‡   Drews, p. 62.
§   Robertson, *Pagan Christs*, p. 164.
¶   Jaan Puhvel, *Comparative Mythology* (Baltimore: Johns Hopkins University Press, 1987). p. 2.

The Christ Myth Theory And Its Problems

> Myth can be transmitted either in its immediate shape, as sacred narrative anchored in theology and interlaced with liturgy and ritual, or in transmuted form, as past narrative that has severed its ties to sacred time and instead functions as an account of purportedly secular, albeit extraordinary happenings... This transposition of myth to heroic saga is a notable mechanism in ancient Indo-European traditions, wherever a certain cultic system has been supplanted in living religion and the superannuated former apparatus falls prey to literary manipulation.[*]

Even so, according to Rylands: "The priests who, after the return from Babylon, redacted the ancient documents in the interest of the monotheistic worship of Jahveh may be supposed to have reduced the status of Joshua, first to that of an angel, and then made a distinction between the angel and Joshua as the actual leader of the Israelites."[†]

Couchoud provides another clue: "He is the scapegoat on whom all spat, who was crowned with scarlet wool and driven into the wilderness (Barnabas vi–viii; the author makes use of a text of Jewish ritual which is unknown to us)."[‡] Here the sharp-eyed Couchoud anticipates John Dominic Crossan[§] in *The Cross that Spoke*, where he demonstrates in astonishing detail how the minutiae of the Levitical scapegoat ritual (offering twin goats to Yahweh and to Azazel) evolved through centuries-long iteration in the Mishnah and in early Christian midrash (especially the Epistle of Barnabas) into the notion of a righteous man being *pierced*, whether by Carabbas' reeds, a crown of thorns, Longinus' spear, or crucifixion nails.

Robertson and others have claimed that the very name "Jesus" is titular and only through common use turned effectively into a proper name. What did "Jesus" denote, then? And here, whether we

---

[*]   *Ibid,* p. 39.
[†]   Gordon Rylands, *Did Jesus Ever Live?* (London: Watts, 1935), p. 39.
[‡]   Couchoud, p. 123.
[§]   John Dominic Crossan, *The Cross that Spoke: The Origins of the Passion Narrative* (San Francisco: Harper & Row, 1988), pp. *117–139.*

are talking about the Old Testament Joshua or the New Testament Jesus is immaterial, since the whole point is that they are supposed to be the same figure. According to Couchoud, "the name of Jesus... means Saviour (*cf.* I Thess. I, 9–10)."¶ It is slightly different with Drews: "Now, as Epiphanius remarks in his 'History of the Heretics,' Jesus bears in the Hebrew language the same meaning as curator, *therapeutes* — that is, physician and curer."** As for Dujardin, "Jesus is in Hebrew Ieshouah, or Ieshou. But 'salvation' in Hebrew is Ieshouah. Jesus is therefore literally Salvation."†† Critics will point out that these theorists are conveniently forgetting the Yahwist theophoric prefix: *Yeshua* equals *Yehoshua*, meaning "Yahweh is salvation" or "Yahweh saves." As we will see, thereby hangs quite a tale.

What about the Old Testament Joshua's patronymic, "son of Nun"? Tasteless Roman Catholic jokes aside, the name remains striking and puzzling. "The patriarch Joshua, who was plainly an ancient god of Palestine and bore the same name as the god of Christianity, is called the son of Nun, which signifies 'son of the fish'."‡‡ From this fact, Dujardin and others posit that Joshua was supposed to be the son of finny Dagon with his merman tail.§§ This alone ought to be enough to make Joshua a god or a demigod, no? Well, maybe not. T.J. Thorburn offers a more modest alternative. "Another... conjecture is, that Joshua, as the son of Nun (... = 'fish,' 'serpent,') was a member of a fish- or perhaps a serpent-clan, fishes and serpents being much confused in ancient

---

¶   Couchoud, p. 203. 1 Thessalonians 1:9–10, "For they themselves report concerning us what a welcome we had among you, and how you turned to God from idols, to serve a living and true God, and to wait for his Son from heaven, whom he raised from the dead, Jesus who delivers us from the wrath to come."

**   Drews, p. 58.

††   Dujardin, p. 47.

‡‡   T.J. Thorburn, *Jesus the Christ: Historical or Mythical?* (Edinburgh: T&T Clark, 1912, p. 161.

§§   Dujardin, p. 54.

times."* "The word *Nun*, Cheyne thinks, is probably a shortened form of *Nahshon*, which *might* mean (he says) 'a little serpent'."† This implies Israelite totemism, "for which there is certainly some evidence."‡ That is, the name Nun could still be that of a god, but "son of Nun" might denote no more than its bearer being dedicated at birth to the service of the fish-totem or deity.

But there is more to it than a name. Robertson, Drews, and others believe they can recognize the original divine stature of Joshua the god in juxtaposition to Joshua the man now depicted in the Bible's official redaction. Joshua himself must have been the Captain of the Lord's host. In Exodus 23:20–24§ it is "promised that an Angel, in or on whom is the 'name' of Yahweh, shall lead Israel" in triumph over the corrupt Canaanite nations. Robertson therefore identifies Joshua himself with this angel, from whom he has been split as a matter of euhemerism.¶ That is, the god Joshua has been demoted to Joshua, human successor to Moses, but also to the angel of Yahweh's army. Originally these two actantial roles were united in the same character; now they are split, two figures being necessary to fill the shoes of a god in the original. But one cannot so easily eradicate a popular object of worship. His memory goes on, and he pops up elsewhere.

---

*   Thorburn, p. 161.

†   *Ibid.*, p. 162.

‡   *Ibid.*

§   "Behold, I send an angel before you, to guard you on the way and to bring you to the place which I have prepared. Give heed to him and hearken to his voice, do not rebel against him, for he will not pardon your transgression; for my name is in him. But if you hearken attentively to his voice and do all that I say, then I will be an enemy to your enemies and an adversary to your adversaries. When my angel goes before you, and brings you in to the Amorites, and the Hittites, and the Perizzites, and the Canaanites, the Hivites, and the Jebusites, and I blot them out, you shall not bow down to their gods, nor serve them, nor do according to their works, but you shall utterly overthrow them and break their pillars in pieces."

¶   Robertson, *Pagan Christs*, p. 163. Similarly, Drews, pp. 56–57.

That personage, again, in virtue of his possession of the magical "name," is in the Talmud identified with the mystic Metatron, who is in turn identifiable with the Logos. Thus the name Joshua = Jesus is already in the [Hex]ateuch associated with the conceptions of Logos, Son of God, and Messiah... Only the hypothesis that in some Palestinian quarters Joshua had the status of a deity can meet the case.[**]

Among Robertson's numerous critics, H.G. Wood did not accept this suggestion.

It should be noted that Mr. Robertson just threw in the conceptions of Son of God and Messiah as a make-weight! But apart from that, the argument... asks us to assume first that the Talmudic speculations concerning the Metatron and the angel of Jahweh, *etc.*, are as old as the Hexateuch, and secondly that being as old they were known to the writers of the Hexateuch.[††]

And I will have to say, even as an admirer of the Christ Myth theory, that Robertson's reasoning looks more cosmetic than anything else. Though the Enoch myth may be older and more influential than anyone before Margaret Barker had thought, Robertson does seem to be casting pretty far with that fly rod! Wood makes the same objection to another odd bit offered as evidence by Robertson, the mention, in a Kabbalistic source, of Joshua as an angelic "Prince of the Presence." Is this not evidence, Robertson demands, that Joshua was still remembered in some quarters as more than mortal? Wood says:

There is a Kabbalistic prayer attached to the Jewish liturgy for the New Year, which contains an obscure reference to Joshua as Prince of the Presence, whatever that may mean.[‡‡] [But] the late piece of

---

[**]   Robertson, *Pagan Christs*, p. 164.
[††]   H.G. Wood, *Did Christ Really Live?* (NY: Macmillan, 1938), pp. 132–133.
[‡‡]   Wood, p. 133.

The Christ Myth Theory And Its Problems

> Jewish angelology in reference to Joshua, the Prince of the Presence... is not even Talmudic, and it is worthless as evidence of any phase of pre-Christian thought.[*]

Mythicists have also thought to associate a Joshua god with the origin of circumcision (or at least an after-the-fact etiology for it). Wood summarizes the argument:

> The reference to the circumcision and the Passover in the book of Joshua, chapter v, suggests that his name was anciently associated with these ordinances. As Mr. Rylands puts it, "Joshua is said to have reinstituted – or as would rather appear instituted – the rite of circumcision, and would therefore in accordance with ancient mythological ideas have been regarded as the god of the rite."[†]

That alone might not imply that, say, Joshua-worshippers regarded circumcision as the sign of a covenant with their god. Added ammunition comes from the Talmud.

> But surely some weight must be given to the passage in the Talmud where circumcision is described as "the week of Jesus the Son"? ... It is in the Babylonian Talmud. Baba Bathra, fol. 60, col. 2, and the best and most recent edition renders it as follows: "A government has come into power... which does not allow us to enter into the 'week of the Son' (according to another version, 'the salvation of the Son.')" ... It is supposed that in the time of Hadrian it was safer to refer to circumcision as 'the week of the Son' or as 'the salvation of the Son" than to mention it openly... No Jew ever called circumcision, the rite or "the week of Jesus the Son."[‡]

Originally there can have been no mention of Joshua ("Jesus") — someone has misunderstood the reference to "salvation or redemption" as an allusion to the meaning of the name Yehoshua.

---

[*]   Wood, p. 136.
[†]   Citing Rylands, *Did Jesus Ever Live?* p.. 38; Wood, p. 130.
[‡]   Wood, p. 138.

Does the Paris Magical Papyrus not mention "Jesus the god of the Hebrews" as a name of power for exorcizing demons? Who can prove that this formula denotes more than the syncretistic stew from which Hellenistic sorcery arose? Does it not merely take for granted the Christian deification of Jesus Christ and his association with the co-opted faith of Judaism? That seems more likely to me if otherwise we are going to have to construct a whole, otherwise unknown pre-Christian Jesus religion for it to be a reference to. Is it worth the trouble?

These data are too fragmentary and equivocal. They might mean what Robertson says they mean, but it is a crap-shoot. Too much else may have been going on. And in case one has not noticed, what we are seeing here is a "preliminary bout" in which Robertson argues that Joshua son of Nun was a god historicized as a human hero, before the "main event" in which he will argue that Jesus of Nazareth was a god historicized as a human hero. It is difficult to make a myth-god Joshua a firm foundation for a myth-god Jesus when the cases are so similar and similarly disputable.

William Benjamin Smith saw in Acts 18:25's reference to a pre-baptized Apollos nonetheless knowing well "the things concerning Jesus" a vestigial reference to a widespread pre-Christian Jesus religion. That must, however, be dismissed as extravagant over-interpretation. How is poor Apollos different from Cornelius? In Acts 10:36, Peter tells Cornelius, "*You know* the word which he sent to Israel, preaching good news of peace by Jesus Christ." In both cases, the author of Acts establishes that a pivotal character has some preliminary knowledge of the Christian message but has not yet been fully initiated into the faith. Does that make any sense in concrete descriptive terms? Can scholars reconstruct some sort of half-Christianity which Apollos or Cornelius, or for that matter the baptized Samaritans of Acts 8:14–16,[§] confessed? No, it is all a

---

§   "Now when the apostles at Jerusalem heard that Samaria had received the word of God, they sent to them Peter and John, who came down and prayed

Lukan device. All that is really missing from the "defective" faith of these would-be Christians is official Jerusalem-apostolic sanction of their conversion. Apollos lacks only one thing: the imprimatur of Paul's colleagues. (Paul, of course, has been established as the obedient delegate of the Jerusalem apostles via Barnabas.) The Samaritans lack only the imposition of the apostles' hands. Cornelius lacks only Peter's blessing for baptism. The business about Apollos is no pre-Lukan fragment about a pre-Christian Jesus cult.

Yahweh himself!

We saw above that there was some confusion about the meaning of the name "Joshua," some making it the equivalent of "savior" or "healer" or "salvation," but that all such guesses conspicuously left out the theophoric element "Yeho-" or "Jehu-." This missing piece, provides, I am persuaded, the crucial clue as to the nature and existence of the pre-Christian worship of Jesus. Archibald Robertson, in a scrupulously fair evaluation of the case for a mythical Jesus, deals with the name issue.

> That "Joshua" was originally a divine name is a legitimate inference from the old song-fragment in Josh. X, 12–13, in which Joshua commands the sun and moon to stand still until the nation have avenged themselves on their enemies. The nearest parallel in Greek literature is in *Iliad* xviii, where the goddess Hera saves the Achaeans from defeat by commanding the sun to set. Ordering the sun and moon about is a divine, not a human job.

But of what god was Joshua the name? On this subject mythicists betray some confusion. J.M. Robertson and Dujardin interpret the name "Joshua" as "saviour" or "salvation."[*] This is inexact. "Jehoshua," "Joshua," or "Jeshua," means "Jahveh is deliverance"

---

for them that they might receive the Holy Spirit; for it had not yet fallen on any of them, but they had only been baptized in the name of the Lord Jesus."

    *   J.M. Robertson, *Christianity and Mythology* (London: Watts, 2nd rev. ed., 1910), p. 107; Dujardin, *Ancient History of the God Jesus*, pp. 47–49.

or "Jahveh saves." If this was originally a divine name it was surely a title of Jahveh himself. "Jahveh saves" can no more have been a separate god from Jahveh than Zeus Soter was a separate god from Zeus. In the old song-book of which Josh. X, 12–13 is a fragment, Jahveh himself doubtless fought in human form, as the Greek gods do in the *Iliad*, and commanded the sun and moon to stand still till victory was won. Later writers got rid of the anthropomorphism by turning Joshua into a human hero and making Jahveh stop the sun and moon at his prayer; but until this metamorphosis was effected there is no evidence that "Joshua" was anything but a title of Jahveh.[†]

How close Archibald Robertson comes to the view espoused by John M. Robertson! Both posit a divine manipulator of the heavenly spheres who was subsequently demoted to the status of a human hero named Joshua (=Jesus). Archibald Robertson's qualm is that this deity was not distinct from Yahweh. And thus he supplies the missing piece from John M. Robertson's puzzle; in seeking to refute Robertson's case, he winds up rehabilitating, correcting it. For, as I will contend, in view of the work of two more recent scholars, the pre-Christian god who became the Christian Jesus must have been Yahweh himself, the son of El Elyon.

William Benjamin Smith[‡] already saw that Jesus is everywhere called *kyrios*, which stands for Yahweh in the Greek Septuagint used by the early Christians. If the Septuagint originally substituted *kyrios* for Yahweh (as synagogue reading required oral substitution of "Adonai" where the Hebrew text had "Yahweh"), the implication of Christian usage of the title is that they wished to identify their savior Jesus as the Old Testament Yahweh. But if, as now seems

---

[†] Archibald Robertson, *Jesus: Myth or History?* Thinker's Library. London: Watts, 1946), p. 95.
[‡] William Benjamin Smith, *Ecce Deus: Studies of Primitive Christianity* (London: Watts, 1912), pp. 135–137.

possible, Jewish copies of the Septuagint had simply transliterated the divine name into Greek characters, then we would have to infer that Christians so closely identified Jesus with Jehovah as to substitute their Lord Jesus for the Tetragrammaton in the Old Testament, a radical move. In either case, we have a direct identification of Jesus Christ with Yahweh the God of Israel. Georg Brandes believed the early Christians had made precisely this identification the very basis for their construction of the fictional-mythic Jesus: Isaiah's suffering servant, Psalms and Wisdom's suffering wise man "became fused into a single figure, that of Jahve himself changed into a god that dies, rises again, and will return to sit in judgment on the world. It is from this... duplication of Jahve into a Jahve-Messiah or a Jahve-Jesus, that Christianity starts."[*]

This version of the pre-Christian Jesus may have seemed to some the least promising, but I regard it as the most promising, especially in view of the work of Geo Widengren and Margaret Barker, neither of whom was or is associated with the Christ Myth theory. Their work cannot be dismissed as axe-grinding on behalf of a pet hypothesis.

> Yahweh was one of the sons of El Elyon; and Jesus in the Gospels was described as a Son of El Elyon, God Most High. In other words, he was described as a heavenly being. Thus the annunciation narrative has the term 'Son of the Most High' (Luke 1, 32)[†] and the demoniac recognized his exorcist as 'Son of the Most High God' (Mark 5, 7).[‡] Jesus is not called the son of Yahweh nor the son of the Lord, but he is called Lord. We also know that whoever wrote the New Testament translated the name Yahweh by *Kyrios*, Lord... This suggests that the Gospel writers, in using the terms 'Lord' and 'Son

---

[*]   Georg Brandes, *Jesus a Myth*. Trans. Edwin Björkman (NY: Albert & Charles Boni, 1926), p. 70.

[†]   "He will be great, and will be called the Son of the Most High; and the Lord God will give to him the throne of his father David."

[‡]   "What have you to do with me, Jesus, Son of the Most High God? I adjure you by God, do not torment me."

of God Most High', saw Jesus as an angel figure, and gave him their version of the sacred name Yahweh.[§]

Not only this, but, as is well known, the Pauline Epistles often cite *kyrios* texts from the Old Testament as if Jesus were their subject. In fact, the hope of the second coming is largely based on simply transferring all the prophetic passages about Yahweh's coming in judgment or salvation to the Christian Jesus.[¶] Finally Barker argues that Trinitarianism represented no syncretist compromise with heathen polytheism, but rather was simply a case of popular religion stubbornly hanging on to very ancient Israelite belief in the great God Yahweh as the son of the Greater God El Elyon, his father ancient in days. Jesus simply was Yahweh recently descended to earth as in the numerous theophany stories of scripture. Barker is assuming an historical Jesus to whom this ancient mythology was applied, but that is a separate issue. The point here is that, as W.B. Smith and Georg Brandes already surmised, the pre-Christian Jesus was Yahweh. When he is thought to have descended as an avatar to earth, he is rightly called "Yahweh Saves."

But what of the distinctive death and resurrection pattern? Robertson and Drews had been forced to surmise their ancient god Joshua to be a fertility god, a reasonable guess, but little more. Is it not, however, even less likely to understand Yahweh as a resurrected deity? Not at all! Geo Widengren explains how

recent research has attempted to prove that there really existed in some Israelite circles a worship of Yahweh as a dying and rising deity, and further that passages in the Old Testament where such mythic reminiscences are found testify to a closer correspondence between Hebrew and Ugaritic phraseology and technical terms than

---

§   Barker, pp. 4–5.
¶   T. Francis Glasson, *The Second Advent: The Origin of the New Testament Doctrine*, (London: Epworth Press, 1947), Chapter 18, "The Coming of the Lord," pp. 162–179.

The Christ Myth Theory And Its Problems

was hitherto recognized. Thus we do not find only the expression
'Yahweh liveth' in some pregnant passages, above all in Ps. Xviii.
47..., an expression exactly corresponding to the cultic cry of jubi-
lation in the R[as] S[hamra] texts. 'Aliyan Baal liveth', I AB iii, 8–9,
but, moreover, the cultic exhortation, 'awake', addressed to the god
in the sleep of death and directed even to Yahweh in Ps. Xxxv. 23;
xliv. 23; lix. 4. A mythic situation, in which Yahweh is thought of as
being dead, is accordingly presupposed in the cult.*

Here is the old religion, from before the Deuteronomic reform, surviving in strength among the people who never took on their lips
the oath ascribed by priestcraft to Abraham, "I swear by Yahweh
El Elyon," as if they were one and the same. Here is the faith of the
crowds who witnessed year by year the thrill of the king reenacting
Yahweh's death in the jaws of the Hydra-like Leviathan (puppeteers
inside a billowing parade costume) and his triumphant resurrection,
bursting forth from within the monster and crushing its heads with
resurrected might! "Yahweh lives! He is risen indeed!" Such faith
does not entirely fade with the ages, especially as it remains ever attested in the Psalter. And one day it was decided that "The Lord has
visited his people!" He was Jesus: Yahweh Saves.

The Peril of Historicizing Jesus

What led to the historicizing of Jesus? Drews[†] pointed out the
simple truth, at least a natural, plausible answer: it had everything
to do with institutional consolidation. Few critics will deny that the
second-century Catholic church fabricated the notion of the apostolic
succession of bishops in order to provide exclusive credentials for
their own teaching. At a time when Gnostics and others claimed,
like Paul, to have direct communications from a heavenly Christ,

---

* Geo Widengren, "Early Hebrew Myths and their Interpretation" in
S.H. Hooke, ed., *Myth, Ritual and Kingship: Essays on the Theory and Prac-
tice of Kingship in the Ancient Near East and in Israel*. (NY: Oxford University
Press, 1958), p. 191.

† Drews, p. 272.

the strategy of Irenaeus was to dismiss all such "revelations" as drunken hallucinations and demonic spewings. Catholic teachings, by contrast, were objectively true, once and for all delivered by a flesh-and-blood historical Jesus to named and credentialed apostles, who in turn passed the teachings on to their successors, the bishops. For this to get off the ground, the church required an historical Jesus who would have flourished only recently, so that "today's" authorities could claim to have "shook the hand that shook the hand." To compete with these tactics, Gnostics, too, began to claim that Jesus Christ had appeared in recent history and commissioned apostles who taught their own teachers (Paul taught Theodas, who taught Valentinus; Peter taught Glaukias, who taught Basilides). "Once the need for apocalyptic prophets had passed, once the atmosphere of secret gnosis should have been swept away, the Christian legend would take on a narrative and popular form, making an easy appeal to the masses."‡

How did the historicization of Jesus proceed? "Later the common people's curiosity and desire for information… resulted in the collection of traditional anecdotes, [*etc.*]… all of which was then boiled together into the strangely composed mess that is called the Gospel according to St. Mark."§

Gospel events have been derived from Old Testament exegesis ("according to the scriptures"): "When these things are said to have happened 'according to the Scriptures,' the … statement is a certificate of their dogmatic necessity, not of their historic actuality."¶

---

‡   Couchoud, p. 108.
§   Brandes , p. 71.
¶   Smith p. 155. *Cf.* Rylands, *Gnostic Christianity*, p. 187, fn 2. Earl Doherty, *The Jesus Puzzle: Did Christianity Begin with a Mythical Christ?* (Ottowa: Canadian Humanist Press, 1999), Chapter 8, "The Word of God in the Holy Book," pp. 77–86. Also Robert M. Price, "New Testament Narrative as Old Testament Midrash" in Jacob Neusner and Alan J. Avery-Peck (eds.), *Encyclopaedia of Midrash: Biblical Interpretation in Formative Judaism* (E.J. Brill, 2005), Volume One, pp. 534–573.

The Sum of the Matter

We have seen that the Christ-Myth claim that Christianity developed from some sort of pre-Christian Jesus or Joshua religion has suffered mainly from reliance on weak (though not absurd) arguments, mostly dependant on the identification of the pre-Christian Jesus with a hypothetical pre-canonical Joshua god, distinct from Yahweh, a debatable doublet of the very case being argued with regard to the Christian Jesus. The evidence for a Joshua deity proved misty and equivocal. But everything implausible in this reconstruction was either avoided or made good in the case of a similar claim ventured by William Benjamin Smith and Georg Brandes, namely that the pre-Christian Jesus was none other than Yahweh himself, as he had been understood in pre-Deuteronomic times: as a dying and rising savior.

Conclusion:
Worse Than Atheism

Stand up, Stand up for Jesus, Opponents of the Cross!

I have found that when the infamous "Christ Myth" theory comes up, the notion that Jesus Christ was pure myth, not an historical figure, many people, already somewhat acclimated to the once-frightening notion of Atheism, are jolted all over again. It rings like Atheism in the ears of Atheists, that is, as Atheism itself *used* to, before they embraced it. There are various possible reasons for this reaction. I want to propose a few of them here.

First, I suspect many Atheists feel some nostalgia or lingering sympathy for vestiges of their now-abandoned Christian faith. They always viewed Jesus as a moral paragon, something of an ancient Mother Theresa or Mahatma Gandhi. (That is, of course, the official Christology of television documentaries that air around Christmas and Easter.) They are close to Neo-Orthodox theologian Rudolf Bultmann who saw the historical Jesus as a prophet of self-assessment and authenticity, subsequently mythologized by his followers, who painted him in the glowing hues of apocalyptic, Gnosticism, and the mystery religions. Many Atheists are glad to demythologize a historical Jesus whom they continue to revere as a moral giant in the Humanist Hall of Fame. And then to hear that he never existed? That, "if you strip away the myth from the man," you will have nothing left but the despised myth...? Well, maybe that's better than finding out he did exist but he was a bum, like JFK. I don't know. Atheists, I very much suspect, want to keep a liberal Protestant or Reform Jewish Jesus, not so much for an icon of their own as a cane to use to whip, at least to twit, orthodox Christians. "You know, your Jesus was more like us than like you."

Or consider this: If Jesus turns out, as the Christ Myth suggests, to have been divine, that is mythical, all the way down, first conceived of as a god, then fictively made human, well then, Atheists must simply reject Jesus as they reject Jehovah, and for the same reasons. Even as the same imaginary entity. There is no human Jesus left over for Humanists to respect. That's "a bit of a blow" even for many who thought they were over religion. I think here, too, of the 1960's Death of God theologian William Hamilton, who disavowed all belief in God but proposed that Christians huddle together under the remaining umbrella, casting their lot with a "merely mortal" Jesus who could still function as a North Star for social, moral, and religious commitment, even if one no longer cherished belief in a God above or a heaven beyond. But suppose even *this* bit of driftwood is yanked from the numb fingers of the castaway ex-Christian? It is like the cold-dawn enlightenment of Atheism all over again.

A second group of Atheists for whom the Christ Myth idea is a shocker would be those who, never having closely examined the theory, assume it is a crackpot idea like Holocaust Denial or disbelief in the moon landing. They don't want to associate the Atheist or Humanist cause with hare-brained schemes of this kind, as its apparent lack of credibility will then be seen to bleed over into Atheism *per se*, and Atheism's detractors will be happy to dismiss the one along with the other, though in fact they are quite different. (Liberal Protestant philosopher of religion John Hick once urged the assembled Atheists and Secularists at a 1985 CFI conference at Ann Arbor not to rest the credibility of the movement upon such termite-riddled supports as Mythicism, a warning G.A. Wells, present at the same event, took some umbrage at!) Christ Mythicism seems to many Atheists a secondary stumbling block in the way of Atheism. Why make it even more difficult for theists to abandon faith than it already is? Why lengthen the line of defense in this way? I say: that worry is misplaced. The non-existence of God and the non-existence of Jesus Christ are separate issues, to be argued in altogether different terms. One may believe in God but no Jesus, or in Jesus but no God, or neither, or both. But they are (or should be) two separate judgment calls.

I do not believe in a free-standing God, one existing outside the dramatic, role-playing context of liturgy. My first problem with personalistic Theism is my inability to accept Idealist metaphysics, the notion that ideas are more real than material instantiations of them, that *concepts* of tables and chairs are more real than *physical* tables and chairs. I think that Comte was correct: the abstract entities of Idealist philosophy are merely faded, bleached-out spirits and gods. My second problem with theism is what seems to me the utter lack of evidence of a just and providential deity's supervision of the world. If these problems could be overcome, I should still have great difficulties with the specific doctrines of the particular religions, though Pantheism and Monism might attract me. I should add, too, that I am a respectful God-denier. That is, I dissent from Theism from within the theological discussion, not from outside it. I would rather speak of the Death of God, along with Nietzsche and Altizer, than the non-existence of God. But none of these considerations bears at all on the likely or unlikely existence of a historical Jesus.

There is no God, and Jesus is his Prophet

It should be obvious that denying the existence of a historical Jesus Christ is an altogether different matter. Theoretically, there might have been a Jesus much like the gospel hero even if there is no God. A prophet, a faith healer, a teacher, even a mystagogue who taught his own divinity: none of these things becomes impossible or historically unlikely if there is no God behind it. It is obvious; I just need to say it in order to get all the options out on the table for comparison. There might have been a Jesus of Nazareth who spoke winsomely of a heavenly Father and his Kingdom of Righteousness even if he was wrong about it. Such a mistaken Jesus might even have set forth moral maxims we would find it wise to follow. There not being a God does not rule out there having been a Jesus.

Likewise, if there had never been a Jesus, that would not constitute any reason for not believing in God. Ask any Jew. I admit, it is obvious, but it is worth saying aloud because of what many suspect is the hidden agenda of the Christ Myth theory. Don't you suspect that some espouse the Christ Myth theory as a kind of "scorched earth" policy? Some want to wage a war against religion on all possible fronts. "Religion can never have done any good! There is no God! And, just to rub your face in it, your sweet and precious Jesus never existed either! Take that, Christian!" I am pretty sure that is the motivation of some, though it remains a suspicion only. Such unfortunate zealots are like Count Dracula, cringing from the sight of the cross. Such neurosis invites outsiders to chalk up our Atheism to mere adolescent rebellion against the inhibiting rules of religion. And for some or even many, no doubt, that may be the truth. Not being a mind-reader, I do not pretend to know.

But you might be such a "party-line" Atheist if you gladly hasten from disbelief in God to accepting the Christ-Myth theory without seriously scrutinizing the evidence and the arguments. "No, don't bother! Sounds good to me! You had me at 'no Jesus'." You might think the Soviet Union officially embraced Mythicism because it was one more hammer to bludgeon religion with. But I doubt it. Rather, it seems Karl Marx was convinced by the arguments of radical New Testament critic Bruno Bauer that Jesus was a fictional character created by the evangelist Mark, based on certain Stoic ideas. Marx did not require the nonexistence of Christ for his opposition to religion. He could have taken the approach of Karl Kautsky, recruiting a historical Jesus as a precursor of Communism, even as Liberation Theology does today. The two are different issues. That's my point. It's not as simple as deducing, "Since there is no God, neither can there be a Son of God."

424

Do You "No" Jesus?

Let me summarize the major factors that lead me to accept the Christ Myth as the most likely hypothesis to explain the data. First, almost every story in the Gospels (and Acts) can be plausibly argued to be borrowed from the Greek Old Testament, Homer, or Euripides. Use Occam's Razor: Which is more likely: that a man fed 5,000 with a handful of loaves and fish, or that a gospel writer rewrote an already ancient myth about Elisha doing the same darn thing?

Second, every detail of the narrated life of Jesus fits the outlines of the Mythic Hero archetype present in all cultures: divine annunciation of the pregnancy, miraculous conception and birth, heralding of the birth by wise men, stellar phenomena marking the event, child prodigy behavior embarrassing the adults, temptation by a devil at the outset of his career, wonders and contests with evil forces, coronation as king, popular acclaim giving way to hostility, death on a hill top, uncertainty as to the place of burial, postmortem appearances, annunciations of a heavenly ascension. Sound familiar? Granted, many of these mythemes get stuck like barnacles to the bow of the biographies of real historical figures, like Caesar Augustus, but in those cases there remains considerable "leftover," secular information tying the figure into contemporary history. All such links in the gospels, *e.g.*, with Herod the Great, Joseph Caiaphas, and Pontius Pilate, are so problematical on internal grounds that most critical scholars, never meaning to espouse Mythicism, reject these features of the story as legendary.

Third, the epistles, regardless of their dates as earlier or later than the gospels, seem to enshrine a different vein of early Christian faith which lacked an earthly Jesus, a Christianity that understood "Jesus" as an honorific throne-name bestowed on a spiritual savior who had been ambushed and killed by the Archons who rule the universe before he rose triumphant over them. Gnosticism, too, continued this tradition. But what we know as Christianity eventually rewrote Jesus

425

into an historical incarnation who suffered at the hands of earthly institutions of religion and government.

It doesn't matter so much that there is no contemporary reference to Jesus the miracle-worker, or even to Jesus the wise man, as there is to Apollonius or to Peregrinus. If we did have such tangential documentation, it would be enough, I admit, to destroy the Christ-Myth theory, and to make us incline, say, to Bultmann's view of a mythicized historical Jesus. I know the literary evidence from the ancient world is fragmentary and that little has survived. So there *might* possibly have been such a letter mentioning Jesus without it having survived the vicissitudes of history. Of course. But the mere possibility is of no help. In the end, no evidence is no evidence.

But you can see, can't you, that none of these considerations bears in any way on the issue of God's existence. Nor, if one could prove that God does exist, that it would make the historical existence of Jesus Christ more likely.

Et Tu, Brute?

Those of us in the skeptical community who incline toward the Christ Myth theory suddenly find the tables turned when we face the same sort of skepticism all Atheists face from religious believers. There is a certain irony here, no doubt of that. But if we were actually to charge our Atheist critics with inconsistency, we would be the ones reducing the Christ Myth theory to a mere deduction from atheism, a subspecies of Atheism. And that is exactly what I reject. So in fact I am never impatient with such critics. I only urge them (as I do Christians) to reexamine the issue and the evidence. For I doubt that many of them have had either the interest or the leisure to do so, and I do not blame them. But I do think it is worth asking if their initial sense of outlandishness may not be a vestige of the way they, as theists, used to take for granted the "truth" they had been taught about God. Automatically finding the Christ Myth theory kooky or outrageous is, I think, a trace of satisfaction with the lingering conventionalism against which we fight so hard as Atheists when the question under debate is not Jesus but God. If you call believers to account for their reluctance to explore the unthinkable lest they should find it thinkable indeed, then you have no right easing back into the same complacency when it comes to the startling notion that Jesus never walked the earth.